DEADLINES FROM THE EDGE

'Over the years I have found myself travelling and working in Africa, the Middle East and Central Asia. The journeys have been to places outside the developed world where some of the major news events of the turn of the millennium have happened. What links them all is that they are journeys out – away from the centre into the geography of the edge. In today's world of instantaneous electronic communications, I have come to see that in these travels I have wandered into an extra dimension, a layer of experience that has only become possible with the invention of television. I have come to see that they have been travels into a new province of the human mind . . . one that exists because of what we see of each other on our television screens . . .'

HAMILTON WENDE is a freelance journalist and television producer who has travelled extensively for the BBC and NBC, as well as Australian and Japanese networks. He is based in Johannesburg.

DEADLINES FROM THE EDGE

Images of War from Congo to Afghanistan

HAMILTON WENDE

VIKING
an imprint of
PENGUIN BOOKS

VIKING

Published by the Penguin Group
80 Strand, London WC2R 0RL, England
Penguin Putnam Inc, 375 Hudson Street, New York, New York 10014, USA
Penguin Books Australia Ltd, 250 Camberwell Road, Camberwell,
Victoria 3124, Australia
Penguin Books Canada Ltd, 10 Alcorn Avenue, Toronto, Ontario,
Canada M4V 3B2
Penguin Books (NZ) Ltd, Cnr Rosedale and Airborne Roads, Albany,
Auckland, New Zealand
Penguin Books India Pvt Ltd, 11 Community Centre, Panchsheel Park,
New Delhi – 110 017 India
Penguin Books (South Africa) (Pty) Ltd, 24 Sturdee Avenue, Rosebank,
Johannesburg 2196, South Africa

Penguin Books (South Africa) (Pty) Ltd, Registered Offices:
Second Floor, 90 Rivonia Road, Sandton 2196, South Africa

First published by Penguin Books (South Africa) (Pty) Ltd 2003

Copyright © Text and Photographs Hamilton Wende 2003
All rights reserved
The moral right of the author has been asserted

ISBN 0 670 04782 1

Typeset by CJH Design in 10.5/13pt Sabon
Cover design: Mouse Design
Printed and bound by CTP Book Printers, Cape Town

Except in the United States of America, this book is sold subject to the condition that it shall not, by way of trade or otherwise, be lent, resold, hired out or otherwise circulated without the publisher's prior consent in any form of binding or cover other than that in which it is published and without a similar condition including this condition being imposed on the subsequent purchaser.

For my darling Sam
with love
and with the joy of sharing our journey

CONTENTS

List of Acronyms	viii
Acknowledgements	ix
Distance	1
A New, and Most Exact, Map	3
A New War Across the Border	9
The Last Days of the Leopard King	55
Season of Hunger	125
Desert Sunsets	155
The Invisible City	195
A Hidden War	207
The Diary of a Ceasefire	263
The Border	280
References	283
Selected Index	286

List of Acronyms

AFDL – Alliance of Democratic Forces for the Liberation of Congo-Zaire
AWACS – Airborne warning and control system
CIA – Central Intelligence Agency (US)
DSP – Presidential Guard / Special Presidential Division (Zaire)
EU – European Union
FAR – Forces Armée Rwandaise / Armed Forces of Rwanda
FAZ – Armed Forces of Zaire
FNLA – Frente Nacional de Libertação de Angola / National Front for the Liberation of Angola
IDF – Israeli Defence Force
MPLA – Movimento Popular de Libertação de Angola / Popular Movement for the Liberation of Angola
MSF – Médecins Sans Frontières
NATO – North Atlantic Treaty Organization
OAU – Organization of African Unity
PDF – Popular Defence Force / *Murahaleen* (Sudan)
RPF – Rwandan Patriotic Front
SARM – Military Action and Intelligence Service (Zaire)
SPLA – Sudanese People's Liberation Army
SPLM – Sudanese People's Liberation Movement
SRRA – Sudan Relief and Rehabilitation Association
UN – United Nations
UNHCR – United National High Commission for Refugees
UNICEF – United Nations Children's Fund
UNITA – União Nacional para a Independência Total de Angola / National Union for the Total Independence of Angola

Acknowledgements

So many journeys, so much witnessed, so much shared: Allan Little, George Alagiah, Milton Nkosi, Fergal Keane, Richard Atkinson, Glenn Middleton, Tim Facey, Jeremy Vine, Byron Blunt, Martin Turner, Connie Maditse, Dan Moiloa, Kate Peyton, Jane Standley, Greg Barrow, Ofeibea Quist-Arcton, Jackie Martens, Regeh Omaar, Patience Mathobela, Hilary Andersson, Barnaby Philips, Ben Brown, Alistair Lyne, Jimi Matthews, Sahm Venter, Claude Colart, Dave Copeland, John 'Dinky' Mkhize, Patrick Muiruri, Martin Seemungal, Francois Marais, Ben Wilson, Tim Lambon, Cecile Antonie, Sue Burt, Dennis Murphy, Justin Balding, Richard Burr, Hoda Kotbe, Mohamed Muslemany, Nina Zacuto – thank you all for the camaraderie of the long days and nights, and for the compassion and the laughter that lie behind the deadlines.

I have spent most of my professional life in a limbo, stubbornly refusing to choose between the power of the image and the deeper, quieter strength of the word.

So thank you to Tony Grant and Mike Popham of the BBC who have run some of these words in another form on their programme *From Our Own Correspondent*.

Thank you to Belinda Hawkins, and Judith Matloff who looked at early drafts, and to Allan and George too for your advice. Special thanks to the Penguin team, to Alison Lowry, Pam Thornley, Claire Heckrath, Jane Ranger, and all of you for your patience, your wisdom and your professionalism.

To Stephen, Marc and Candace who have also ended up in this business, thanks to the three of you for what we've shared – over all the years. And to Colleen and Daryl, too, you've both been there for me so many times.

To my parents, thanks to you both for – well, everything. Mom, you taught us to love the power of stories; and Dad, you taught us the care and the patience needed to make things.

To Jena and James and Nicholas, we love you all so much. Thank you for teaching us to see the world again in such a wondrous new light.

DISTANCE

I am alone, lost in the air-conditioned hum of a seventh-floor hotel room anywhere in the world. I cannot sleep tonight. When I close my eyes, my head is filled with the white noise of insomnia. Outside, every other sound is sharp and magnified. Each tiny click and shudder echoes through the dark, empty room. My head is spinning with images. Finally, I get up and walk to the window. I draw the heavy hotel curtain aside and look out into the distant night where the city lights end and the flow of memory begins.

Somewhere out there the world holds the mist in the valleys of the green foothills of the Ruwenzori – the Mountains of the Moon. A single heron slowly wings its way across the morning clouds. Far away in the depths of the hotel corridors a telephone rings and no one answers.

It seems tonight that I can almost hear the wild, terrifying, exhilarating crackle and scream of tracer fire across the night sky in a country once called Zaire. In Rwanda, I can hear the distant thud of mortars, and see the black smoke rising on the horizon to meet the thin red dawn. A human thighbone lies on the quiet shady floor of a eucalyptus grove, a brown tendril of leathery flesh flowing out of the whiteness of it. A frangipani tree flowers above the worn-down stone where the killers sharpened their machetes. A spiral of incense smoke drifts out across the cold, ancient stone in the Church of the Holy Sepulchre in Jerusalem where they say the body of Jesus lay.

The pale green of the desert scrub stretches out for miles in front of us as we drive out of Kuwait City towards the Iraqi border. White skulls lie jumbled and broken in the long grass in the Sudan.

A flock of black-headed sacred ibis wheels in the golden afternoon light that hangs above a bush runway somewhere in the savanna of East Africa.

Image upon disconnected image, whirling through my mind tonight. How many journeys have begun like this, with me unable to sleep?

Behind me in the room is the television set. The screen is grey and flat, silent in the darkness. I point the remote at the set and push the button. There is the reassuring click and the hum of static as the television warms up. Faint images flicker on the screen for a few seconds before they reach their full brightness. The screen bursts alive with colour and sound.

I wrap the hotel dressing gown around me and sit on the edge of the bed, waiting for the screen to work its magic, for its hypnotic force to drag me into its bright and shining world. In the lonely insomniac darkness of the room the gleaming screen is a source of light and emotional warmth in the same way fire was to humans for thousands of generations. The constantly shifting images are like flickering flames. We are so easily captivated by what we see – the endless writhing of light and colour, our twenty-first century version of the shadows on the wall of Plato's cave.

But it is in the dark spaces that flash between the electronic pixels where the true meaning of television lies. In those fleeting absences lie the shadowlands of secrets unrevealed and dreams undreamt.

Tonight the screen is a household god, a cold Janus face looking back out at me as I peer bleary-eyed into its world of ghostly images. I have filmed so many of the things you will never see, and so many of the things you never want to see. So much suffering, so much blood, so many deaths – all the things you can turn off with the push of a button.

When I began working in television I was much younger. I wanted to see the world and to witness something of life as it is lived in its different ways. I wanted to experience both the horror and the beauty of life, because I thought that by being there when things happened, I would one day understand why they happened. To travel and work as part of a television crew seemed to me the best way to do that.

But no journey ever takes you exactly where you want to go, and all travellers one day find themselves in a place they did not expect to be. Somehow, in searching for the world, I ended up all too often getting caught in the space that exists between two worlds, worlds as far apart as it is possible to get in this life, connected to each other only by the cold grey curve of the screen.

Somewhere out there that same distance haunts my dreams, the distance that wakes me in hotel rooms in the middle of the night, reaching out in the darkness for the television remote.

A NEW, AND MOST EXACT, MAP

I was twelve years old when my father died. He was far away in America where I was born, but I was living with my mother and stepfather in South Africa. He didn't leave much money, and it was only when I was in my late twenties and living in New York that the final settlement from his will was made available to me. He left me several hundred dollars – an amount that would have sunk into my overdraft without trace. I decided instead to use it to buy something to remember him by.

It was autumn. That magnificent time of the year in Manhattan when the trees in the parks turn brown and yellow and crimson. The leaves flicker in the afternoon light before they unexpectedly spiral down on to the ground. The cool air sweeps in off the Hudson and the East rivers and blows away the greasy restaurant and garbage smells of the summer heat. The city is fresh and clean and people walk briskly and businesslike again. They've given up their depressed summer thoughts – brought on by the hot concrete and the grey cloying fog of pollution – of moving out into the shaded suburbs or to a smaller city somewhere.

Suddenly they are kinder and more open than they have been all year. In the autumn everyone suddenly remembers again why they came to New York in the first place, and why they want to stay . . . well, for just another year or two, at least.

It was my favourite time of the year in the city. I had a little money in the bank that I knew I could spend. I couldn't resist the temptation of joining that invigorated flow of people moving through the streets. I took the afternoon off work from the school where I was teaching English, slipped my *faux*-Burberry raincoat over my shoulders and stepped out on to the sidewalk.

I had no idea what I should get to remember my father by. The truth is, I never knew him well. I saw him only once in the years between my parents' divorce, when I was five, and the day he died. Still, I remembered him as kind and gentle. I wanted to find something that I would like, but that

would also honour his memory.

I walked up and down the grid of Manhattan's streets and avenues all that afternoon, enjoying the day but not finding anything that suited me. At first I thought I might buy an old book, or a lithograph of early New York, but everything I saw was either too expensive or somehow just not quite right.

On First Avenue – I think it was – I came across a store that specialized in antique maps.

In the window was an old map of Africa. Printed in London just before the turn of the eighteenth century, it was a surprisingly accurate representation of the continent. Somehow, considering that my life had been spent living partly in America and partly in Africa, it seemed the right thing to buy. The owner of the store was firm about one thing: it had to be framed in black with a narrow trim of gold.

'That is the way they did it then,' he said. 'And I recommend to all my customers that they do it this way.'

The logic of his appeal was inescapable. I had become one of his customers. It would not do, now, to begin suggesting alternatives.

'Fine, we'll frame it that way,' the owner said, peering at me over the tops of his bifocals. 'Come back in a week. It'll be ready for you then.'

That map has hung on our wall ever since.

'*A new and moſt exact map of AFRICA. Deſcribed by N.I. Viſcher and don into Engliſh. Enlarged and Corrected acording to I Bleau and Others With the Habits of ye people & ye manner of ye Cheife sitties. ye like neua before.*
       LONDON by ye White
Printed Colloured and areto befould by Iohn Ouerton at horse meere ye Fountaine Tavern without Newgate.'

It has prompted endless conversations as people stare at the neat copperplate handwriting and the engravings of people, places, ships and animals that fill the stained, creased paper.

When you look carefully, the first thing you notice is that it is only the position of the river mouths which bear any resemblance to the geography of the great rivers we know today. *Nilus, Niger, Congo*: from the coastline you can trace their flow through imaginary mountain ranges into hidden, mythical lakes.

The ocean has traditionally been the symbol of the unknown, but for the makers of this map it was the other way around. The routes across the seas had by then been charted for centuries. At the turn of the eighteenth century, longitude was still a tentative matter of dead reckoning and hopeful guesswork. Latitude, based on the position of the sun and the stars, was a more precise measure.

Despite these limitations, the Portuguese caravels, the Dutch trading ships and the English Men of War had been sailing the sea paths from Europe all the way across the coasts of Asia to the isolated ports of Japan for nearly two centuries.

The true flow of those rivers to the ocean from the interior of the vast continent of Africa was the real unknown to those ancient sailors. The maps they spread out on the polished tables in the captain's cabin were no help to them. The outline of the continent was clear. It hardly differs from the satellite pictures we see today. But the spidery black ink of the coastline stood as a border between two worlds – between the growing world of the caravels and the trade routes, and the then completely unknown interior of Africa.

Some of the places we know today do exist on that map. Cairo is *Cair*; *Loanda* is there in Angola; *Tunis* and *Tangiers* are spelt the way we would do so today. There is *C. de Bona Spei* or the Cape of Good Hope. *LI BYA* is buried far in the west with an enigmatic note saying: *Deghir now called Sarra which fignifieth Defert*. Surprisingly, there is no Timbuktu, but there is a Congo, Guinea, *Biafara* and Benin – *'whose King is adored by the people for a God and will not bee feene they alfo believe that he doeth not eat'*

There are also sheer absurdities: there is an engraving of an elephant swallowing the head of a rhinoceros; *Here are Amazones*, is written across one blank space; the Nile emerges from two-thirds of the way down the continent, from the vast *Zaire lake* where, of course, there are lurking both *tritons and sirens*.

Still, despite these far-fetched inventions, the equator and those faded lines of latitude and longitude are not too far off the modern positions. If you followed their coordinates today with an electronic GPS machine, they would take you to much the same place on the continent that the ancient sailors might have found by the stars and with their chronographs and their brass sextants. What you might find there, of course, will have changed beyond recognition.

The map on my wall, then, is a kind of halfway station. Its well-thumbed centre, its edges now just beginning to crumble, its ornate, engraved compass roses somehow invite the mind to linger between the past and the present, between knowledge and the imagination, between ways of knowing and ways of seeing.

For years now, that ancient map on my wall has stood as a silent witness to my coming and going across Africa and, more lately, across the wider world. It has come to stand for something more than sentiment, though. I have come to see that, today, we who work in television are in the constant process of creating maps. New, ambiguous charts that shift and change constantly.

The images we film are creating a vast map of the world that flickers and hums behind the curved lines of a TV screen or a computer terminal. It is unfixed territory for us today, just as the old, unknown world of geography was for those ancient sailors and the Africans who greeted them warily when they first appeared on the horizon.

This new map of the world is not defined by lines of latitude and longitude – the minute, myriad points of intersection in this new world are the television cameras, the satellite dishes, the cellphones, the laptop computers that are the tools of our information age. These machines are the gateways into the matrix. They are the doors leading into the electronic corridors where the world looks in at itself at a thousand different points and out again towards a thousand more. It is a moving, constantly changing hall of mirrors, a vast chamber of echoes – a blurred, uncertain area where understanding and the imagination swirl and mingle endlessly.

I will never forget the first radio I owned as a child. I loved turning it on at night when the door was closed and I was supposed to be asleep. There was something compelling in the glow that emitted from the bulb underneath the face. I was fascinated by the red cursor that slipped across as I searched for a station – a tiny ship sailing at my command through a sea of pale green light, guiding me far away, deep into the night outside, a solitary voyage to all the world that lay in the darkness beyond.

There were nights when I had had enough of pop music, quiz shows and radio dramas. Those nights all I wanted to do was listen to the static at the farthest end of the tuning bar. I put the radio on the pillow next to my head and turned the volume as low as I could. The static was exciting. Every now and then, amongst its chaos of hisses and crackles, I would hear a sudden snatch of a foreign language: Portuguese, perhaps, from the moonlit beaches of Angola or Mozambique, or French from the vast, troubled forests of the Congo. Sometimes the rapid cadences of an African language would tumble out, or a snatch of unfamiliar music and song and then, as quickly as they had appeared, the voices would fade away again, drifting into the hiss of the radio night. The static didn't seem empty to me. It was filled with life and with possibilities.

Television has multiplied this experience many times over. Millions of people across the world now flip through the dozens of channels on their satellite dishes, surfing the waves of information and images that bombard us constantly, trying to navigate their own way through the vast sea of colour and light that seethes through the world in which we live.

The people in the rich, developed world peer nervously at the images on their screens of the poor countries that surround them, while those people who live in these poor countries at the edge stare back at their screens at the glittering opulence of London, Tokyo and, of course, New York.

Over the years, I have found myself travelling and working as a television journalist in Africa, the Middle East and Central Asia. The journeys I have made have been varied. They have been visits to places outside the developed world where some of the major news events of the turn of the millennium have happened. What links them all is that they are journeys out – away from the centre into the geography of the edge.

They have been physical journeys. Anyone who has suffered the shattering and humiliating experience of a long-haul economy class flight will know that it still takes money, time and often exhausting effort to move from one place on the globe to another. The crossover in meaning between the word 'travel' and 'travail' or the French *'travail'*, work, is as valid today as it was in the days when tiny sailing ships ploughed through the high seas and dromedary trains plodded across the steppes.

But in today's world of instantaneous electronic communications, I have come to see that in these travels I have wandered into an extra dimension, a layer of experience that has only become possible with the invention of television. I have come to see that they have been travels into a new province of the human mind. One that exists because of what we see of each other on our television screens.

It is a place where anything might happen. An uncharted territory where our different worlds intersect all too often only in the dark hollow at the end of a rifle barrel. Or, as we know so horribly now, in the shattered glass and twisted steel and flames rising above the skyline of Manhattan.

RWANDA

A NEW WAR ACROSS THE BORDER

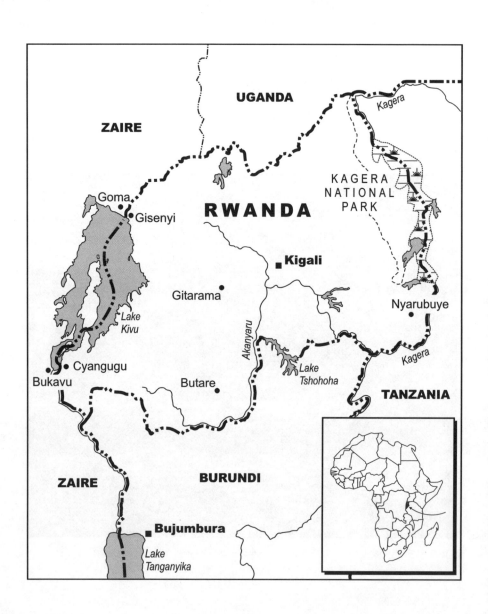

Arriving

Misty layers of rain cloud were building up over the distant blue hills. The image of the brown vastness of Lake Victoria was still fresh in my mind, the fishing canoes tiny and bobbing in and out of the silvery ripples that lined its surface.

The plane descended through the thin air of the African highlands. I could see the rusting tin roofs of the shanties and the green patches of manioc on the hillsides. As we came lower, I watched the people walking on the red earth footpaths that spread out through the banana groves, following the contours of the slopes. The pathways reminded me of the lines on a giant hand, etched deep into the surface of the earth by the slow erosion of countless comings and goings.

We landed and taxied down the runway. Through the narrow porthole I could see the long savanna grass, green with the recent rains, growing up to the edge of the tarmac. Four soldiers dressed in camouflage and carrying AK-47s stood outside the glass and concrete terminal building. Above them was a jagged hole in the wall surrounded by long feathers of black soot burned into the concrete – the entry point of a rocket grenade. There were bullet holes around the glass entrance doors.

We taxied in next to the only other plane on the apron. A huge United Nations Antonov with the flag of one of the new post-Soviet republics painted on its tail.

I climbed down the steel and aluminium gangway, acutely conscious of the rickety steps bouncing erratically under the heavy tromp of the passengers' feet. The cool fresh air filled my lungs. I could feel it flowing into my head, clearing my thoughts. I had spoken to no one on the flight. I had nothing to say. From the moment the pilot announced that we had crossed the border, I had slipped into a world of my own, a kind of daze where everything around me seemed unreal.

I could hardly believe I was in Rwanda. It was October 1996. After covering the genocide there in 1994, I had always said I would never go back.

There was a radio playing in the taxi on the way to the hotel. The song was a teenybopper disco tune, a heavy seductive beat that filled the interior of the car.

Every now and then the driver would glance back at us in the rear-view mirror. Looking for a good tip, he greeted us with a forced cheerfulness, and was only prevented from launching into a monologue of commentary by our own obvious silence. The music was his attempt to please us, but instead it reminded me of how the radio had been used to broadcast the messages of hate that had fuelled the murder.

I was sure, too, that the driver had his own memories of the genocide. Every single person I have ever met in Rwanda, Hutu or Tutsi, has had at least one member of their family murdered by someone of the other ethnic group.

It takes a moment for that to sink in – but try to imagine the layers of pain and rage, and fear. One has to understand the vast network of memory that echoes beneath the surface of daily life in Rwanda.

I once met a man who admitted to having taken part in the killing. His name was Denis Bagaruka. He sat in the prosecutor's office of the tiny rural commune of Rusumo in south-eastern Rwanda. Denis was a tall, striking man with a handsome, angular face. I remember him sitting there on a wooden bench in blue overalls with the sleeves cut off above the elbow.

He seemed calm, even self-possessed, as he leaned back against the stained, dirty wall. It was only when you looked into his eyes that you could see the troubled emptiness that lay in their depths. His dossier was on the desk nearby on top of a huge pile of plain white folders. His name was written on the outside in neat handwriting. In the centre of the folder a single word described the crime he had confessed to: 'Genocide'.

Denis, a Hutu, had taken part in the killing of Tutsis in the churchyard of Nyarubuye – 'The Place of Stones' – a remote Catholic church deep in the hills nearby. The killing had taken place over four days, beginning April 17, 1994. No one knows for certain how many people were killed in that time, but between three and four thousand people had gathered there in the hope of finding protection from the killers. Herded together and trapped by the brick walls of the churchyard, the Tutsis made easy victims. There was only a handful of survivors.

In June 1994, only a few weeks after the slaughter, I had been to the haunted churchyard of Nyarubuye and witnessed the piles of rotting bodies that lay as mute evidence of the cruelty of the killers. I remembered the rotting bodies with their severed hands, their wide-open throats, torn and mutilated, and their neatly sliced skulls. I would never forget them.

I wanted that day to know from Denis how it had been possible for him to do what he and the others had done.

'No one survived,' he told us. 'Everyone was killed. We couldn't spare the children's lives. Our orders were to kill everyone.'

I knew this. I was hoping to find some different answers. I wanted to know how . . . how did it happen? What did you feel? I remember looking into Denis Bagaruka's eyes. They were not the blank, stereotyped orbs of the cheap thriller novel. They were the eyes of a man, lost now forever, haunted by the terrible distance that lay between him and the world around – by the distance that lay between him and us. His eyes did not ask for pity, and I certainly had none to give him, but in the steady frankness of his gaze I could not help but see another human being.

On an impulse, I asked him the strangest question I have ever asked anyone. 'Was it hard work?'

He stared at us while the question was translated, and then he replied calmly and fell silent as the answer was relayed back to us.

The translator was stunned; a mist of confused, angry tears filled her eyes. 'It was a . . . a most extraordinary answer. I don't know quite how to translate it . . . "Yes, it was hard work," he said. "We got very tired doing it." '

Later we had Denis' exact words translated for us. 'It was tiring work. They would beat you or fine you, therefore it was compulsory to go. Even if you were ill you had to go or ask permission to be excused. It was an absolute order.

'We heard the radio telling us to be strong and to cut down the tall trees. Our local leader explained that these trees were the Tutsis. We were listening to the radio and because of that and what the soldiers were urging we started to kill our neighbours.'

With the radio blaring in the background, I gazed out the window as we drove through town. Just exactly where we were driving, on one of the main roads of Kigali, the capital city, I remembered passing through the roadblocks manned by the Hutu extremist militia, known as the *interahamwe*, in an armoured UN vehicle in 1994. It was early in the day, just after 8:00 am, and already the soldiers and their civilian allies were drunk. They stared at us through the bulletproof glass with total menace. A little further up the road I saw a young boy, no more than ten years old, carrying an obsolete colonial-issue .303 rifle. The look of hatred on his young face had shocked me profoundly.

Much later, at the Rwanda TV station, I was shown footage of this very street taken by an unknown cameraman who had obviously been in league with the extremists. They were horrific pictures, images that were never broadcast, and probably never will be. The footage showed the bodies of people who had been apprehended at the roadblocks and discovered to be, or were accused of being, Tutsis.

The side of this road was lined with hundreds of fresh corpses still bleeding into the gutters from their slashed throats and crushed heads. Some were still alive – you could tell by the red bubbles forming in the corners of their mouths. I hadn't asked to see such things. We were looking in the Rwandan TV tape library for footage of a political leader. We had to spool quickly through a large number of tapes and those images were on an unmarked tape. Looking around me in that room, I realized that the library was filled with unmarked tapes.

That day, though, my first back in Rwanda, those images seemed unreal. The city today was filled with the vibrancy of a normal African capital. There were children walking along the road, smiling and waving; women carrying baskets of fruit and vegetables on their heads; men pushing bicycles laden with charcoal and bags of corn.

There was a part of me that could hardly believe it was true, and an equal part of me that wanted to believe it would always be this way now. I remembered the words of a young American aid worker I had talked to recently: 'The new government is serious about stopping the cycle of violence.'

But now, in October 1996, there was a new war across the border in neighbouring Zaire. The rebellion against the ageing dictator Mobutu Sese Seko had finally begun. The fighting was in its early stages, but it was growing rapidly. Despite the hopes that so many people held out for the fragile peace in Rwanda, a new cycle of violence was again beginning on its borders, only two years after the genocide had been brought to an end.

We arrived at the Umubano Hotel. Everyone still called it by its old name, The Meridien, but the Rwandan government had taken it over after its European owners had quietly exited. It was still in a somewhat ramshackle state, having been on the front lines in the fight for Kigali in 1994. The buffet on the top floor of the hotel was the best in Kigali, the bar was operating and the swimming pool was filled with sparkling blue water. The carpets on floors inside were filthy with large unpleasant stains. It was better not to try and imagine what their origins were.

Many of the doors still had splintered holes in them. The killers searching for Tutsi victims had forced them open. The horrible aluminium railing on the balcony outside my room had the twisted oval holes caused by high-velocity assault rifle bullets. The phones didn't always work and room service was erratic and usually just a polite fiction. But every room had a TV with excellent reception of CNN, BBC World and Canal Plus.

I met with some of the other journalists at the edge of the pool as the sun was going down behind the green hills of Kigali. I needed to catch up on the latest news of what was happening across the border in Zaire.

The revolt against Mobutu had broken out a week or so before. Its roots lay in the waves of violence that the Rwandan genocide had unleashed. One of the biggest upheavals in Eastern Zaire was the mass movement of nearly a million Hutu refugees who had fled Rwanda in the wake of the Rwandan Patriotic Front (RPF) invasion and takeover of the country in 1994. At this point, in October 1996, the refugees were living in massive, semi-permanent camps on the Rwanda-Zaire border.

The world had watched in 1994 as they poured out of Rwanda, but unlike most refugees the world over, they were not mere victims of a civil war. Of course, there were the innocent among them, but thousands of those who fled across the border were members of the extremist government, the army and the *interahamwe*. They were responsible for the massacres, they had urged and even forced thousands of Hutu peasants like Denis Bagaruka to take part in the killing. The Rwandan genocide was a crime in which hundreds of thousands of people were guilty, most of whom were now living in the refugee camps in Zaire.

From those same camps after 1994, the extremists continued with their plans and their efforts to eliminate Tutsis from the face of the earth. One of their first acts, after setting up a government in exile inside the camps, was to impose a tax on the food donated by the international community. After the aid workers had distributed the grain, the refugees were forced to hand a portion of it over to the extremists. They then took the grain and sold it to the local Zaireans, who often had less to eat than the refugees. The money from selling the aid grain was used to buy weapons. The weapons were given to the remnants of the FAR (Forces Armée Rwandaise or Armed Forces of Rwanda) and *interahamwe* who were roaming the rainforest and making repeated guerrilla raids into RPF-controlled Rwanda, killing Tutsis and sowing as much mayhem as they could.

Initially restrained in their response, there was no denying that the RPF had become increasingly brutal in their reprisals against Hutus in Rwanda suspected of collaborating with the *interahamwe*. Most observers felt that the RPF government was trying, though, unlike the Hutu extremists who still talked of eliminating the Tutsi. The new government talked about national reconciliation.

They arrested suspected *genocidaire* (a coinage in French meaning 'those who have committed genocide'). Hundreds of thousands of them languished in overcrowded prisons awaiting trial for suspected involvement in the genocide. It was not a perfect solution, but at least there were no mass reprisals as so many people had predicted. There was some hope that Rwanda might slowly begin to break the cycle of killing and revenge that had marred so much of its post-independence history.

The camps and the fact that nearly one million of Rwanda's people were living in them as refugees outside their own country was a massive obstacle to achieving this.

But the growing war in Zaire was complicating matters. The rebellion was begun by ethnic Tutsis who had lived in the area of Kivu province in Zaire since the eighteenth century. Known as the 'Banyamulenge', in recent years they had been increasingly discriminated against by the Mobutu regime. The 300 000 or so Banyamulenge had their Zairean citizenship revoked as far back as 1981. Since then they had constantly been under the threat of having their land taken away and being expelled from the country. The final straw came in late 1996 when the Zairean army, assisted by the *interahamwe* launched a pogrom against the Tutsis. An estimated 15 000 Tutsis were killed and tens of thousands more driven from their homes and their land. They had now decided to fight back.

'The situation is changing rapidly,' one of the journalists said, leaning forward in the fading light and pouring a fresh glass of the local Primus beer. 'As far as we can tell, the Banyamulenge are as close as 30 kilometres away from Bukavu. The reports are that most of the Zaireans have fled, leaving only some units of the DSP (Presidential Guard) and the ex-FAR and *interahamwe*. The story is not yet in Goma. It is in southern Kivu province and will soon be in Bukavu.'

'The rebellion is growing,' a photographer said. His cameras were spread out on the round concrete table in front of him. He leaned forward and rolled a cigarette.

'This could be the break up of Zaire,' one of the other journalists added. 'The central authority is weakened. People will take advantage of it. Look at the break up of the Soviet Union. It's the same here.'

'Mobutu is hiring mercenaries wherever he can get them,' said a British journalist. 'There is even a rumour that Bob Denard is in Kinshasa. He's missing from his village in France and they say he's in Kinshasa, getting ready to raise a new army of mercenaries for Mobutu's final showdown.'

'All the borders are closed now,' the photographer added glumly.

'It's going to be a full-scale war,' somebody else said as the last of the twilight slipped away behind the hills. I remembered the same horizon filled with the echoes of gunfire, the distant boom of mortars and the flare of tracer rising into the sky in the hazy greyness of first light. The horizon was silent now; there was only the comforting sound of crickets filling the cool evening air. I watched the waiters come and go with trays of drinks around the turquoise glow of the lighted swimming pool.

A string of colourful party lights winked on above the outdoor bar and a group of trendy young Rwandans were laughing above their cold bottled

Heineken. There was music gently ebbing across the dark expanse of the hotel lawn.

Through the Forest

'They shoved a grenade, a fucking *hand grenade* into his mouth,' the photographer was saying. He paused with his fork hanging over his omelette. 'Five Zairean soldiers held up a BBC guy and his cameraman on the road in Kivu. They took all their money. They were lucky to get out alive.'

Reuters cameraman Patrick Muiruri raised his eyebrows at me over the edge of his coffee cup. The two of us were to set off after breakfast for the southern Rwanda-Zaire border at Cyangugu, the Rwandan town at the bottom of Lake Kivu, just opposite Bukavu.

'The information coming out of Bukavu is unclear,' Reuters coordinator Victor Antonie said somewhat frantically while the porters were throwing our luggage into the car we had rented. 'You can't get across the border, so you're going to have to wait it out in Cyangugu. But the first news pictures you get, you get the tapes back here.'

The main road leading west out of Kigali was crammed with people carrying on with their ordinary lives. Men pushed bicycles loaded with bulging bags of charcoal, sugar or maize meal. Women in colourful dresses walked slowly, carrying sacks of clothing, huge yellow bunches of bananas or wide-mouthed baskets filled with fruit, dried fish or sugar cane, each bundle balanced precariously on top of their heads,

All along the edges of the road were tiny boys armed with slender poles six or eight feet long. They confidently herded the large Ankole cattle with their long, curved horns.

They are the same wide, arched horns that you see on the cattle in Egyptian carvings on the walls of the pyramids and temples. They are the descendants of the seven kine 'fatfleshed and well favoured' that came up out of the river in the dream that a troubled Pharoah told Joseph about.

Recent DNA testing shows that the ancestors of these animals were brought into Africa by migrants from central Asia long before the advent of recorded time. Herds of these cattle have been chased by small boys up and down the Nile valley and through the fertile lands of its headwaters for over 10 000 years now.

It seemed hard to imagine that this was the road leading to a brutal, modern war. But many of the houses and shops were pockmarked with bullet scars. We drove past shattered buildings that stood as testimony to the fierce battles that raged during the genocide.

In 1994 I had filmed the RPF dropping mortars on the Rwandan government army. It was exactly this area where the bombs had landed. What was a marketplace now had been the front line only two years before.

Our driver, Gustave Murenzi, could speak only a little English and Patrick and I could not speak more than a few words of French.

In the car, Gustave haltingly told us something of his own story. 'The *interahamwe* wanted to kill us,' he said. 'Now I am starting again. The *interahamwe* say they will come back by fighting. We are waiting for them – because they want to kill me.'

Patrick was a very experienced cameraman and journalist. He had covered the US invasion of Somalia, the civil war in Sudan, and had worked all through the genocide in Rwanda in 1994. He was married, and his wife had recently given birth to their first child.

It was a beautiful drive through the deep shaded valleys of Rwanda. Gustave cranked up the music on his crackling, tinny sound system as we wound our way through the layers of rounded green hills covered in eucalyptus, banana and the occasional tea plantation.

People were wandering up and down the pathways and fields that crisscrossed the hills. Both men and women were hoeing in the fields. Elsewhere men were chopping wood, and women were carrying water. In the shaded valleys where the sun had not yet reached, traces of morning mist clung to the soft red earth. The pale blue smoke of charcoal fires rose up against the bright sky; we could hear cattle lowing and children laughing.

We passed the town of Gitarama which had seen some of the fiercest fighting two years before as the Rwandan government army held firm here, hoping to delay the advance of the RPF rebels.

What had once been a three or four-storey concrete building lay crushed at the crossroads. It had been reduced to layers of dust and flattened concrete slabs by mortar shells. I wondered at the fate of the soldiers trapped inside its increasingly fragile walls as the battle raged and shell after shell pounded the superstructure.

Already weeds and grass were growing in the cracks and hollows left by the force of the explosives.

I had seen death from a mortar shell before on the front lines in 1994 when the RPF were taking Kigali, block by grim block. I walked into a tiny shop front just off the street. I entered the room half-dazed with exhaustion and the horror of all that I had already seen.

I remember seeing the gaping hole in the tin roof, and looking at the holes and deep gouges in the plaster. There was a huge splash of blood on the wall opposite me that had dried in awful waves of brown concentric rings. In the corner of the room there was a pile of rags, and half-concealed beneath it, the drying, twisted body of a soldier in camouflage uniform. I hardly noticed the smell, so used to death had we become.

I could see the signs of battle all around me: the blasted roof, the shrapnel scars in the walls, the bloodstains, the dead soldier. It was all a confused jumble of impressions. For months it stayed with me, a random swirling of memory and horror.

A few kilometres further down the road we came to one of the last surviving fragments of the great rainforest that had once covered most of Rwanda.

The green layers of forest-covered mountains stretched into the misty sky as far as the eye could see. They plunged precipitously away from the damp roadway. A single skid would be enough to send our car tumbling down, smashing into the broad trunks of the hardwood trees clinging to the rocky outcrops.

It was in the shaded depths of these rainforests that the earliest human inhabitants of Rwanda, the BaTwa, the pygmies, first set up their shelters of leaves and bent branches against the cool, wet rains of central Africa. As far as anyone knows, the Twa people have been in Rwanda since the first humans began spreading out and inhabiting the savannas and forests of Africa. Today the BaTwa in Rwanda make up only one per cent of the population. They have lost their original language and they speak the same language that the Tutsis and the Hutus speak, Kinyarwanda. As a tiny, marginalized population, they have little or no political power. Hutu extremists targeted them along with the Tutsis for extinction during the 1994 genocide.

The modern history of Rwanda begins in what corresponds roughly to the late medieval period of Europe. Over the course of centuries both Hutus and Tutsis migrated into the forested hills. So much has been written about the tortured relationship between them. Victorian writers favoured a 'Hamitic' racial theory which held that the taller and more angular-featured Tutsis, who made up only 12 to 15 per cent of the population, were immigrants of a 'superior' race, perhaps from Ethiopia or even as far away as the Ancient Near East. The largely shorter, more squat Hutus were seen as a lower race, easily conquered and subdued by the invaders from the North.

The problem with this theory is that wherever they came from in the past, today – and for all of historical memory – Hutus and Tutsis cannot be seen as distinct ethnic groups. They speak the same language, intermarriage is common, they do not live in separate regions, but amongst one another on the hills, even the traditional definition of a 'Hutu' and a 'Tutsi' was fluid. It was possible for a Hutu to rise into the aristocratic ranks of the Tutsi or for a Tutsi to sink to Hutu status. The only firm difference between them was that Tutsis owned cattle and Hutus cultivated the land. The ultimate origins of this distinction are so lost in the mists of time and the uncertainties of the oral tradition that it is impossible to define exactly how this difference emerged.

It was true that the Mwami, the supreme, semi-divine emperor, was always a Tutsi, but some of the other local rulers were cattle and land-owning Tutsis who had once been Hutus. The Hutus owed complete loyalty to the Mwami and to the Tutsi power structure, but the hegemony was never defined in racial terms. The basic structure of Rwandan society was aristocratic but it was made up of a complex system of clan and family alliances.

The immediate roots of the waves of killing and revenge that have swept this region lie in the last years of Belgian rule. In 1959, the last Mwami to rule in Rwanda died. In the days that followed, a number of prominent Hutu leaders were murdered by a monarchist Tutsi clan hoping to consolidate their power over the country. The anger that had been there for so long finally broke out. There was a massive Hutu uprising, the first in modern times. Some 100 000 Tutsis were killed and tens of thousands of others fled to Uganda and other neighbouring countries.

The Tutsi elite, being largely better-educated, had enthusiastically adopted the new ideas of independence that were sweeping the continent. This did not suit the Belgians and they switched their support and allegiance to the mass-based Hutu politicians.

In 1962, when Rwanda gained independence, the main Hutu party, Parmehutu, took power. The Tutsi monarchy was abolished, and the once dominant Tutsi became a politically impotent minority. This, predictably perhaps, led to invasion by Tutsi exiles based in Uganda.

They got to within 20 kilometres of Kigali before they were forced back. A wave of revenge killings against Tutsis broke out across the country, causing thousands more to flee. It was this 1959 and 1962 generation of refugees who formed the basis of the Rwandan Patriotic Front.

In October 1990, the RPF invaded northern Rwanda again from their bases in Uganda.

After an initial surge of killing of Tutsis suspected of collaborating with the RPF invasion, the civil war against the Hutu-dominated Rwandan government continued sporadically through the early 1990s. In April 1994, the plane carrying Juvenal Habyarimana, the president of Rwanda, and Cyprien Ntaryamira, the president of Burundi, was shot down as it was coming in to land in Kigali.

Still today, no one knows who was responsible. There is much evidence to suggest that Habyarimana was shot down by extremists in his own Presidential Guard who felt that he was giving away too much to the RPF in the peace talks that had been initiated to end the civil war. As soon as the plane crashed, killing both presidents, roadblocks were set up. The Hutu extremists started moving from door to door in the city, armed with prepared lists of names of Tutsis and Hutu moderates. Hundreds of people were slaughtered within an hour of the presidents' plane having been shot down.

By nightfall, the killing had spread to cities and towns all over Rwanda. The genocide had begun.

The silent immensity of the forest seemed to fill the car. Gustave drove slowly along the narrow road. The surface was wet from the humidity. It doubled back and forth through the tortuous hills, forcing us up and down a series of hairpin bends. Fronds of enormous ferns dripped over the edge of the tarmac. Lianas and tree moss hung off the branches of vast mahogany and ebony trees. Swirls of cool grey mist tumbled down into the shaded valleys.

We turned a bend in the road and four colobus monkeys, covered in jet-black fur with silver-white streaks, bounded across the road and leaped into the trees. All over the continent these beautiful pelts had been sought for ceremonial garb for chieftains and shamans. In the nineteenth century the monkeys were killed for trimming on the coats of fashionable New Yorkers and Parisians. Today, though, the main threat to the survival of these creatures is the bush meat industry and the rapid deforestation of their natural habitat.

They cried raucously as they swung away through the branches. Within moments, the only sign of them was a rippled movement in the broad forest canopy. The silence was broken only by a few bird calls, echoing deep and far away across the valleys.

We came to a dip in the road, narrow and surrounded by huge trees. There was snow on the road, a white scattering like tiny clouds hidden among the dense vegetation. It was smashed to a grey pulp by each car that came through. The air around us was cool, but not particularly cold. At the crest of the hill that lay beyond, the sun emerged from behind the clouds for a few moments, its rays spreading out across the distant layers of forested hills.

For a few brief moments the sunlight broke through the forest canopy and shone through to the rotting, fertile ground. Its hard straight beams and angular shadows made me think of the carvings on the musical instruments and the fetishes that one could see for sale in the streets of Kigali.

The carvings, it seemed to me, reflected the way light broke up in the forest. The tall horizontals, cut by sharp oblique angles, were like the fractured beams of sunlight shining through the cluttered tangle of overgrowth. The deep, hooded expressions were like faces emerging from the shadowy gloom between the trees. They spoke so eloquently of a world unknown to people like me from a modern, electronically lit city.

In the mid-nineteenth century Speke and Burton had come through the southernmost tip of this very forest, in the days when the trees stretched south and west for hundreds of miles. Their expedition halted on the banks of Lake Tanganyika only a hundred kilometres or so south of where we were. By the time they got that far, Speke had almost lost the hearing in one of his ears. While sleeping in his tent one night, a beetle climbed into his ear. Speke tried to dig it out with a penknife and damaged his ear. For months afterwards he marched grimly through the African bush, his face swollen and pus dribbling from his damaged and infected ear.

Burton was determined to push on. They stopped eventually at Uvira, at the extreme northern end of Lake Tanganyika. They wanted to push on to the mouth of the Rusizi river, but their followers refused to go on.

Uvira was the limit of the Arab slave-trading caravans and their African companions feared the hostile tribes that lay beyond. They were forced, in the end, to return to Ujiji, further south on the east bank of Lake Tanganyika.

There was real danger in the forest around us. Its cool hidden depths were the main route that the *interahamwe* bands used to infiltrate RPF-ruled Rwanda from the camps in Zaire. The road was guarded by soldiers dressed in camouflage uniforms and their trademark black gumboots. But this was an army whose resources were stretched to the limit. The RPF was guarding the road in *pairs*. They had no large machine guns, armoured vehicles or other heavy weapons. They carried only their Kalashnikovs and the occasional grenade or bayonet fastened to their belts. Each pair would be an easy target for an ambush coming out of the thick forest. No doubt these soldiers knew the pathways through the trees as well as their enemies did, but almost every day now there were attacks on Tutsis and RPF troops inside Rwanda. There was no reason to assume that the extremists would not attack journalists. They mostly hated the press now, after the extensive coverage that had been given to the genocide two years before. Gustave was a Tutsi. He could expect no mercy if we were ambushed or kidnapped. 'Night,' he said to us in his halting English. 'Night in *la forêt* is not good. There are many *interahamwe*.'

We were getting close to Cyangugu now. We came around a bend. There was a TV journalist standing at the edge of the road. She was holding a microphone and talking into the camera.

We stopped and got out to speak to her. You could see the town of Cyangugu nestling in the green hills on the Rwandan side of the border. Lake Kivu and the Rusizi river gleamed turquoise in the sun. On the other side of their banks was the Zairean town of Bukavu. We could see the white colonial cathedral on the hill above the town and the houses nestling on the sloping hillsides.

The view into Zaire was hazy, but the plumes of pale smoke rising into the sky in the terrain beyond the town were clear. They were tall, billowing columns, narrow where they came up from the ground, and spreading wide as they dissipated in the high, thin air. There were two or three tiny puffs of smoke suddenly curling up from the green landscape. A few moments later we heard the muted *crummp, crummp* of mortar shells exploding. The faraway blasts echoed for a moment, hanging in the cool forest air. Then the sound of birds filled the silent damp roadway.

We drove on. The forest petered out and gave way to huts and cultivated fields. The UN had set up a camp in expectation of the flood of refugees that they anticipated would soon come across the border. The blue plastic shelters had been erected in neat rows on the hillside, empty and waiting to be filled with people.

As we descended towards the low altitude of the lake, the road switched back on itself through the steep contours of the mountainsides. The car strained at every bend, the wheels just holding on to the surface.

Gustave reached over to the dashboard and changed the stations on the radio. We were close enough to the border to pick up the station from Kivu province in Zaire. There was an announcement in French and Swahili: 'The governor of South Kivu appeals to the people to be calm. Reopen your businesses. Ignore Radio Rwanda which is telling lies. The Tutsis are getting ready to invade and attack the refugees.'

In the front seat, Patrick shifted his weight awkwardly.

'Signs of panic, hey?' he said, cocking one eyebrow under his baseball cap. 'When you start appealing to the populace to stay calm.'

We stopped at the Hotel Kivu. We booked rooms and went on to the small concrete balcony for lunch. Just below ran the Rusizi river. The water was as clear and green as jade, filtered by the porous volcanic rock that made up the geology of these hills. From the balcony you could see where the Rusizi flowed through the last remnants of the forest into Lake Kivu. The river and the lake formed the border between Zaire and Rwanda. An old bridge, called Rusizi I, connected the two countries. Further upstream was another bridge, Rusizi II. Rusizi I was a steel structure made of criss-crossing beams and trusses. It had been built in the colonial days by the Belgians, and was still the main source of contact between Rwanda and her increasingly hostile neighbour, Zaire.

Patrick and I ordered lunch: sandwiches and Cokes. Zaire was a steep, grassy hillside on the other bank of the river. It looked close enough, almost, to reach out and touch. The border was closed, but somehow we would have to find a way to get across. There was a war going on behind that grassy hillside.

For the moment, though, there was nothing we could do to get over. The distant mortars had fallen silent. Perhaps it was that we were low now and the sound of their explosions was muffled by the hills around us.

We waited for our lunch. On an outcrop of rock in the middle of the river some young boys were fishing. They flicked long white poles in and out of the water, chatting offhandedly to one another. Every now and then one would call out joyfully and swing his pole back wildly. You could see a tiny glint of silver, whirling and twisting at the end of his line. With a deft movement of the fingers, the fish was plucked off the hook and left to flap its minute fins against the rock.

'You are journalists?' a man sitting at a table opposite us asked. 'The Zairean soldiers are getting scared. Some of them have been saying to us: "I'm not a bad guy, so treat me well when I come across the river."'

'Is the situation getting worse, then?' Patrick asked.

'They say that so many guns are coming from Angola. The Banyamulenge are growing. Now four more tribes have joined their movement. Every day, the battle grows stronger –'

He was interrupted by a whirl of activity at the doorway. Four white journalists burst on to the balcony. They were filthy and covered in sweat. Their faces were red and sunburned. They were distracted, high on adrenalin and worse. I could see in their eyes the jittery edge of fear.

They shook hands with us briefly. They dragged out the chairs at our table and sat down heavily, exhausted and relieved at the same time. One of them, a TV cameraman, put his camera down and lit a cigarette. I could see the hands of another trembling as he grabbed at the mineral water the waiter had brought. Within moments, their story began tumbling out.

'We've just been stuck in a ditch for hours.'

'They pinned us down. Every time we tried to move, they opened up on us.'

'The Zairean officers *must* have known who we were. They were watching us with binoculars from the hill tops.'

'They were fucking us around, sending us a message from over the border.'

'Finally the RPF saw what was going on. They gave us covering fire.'

'One by one, we managed to get out, going from point of cover to point of cover.'

Slowly they began to calm down and the atmosphere around the table relaxed. We introduced ourselves.

'You guys have got to be careful,' their producer Tony said.

'Journalists are not neutral to those guys across the border,' his cameraman added. He was a South African from Durban called Alistair Lyne. He took a deep drag of his cigarette and swept his long blond hair back from his red, sweat-stained face.

'From now on, we've got to assume that we're the targets as much as anyone else.'

'Where are you staying?' Tony asked.

'Here,' Patrick said. 'In the hotel.'

'Fuck that,' Alistair said. He pointed across to where the road in Zaire curved around a hill and ran down the slope to meet the bridge. 'Last night there was a firefight only 50 metres from here. It's too dangerous.'

'There's a monastery on the hillside above town,' Tony said. 'That's where we're staying. It's much safer.'

The 'monastery' was actually a nunnery. It was high on the hillside overlooking both Cyangugu and Bukavu. From up at the nunnery you could see how little lay between them – just the calm, still waters of Lake Kivu and the Rusizi river catching the rays of the late afternoon sun. In the clear air, higher up, we could hear again the faint sound of gunfire and the 'boom' of a single mortar or hand grenade.

Ernest Hemingway came here once. Bukavu was called Costermansville then. It was in 1954, in the last years of the Belgian era. He was in the latter half of his life, seeking escape from all his own wars, and from the Western Europe of his youth, still dazed and recovering from the devastation of World War II. He had just published *The Old Man and The Sea*, perhaps his most famous book. Later in the year he would hear that he had won the Nobel Prize. Still, the years of heavy drinking and hard living were beginning to take their toll. He was only fifty-five, but was constantly plagued by a succession of minor ailments.

In 1954, the Costermansville that Hemingway saw was, at least on the surface, a place of peace and beauty:

> We landed at a very fine airstrip at the town of Costermansville situated on Lake Kivu. There is a first-class hotel with excellent food and accommodation and a view over the lake. The lake is one of the most beautiful I have ever seen. It is impossible to compare lakes accurately, but I would think that with its islands, broken outline, colour of water, it would be certainly as beautiful as Lago Maggiore or Lago di Garda. It is certainly much more beautiful than Lago di Como and I am quite sure that it contains less dead bodies, of human beings at any rate.
>
> In the morning, which was bright and lovely, we repaired the generator and the plane was thoroughly checked and we proceeded north . . .

The next day their plane crashed after they had circled the Murchison Falls in Uganda. Hemingway damaged his shoulder, and his wife Mary cracked her ribs. The wreckage was spotted and the news went out that the Hemingways had been killed. A river boat had found them, though, and took them down the Victoria Nile to Lake Albert where another plane was waiting to fly them to Kampala. Before it could take off, the plane hit a bump in the runway and burst into flames. The pilot got Mary clear, but Ernest had to force his way through a jammed door with his head and painful shoulder.

This time he sustained a full-scale concussion, damaged vertebrae, a ruptured liver, spleen and kidney. He lost part of his hearing and his vision and sustained first-degree burns on his face, arms and head. He dictated the jocular, superficial piece about his trip to Africa while he was in hospital in Nairobi. The truth was, though, that he had been badly injured and never really recovered. It was only five short, illness-ridden years after this African trip that he got up early one Sunday morning at his house in Idaho and fetched the double-barrelled shotgun that he pressed against his own forehead.

By dawn on April 7, 1994, the morning after the Presidential plane had been shot down and the killings had begun in Kigali, the *préfet* of Cyangugu, Emmanuel Bangambiki, had sealed the border to Bukavu, preventing Tutsis from escaping to Zaire. The *préfet* acted quickly. The steep hills and deep valleys surrounding the town made escape into the forest difficult.

The massacres in Cyangugu took place so swiftly that very few Tutsis had time to gather together and defend themselves. Many of the bodies were thrown in the lake. The sapphire waters that so struck Hemingway had lost their serene innocence forever. There were more bodies in Lake Kivu than there had ever been in Lake Como.

'Go back to Ethiopia, where you came from,' the killers cried as they threw the corpses into the water. For weeks afterwards, the rivers and lakes of Rwanda were cluttered with bloated, decaying bodies. Tens of thousands of them floated all the way to Lake Victoria.

The killing in Cyangugu was brutally efficient. An estimated 90 per cent of the Tutsis in Cyangugu prefecture were murdered before the tables turned with the RPF invasion and the extremists themselves fled into Zaire. There, from the camps that had given them refuge, they were now coming over the border to continue the fight against Tutsis.

We went to bed early that first night in Cyangugu. The lake stretched out as a black hole of darkness below. Across the water we could see the lights of Bukavu twinkling in the night. The distant shooting stopped and there was just the sound of insects and frogs in the streams and ponds around us.

There is a memory of another night, another journey – my first night in Rwanda in 1994. We had crossed over that afternoon travelling south from

Uganda and were camped out in a house in a town on the outermost edge of the war. In the early evening we could see the flashes of artillery fire on the horizon in the direction of Kigali.

As the stars came out, silence descended and we were left alone in the cool darkness of the African night. There were piles of empty machine gun shells in the garden, and dried hard kernels of corn scattered across the concrete floor of the house. We were filled with a mingled sense of fear and quiet relief that we were behind the front lines, away from the fighting. On the balcony outside there was the muted static of someone trying to find a rebel radio station on a shortwave radio.

We were clustered inside the house, eating food out of tins by the light of a candle. The talk amongst us moved to the war and the state of things as they were now.

'It is impossible to be certain of anything in war,' Lieutenant Frank said. 'Impossible. The front lines are always shifting.'

Pictures of War

I woke to the sound of bells pealing out from the chapel. I could hear the faint sound of the nuns singing. Their hymns drifted through the chorus of birdsong that filled the simple garden.

In the distance there was a single burst of machine gun fire inside Zaire. It echoed across the expanse of the lake. Then nothing. I wrapped a kikoi around my waist and took a shower under the cold water taps that the nunnery provided.

Patrick and I went for breakfast at the Hotel Kivu. It was too early in the morning for fishing in the river, but some Zairean women were hoeing the steep slope on the other side. It was about 7:45 am. We had almost finished our omelettes when a sustained burst of machine gun fire broke out further down the river. There was more shooting. And more, far away still, but evidence of renewed fighting. The women on the bank didn't even look up, they continued hoeing the ground, used to the ebb and flow of the skirmishes and judging that it did not yet threaten them.

'The Zairean military camp is up in that direction,' Patrick said. 'I think that's where it's coming from.'

We paid for our breakfast and drove up the river towards Rusizi II where there was a vantage point looking down into Zaire and into Camp Panzi, the military camp. The other crew had arrived at this hill top before us. We stood side by side and filmed what we could of the situation in Zaire. Tiny figures moved back and forth across the hillsides on the other side of the border. There was smoke rising from half a dozen places. We could hear the sounds of shelling and machine gun fire, but it was sporadic.

A single truck, its open back crammed with people, crawled slowly along a dirt road between the town of Bukavu and Camp Panzi. No doubt they had the impression they were moving fast, but from our high vantage point they were moving agonizingly slowly. Who were they? Where were they going? Were they fleeing from or eagerly rushing towards some point of conflict? We couldn't tell. There was a sudden upsurge of fighting on the far side of town, two, three more columns of white smoke billowed up into the sky.

In the distance we could see people running helter-skelter across the rounded peak of a hill as the sound of gunfire echoed around them. Men with guns were sprinting in the streets. Fires had broken out among the houses.

The shooting faded by lunchtime. We did not know where it had gone, but it was no longer within view of our cameras. The hillsides across the border had fallen silent, the columns of smoke had drifted up and away into the clear, empty sky.

That afternoon we went to the small refugee camp just outside Cyangugu to interview the growing trickle of people who had fled across the border. People crowded around us in the centre of the camp.

A woman was holding an infant in her arms. 'I lost three of my children,' she told us. Her eyes were filled with a kind of dreamy, exhausted look as if they were somehow sheltering her from the reality of what had happened. 'I don't know where they are.'

She began to cry. 'They are gone,' she said.

A young man pushed himself forward in the crowd. He had spent three days as a prisoner of the Zairean army. 'The soldiers beat us every day. They told us they were going to kill all the Tutsis.'

Next to him a teenage girl shook her head slowly. 'We had to leave.'

She slowly let her fingers run down over her nose and cheekbones. 'I have the features of a Tutsi.'

'What about the army?' I asked.

'The army left two days ago,' another woman answered. 'They were shooting everywhere and looting houses. They left the bodies lying in the streets. Now it is only bands of young men who control the town. They are roaming the streets with machetes and clubs and spears. They will kill us if we stay.' I asked for her name. Suddenly, she was close to tears. 'No,' she said. 'I cannot tell you that. You will put it out on the television and then they will look for me.'

'We need something different today,' Patrick said the next morning on the balcony of the Hotel Kivu. In the last twenty-four hours, Bukavu had become the place where things were happening. The brutal, irregular rhythms of war had brought the fighting to within kilometres of us.

Suddenly there was a burst of machine gun fire across the border. It rapidly grew louder, coming down the valley in successive waves of firing. The thudding reports of heavy gunfire echoed back and forth off the steep hillsides.

In moments it was very close to us. Now we could hear the sound of gunfire, and the whine of bullets overhead.

Patrick looked at me. 'They're in the centre of town. This must mean the fall of Bukavu.'

We decided to try and get up to the high ground where we could film. We climbed into the car and set off towards our base at the nunnery.

A huge column of water spurted up out of the centre of the lake, followed by a muffled, watery thud. It was so close we could feel the fine spray of water falling on us through the open window of the car.

'Christ,' Patrick said. 'The Zaireans are lobbing mortars across the border.'

There was a high-pitched whine and another explosion in the hills beyond Cyangugu.

'They're getting their range,' Patrick said calmly. 'The first one was short. The second one long. They're probably going for the bridge.'

On the road to the nunnery there was an RPF checkpoint. The soldiers were hunkered down behind whatever cover they could find. They were pointing their AK-47s and a single grenade launcher towards Zaire. They were watching developments. We could hear the sound of another mortar landing as they waved us on angrily.

'We've got to get out of this car,' Patrick said. 'It's a perfect target.'

Gustave seemed to be taking events in his stride. 'I will park at the monastery,' he said, looking at Patrick in the front seat.

At the nunnery people were taking cover as the mortar shells screamed overhead. Patrick and I went to the edge of the lawn to see what we could film below in Bukavu.

Heavy machine gun fire erupted from a hill top just behind the nunnery.

'Fucking hell,' Patrick said. 'That came from this side. Both sides are shooting across the border.'

Tony, the other producer, was at the nunnery. With him was a young American print journalist who had arrived only a few hours before. He had spent some time covering the war in Chechnya and was clearly badly shell-shocked.

A mortar shell burst directly above us with a loud crack. I heard the whirring of shrapnel spinning just over the top of my head. It was a strangely comforting sound, the fact that I had heard it meant it had missed me. But all the same, in that moment, I had come close to death. My brain registered all these thoughts, but there was no time to think further than this. The nuns were crouching behind a brick wall. Gustave had joined them. He took out a cigarette and lit it. He was laughing strangely, but I saw his hands were shaking.

My hands were shaking too, after the shrapnel. We were all scared. The war was no longer a distant set of images on a hillside. It was suddenly real and exploding all around us. We had to decide how to act. We needed pictures, but at the same time none of us was willing to take unnecessary risks. Tony and I agreed to pool our pictures. We didn't even know where Alistair and Chris were. They could be trapped, under fire, like the other day. This was no time for playing competitive news games with people's lives.

'What should we do now?' Tony asked.

'There's an RPF post on that hill,' I said pointing off to the right of the nunnery buildings.

'Outgoing fire attracts incoming,' Patrick said. 'We've got to get away from that machine gun post.'

'Let's go up that hill,' I said pointing to the left. 'It's away from the outgoing fire. We can film from the trees.'

Patrick looked at us. 'Remember, I'm the only black guy here. And I'm the one with the camera. I don't want anybody thinking I'm a soldier with a gun.'

Suddenly the American journalist erupted. '*We gotta get the fuck outa here. Once the shelling starts, they're going to fucking destroy this building and everything around it. We gotta get out of here, fast.*'

'Just calm down,' I said. 'We're going to be fine.' I was conscious that my voice was shaky. 'We've got to think about what to do.'

'We need pictures,' Tony snapped.

'What do you think, Patrick?' I asked.

'Let's try the hill,' he said. 'We're getting no pictures from here. But we walk slowly. No running. I don't want to do anything that looks suspicious.'

The hillside was a lot steeper than we anticipated. The mortars were coming in rapidly. They were screaming overhead and bursting in the air or on the ground a little way ahead. Patrick managed to squeeze off a couple of shots of the distant fighting in Bukavu and of shells landing in the lake and on the Rwandan side of the border.

We were halfway up the hill when a shattering blast of heavy fire erupted from among the trees at the crest.

'Fuck it,' Tony said. 'The RPF have set up another machine gun.'

Patrick was rolling the camera. The sound of the firing that would be picked up by the microphone made for very dramatic footage.

'We're caught between two outgoing positions,' Tony said. 'It's the worst possible place to be.'

We were all scared. It wasn't the first time any of us had filmed combat. We all carried our own fears, layered into each moment of our lives – and suddenly now brought frighteningly to the surface. We had to think ahead to what might happen and try to plan for it. The American had been in Grozny when the Russians bombarded it. There the Russian artillery did pound buildings to rubble, killing everyone unlucky enough to be caught inside them. The same thing was theoretically possible here, although we knew it was unlikely. The biggest danger in this war was not being pounded to rubble, but being caught in the wild spray of crossfire.

The firing was heavy now. The Rwandans were pouring in high velocity anti-aircraft shells. The Zaireans were replying with mortars and the occasional burst of their own heavy machine guns. We could see the red flares of the tracer flying over the lake.

'We've got to get away from this position,' Patrick said. 'We can't stay here.'

We had two options. To go up, or to go down. If we went down the hill we would be safe, but we would have no chance of filming anything. All we would see would be the green hills around us. Going up wasn't much better, but it held out the best possibility of getting pictures.

We decided to go up. There was a hill between the two outgoing posts which were now hammering out fire in regular bursts. It was exhausting work climbing the slope. We ducked and crouched a few times as bullets or mortar shrapnel flew overhead.

The situation was dangerous, but Patrick, Tony and I were anxious about not getting pictures.

This was a major escalation of the war. It was the first time that Rwandan and Zairean forces had exchanged fire across their common border and we knew that the incident would flash on TV screens around the world.

It was not that we were being brave or foolhardy. It was just the nature of television. In the world of the television screen, if there were no pictures, nothing had happened. No matter how many buildings were pounded to rubble, no matter how many people died in the fighting today, it would all mean very little without pictures.

Exhausted, we reached the top of the hill. The firing hadn't slackened at all. Patrick squeezed off a few more shots. He was trembling with fatigue and adrenalin. I had carried the camera part of the way up the hill for him, but it was incredibly heavy. We had had to leave the tripod behind at the nunnery, so it was difficult for Patrick to get steady shots of the fighting taking place in the town below us.

A volley of mortar shells screamed overhead. We ducked behind the crest of the hill. We couldn't stay on the ridge because we made an unmistakable silhouette and a target for Zairean machine gunners.

Then the rain started. It was a slow, steady downpour that shut everything from view. The firing continued, shells flying overhead, machine gun fire hammering out from both sides of us. We hunkered down in the soft mud, listening to the sounds of battle.

'What do we do now?' Tony asked.

'I can't film anything in the rain,' Patrick said. 'There's nothing to see.'

We were panting heavily, exhausted from running up the steep hills. We were now thoroughly soaked and bullets were flying all around us. We had some good pictures. The sound we had recorded of the massive amount of firepower was very dramatic. We had a great story.

'We're stuck here now, at least until the rain stops,' I said jokingly.

'Until the rain stops!' The American journalist was incredulous. He clearly did not appreciate my irony. His hair was plastered untidily to his forehead and rain dripped off the edge of his nose. We were all in a similar state.

The night sky was washed clear. We got the tapes on the road to Kigali. In a couple of hours our pictures would be flashed all over the world. The American journalist got the story for his magazine. They devoted a full page to his eyewitness account.

The nuns gave us chips and eggs and bread for dinner, an act of kindness we hadn't expected. Somebody had a bottle of Chardonnay from the Business Class lounge at Jo'burg airport. We ate by candlelight because there was still sporadic firing going on across the lake and we didn't want to turn on the electric lights and make a target of ourselves.

Bukavu was plunged into complete darkness, but we could see the tracer flying up into the night. It made trails of red fire that spiralled up like streams of fairy lights. Once, a solid stream came pouring out of the darkness straight towards our rooms at the nunnery. We hit the floor, scrabbling on the hard, unyielding concrete, but the tracery of light burnt itself out somewhere over the lake and the bullets that followed dropped away into the cold, still water.

It was a beautiful night, fresh from the afternoon rain. We stayed up late, filing stories on the satellite phones, calling the editorial desk in London with names and places to accompany our pictures. Our pictures were running, TV stations all over the world were picking up the images we had shot, and everyone in London wanted to know if we were all right.

The faint, bluish glow from the digital display on our satellite phone flickered comfortingly in the darkness as we called around the world. It was a strange, unearthly feeling to be watching the tracer fire far below and hear the echo on the line as we spoke to London, New York, Paris, Jo'burg.

We could only imagine what hell was being played out in the shadows across the border. Just before midnight, fires broke out on the horizon. The hillsides were black as ink, but somebody was setting fire to huts in a village. At first there would be a tiny point of orange light, and then the fire would flare up into a ball of flame as the flimsy straw roof ignited. Then it would die out suddenly. A few seconds later there was another tiny orange point of light, and another, the distant flaring balls of flame dying out, one by one, in a long row across the darkened hill tops.

Silence

From early the next morning more journalists began pouring in, looking for pictures of the war. At dawn there was sporadic firing across the border and dozens of people were now fleeing into Rwanda across the bridge at Rusizi I. Then there was silence. The shooting had stopped. We wondered what had happened across the border.

The announcers on the radio claimed that the Zairean army was in full flight away from the area around Bukavu. Other journalists were talking of a 'punitive strike' by the RPF against the Zaireans and the Rwandan extremists.

But I couldn't help thinking of something Gustave had told me the night before.

'The soldiers,' he had said, meaning the RPF and pointing at Patrick. 'They saw him moving in the trees and they wanted to shoot him. Then they saw you whites, and they realized you were journalists. So they didn't shoot.'

Patrick knew the risks better than any of us, and yet he had tried harder than any of us to film what he could of yesterday's battle.

Now there were eight or nine TV crews in town, plus a score of journalists and photographers. All of them were clustered around the bridge, waiting for the refugees to come across. Everybody needed pictures and a place to stay. The nunnery and the Hotel Kivu were full. There was no chance of lunch at the Hotel Kivu, though – not today, anyway. In the bombardment the hotel had been hit by a rocket grenade, and there was glass and shattered brickwork all over the tiny foyer. A group of journalists had been caught in the hotel as mortar and machine gun fire hammered all around them. It had been a close thing for them.

A slow but steady stream of refugees began coming over the narrow bridge. The adults were carrying bundles on their heads or strapped to their backs. The children stared around them, wide-eyed and overawed by the new world they were walking into.

An older man with distinguished-looking grey temples agreed to speak to us. He had come across the border with his daughter and her two children. 'When the fighting began we locked ourselves in our house. We were determined not to leave. We stayed there for two days, but then we heard people speaking Kinyarwanda. We called out in our own language to them. They came and escorted us to the Rwandan border.'

'Were they Rwandans or Banyamulenge?' we asked. The man shook his head and turned away.

A photographer was standing next to us at the bridge. He had arrived just that morning. His previous assignment had been working in the former Yugoslavia but, for today, the pictures out of Bukavu were eclipsing those out of Bosnia.

'I heard from one of the top military men in Kigali that if the shelling continues, the Rwandans will go in and take them out.'

Patrick laughed. 'They must have already done it. All that heavy firing yesterday must have been covering fire for their men.'

We drove to the *gendarmerie*. On the road we saw that some of the shops and houses in town had been hit by mortar shells the day before. The attack had shattered the thin veneer of calm the town lived under. Groups of men, women and children stood around the remains of the shell blasts.

The barracks were on a hill overlooking Bukavu and Cyangugu and the fabric of destruction that now connected the two towns. We could see the suburbs of both towns spreading out below us. Cyangugu was bright in the morning sun, while plumes of white and black smoke rose from the houses of Bukavu.

Some of the mortar shells from yesterday had found their mark. A few of the buildings had been hit. Gaping holes had been torn into the brickwork and sheets of corrugated iron had been thrown off the rafters. Some of the cars and trucks nearby had been pierced by shrapnel, and their windscreens shattered.

They took us first to the hospital compound. Four of the wounded soldiers were lying on old iron bedsteads. One of them was on a thin foam mattress on the concrete floor. The bare walls were stained and dirty, but the bandages were clean and neat. The wounds were light, the white bandages covered places where hot shrapnel had sliced into arms and legs.

One man had a shattered eardrum from the impact of the sound waves of the explosion of a mortar shell. There was a bandage around his head to stop the bleeding from deep inside his ear.

We were allowed to film, but we were not allowed to ask the soldiers any questions. The man with the shattered eardrum stared at us as Patrick filmed him. He looked dazed and angry. The torn arms and legs of the others would heal quickly enough, leaving their scars on the skin. But the eardrum would never heal completely. His scars would be inside, layered into the silences of his life. The violence of the bomb would be present in every word of anger, or love, he misunderstood, in every note of music or laughter that passed through his life unheard.

Outside, in the bright morning sun, we found Lieutenant-Colonel Firmin Kagame. He agreed to speak to us. He was the Cyangugu area commander for the Rwandan army. We put him in front of the camera with the delicate plumes of smoke rising up from Bukavu in the background.

'We crossed over last night,' Colonel Kagame said, staring confidently at the gleaming eye of the camera lens. 'We drove them back. I sent in a good force to do it.'

It was clear and unambiguous. There was no longer any mystery to the end of the shooting and the sudden silence that lay across the border.

Colonel Kagame went on: 'Two civilians were injured and one killed yesterday. After they hit our territory and injured and killed civilians we were forced to retaliate. We sent in a force to destabilize them and push them back to where they could no longer affect us. They are now pushed far away and we are not worried about them.'

We rushed back to the nunnery and from there we sent the tapes back to Kigali. A senior Rwandan army officer had finally confirmed, on camera, that his troops were actively involved in the fighting across the border.

But he did not explain everything. Colonel Kagame understood the power of our camera. He refused to answer too many questions. His words were carefully chosen. What he told us represented a hierarchy of command and specific orders stretching down from the highest levels of the Rwandan government.

We had to report whatever news we could find, but, in doing so, we were becoming part of the Rwandan army *strategy*. Yesterday the Rwandans had sent in their strike force; this morning, they were using us to send out their message.

Silence descended on the other side of the border. No women hoed the fields while we ate our omelettes on the balcony of the Hotel Kivu, and no young boys came to catch silver fish in the clear blue water of the Rusizi river. We saw no soldiers, no vehicles. Twice a small propeller plane flew over, the sound of its engine sawing into the air high above us, and fading away into nothing as it disappeared behind the small white clouds. We stood on the lawn of the nunnery craning our necks upward to see it. The flight path of the plane followed the line of the border on the ground and through the centre of the lake precisely. It never swerved or deviated into the territory of either Rwanda or Zaire. It must have had Rwandan permission to fly, but I wondered who controlled the airspace that lay directly above the border. Who, now, was left in Zaire to give permission to fly in this region of its airspace?

The plane and its slow, soaring journey, like everything here, had a meaning. But what that meaning was we could not know.

The fall of Bukavu to the Banyamulenge marked an intermediate stage in the war. The biggest question mark lay over the one million refugees who were still in Zaire. Some were still in the camps north of Lake Kivu in Goma, but hundreds of thousands had been driven out of the camps in Bukavu and further south. What would they do? Where would they go? The most obvious route for those in the south to follow if they chose to come home was the bridge across the Rusizi river at Cyangugu.

A tiny number of refugees trickled over the bridge at Rusizi I every day. From them we learned something of what had really happened beneath the distant plumes of smoke and the sounds of battle. Their stories were fragments of truth, as muted as the far-off gunfire in the shadowed valleys had been. The reality of the horror they had experienced was almost incommunicable.

'We lived near the border,' young Christian told us. 'The Banyamulenge came at night. We were frightened all night with the shooting. By the next morning, the Banyamulenge were in charge. We saw four dead people on the road.' He stopped for a moment and looked into the camera. His mother and father were standing next to him as he spoke. 'One of the dead people was my brother,' Christian said quietly.

Christian and his family were Hutus. 'We didn't have time to bury him. The Banyamulenge said we had to leave.'

'There was fighting all night,' Nyira told us. 'And we decided to come across the border. The Zairean soldiers arrested us at immigration. They took all our money and my jacket. They locked us in a cell. We were there with all the other Rwandans until the Rwandan soldiers came and let us out. For four days we had no food. In Bukavu things are terrible now. I saw many wounded people. There is no food; no water. I saw people begging for food, others are hiding in the hills.'

The refugees were mixed, a microcosm of all the suffering and anger that Rwandans carried with them wherever they went. Now the hatred was spreading into Zaire. Mutware was a Munyamulenge, an ethnic Tutsi from Zaire.

'When the troubles began I was in jail for forty-eight days. It was a terrible time. Many people were sick. Every day they beat us. The Zairean soldiers told us they were going to kill all the Tutsis. When we were in jail we heard that the soldiers took some of the students who were Banyamulenge into the park and killed them. When the Banyamulenge soldiers took Bukavu, the guards ran away. They left us with no food and no water. Finally we managed to break the door down and get out.

'When we met the Banyamulenge soldiers we were scared. But they told us not to worry. They let us come to Rwanda. The town is quiet, everybody is terrified. They are hiding in their houses. There is nothing, no food, no electricity and the people are very hungry. We saw so many bodies in the streets.'

Finally, a definable leader had emerged in the rebellion across the border. His name was Laurent Kabila. No one knew much about him. He was a shadowy figure from the past, from the time when Zaire was still called by its old name, the Congo. He had been a close follower of Patrice Lumumba. After the death of Lumumba, Kabila had disappeared into obscurity. He had been involved in some diamond trading and in an obscure Marxist rebellion somewhere in Kivu province in the 1970s. But the years in between the heady days of Lumumba and now were mostly an unknown quantity.

Laurent Kabila was an enigma. Nobody had seen him yet. He issued statements to the press only by satellite phone. He had set up his new revolutionary headquarters across the lake from us in Bukavu. One of his first acts from there as the official leader of the rebellion was to promise a ceasefire for three weeks.

President Mobutu was at his luxury residence at Roquebrune-Cap-Martin on the French Riviera.

'The ceasefire is confirmed,' the radio told us.

Crossing Over

On the first day of the ceasefire the shooting started again. Distant booms of mortar and machine gun fire echoed from the direction of Bukavu airport. It was one of the last places that the rebels had not taken control of.

'They must be mopping up resistance there,' Patrick said. We were sitting on the balcony of the Hotel Kivu. A Belgian journalist, Claude, the only one of us who could write decent French, had a piece of paper in front of him. The rest of us were gathered around him in a semicircle. We were writing a letter to Laurent Kabila, asking him for permission to visit Bukavu, the new capital of the *zone libérée*.

It seemed ironic that we, who had the most sophisticated electronic communications in the whole region, had been reduced to this, the writing of a letter. We hoped to have it delivered by hand.

There was something faintly absurd about our undertaking. We were all gathered around Claude like a gang of schoolboys and girls clustered anxiously around the cleverest pupil preparing a homework assignment.

'How do we address him?' somebody asked.

'As *monsieur*,' Claude said firmly.

'Is that really appropriate?' somebody else chipped in. 'He's running a revolution.'

Claude looked up from the paper in front of him. 'Do you speak French?'

'No, not really.'

'Then let me write it.'

Finally, the letter was finished. Claude put it in an envelope and sealed it. He wrote in large, careful letters on the front: *Monsieur Laurent Kabila*. There were about half a dozen of us in the group. Most of us were TV journalists or photographers armed with cameras, tripods, and microphones. We all trooped off behind Claude and the letter to the bridge at Rusizi I.

First, we came to the Rwandan immigration post. There was a single official in the tiny hut at the entrance to the bridge. Refugees had been coming into Rwanda for days now, but no one had tried to cross the other way, back into Zaire.

The Rwandan official stared at us through the narrow horizontal opening in the wall above the passport counter. He muttered something to Claude.

'It will cost us each twenty dollars for visas to come back to Rwanda,' Claude shouted.

'We'll pay.' We handed over our passports and waited while the official painstakingly stamped each one with an exit stamp.

We walked across the Rusizi bridge. The road leading up the hill in front of us was empty and damp with the recent rain. We could see nothing beyond the bend. We walked a few hundred metres in silence. The few journalists who had been trapped in Bukavu when the fighting broke out had not been heard from for days now. It was possible that they had been arrested by the rebels.

Suddenly, on the road in front of us were six heavily armed men. These were the first rebels anyone had seen. Two of them were wearing the red berets of the Zairean Presidential Guard and one had a black beret from the special forces. They were all carrying automatic weapons. One of the rebels was wearing a long flowing African robe and a black bomber jacket with a sheepskin collar. The strangest rebel was wearing gumboots, a silky black dress and a snow-white woman's sweater. He wore a shimmering bracelet of costume jewellery on his wrist. His rifle was slung over his shoulder.

The rebels were as uncertain of what to do as we were. They stood at the highest point of the hill where the road flattened out and disappeared.

We halted where we were and shouted up to them, first in English.

'Hello,' we yelled. There was no response.

'*Bonjour*,' Claude said. Still they stared at us. Their faces were suspicious, hostile.

One of the rebels in a camouflage uniform began to walk towards us. The man in the dress followed him. The man in the uniform spoke a little English. He found our group as strange as we found his. He couldn't understand why a group of mostly white people wanted to come into Zaire. He seemed nervous and unsure of his responsibilities as the guardian of an international frontier.

The man in the dress lit a cigarette. He held it up between two fingers in an exaggeratedly feminine way. His gumboots clumped on the tarmac as he circled around our group, occasionally dragging at the cigarette. He had long dark eyelashes and soft, curious brown eyes that looked each one of us up and down in turn.

'Are you tourists?' The man in the camouflage uniform blurted out.

Claude handed him the envelope. The rebel tore it open with his finger, nearly ripping the letter. The other four rebels came down from the top of the hill. They all gathered around the letter. The rebel with the cigarette was peering curiously over the shoulders of the others. One of them spoke to Claude in French.

'He won't deliver the letter,' Claude told us. 'He says he has never heard of Laurent Kabila.'

The man folded up the letter and shoved it into his camouflage tunic. He looked angry.

'Go,' he said.

'*Monsieur* –' Claude began.

He waved the back of his hand at us. 'Go, go! *Retournez!*'

There were reports of streetfighting in Goma. The war was moving north rapidly. As the war grew inside the borders of Zaire, it spread to other neighbouring countries. Zaire now had broken off diplomatic ties with Rwanda, Burundi and Uganda. All three countries were suspected of supporting the rebels. President Mobutu was in Switzerland.

Somebody must have delivered the letter. This time word had got out that a border crossing might be possible. There were eleven journalists, cameras and equipment, a number of rebels and only one Land Rover. We were under the care of the rebels. There was no question of our being able to take our own vehicles. We would be allowed in for one day only. Laurent Kabila was holding a rally that we would be allowed to film.

I ended up on the roof of the Land Rover, clinging on with my fingers as we drove through the deserted streets of Bukavu. The roads were potholed and filled with stinking water, the street lights hanging at crazy angles, rubbish piled on the sidewalks. This was evidence of normality in Mobutu's Zaire.

Claude negotiated an hour for us to film around town. The rebels dropped us off and let us make our own way around the battered streets of the town.

On top of the damage of Mobutu's rule was the carnage of war. A steel helmet lay abandoned in the street. From where it lay on the rough, ill-maintained surface of the street, you could see all the way to the hospital. A single red cross adorned its white walls. The entire corner of the hospital building had been torn away by shellfire. Concrete beams and reinforcing steel hung into the air like shattered bones and exposed nerves. The shop behind it had small tendrils of black soot flowing down the walls. There was no roof and the inside had been gutted by fire.

All the shops had been broken into and stripped. There was no bread in town, as the *boulangerie* had been looted. The heavy iron burglar bars over the windows and doors were broken and twisted. Every single pane of a huge window at a fuel station had been shattered by the blast of a nearby explosion. The glass lay on the concrete apron, glinting in the sun. Paper money with Mobutu's face on it lay scattered on the streets, collecting in the filthy gutters. In Mobutu's Zaire, a 500 zaire bill was worth less than one US cent. In Laurent Kabila's liberated zone it was worth nothing at all. In fact, possessing something with Mobutu's face on it now might cost you your freedom, or perhaps even your life.

One of the rebels with us pointed to a pothole in the street. 'Can you see the condition of Zaire? This is why we are fighting.'

Some 500 people had been killed in the fighting for Bukavu. We walked up to the highest point in the town where the cathedral was. There was blood on the gravel road leading up to it. A Mazda sedan had been hit by machine gun fire. A white Suzuki Samurai lay halfway up the hill. Its tyres were flat and its doors hung open. Bloodstained clothes and abandoned boots lay scattered around it. The back seats had been removed and a thick crust of dried blood lay in frozen runnels along the paintwork. The front seats were black with days-old gore. Foam rubber and fragments of steel stuck out through the back of the seats. On the floor lay a pen, some buttons, an empty plastic bottle of mineral water – the remnants of the last moments of life before violent, sudden death. They must have been Zairean army officers in this expensive car, the only people permitted to drive around town while the fighting was going on. I found myself wondering what they had been doing, saying, and thinking in those very last seconds before . . .

The windscreen was shattered where the bullets had smashed into the car as it was driving up the hill. They had been fired by a large calibre anti-aircraft machine gun. It was impossible to imagine that a human body would have survived their high-velocity impact.

The remains of the windscreen framed the cathedral in an eerily beautiful tableau. Their ragged edges were like a cave of ice surrounding the curved dome and the tall cross at its peak. Behind the cathedral we could see the green terraced hills of Rwanda. On their slopes were the white buildings of the nunnery and the hill tops above them. The gaping hole of the windscreen was in the direct line of fire of the Rwandan machine guns that had opened up above us.

I was looking at the last thing those Zairean officers had seen before they had been blasted out of this life. I could not help thinking that, with the help of a pair of binoculars, they would have been able to see us that day, scrambling up the muddy hillside towards the machine gun post.

There was another 4x4 abandoned at the edge of the cathedral. It was a UN vehicle that must have been commandeered by the Zaireans when the fighting was at its peak. It was slewed around, one tyre flat, the UN numberplate hanging loose. The car had not been hit, but it had failed someone who had tried to flee. The car was facing down the hill, but something in the engine must have stalled at the last minute, the machine changing people's fate, at the last minute snatching away the hope of speed and leaving them on foot, to hide or fight as best they could.

All around the cathedral was evidence of war: abandoned uniforms, empty mortar and machine gun shells, ammunition boxes torn open with bayonets and screwdrivers. From this high point one could see the whole of Cyangugu spread out below. Everything that moved across the border was visible. No wonder, when the time came, the Rwandans had hit this place as hard as they could. It was a high point that controlled the ground for twenty or more kilometres in a radius around it.

Gathered on the steps of the cathedral was a pathetic group of refugees. Their few possessions were rolled up in bundles and stored in nooks and crannies around the building. A few piles of cooking pots and jerry cans of water were evidence that the people had nowhere else to go. A young woman was staring at us. She had a rag wrapped around her face. The people standing around her waved us over. She pulled the rag down to reveal a ragged gash at the edge of her lips. It had cut deep into the flesh on her jaw.

She spoke to the camera in halting, pain-filled phrases that were translated for us. Her name was Ngabonziza. She was a Zairean Tutsi. 'The *interahamwe* found me in the street. They cut me like this with a machete. But somehow I managed to escape. I came here hoping to be safe.'

A simple story. The people standing around us were nodding as she spoke. Ngabonziza had given us nothing but the barest outline of her experience. But she had wanted to speak to us. When she had finished speaking, she replaced the rag around her wound. Her warm, dark eyes were filled with a mixture of pride and agony.

People were already gathering in front of the central post office in Bukavu by the time we arrived. It was a colonial building dating from the late 1950s – a dull façade of concrete and horizontal lines, crumbling in the tropical humidity. The post boxes had all been torn open. Their tiny aluminium doors hung open. There were cobwebs in some of the boxes. I could see a bird's nest among the shelves in the empty mail sorting room.

A goat ran along the edge of the concrete steps and disappeared around the side of the building.

Soon there were 6 000 to 8 000 people crammed into the square in front of the post office. They were standing on the roofs of nearby buildings, hanging on to lamp posts; half a dozen young men were holding on to the branches of a single low tree that stood in the middle of the square.

There was a strangely mixed atmosphere of excitement and sullenness amongst the people – mostly men – gathered in the growing heat of the day. They wanted to see this new man who had come. For most of the people standing here today, Mobutu had ruled their lives since birth. He was more than a distant, corrupt president. Over three decades of his rule, Mobutu had become a fact of life, an immovable condition of the world here. In fact, it was not Mobutu himself who had controlled them, but rather it was the lack of any rule that governed their lives. Mobutu was an immovable absence – a dark hole that surrounded them, the corruption and brutality that lingered at the edge of everything in Zaire sucking in all their energy and hope for the future.

Now he was gone from here. And no one knew yet what it was that would replace him. Who was Laurent Kabila? What would he do for them?

We could feel the sense of coercion that lingered in the air. Yes, the crowd was curious, but they were also there because they didn't know what to expect from this new man. It was better to go to the rally, because there was no telling what might happen if it became known that you didn't go.

The atmosphere was filled with an oblique fear. There might be violence today. It was better for the women and children to stay at home.

A convoy of vehicles arrived. A loud cheer went up. The people around me began clapping and whistling. The convoy pushed its way slowly through the crowd, the people pushing each other aside to make way for it.

Laurent Kabila stepped out of one of the jeeps. He was bare headed and wore a 1960s-style safari suit. A swathe of bodyguards swept out of the vehicles at the same time. They were carrying Kalashnikovs and were all wearing black berets, camouflage uniforms and sunglasses. Laurent Kabila climbed the steps of the post office to where our microphones had been set up. His bodyguards formed a semicircle facing the crowd. A group of senior rebel officers climbed out of the other vehicles and gathered behind Kabila. They were wearing camouflage, gold braid and brightly coloured berets. 'I am a philosopher, politician and soldier,' was how Laurent Kabila was describing himself now. 'It is the perfect combination for a revolutionary.'

Kabila stood silently in front of the bank of microphones for a few moments. I wondered what was going through his mind.

He had waited so long for this moment. Decades of obscurity lay behind him. Now was his time. This was his first rally as leader of the Alliance of Democratic Forces for the Liberation of Congo-Zaire (AFDL). From the moment he spoke to us and our cameras, the world would know of his revolution. In front of him lay the savannas and the forests of the country he meant to conquer, and contained within their vastness was all the promise of his new republic.

Somewhere in the shadowy distance across the ocean lay his adversary, Mobutu Sese Seko, the president who had created Zaire, an enormous empire of anarchy that stretched across the continent, a country the size of western Europe whose riches he had milked for nearly three decades.

When Laurent Kabila began to speak, he would be speaking to two audiences: to the nervous people lined up in the sun in front of him, and to the viewers that our gleaming rows of cameras would bring pictures to. The newly re-elected President Clinton would soon be seeing Laurent Kabila, John Major would be seeing him, Jacques Chirac would be watching him and listening carefully to every word he said.

But I suspected that the man who mattered most to Laurent Kabila was Mobutu Sese Seko. The revolution was far from secure. Mobutu had once been a competent battlefield commander who had put down more than one revolt against his rule. He had proved himself to be physically brave by often appearing in person on the front lines to encourage the troops. Every day now there was talk of a counter-attack against the AFDL. It seemed unlikely that the disorganized rabble of the Zairean army would succeed, but it was not impossible. Mobutu had done it before.

Kabila smiled and drew in a breath. '*Jambo sana*,' he thundered into the microphone. He was speaking in Swahili, the lingua franca of the East of the continent. He was deliberately snubbing the Lingala-speakers from Kinshasa in the West. It was an affirmation of identity for the people from the East. But it was also a statement meant for us and for our TV cameras. He was not speaking in French or English. The opening words of his revolution were in an African language. The era of post-colonialism was dead. His revolution would be an African revolution fought by Africans for Africa. This time the outside world would not dictate to the continent what was good for it. Africa would speak its own languages and the outside world would have to find its own way to understand.

It was a masterful beginning. The crowd roared its approval. Kabila was smiling broadly.

'How many people want me to speak in Swahili?' The crowd raised its arms, waving them in approval. Whistles broke out. People began clapping.

'I am Laurent Kabila of Zaire-Congo . . .' The crowd cheered him wildly.

A man standing in the crowd next to me saw me writing in my notebook. 'Tell the president we want food – money,' he said bitterly and looked away. *Tell the president* . . . despite his anger he had already accepted Laurent Kabila as his new ruler.

On the podium Laurent Kabila was raising his right hand high above his head. He brought it down suddenly, in a crushing gesture of power and defiance.

'We have had thirty-five years of dictatorship in this country. We will push on towards Kinshasa and Gbadolite. From tomorrow we will open a recruiting office in Bukavu. It will be hard going, but we will go on together.'

He brought his voice to a crescendo: 'Are you ready?'

The arms of the crowd were waving in the air. The young men smiling and laughing with excitement. The answer came thundering back.

'*We've been ready for a long time.*'

Exodus

We were getting only one side of the story. There were over one million Hutu refugees trapped here in Eastern Zaire. Among the hundreds of thousands of those guilty of genocide, there were hundreds of thousands of the innocent.

Part of the problem was the difficulty with war reporting anywhere. We could only report what we saw or, even more crucially, we could only show what we could film with our cameras. In a war, the front lines might be constantly shifting, but no matter where they lay, you could never cross them. You were stuck on one side or the other.

The one million Hutus and their fate were rapidly becoming the new story. Where were they? We knew from the aid agencies that hundreds of thousands were crammed into Mugunga camp north of us in Goma. But the aid agencies were almost overwhelmed by the scale of the problem that had descended on them. The camps here in the south were empty. Hundreds of thousands of people were on the move in the forests that covered this region of Africa. There was talk of setting up humanitarian corridors through the forest to allow the refugees to go back to Rwanda. But nothing concrete had been achieved. The UN had sent a Canadian envoy, Raymond Chrétien, to the region. 'We simply must attempt to arrange some kind of an immediate ceasefire in the Great Lakes.' It was a statement of precisely calculated meaninglessness. '*Attempt to arrange some kind of an immediate ceasefire* . . .' the words ran, tumbled, into one another, tripped up by their own vagueness. There was nothing that could be done. The French called for action, but the Rwandans didn't trust them an inch. The Zaireans, in turn, were suspicious of the Americans who were openly supportive of the Rwandans.

The rebels had a name now, the AFDL, the Alliance of Democratic Forces for the Liberation of Congo-Zaire, and they were on the march, aided by their allies the Burundians, the Ugandans and the Rwandans. The war was growing by the day. The Zairean army was fleeing. The one million Hutu refugees were caught up in this growing maelstrom of conflict, moving up and down the Great Lakes region. Some reports already talked of the refugees being attacked and forced deeper and deeper into the forest. There was at least one report of firing coming *out* of a refugee column. The former Rwandan army and the *interahamwe* forces hidden amongst the refugees would certainly not meekly allow themselves to be attacked by their enemies.

It was now clear that among the distant shelling and plumes of smoke that we had seen from a distance, had been attacks on the refugee camps by the Rwandans and the Banyamulenge. The attacks had driven the refugees out of the camps and forced them on to the roads and into the forest. There had also been attacks on the camp of Kibumba, near Goma, which had driven more refugees into Mugunga camp.

Tiny Rwanda was now effectively at war with Zaire. The next step in the conflict was to solve the question of the refugees. It was no secret that the Rwandans wanted the camps closed and the refugees home. The new vice-president and head of the Rwandan army, Paul Kagame, had warned the international community repeatedly that Rwanda would not tolerate the permanent existence of the camps, which were such a threat to the security of the new Rwanda. Kagame knew from first-hand experience how the dreams of refugees living together in camps constantly turned towards coming home and taking power again. 'I grew up in a refugee camp,' he told journalists often.

It was obvious that the Rwandans had a two-pronged strategy. The first element was that of military success. The second was to win the diplomatic war. Through us and our cameras, they were communicating their moves to the world, step by careful step.

No one else, though, seemed to know what to do. There was talk in the Security Council of a multinational force to protect the humanitarian corridors. The only problem was that no one in the world seemed to want to send their soldiers to the forests of central Africa. The rebels were saying they would only accept a force made up of African troops anyway.

The fighting grew fiercer every day, while the refugees disappeared into the forest or poured into Mugunga. 'We are on the brink of a catastrophe,' Sadako Ogata, UN High Commissioner for Refugees, was saying to anybody who would listen. 'There is no time to waste.'

Raymond Chrétien had become more specific. 'It's a war,' he said. 'It's started.' That was old news. The Rwandans and their ally, Laurent Kabila, were miles ahead of everyone else.

In Mobutu's realm chaos reigned. Riots had broken out in Kinshasa yet again. Students had stormed the parliament buildings demanding the resignation of the half-Tutsi Prime Minister, Kengo wa Dondo. They raged through the city, stealing cars. A group of them attempted to loot the house of the governor of the central bank. The mobs on the streets attacked 'Tutsi-looking' people yet again and stormed the Rwandan Embassy. The Zairean Parliament's solution to the attacks was to call for all Tutsis to be removed from government jobs.

The war here in the East was moving rapidly. Heavy gunfire was being reported all around Goma. A battle was taking place for the airport, five kilometres north of the town.

Over the weekend of 2 and 3 November, the battle for Goma exploded. The sound of gunfire had grown all night on the Friday. In a lull in the fighting in the early morning, a group of *interahamwe* appeared at the border post on the road that connected the Rwandan town of Gisenyi with Goma. They stood, stark naked, armed with assault rifles, at the red and white striped boom that marked the border between the two countries. Some of the men had small clumps of leaves tied to their rifles. They were a talisman of some sort, designed to protect the owner from his enemies.

The young men began a crude, stamping dance. They waved their buttocks and genitals at the Rwandan soldiers who manned the border post. It was the supreme insult.

The cameras went mad. The satellite dish had been moved to Goma now. Within minutes, pictures of naked Africans with guns dancing on an international frontier were beamed around the world. In the years that have followed, whenever I have found somebody interested in talking about the beginning of the rebellion in eastern Zaire, these are some of the few images that people remember. 'Those naked men, dancing . . .' they say, shaking their heads.

And yet, those young men wanted to be seen. They knew they were being filmed. The moment they began their dance in the rich, early morning light of the African highlands they were stepping into the vortex of television. The pictures of them would run, and run and run all across the world.

The Tutsi soldiers of the RPF stared impassively over their machine guns and rocket grenade launchers at the naked dancers. They were waiting for their moment. Soon they would be in control of that border post and the *interahamwe* and their Zairean allies would have been killed or have fled deep into the forest.

As the dance was going on, the AFDL rebels were moving into the outskirts of Goma. At mid-morning, the first howls of artillery roared overhead. It was a carefully planned battle. The Rwandans fired at Zairean and *interahamwe* military posts. The grey bursts of explosions were filmed among a clump of eucalyptus trees at the edge of Goma. More shells followed. The Zaireans responded with mortar fire. A shell landed near the central market of Gisenyi, panicking the civilians and refugees gathered there.

After the artillery bombardment, the next stage was for the RPF troops to storm the frontier. Some units crossed Lake Kivu by boat; but the main bulk of the troops simply lifted up the red and white barrier and drove through the abandoned border post.

There was sporadic fighting as the Rwandans took control of Goma. Afterwards, some 400 bodies, most of them civilians, were found scattered around town. By the end of the weekend, the situation had reached a stalemate. Rwanda and the AFDL were in control of Bukavu and Goma, the two major towns in eastern Zaire. All aid workers had been expelled from the areas controlled by the AFDL.

The next phase in the Rwandan military strategy was to seal off the camps. No aid supplies were able to get into Mugunga camp where an estimated 400 000 refugees were now living. Another 500 000 refugees were moving in the region. Many of them were hiding in the forests. We could see nothing of what was happening. In an effort to get some pictures, a group of journalists chartered a plane to fly to Kisangani and to fly over the camps at the same time. The pictures showed a blurred landscape with some refugees, but no more detail.

The French government was demanding that the international community act. The Spanish announced they were ready to send troops to man the international humanitarian corridors. Laurent Kabila was firm in his rejection of non-African troops. President Mobutu from his luxury home in Nice announced that he welcomed foreign military intervention.

In the first days after the fighting in Goma had ended, a small trickle of refugees began to stumble back into Rwanda. The vast majority of them were still caught in Zaire, either crammed into Mugunga or shuffling deeper and deeper into the forest, surrounded by the growing fighting between the rebels and the Zaireans. One of the refugees who had come back told us about the fate of those still in Zaire. 'They have begun to die on the side of the road,' he said.

The Reuters team was being beefed up with new people coming in from Paris, London and Nairobi. Somehow, in the shuffle of personnel, I as a freelancer wasn't needed. On the other hand, one of my regular clients, the BBC, needed a producer to join their team.

Patrick had already been shifted somewhere else in the region. I drove back to Kigali with Gustave.

We talked in the car for a while in our own peculiar patois of his limited English and my scarcely existent French. He told me some more of his own story. Gustave was about my own age, thirty-five, and had first fled Rwanda during the anti-Tutsi pogroms in 1973 when Gregoire Kayibanda, who had been president of Rwanda since independence in 1962, was ousted in a coup by a young army officer, Major General Juvenal Habyarimana.

Gustave never saw Rwanda after that. He grew up in a refugee camp in Burundi. In 1994, when the RPF took Rwanda, Gustave decided to come back to his native land. He was a decent man, impeccably honest and hard-working. This driving job was the first opening he had ever had to make something of his life, and he was determined to make the most of the opportunity. He hoped one day to own his own car, so that the profits would be his, and not somebody else's. Gustave was not married yet, but he hoped to be one day. With our limited ability to speak each other's languages, there wasn't much more we could say to one another.

We reached the outskirts of Kigali just as the shadows on the hills were growing deep over the steep, green valleys. Gustave was pushing now, trying to get us back to town before dark. We came to a low rise. On the road in front of us, two young boys were standing motionless in the middle of the tarmac. Gustave blew the horn. Once. Twice. The boys didn't move.

Gustave took his cigarette out of his mouth and hastily stubbed it in the ashtray.

'What's wrong?' I asked.

'Wait, wait,' Gustave said. He put his hand out to reassure me. He slowed the car right down and stopped just behind the boys at the crest of the hill. He switched off the engine. A policeman with an AK-47 was standing to attention at the side of the road. Two women working in a field nearby were standing with their hoes, their bodies frozen.

In front of the commune office two policemen were taking down the flag at sunset.

'In Rwanda, Burundi, we must always stop when the flag comes down,' Gustave told me.

We sat in the car together watching the policemen tug at the halyards on the flagpole in the growing dusk. I was worried about cars coming the other way, but there was nothing for it. We had to wait until the flag was neatly folded and carried into the commune offices. The policeman shouldered his rifle and began walking along the road. The women picked up their hoes and started talking as they wandered away from the field and the day's work. Gustave turned the key in the ignition and we set off down the road towards Kigali. The first lights began to wink on as we drew into the outer suburbs.

Gustave never spoke of the genocide itself. He would avoid the subject and somehow I never did get to find out what had happened to his family in all the years of their ordeal from the slaughter in 1973, and again in 1994. He would often fall into long silences, just staring ahead at the road.

There were huge, empty spaces in Gustave's life. Memories of things that could never be shared, or understood, by people who came from outside. He made me see one thing, though: Rwanda might be a hellhole for people like me; but for Gustave, Rwanda, as it was today, was the only chance he would ever have.

There was talk at breakfast of the spreading ripples of the war. Reports had been coming from Kisangani, the city on the bend of the great Zaire river, the second largest city in Zaire, deep inside the forest some 500 kilometres from Goma. The Zairean army was reportedly already fleeing there. There was rioting and looting in the streets.

But there was only one major story now: the one million refugees trapped inside Zaire. *Where were they?* was the question on everybody's lips.

Between 350 000 and 400 000 were, according to the best estimates, eking out a tenuous existence in Mugunga camp. They were surrounded by armed *interahamwe* units who had formed a defensive line from Kibumba camp slightly north to Mugunga. In effect, they were holding the refugees hostage, preventing them from returning to Rwanda. *They may have the land,* was the common retort from the Hutu extremists in exile, directed against the RPF, *but we have the people. How can you say you have conquered a country when it has no people?*

The people, then, were what the fate of this country hinged on. The only problem was, nobody knew where nearly 600 000 of them were. Laurent Kabila had been clear on the subject. 'We don't know where they are,' he told a press conference in Bukavu.

The UN was no help either. 'A million people,' a spokesperson for UNHCR said, 'a medium-sized city, has just disappeared. They've gone across the front lines and into that great Central African abyss.'

Vague fragmentary stories were drifting back over the border. Stories of hunger, thirst, fighting, disease. The Zairean soldiers fleeing the AFDL advance were said to be looting and robbing the refugees.

For two years, this one million people had lived in a Rwanda of exile, a country that existed only in the imagination and in the paranoia of their leaders. To close this cycle and bring them home was the task that faced the new rulers of Rwanda. Mugunga and the 500 000 to 750 000 refugees crammed into it was the last stand of the Hutu extremists.

On Thursday November 14, heavy firing broke out in Goma. The Rwandans and the rebels were launching an assault on the *interahamwe* defences in Mugunga. The fighting continued into the next day. On Friday, a determined, calculated rain of mortar shells fell on to the *interahamwe* lines for six hours.

The storm broke. In two days, the Rwandans and the AFDL rebels managed to achieve what the international community had not done for over two years: they broke the hold of the extremists over the mass of Hutu refugees. Seven hundred thousand people picked up their belongings and began to walk home.

I don't imagine I will ever live to see anything like it again. The United Nations estimated that 12 000 people an hour were pouring through the border post at Gisenyi.

The first thing that struck me was the colours. Red, yellow, blue, green, silver, brown . . . this vast sea of humanity shimmering with colour and life as it moved through the hills of its native land.

The feet struck me next. Hundreds of thousands of bare, calloused feet slowly moving on the tarmac, and in the mud and stone on the side of the road. From the moment we saw the first refugees on the road, we had to remind ourselves that there were both the guilty and the innocent among them, that they brought with them as much hatred as they brought hope, and that it would be years before Rwanda was free of that hatred – if it ever was.

It was an extraordinary sight. We were at the end of the twentieth century, and only in Africa could such a moving spectacle still be witnessed. To stand on a high point and watch this seemingly endless flow of human beings pass by on foot was to witness the movement of a People in a way that was as slow and ancient as human history itself.

Thousands of kilometres of videotape ran over the magnetic heads of the cameras, recording this grim, determined migration. The satellite dishes had been moved to Gisenyi and the images poured into space. They bounced back to earth, filling screens across the world. We filmed and rushed back to the hotel room with the tapes. The tape editors worked until two or three in the morning, cutting and editing our stories, running up the stairs to the satellite dish. They jammed the tapes into the playout machines and watched as these images of a biblical journey of humanity spooled out into space.

We were exhausted, exhilarated, overwhelmed by the sheer scale of it. The first small groups were clumped in tens and twenties, straggling down the road carrying their bundles on their heads. They were tiny figures against the vast cloud-covered backdrop of Karisimbi volcano. Then they began to come in their hundreds, children and the lame walking slowly among the healthy adults. The condition of the refugees was good. The wealth of the West had fed the camps for over two years. The aid agencies had treated diseases, inoculated the children, and fed everyone a balanced diet. The nutritional levels of people in the camps were higher than those of the Zairean people living in the villages around them.

Then they came in their thousands, jamming the road and spilling out into the fields and trees on either side. Every now and then a ramshackle car or truck, piled high with people and their belongings, would nose its way slowly through the crowd. But where the river of people was at its thickest, the cars and trucks simply stopped and the drivers watched helplessly as the people streamed by on every side.

Then the rain started. The skies turned grey and cold and the green fields and hillsides turned red with mud as the people's feet churned up the soil. Smoke rose from the small houses and shacks nearby as the people who had stayed in Rwanda, or who had come back after 1994, began to stoke fires to cook their evening meals. No one had anything to share with the refugees. They came to stand at their doorways to watch the flow of people pass by through the silver rain. No greetings were exchanged. No hands were extended in welcome. The people who had houses stood at their doorways to make sure that nothing could be misunderstood. *These houses are occupied. If this was your house before, it is no longer yours now. Move on elsewhere.*

A small girl was selling roast sweet potatoes. Her fire sputtered and turned smoky in the rain. Her eyes were wide as she watched the refugees tramp past her, endlessly, still coming long after she had nothing left to sell.

One of the refugees stopped and spoke to me. The rain sputtered on the plastic sheeting on the bundle on his head. It blotted the ink in my notebook, turning the writing into small violet splotches.

'I'm tired,' he said, looking around him. 'But the country hasn't changed.'

My driver, a young Tutsi called Jean-Paul, was handing out his own money – 100 Rwandan francs at a time. He was one of the Tutsis who, like Gustave, had returned after 1994, hoping for a fresh start.

It was a small amount of money he was giving, but it was something, at least. I knew also that the currency in Rwanda had been changed after the RPF had taken over the country. Any money that these people had saved from the old days was worthless. The vast majority of people were coming home penniless.

I watched Jean-Paul for a few moments in the rain. He seemed to be singling out women with children. He handed a new gleaming note to a mother carrying a baby, another to a grandmother leading a child sobbing in the sudden coldness of the rain.

Jean-Paul seemed embarrassed to find me watching him. 'I was a refugee once,' he said, shrugging his shoulders.

People began sitting down at the side of the road. They could go no further, not that night, anyway. A little further away, a group of refugees had found a field of cassava. They started digging out the tubers. A whole season's harvest. The family who owned the field watched helplessly from the threshold of their doorway.

Most of the refugees were not so lucky. I saw an old man stripping leaves off a tree. Nearby his family were struggling to light a fire of green wood in the damp rain. They had a blackened pot of water that they wanted to boil.

Further down the road John Habimana and his family were cooking some beans and maize. He agreed to speak to us and our camera. 'I am happy to be back,' he said. 'Because I have food. If I stayed there I would die. Many people died in Zaire because they had no food. I didn't come to Rwanda before because I thought that there wasn't safety. But now I find there is. The RPF is no problem for me.'

A young student had found some green bananas. He was roasting them over a smoky fire. Nearby a pair of RPF soldiers stood at the side of the road, their Kalashnikovs strung over their shoulders as they watched the people walking past them.

'I am not happy to be back,' the student told us. 'We left our leadership behind. I was forced to return because of the war.'

Ayob, our translator, had a Tutsi father and a Hutu mother, and found himself constantly torn between the extreme poles of his country. 'Most of the refugees feel that way,' he told us, when the interview was over.

The rain stopped. The setting sun came out behind the clouds, turning the sky a deep gold. We could see Gisenyi and the northern end of Lake Kivu silver and flat in the rich light. The smoke from countless cooking fires swirled up above the rounded hills.

Still people were walking even as darkness began to fall. Slowly, though, a kind of peace fell over the multitude. You could hear people talking in soft voices, and laughter from around the cooking fires.

The hotel in Gisenyi was hopelessly crowded with journalists, aid workers and Rwandan army officers. We were all crammed in, three or four to a room. Somehow we made do with sleeping bags and blankets and camping mattresses. The corridors were piled high with the silver cases that held edit packs, satellite phones, monitors, radio sound mixers. There were cases of tinned food and bottled water squeezed in among them. Every floor was a swirling hive of activity – journalists, camerapeople and photographers were running back and forth along the threadbare carpets rushing to meet deadlines in Europe and America.

We worked late that night, feeding stories down the satellite pathways to London. The world was fascinated by this mass evacuation of people finally coming home. Some time around midnight, exhausted by the blur of colour and sound that had been spooling back and forth on the edit machines, I went down to the hotel bar for a drink. We had just finished editing a story for BBC World TV. I had taken it up to the satellite engineers about seven or eight minutes before and had watched it being played out over the TV monitors connected to the satellite dish.

The bar was filled with Rwandan army officers. They had filled all the chairs and stools in the bar and were drinking lemonade and mineral water. They were in the bar for one reason only – to watch the satellite TV the hotel offered as one of its facilities. Flickering above their heads was the whole world of colour and sound that we had been recording all that day. Space on a communications satellite is sold in ten-minute increments. All that day and late into the night, every slot had been filled. Every ten minutes a new TV story was being sent out into space. Many of them were bouncing back, to . . . well, the satellite receiving dish on the roof of the Meridien Hotel in Gisenyi.

We had brought the matrix to Gisenyi. The gateway was on the roof above our heads. I watched the Rwandan army officers watch the pictures we had filmed only a few hundred metres away. This exodus was the culmination of their strategy, of their mortar shells and their artillery bombardments.

I thought of how carefully they had planned everything, and of how skilfully they had used us and our pictures to aid them in their objectives. It had been a masterfully conceived strategy to bring their people home.

But now, I reflected, they had reached the point of the unknown. The fate of their country would be determined by the echoes of memory that those 700 000 people were bringing with them. An end to the killing would depend on how, and on whether, the memories of hate could be reconciled.

Rwandans would carry their past with them into eternity in the millions of images of their country that had been recorded over the last two and a half years.

So much violence, so much fear, so much hate, so much cruelty was frozen now, stored forever on the magnetic tapes of TV stations all over the world. Would these images become the talismans of hate carried by generation after generation? Would the future of Rwanda forever be held hostage to what could be shown on a television screen at the push of a button?

Which images would determine the future history of this country? Those of the slaughter, or those of the People coming home?

The Rwandan army officers sipped their lemonade and stared at the flickering screen in silence, watching this exodus bouncing back towards them through the cold immensity of space.

Rwanda. *Near Rusizi II was a high vantage point looking down into Zaire. We stood side by side with the other crew and filmed what we could of the situation in Zaire.*

Rwanda. *Trapped in the line of fire. Cameraman Patrick Muiruri takes shelter from mortar fire on a hillside above Cyangugu.*

Rwanda. *From Mugunga camp near Goma 700 000 Rwandan refugees picked up their belongings and began to walk home. It was a grim, determined migration.*

Zaire. Bukavu: The remains of the windscreen framed the cathedral in an eerily beautiful tableau, their ragged edges like a cave of ice surrounding the curved dome and the tall cross at its peak.

Zaire. Bukavu: A crowd of six to eight thousand people crammed into the square in front of the post office to listen to Laurent Kabila address his first rally as leader of the AFDL.

Kinshasa. *Laurent Kabila's AFDL rebels march steadily down the streets . . . they are heavily armed with mortar tubes, rocket grenades and machine guns. Many are barefoot, but they are disciplined as they march.*

Kinshasa. *The days of the Leopard King are over. A group of a dozen men dance and yell outside government offices. They have found a Zairean flag and are tearing it to pieces.*

Kinshasa. *What is it that created this monstrosity? Mobutu's mansion is silent and abandoned. It is a haunting, almost wondrously malignant sight . . .*

Sudan. *The face of famine. The 18-year-old who pleaded with aid workers to be allowed into the feeding centre in Panthou. But the centre had been set up to treat malnourished children under the age of five, and he was turned away.*

Sudan. *The starving and the desperately ill gathered on the edges of the main street in Tonj . . . a group of emaciated children sat listlessly on a veranda; a grandfather lay stretched out, unmoving, across the steps.*

Kuwait. *The Iraqi tank graveyard left behind after the 1991 Gulf War. Acres of devastated military hardware bear testimony to the destructive power of the American and coalition forces.*

Kuwait. *The shattered remains of a building hit by Allied fire during the Gulf War.*

ZAIRE

THE LAST DAYS OF THE LEOPARD KING

In the months that followed the return of the refugees from Zaire to Rwanda, the rebellion against the rule of Mobutu Sese Seko grew faster and faster.

I watched from Johannesburg as the war progressed across the vast extent of Zaire. Shabunda, Walikale, Kalemie . . . the fall of each town marked the advance of the rebels. It was with growing frustration that I heard on the radio and TV reports and read in the newspapers as each one of these towns fell to the army of Laurent Kabila.

I remembered Kabila's triumphant rally so well. 'We are ready to march to Kinshasa' the crowds who had greeted him in the square in front of the post office had yelled, punching their fists into the air.

It had seemed a far-off dream then – a thousand miles of rainforest and Mobutu's army lay between them and Kinshasa. But that was only five months ago. Now the AFDL under Kabila's command was rapidly taking over the country.

His success seemed all the greater when one remembered that Laurent Kabila was a minor figure from the earliest days of the country's liberation from the Belgians. As the months had passed I had learned more of his story. Just after the independence of the Congo in 1960 Kabila was based in the far eastern province of Kivu and he fled into the bush when Mobutu, with the help of the CIA, organized a coup against Lumumba, who died a few days later at the hands of his Belgian captors.

Kabila rebelled against Mobutu in 1964. Che Guevara, who spent a short time with Kabila in the mid 1960s, was disillusioned by the African leader's attitude. He described Kabila as having the potential to be a leader of the masses but, instead, he spent most of his time not at the front line, but moving from 'saloon to whorehouse'.

Less than a year later Kabila's uprising was crushed. In 1967, Kabila set up the tiny People's Revolutionary Party (PRP) which went on in the 1970s to create a Marxist self-declared statelet in the Fizi mountains of south Kivu province, surviving on gold and ivory trading. Mobutu's troops finally drove him out in the 1980s and Kabila disappeared into obscurity, selling gold in the capital of Tanzania, Dar es Salaam.

In October 1996, revolt broke out among the Banyamulenge and, while no one was quite sure how it had happened exactly, Kabila had appeared to lead this rebellion.

It was a successful comeback. The tide of battle was turning rapidly in his and his Ugandan and Rwandan allies' favour. Kisangani, Zaire's third largest city, located on the bend in the great river and defended in its last days by a bizarre, desperate group of mercenaries from the former Yugoslavia and France, had fallen easily to the rebels on March 15, 1997.

Everywhere now Mobutu's troops, known as the FAZ (Armed Forces of Zaire), were fleeing in the face of the rebel advance, stopping only long enough to loot the towns they left empty for Kabila's soldiers to march into.

This war was causing massive realignments of forces on the African continent. Before the anti-Mobutu uprising in Kivu there were wars or simmering conflicts in five of the nine countries that border Zaire. In the Central African Republic, Rwanda, Burundi, Sudan and Uganda, there were destabilizing conflicts in which events in Zaire were somehow involved.

Now it was not only Rwanda and Uganda who were assisting Kabila with a very big nod from America. He was also getting at least moral support from Eritrea and Ethiopia – then at peace with one another, but supporters of the Southern Sudanese rebels and opposed to the radical Islamist government of Sudan, a government viewed with extreme suspicion by the US.

Zimbabwe was providing Kabila with arms, planes, boots and rations. Soon the Zimbabwean aid extended further – to providing intelligence and even active air support.

Zambia was allowing Kabila's rebels to use its territory as a base for their attacks. The MPLA government in Angola was sending guns and men to die for Kabila. Their bitter enemies, the rebel UNITA movement, had plans to mount a defence of Kinshasa for Mobutu.

France was largely on the side of Mobutu, if only for the sake of defending *La Francophonie* against the AFDL rebels' Anglophone allies from Uganda and Rwanda. The remains of the Hutu extremist *interahamwe* militias and the old Hutu-dominated FAR (Armed Forces of Rwanda) were fighting openly for Mobutu, and were probably his most effective allies. Their old leader, the previous president of Rwanda, Juvenal Habyarimana, who had been shot down in the mysterious plane crash that started the Rwandan genocide, had been a close personal friend of Mobutu. They were so close that, after the plane crash, Mobutu had Habyarimana's body brought to his palace in Gbadolite and buried there. The *interahamwe* were being aided by the Hutu rebels in Burundi, who had strong links to Tanzania and the Tanzanian army.

Libya and the Sudanese government were sending help to Mobutu; while the Sudanese rebels on the border of Zaire were helping Uganda and the AFDL rebels.

Chad was reportedly on the verge of sending troops to aid the rebels. Morocco was allegedly sending guns to Mobutu, but refused to provide further aid. Who knew exactly where the Francophone Central African Republic bordering Zaire in the north stood? And what about the People's Republic of the Congo, just across the river from Zaire, whose president, Pascal Lissouba, was openly supportive of Mobutu? It was certain that neither country was sitting quietly on the sidelines.

Some were saying that in Europe this would have been called a World War – and Kinshasa was at the heart of it.

For weeks, as Kabila's army advanced through the forest towards Kinshasa, I fretted in Johannesburg, wanting to join the growing numbers of my colleagues who were flying up to Kinshasa.

In the early part of 1997, I went to Zimbabwe, Kenya and Eritrea to work on a documentary on eye surgery in Africa. I could not escape the war raging in Zaire. In Nairobi, a new cocktail, blood-red in colour, was being served at the bars. It was called the 'Kabila', and there was talk of President Moi going the same way as Mobutu. In Asmara, the capital of Eritrea, the Sudanese rebels based there were steeling themselves for the possibility of the war spilling over into their region.

Almost every night before I went to sleep in the vast echoing bedchamber of my colonial hotel room in Asmara, I pulled out my shortwave radio and searched through the hiss of the static, trying to find news of what was happening in Zaire.

I waited, growing more anxious by the day. Lubumbashi, the largest city in the country and the centre of the strategic copper-producing Shaba province, was on a knife-edge.

Mbuji-Mayi, the city at the centre of Zaire's diamond industry, fell on April 4. Kamina, the vast old Belgian army base fell soon after.

The rebels' advance was unstoppable. It seemed certain now that they would be in Kinshasa in a matter of weeks, and I was stuck in Jo'burg. My wife remained calm. She is used to the fluctuations of my uncertain soul, the gnawing journalistic madness of 'anywhere but here'.

'Don't worry,' she said. 'Something will come up.'

I was at home making dinner when the phone rang. It was Allan Little, one of the Africa correspondents for the BBC. He was on holiday in the US, and London had called him to cut his holiday short and get to Zaire.

'Can you come to Kinshasa?' he asked. 'We're going to need another producer there.'

'Oh really?' I asked. 'Yes, well, as it turns out . . .' We talked for a few minutes about logistics. Kinshasa was going to be a big story, vying with the chaos in Albania for the world headlines. CNN had moved in, and so had the other big American networks. The EBU (European Broadcasting Union) was a putting a satellite dish on the roof of the Memling Hotel. The Swedes were there, the Swiss, the Germans, the Japanese . . .

As soon as EBU had their dish up and running, there would be lots of live coverage. The team would assemble in Kinshasa over the next week or so. Allan and George Alagiah would be the correspondents. Martin Turner from Johannesburg would be the chief producer for both radio and TV. Milton Nkosi, also from the Jo'burg bureau and one of my oldest friends in journalism, and I would be the other producers.

Lubumbashi fell two days later, on April 9, 1997. The call from Allan had come just in time.

Leaving

I had less than forty-eight hours to get ready, and I was bringing in a lot of valuable equipment and quite a bit of cash. I spoke to Milton on the phone. He was already in Kinshasa.

I heard him chuckling on the other end of the echoing satellite phone line. 'It's the worst airport in Africa,' he said. 'But don't worry, everything will be all right. It *will* be chaos, that I can promise you, but whatever happens, you're not going to be physically harmed. Just go with the flow and hold on to your passport. Jean Marie will be there to meet you.'

'How will I recognize him?'

'You can't miss him. He is the biggest man you've ever seen.'

'CHAOS ERUPTS IN KINSHASA AS REBELS ADVANCE'
(Headline of *The Star*, in Johannesburg, April 10, 1997)

SA 052 on Friday April 11 is one of the last scheduled flights into Kinshasa. The Africa press corps is not that big a fraternity and I am on the plane with old friends.

'We're on the last flight to hell,' Chevan Rayson of AP TN, says.

'It's going to be fine,' Sahm Venter replies, adjusting her money belt hidden under her jeans and holding up her glass of champagne that the crew have served us while we wait. 'We've got the biggest man in the world waiting to meet us at Ndjili.'

'Not Jean Marie?' Jimi Matthews of Reuters says.

'Yes. It is.'

'He's meeting me too,' someone else adds.

'Me, too,' I say.

'You see, I told you we'd be fine,' Sahm says.

Huge pillars of white cloud hang in the blue sky. The earth below is a patchwork of green and brown. We descend into the cloud. Thin plumes of smoke rise up into the sky from the villages; the green hills disappear into the vastness of the forest.

Emerging out of the forest, glowing bronze and orange in the hazy light of the late afternoon sun, is the River. The Congo, now renamed the Zaire. The meandering heart of this vast land. We turn in the sky and the light on the water changes to silver. Islands, dark green with vegetation, are in the middle of the stream, and dugout canoes like pointed matchsticks drift on the current. Then the river is behind us and we are passing over the shanty towns that lie on the outskirts of the city.

Soldiers guard the runway; they stand in groups, wearing sunglasses and carrying AK-47s. With a bump, we land and taxi down the runway. In front of us lie the scruffy white terminal buildings. On the roof is a tattered Zairean flag: a green background with the yellow sun in the centre and a powerful, muscular black arm holding a flaming red torch of hope in the centre.

As the plane parks on the tarmac, a horde of people rush out from the terminal building. They surge forward to meet us as we descend the steps. Most of them are waving their hands and imploring us to hire them. Their faces are taut and suffused with the barely submerged fear that hunger and desperation brings.

'*Monsieur, bagage!*'

'*Taxi!*'

'*Passport!*'

Jean Marie is certainly the biggest man at Ndjili airport, and that is enough for us. He beats off the competition, takes our passports and fifty dollars each.

We stand sweating in the humid heat until he returns with our passports, each containing an illegible purple smudge and a scribbled date above it. We are free to enter the crumbling empire of President *Maréchal* Mobutu Sese Seko Koko Ngbendu wa za Banga, 'the All-Powerful Warrior Who, by His Endurance and Inflexible Will to Win, Goes from Conquest to Conquest, Leaving Fire in his Wake'.

Milton is already at reception at the Hotel Memling, waiting with my key. We hug.

'You made it,' he says delightedly. 'Welcome to Kinshasa.'

Allan is there, too. He strides across the lobby to greet me.

'Tony,' he says in his muted Scots brogue that carries the full weight of his affection. Cameraman Glenn Middleton is there. In fact, the lobby is filled with old friends. Milton introduces me to one of our local fixers, Clyde Salumu. Clyde is a tall, elegantly dressed Zairean who is studying journalism at college in Kinshasa. He is only in his mid-twenties, but he carries himself with the confidence of someone much older. He speaks at least three languages fluently and, over the weeks to come, is to prove himself an invaluable member of our team, helping with everything from translating and arranging visas to organizing interviews.

It's going to be a massive story. The chaos that I had read of in the newspaper back in Jo'burg has kept everyone busy. The political situation in Kinshasa is fluid. Just after returning from France for his most recent bout of treatment for prostate cancer, Mobutu named an old political rival of his, Etienne Tshisikedi, prime minister in place of an old loyalist and hardliner against the rebels, Leon Kengo wa Dondo. Kengo wa Dondo had resigned on March 24, but Mobutu asked him to stay on until someone could take his place. Tshisikedi is popular with the people, and Mobutu was forced to appoint him prime minister only a bare week ago in the hopes of creating some sort of genuinely popular government to oppose the advancing rebels.

Desperate measures. Too little, too late. Tshisikedi was determined to demonstrate his independence. The day after taking office, he announced that he would dissolve the pro-Mobutu parliament, and named a parliament of his own loyalists. He even went as far as offering the AFDL rebels posts in the new parliament, calling Laurent Kabila 'my brother', but the offer was rejected.

Mobutu was furious. On Tuesday this week, while Tshisikedi supporters clashed with the army in Kinshasa and the rebels battled for control of Lubumbashi with units of Mobutu's Presidential Guard – the only troops to put up a fight – Mobutu declared a state of emergency. That afternoon the radio confirmed the appointment as prime minister of Army Chief of Staff, General Likulia Bolongo, replacing Tshisikedi, and five other generals to govern the provinces still theoretically under government control.

On Wednesday, as the rebels took control of Lubumbashi, thousands of Tshisikedi supporters gathered outside his house in Kinshasa waving branches with green leaves to march with him to occupy the office of the prime minister. The branches proclaim peace, but, of course, like in all crowds, the violent impulse born of anger and frustration is there, lurking, biding its time . . .

It was the soldiers who unleashed it. Glenn was filming the march as the army, led by Mobutu's son, Captain Kongulu Mobutu, attacked. First they fired teargas and then they charged in with rifle butts. They chased the people who fled, running some of them down, punching, kicking and hitting them with rifle butts. Foreign journalists were deliberately attacked too. At least one group, a camera crew working for APTN, was beaten; the windows of their car were smashed. The soldiers even hit Tshisikedi himself on the face and neck. He was detained for a while and then released.

The Americans have been among Mobutu's closest supporter for decades, but today the State Department spokesman in the US, Nicholas Burns, said: 'The era of Mobutu is over.'

It is the weekend now. On Monday Tshisikedi supporters are planning a *ville morte* – a stayaway – but I prefer the literal translation from the French – a dead city.

Monday will be a busy day for all of us. I trust my colleagues implicitly. All of us have covered at least one war before, but Kinshasa is a city moving rapidly towards the edge and every day brings the possibility of chaos closer.

Interlude

The story of the fall of Joseph Désiré Mobutu and the rise of his nemesis, Laurent Kabila, is the story of an old, outdated vision of Africa and the rise of a new way of seeing the continent. Laurent Kabila was a flawed man, and his revolution led to at least as much chaos in the Congo as existed in the old Zaire. But there was a dream buried in the centre of the chaos. I had caught a glimpse of it months before in Bukavu when Laurent Kabila stood at the podium in front of the crowd outside the post office and roared in Swahili: *Jambo Sana!*

It was, above everything else, an African vision of an African future. For all its bloodshed, and for all its tragic mistakes and failures, it remains a watershed moment in the history of the continent. It was the beginning of the twenty-first century in Africa.

It was the end of the crumbling empire of President *Maréchal* Mobutu.

Mobutu's hallucinations were the visions of nineteenth-century Europe, corrupted and debased, and forced on to Africa's second largest country.

They began a long time ago, with an image that was a fantasy.

'I am Lord of lords. Under heaven, I surpass in riches and virtue and power all other kings upon the whole earth.' So ran the text of a letter that circulated the cities and illiterate castles of Europe in 1165. It purported to be from the legendary Christian king, Prester John. In his realm, it was said, giant ants the size of dogs dug gold which slaves loaded on to elephants, hippopotami and camels. His palace had a roof of ebony, windows of crystal and was lit by shining golden apples. Thirty thousand men a day dined at the king's table made of gold and amethyst and sat on pillars of ivory . . . such was the image of Africa that filled Europe's imagination for 300 years.

Besides the faded legend of a mystical king, there was the lure of something else, something far more real – the hope of finding the source of the African gold that had been coming out of the desert on camel trains since the days of ancient Rome. From 1422, Henry the Navigator began sending expeditions down the west coast of Africa. They found no gold, but they brought back growing numbers of slaves. In 1483 a single caravel, captained by Diogo Cão, arrived off the mouth of a great river. There he came to the court of the Mani Kongo, ruler of the Bakongo empire.

Ambassadors were exchanged with Lisbon. The king's son was baptized and took the Christian name Affonso. A promising start, but by 1526 King Affonso wrote to King John II of Portugal of the cruelty of the European slave traders: 'As soon as they are taken by the white men, they are immediately ironed and branded with fire.' Their ravages had become so widespread that Affonso pleaded that 'we cannot reckon how great the damage is'.

There was to be no end to it. Portuguese slavers travelled along the coast and deep into the interior, seizing ten of thousands of Africans and shipping them across the Atlantic. But even here, right at the very beginning, this was a twisted tale of double betrayal. Affonso and his Bakongo warriors captured many of the slaves themselves from among their own subjects and from the surrounding peoples. They sold them to the Portuguese traders for a handsome profit and an expanding kingdom.

The greed and cruelty of the slave trade was a cancer that ate away at the heart of the Congo. One by one, the local African kingdoms were destroyed, the Bakongo among them. By the late 1600s the entire region was in a state of constant terror and turmoil from which it has still not recovered today.

In 1885, the European powers at the great colonial Berlin Conference granted King Leopold of Belgium's Congo Free State legitimacy. It was the personal possession of the king himself. Here, at last, was the apotheosis of the white man's dream of finding wealth in Africa. The new country had 2 700 kilometres of navigable waterways, a population of nearly ten million people and an unimaginable plethora of resources: hardwood timber, vast reserves of copper, immense rubber plantations at the time when the automobile was coming into being, incalculable acres of potential farmland, palm-oil, ivory, diamonds, gold, manganese, uranium . . . the list is endless and it was all owned by one man. One man, whose brutal rule became a symbol for all the horrors of European colonization.

Under Leopold, ivory and rubber, especially rubber, became his personal monopolies. The Casement Report of 1903 detailed the atrocities of Leopold's rule. Congolese became virtual slaves on the plantations. They were beaten, tied to trees, even forced to drink white men's urine. If they did not reach their quotas, their hands were cut off and presented to Leopold's agents in baskets as proof that the foremen had not been 'soft'. At least as many as eight million people died under the cruelties of his regime.

As more reports began to filter out, a horrified Belgian public and parliament demanded that he hand over his fiefdom. In 1908, the Congo became a Belgian colony. The new system was little better than the old. The atrocities were less frequent, but terrible abuses were still visited on the Congolese. In 1960, spooked by riots in the colonial capital Leopoldville, the Belgians hastily handed over control of the independent Republic of the Congo to its new Prime Minister, Patrice Lumumba.

Ten days after Independence, Joseph Désiré Mobutu, who had served seven years in the notorious colonial *Force Publique* and had risen to the rank of sergeant – the highest rank a black man could achieve – was given the rank of colonel and made Chief of Staff of the Congolese Army. Two and a half months later, in September 1960, the new Colonel Mobutu seized the attention of the world by putting his prime minister under house arrest.

Lumumba fled towards Stanleyville, now Kisangani, on September 27, but he never got that far. He was captured and arrived in Lubumbashi in the southern Katanga province so badly beaten by his Baluba guards during the flight that he and two other colleagues, Joseph Okito and Maurice Mpolo, could hardly stand. Mobutu always denied it, but, in the years since then, new evidence has emerged that he, the CIA and the Belgians had a hand in the assassination of Lumumba.

Mobutu seized total control in 1965, ousting President Joseph Kasavubu and declaring himself President instead. In 1972, he changed his name to Mobutu Sese Seko. He renamed the country Zaire – a Portuguese corruption of the Lingala name for the mighty Congo river – *nzere-nzadi*, the river that swallows all rivers.

After thirty-two years in power, he was Africa's longest-reigning dictator. He is believed to have amassed a personal fortune of $4-billion, equal to the national debt of Zaire. Mobutu came to power at the height of the Cold War. This was the key to his rise to absolute power. His major allies were France, Belgium and the US, but time and again, when it suited him, he was able to play them off against the Russians and the Chinese. Over the years, he was able to squeeze billions in 'aid' and use it to build a network of influence in central and southern Africa that was unrivalled.

Mobutu became a vicious parody of Prester John. His opulence and extravagance were unrivalled. So grotesque did his vision of himself become that every night on Zairean television he was shown descending from the clouds, like God himself.

Better than anyone, Mobutu understood how power feeds off the image. In his last months, as his power waned and his fantasies collapsed so, too, day by day, his image faded into nothingness.

Dead City

In Lingala, the language of the river, the lingua franca of Zaire, they call the water hyacinth 'the new thing on the river'. Water hyacinth is not native to Africa; it comes from South America. It is a plant invader; and it only appeared in the second half of the twentieth century – the legacy of some Belgian colonial sentimentalist who wanted pretty white flowers for his garden fishpond.

The hyacinth now is an enemy of the Zairean people and of the river they live on. It grows faster than people can clear it, doubling the area it covers every few days, choking small inlets, surrounding islands, blocking off the light and air from the brown depths, starving the water of nutrients and killing the fish.

It struck me from the first night I spent in Zaire that this is how it was in the broad avenues and muddy alleys of Kinshasa as we waited for the end of Mobutu and the coming of Laurent Kabila – the new man who would rule the river. Day by day the fear and rumours grew, choking the streets, surrounding the hotels and the shops and the restaurants; day by day, stripping this city of all pretence, killing off the illusions, and laying bare the truths that could no longer stay hidden.

That first weekend is quiet. I take the time to settle into my room, 712, at the Hotel Memling. (I wrote the price of it in my notebook: *Chambre simple Nouveau Zaires 323,565,00.00*. I think that was the equivalent of about US$150.00, but my mind never did quite get used to dealing in billions when paying the price of a meal for four at a restaurant, or for a few days' car hire.)

Room 712 is to become my home for nearly two months. In an attempt to ride above the chaos and to keep the order of events clear in my head, I buy a colourful diocese map of Zaire published by the Catholic church from a street vendor. I stick it on the wall in front of my bed and, each day, I mark off the towns that are taken as Laurent Kabila's rebels draw nearer. It is not an entirely successful undertaking, because every time it rains the humidity levels soar and the corners of the map curl up against the red camera tape holding it to the wall and it falls down in a crumpled heap on the floor.

The Memling is located in downtown Kinshasa. Not as luxurious as its rival, the Intercontinental across town, the inside of our architectural monstrosity is still a slightly unreal refuge from the squalor and poverty of the city around us. Every day there is an enormous buffet for lunch spread out on the tables of the restaurant, the swimming pool is a sapphire jewel against the mouldy concrete of the buildings surrounding it, the beer is always cold and you can drink it while hungry street kids come up like ghosts in the heat outside and push their noses up against the tinted glass of the bar windows.

Everything in the hotel is brand new. At first, I imagine it is an example of one of the last foreign investments that has flourished in and around the Mobutu elite. It is partly that, of course, but the reason everything is so new is that the hotel was pillaged in 1993 when the army went on a rampage because they had not been paid their salary of less than US$1.00 for months. The Memling was singled out because of its association with foreign capital and the Mobutu cabal. Everything was taken, even the light sockets set into the walls were torn out with bayonets and pliers. Finally, French and Belgian soldiers restored order to the streets of the city. No one knows exactly how many people were killed in the rampage, but estimates range from 300 to 1 000.

It is an ominous warning of what could happen to us when the end days come, and the soldiers have given up all pretence of defending Kinshasa. Despite the luxury of our haven, we are not safe from them. In fact, its very opulence may be our undoing. We, too, fear what the entire city, from the rich to the poor, fears – that the soldiers will go on one final brutal spree of looting in the last hours before Kabila's AFDL forces arrive.

The hotel is extremely vulnerable. The main doors are glass. They are protected by a sliding security gate, but I have seen mobs at work before and I know it is far too flimsy. It will give us, at most, ten minutes' grace before a determined mob has torn it off its hinges. Anyway, the ground floor of the hotel is surrounded by the tinted glass windows. They keep out the street kids successfully, but it won't need a mob of soldiers to break them down, half a dozen rowdy youths would be enough to invade the hotel.

Sunday morning, April 13, 1997 we gather in the BBC office set up in room 405 with our colleagues Milton Nkosi and Martin Turner. The tension in the city is growing. Opposition leader Etienne Tshisikedi has arranged a *ville morte*, a stayaway, for Monday.

Ben Wilson from Australian TV starts the conversation. 'Things are beginning to happen. There are rumours that "elements" are telling people near the airport to move out.'

'Yes,' says Clyde. 'And the driver's getting anxious. He thinks that on Monday when there is the *ville morte*, the crowd may attack us for driving in the streets.'

That Sunday morning in the hotel lobby I hear news of a press conference at the rebel headquarters in the city of Goma in the far east of the country. Earlier in the week, Kabila had unilaterally declared a three-day pause in the fighting to allow Mobutu time to resign. The deadline has come and gone.

'It is a kind of a joke,' Mobutu had declared. 'I am the head of state of Zaire. I don't have to receive ultimatums from the chief of a gang.' Instead Mobutu had suggested that Kabila ask politely to speak to him, like this: ' "Mister President of the Republic of Zaire, it is my intention to meet with you." That is polite.'

'We won't give Mobutu another chance,' Bizima Karaha, the AFDL 'foreign minister', says in reply today. 'There will never be another ceasefire. We want him to leave the country and then we can negotiate a ceasefire.'

And then there are reports that the rebels have already reached Bandundu, only a few hundred kilometres from Kinshasa. The reports are not confirmed, but they cannot be ignored.

Allan Little's local network Telecell mobile phone rings while we are at lunch at the *Cercle Asiatic*. It is London. 'We have to do a piece,' Allan says. 'The bulletins are empty.' We rush back to the hotel and edit a TV piece that afternoon.

Clyde is sitting in one of the hotel chairs behind us, watching the editing process. We welcome his presence there. It is not often that we have someone from our vast, normally faceless audience right there in the room with us while we work. At one point, when Kabila's face comes up on the screen, Clyde says to us: 'At first, after Bukavu fell, people didn't like Kabila because they said he came from Rwanda. But now Kabila represents change. We all want change, whether it comes from Heaven or whether it comes from Hell.'

That evening there is a letter addressed to 'B.B.C.' at reception. It is handwritten in French. It claims to be from the AFDL. Despite the crude lettering, there is something genuine about it. The staff at the reception deny having seen anyone come in with a letter.

'Radio is why we got this,' Allan says. 'Nothing can beat the power of radio in Africa.'

He translates it for me in snatches: 'We are waiting to take Kinshasa . . . We have already prepared the ground . . . There will be no bloodshed.'

Allan looks at me. His face is lit with excitement as he holds up the letter. 'You know what this means, don't you?'

I look back at him. 'What?' I ask.

'*They're already here*. They've done the same thing in every town they've taken. They slowly start spreading the word around, preparing the ground. Then they act suddenly, and the battle is over very quickly.'

Monday, April 14. The day of the Dead City is a grey, overcast day. I look out my hotel window and see a single car moving down the wide, deserted Boulevard de 30 Juin – named after Independence Day. The day in 1960 when King Baudouin of Belgium, dressed in ceremonial finery and holding a sword, rode in a huge white convertible down this same boulevard, then called *Avenue Albert*. A nameless black youth dashed out of the crowd and snatched his sword away. The gendarmes gave chase, but the youth disappeared into the cheering, laughing crowd of Congolese.

That same day Baudouin sat and listened to an angry Patrice Lumumba declare: 'Who could forget the hangings and the shootings in which perished so many of our brethren? We have experienced contempt, insults and blows that we endured morning, noon and evening. We have seen that the law was never the same for whites as for blacks, accommodating the first, cruel and inhuman for the other.' And then the famous, ringing declaration. 'We are going to show the world what the black man can do when he works in freedom, and we are going to make of the Congo the centre of the sun's radiance for all of Africa.'

I cannot help wondering how different the Congo, and Africa, would have been if Lumumba had not been killed. It is too late to think of that now, but somehow, looking down on to the deserted streets that morning, it seems to me that history has come full circle; that their silence is telling Sergeant Joseph Désiré Mobutu that it is time to go.

All that remains is for someone to snatch his sword away.

We gather outside the hotel. Clyde has arranged a driver with a minibus. We pile inside and set off down the Boulevard 30 Juin in the direction of Etienne Tshisikedi's house.

The city is deserted, except for the army patrols that move up and down the streets in their jeeps. The *ville morte* is an obvious success; people are staying away in protest.

The central market is empty. A portrait of Mobutu painted on a concrete stand stares down on the rows of deserted stalls, their wooden framework skeletal against the overcast sky.

After we have filmed the empty market, we drive into the suburbs of the city, where the former colonial masters lived. The tree-lined boulevards are overgrown now, and broken streetlamps lie across the traffic circles. Both the old mansions, and the new ones, built by Mobutu's elite, are surrounded by high walls, paint peeling in the tropical humidity, and topped by broken glass set in cement.

We come across a few dozen youths wandering the streets. They are friendly and they shout and wave at us, the foreign journalists who have come to record their day of protest and, perhaps, if things turn out well, their moments of glory.

More and more supporters throng the streets as we draw near to the street where Tshisikedi lives. When we finally arrive, there is a huge log placed across the road to stop the army vehicles coming any closer.

We stop, too, and get out to walk the short distance to Tshisikedi's house. His supporters gather around us in the thin morning mist that swirls off the river as we approach the house. They are excited and friendly. So far the army and the police have not appeared. Perhaps they will not come at all. Pictures last week of the Zairean military clubbing their own people have been shown all over the world. It cannot have looked good for Mobutu, perhaps he wants to avoid further embarrassment.

We come to the walled compound where Tshisikedi lives. 'We would like to see Mr Tshisikedi.'

The guards outside shake their heads. 'It is impossible.'

'Why?'

'Today is *ville morte*. He is resting.'

We ask a few more times. Clyde tries hard to persuade them, but it is impossible.

We turn and walk back to the car. Just after we step around the log across the road a young man rushes up to us. He is shouting.

A pall of black smoke hangs in the air just a short distance in front of us. 'He says they are burning tyres,' Clyde tells us.

We run down the road to where the smoke is coming from. As we get there, the police and soldiers arrive with sirens blaring. Glenn and Clyde are already 150 metres ahead. Clyde will suffer the most if he is caught. Glenn is down on one knee filming as they screech to a halt in their jeeps and jump out with their rifles at the ready. Despite the adrenalin that is suddenly pumping through my veins, I have to smile. In his calm, experienced way, he is making himself inconspicuous, but at the same time he getting the shots that will lead news bulletins.

The crowds panic and scatter, running wildly through the overgrown streets as the soldiers chase after them with their rifle butts. I look back at Glenn and Clyde. They are no longer there. I can see that Allan is as scared as I am. These soldiers might have won the last few battles against their own people, but they are on the losing side of history and they know it.

The thought of Glenn and Clyde being arrested by these confused and vengeful soldiers is frightening because they are so unpredictable.

Where are they?

We drive slowly through the thick, black smoke and the fleeing people, both of us tense. Soldiers rush past us, yelling at the crowd. We are on the other side of the smoke; and there they are. Glenn, ever the professional, is kneeling on the ground putting a fresh tape in the camera so that if the soldiers do confiscate it, the real footage will be safe. Clyde has stayed with him all the time. The brief moment of anxiety has passed; it is good to see that they are okay.

We drive back to the hotel to file a piece for the One O'Clock News. All down the empty boulevard police and army cars are rushing to and fro. On the skyline of the city we can see plumes of black smoke rising into the air.

In the lobby of the hotel we hear a flurry of stories from other journalists. Somebody's driver ran away when the army appeared, abandoning the car and the soldiers simply kicked him and took it. A Belgian correspondent was arrested. A breathless TV crew say they were fired at; others say that the soldiers fired into the air.

We rush up to room 405 to edit Glenn's pictures for the lunchtime bulletin in faraway London. Here, in Kinshasa, the sirens are still echoing across the city.

Telecells

In years to come historians will record that the first war in the world in which cellphones were an indispensable tool of the conflict took place in Africa.

Madame Pepe was the manager who ran the Telecell network in Kinshasa. With Mobutu's demise, business boomed for her and the company she worked for. The power of the technology they controlled made everyone dependent on them in one way or another. The land line telephone system in Kinshasa was atrocious. It was hardly even worth the bother attempting to make a call. Everyone relied on Madame Pepe's Telecells. The network jammed occasionally but, other than that, it was the only reliable means of communicating. I don't know whether the Big Man himself actually had a Telecell. However, certainly everyone beneath him, including his sons Nzanga and Kongulu had one.

The technology was already outdated in the West, but, by and large, it worked fine. The handsets were huge, chunky blocks of plastic and green backlit screens with hard rubbery aerials that jabbed you in the hip – rather like a soldier's rifle barrel – when you made the mistake of trying to keep the handset in your pocket.

The batteries were temperamental – some would last for days, others would last for an hour at most. But without a Telecell it was almost impossible to work effectively, largely because everyone else had one.

It was not only us journalists who relied on our Telecells. The diplomats and politicians all carried them, the generals in the army issued what orders they could to their subordinates on their Telecells, and the businesspeople who kept the city ticking over relied on them entirely.

The Telecells were crucial to the running of the country, they even made it possible to regulate the exchange rate of the endlessly fluctuating value of the Nouveau Zaire to the US dollar. Just near the American Embassy was the street where the money changers did business. They were mostly women wearing the colourful dresses that were once Zaire's national costume. Everyone called it 'Wall Street'. The women would wave huge wads of dirty notes at you as you passed by, hoping that you would stop and change some foreign currency with them.

The value of the notes changed constantly. Now the rate was even more volatile than usual, as people were terrified of what would happen to their money when the rebels marched into town. Everybody wanted to be holding as many dollars as possible.

To make things worse, Mobutu's government had in January introduced a large number of NZ 100 000 notes, and even some 500 000 notes in order to compensate the civil servants who hadn't been paid for months.

Within days of the bills circulating on the streets, the people of Kinshasa had started calling them the 'prostate' as they hit the streets at about the same time as Mobutu underwent his first round of surgery for prostate cancer. The *Maréchal* might have held the power of life and death over his subjects in his decaying Wonderland, but not even he could change the rules of economics. The poor civil servants who had once counted themselves lucky to have a job and who now, as the end came nearer, were looked on with increasing animosity by other Zaireans, had been fobbed off with the 100 000 zaire notes. They had no choice, but by accepting the government's new notes as payment for their salary arrears they found themselves trapped.

The sharp-eyed women of Wall Street were deeply suspicious of the new notes and of the man in miltary uniform whose face glared at them from their shiny clean surfaces. At first, the women refused to have anything to do with the notes at all. Now, apparently, they would take them at more than double the exchange rate for the older, more trustworthy, small denomination bills. The Nouveau Zaire, when it was introduced in 1993, had started its spiralling life at three to the dollar. Now on Wall Street, to get one creased and dirty greenback, you had to present the women with 162 000 small denomination zaires, and the rate was rising fast. Until recently, the women of Wall Street with their canny trading skills had managed to keep the inflation rate relatively low at about 5 per cent in Kinshasa itself. The overall inflation rate countrywide, however, was estimated to be about 600 per cent, which meant that the value of the zaire decreased usually a few times a day. Zaire was an immense commonwealth of confusion. The rate for the zaire, in addition to changing constantly, was also different in Kinshasa to the rate in Lubumbashi or in Kisangani. In the diamond-rich province of East Kasai they accepted only the *old* zaires anyway, at a rate of 16 million to the dollar. And that was *before* the AFDL had taken over more than half the country.

'How do you manage to keep track of it all?' I asked a man whom I shall call Salim, an Asian businessman we had got to know, when I was having lunch with him at a fancy restaurant in Kinshasa.

Salim smiled and lifted his Telecell off the starched white linen tablecloth. 'We have somebody down on Wall Street with one of these. We call him a few times a day to find out what the dollar trading rate is at that time of the day. Then we phone each other and then we call our partners around the country and we let them know what the rate is. That's how we keep track.'

It is Tuesday, the second day of the *ville morte* declared by Tshisikedi's supporters. I am preparing for the beefing up of our team with the arrival of correspondent George Alagiah, and cameraman Byron Blunt from Johannesburg. I have just finished paying homage at Madame Pepe's office, hoping to get at least one more phone for George and perhaps one for Byron too. Alphonse is driving me back to the hotel when a silver minibus roars past us. Hanging all over the outside are students from the university. In the darkness inside, I can see the faces of Chevan Rayson from AP and Spokes Mashiyane, a colleague from WTN. There are a couple of other faces that I can't see clearly.

Immediately I dial Sahm Venter, the AP TN bureau chief.

'I've just seen Chevan and some others being carted away in a minibus,' I tell her.

'I know. We're on to it,' she says and hangs up.

By the time I reach the hotel, they have already been released. Sahm has been at work on her own Telecell. The journalists were filming on the grounds of the university campus and were 'arrested' by pro-Mobutu students for interviewing anti-Mobutu students. The pro-Mobutu students then forced the driver of the silver minibus to take them to the army. That had been a tense time for Chevan and Spokes and the others as they didn't know what the army's reaction would be. Caught up in the spirit of the moment, the students clearly hadn't bargained on the army's reaction either. When they arrived at the barracks, the soldiers released the journalists. As a reward for their loyalty to the *Maréchal*, they arrested the students and started beating them.

Of course we are relieved to know that our colleagues are safe, but there is also something ominous in the soldiers' reactions. The day before, they had been hell-bent on arresting and even beating journalists; today they are releasing journalists and beating pro-Mobutu students. No one can predict how the soldiers will react to any given situation. The only thing that is certain is that they will act violently towards somebody. Our Telecells mean that we are not entirely at their mercy.

The foreigners have begun leaving in large numbers; what had been a trickle of mostly wives and children has become a flood now. Embassies are keeping on only essential staff. Everybody is doing stories on the expatriates who are closing factories, locking up their houses, selling the last of the stock in their shops. Of course, it is not only the expats who are fleeing. More and more wealthy Zaireans are going on 'holiday'. Flights are irregular, but the airport is still open. They smile when we interview them in the long lines at Ndjili airport on the outskirts of Kinshasa. They tell us they have faith in their country. They will never abandon it, they say. It is only their frightened eyes and their bulging suitcases that tell a different story.

Others drive out of the city in their shiny, air-conditioned 4x4s, taking the ferry across the river to Brazzaville where the hotels are open and the foreign troops – Belgian, French, British, US, and a small number of South Africans – are waiting to rush in to save the foreigners the moment the *pillage* begins in Kinshasa.

A few missionaries remain behind in the city, trusting in their reputation with the people and in their God, but most of those people who can get out, are leaving. The rest of us are staying behind, and waiting.

We have to remember that when the story is over we will be leaving, but for Clyde and the other Zaireans we are working with, this story is their story. The way it turns out will define much, perhaps everything, in their lives. Clyde particularly shares the excitement of the unfolding drama along with us but, for him, it is always tempered by the dangers of what might happen. By chance his own story mirrors so much of what is happening around us. He is an only child born in Kivu. When he was still very young, his mother brought him to Kinshasa looking for a better life for herself and her son. She raised him in the slums of what, in colonial times, was the old African quarter known as the *cité*, as opposed to the white quarter known as the *ville*.

Clyde never talks of his father, but he grew up speaking Swahili, the language of the East, although living here in the West in Kinshasa. It always marked him as someone different. Many of his relatives in the East are Tutsis and in today's Zaire that has grown from being a difference into a serious handicap. He speaks Lingala, French and English fluently. He is what is known as a Kinois, a Kinshasa resident. The city and all that goes with it, not Kivu, is his home now. He will never go back to the East. What happens to the city happens to Clyde, and through him, and the others like him, we learn so much about what is really going on in this city outside the air-conditioned bubble of our hotel.

The Leopard King

All of us in the city are growing more obsessed with the coming of the rebels as each day passes. *Radio Trottoir* – pavement radio – the nickname Kinshasans give to the rumours that circulate through the streets, claims they are coming soon, any day now. The people of Kinshasa see Kabila and his AFDL forces as liberators. They say so openly to us and our cameras in the streets and then they turn away and go about their business as best they can, waiting for the fateful day when the rebels come.

They are scared, and many of them are growing hungry as food supplies run short and prices rise. At long last, though, some have begun to hope and to speak their minds.

Always wary of the uniformed thugs of the army, we spend the days filming in the jostling streets filled with people wearing their colourful shirts and dresses. We take our microphones to the markets where you can buy anything from smoked monkey parts, trussed-up iguanas and crocodiles with wired-up jaws destined for the cooking pot to a sealed beam headlamp for your 4x4 vehicle. Here the vibrancy of Africa swirls all around you. In the smaller corners of the market women sit under makeshift shelters of palm fronds and sell tiny mirrors, toothpaste, piles of sugar gleaming in the sun or a few small tomatoes.

The people come up to us all the time now, despite their fear of the army. Everywhere their message is the same:

'We are starving to death, and we do not get good salaries.'

'People are sick and tired of Mobutu in government. They want change and they want it now.'

'We will fight. If the soldiers of Mobutu kill us, good, we will accept that. But we will fight for our liberty.'

Brave words, angry words, desperate words. They contrast so fiercely with the words of *Papa Maréchal* himself in March when he finally returned to his adoring nation from his convalescence in France.

When he came back, he did not allow his people to see him themselves, but two days later, after meeting with South African Deputy President Thabo Mbeki, he spoke to the cold eyes of our waiting cameras.

His voice was trembling and hoarse, betraying the weakness of his physical, human illness, but the words were strong and ringing with confidence: *'Je m'appelle Mobutu* . . . My name is Mobutu. I am back.'

Above all, he was fighting for control of his image. His right hand was raised, not in a fist, but with the fingers lightly held together; a kingly gesture, a gesture of contempt. The leopard-skin hat was tilted at a cocky angle. His eyes were steady as they looked over the pushing, sweating crowd of journalists gathered below him.

The right hand came down, swiftly, arrogantly. 'I am back, not to take care of my own fortune and interests, as you often say, but to take care of the country's highest interests: our unity and territorial integrity.'

The wily old Leopard King, trapped in his own lair, fighting back. But his words and his image no longer have the power they once had.

Je m'appelle Mobutu.

It sounds empty and today he looks ridiculous. Once Mobutu had strolled boldly, visibly risking his life, amongst his troops on the front lines of the rebellions against his rule. Now he cannot muster his troops to provide even one small victory against the advancing rebel forces of one of his oldest enemies, Laurent Kabila, a man all but invisible for the three decades of Mobutu's rule.

The image of the Leopard King is one of weakness and decay. But still it rules this city. In a younger incarnation he still emerges from the clouds on television every night. It is only words that dare challenge his sway.

The most obvious are the frenzied cries of the mobs under their palm leaves. The streets echo with their anger.

MOBUTU IS A THIEF AND A MURDERER! DOWN WITH MOBUTU! DOWN!

At other times we sit in chairs on neatly mowed lawns on the banks of the swiftly flowing river with the soldiers walking up and down in the long grass at the edge of the water and the clumps of hyacinth floating and spinning on the muddy grey currents. Here we enter the calm, unreal atmosphere of press conferences and ambassadorial briefings.

'This is off the record, of course, but I estimate we have a six week window before we have to start evacuating.'

But, most of all, the words that surround us are the ones we hear from the whispered rumours that scurry through this city.

'The Chinese are coming. They are sending 500 troops to help in the defence of Kinshasa.' It sounds absurd, but suddenly everyone is talking about Chinese soldiers.

'Someone has discovered a chemical weapons testing plant on the road to

Matadi. It's near an old picnic spot.'

Near an old picnic spot . . . it's just ridiculous. But, then again, chemical weapons are not that difficult to obtain or even to manufacture. The crudest of artillery shells can be adapted with very little difficulty to carry simple chemical, or even biological, warheads. Anything is possible in this world if you possess both money and imagination. Mobutu has plenty of money and an imagination fevered enough to allow his image to emerge from heavenly clouds every night on national television.

Then comes a report from Lubumbashi – still only words: The AFDL finance minister Mawapanga Mwana Nanga says: 'Mobutu and his henchmen are planning to kill expatriates in Kinshasa with the help of the Military Action and Intelligence Service (SARM) and Special Presidential Division (DSP).' He claims that killing whites will bring in the foreign troops waiting on the other side of the river in Brazzaville. 'This plan,' he goes on, 'is well-conceived and is to be carried out soon.'

Did the words come first from Lubumbashi or from Kinshasa? How did they move so quickly across the forest? Who should we believe? It is an outrageous claim, but it is the sort of last-ditch thing that a deluded tyrant like Mobutu might dream up. There is a certain logic to it. An armed force of Belgian, French and US troops in control of Kinshasa would complicate the rebels' plans enormously. In addition, the rebels' pronouncements of the course of the fighting have been pretty accurate so far.

A few of us decide to contact the Israeli-run security firm that protects most of the diplomats and businessmen in town. We sit down at the gleaming opal poolside with an enormous, smiling man. His salesman-like manner and obvious physical strength and fitness inspire the sort of confidence we want. Before the meeting begins, he stretches his muscular arm down to his briefcase to turn off his two-way radio and his Telecell. Our needs now have his full attention.

'How much would it cost to secure the hotel?' we ask him.

He smiles, and puts his elbows on the table in front of him.

'It is impossible to secure this hotel,' he says, still smiling.

'But why not?'

'It is too late.' He gestures around him at the plate glass windows, the low wall around the pool, the marble lobby. 'I would need at least twenty men, maybe more. I don't have the men. There's nothing I can do for you.'

Later that evening, in Beijing, the Chinese Foreign Ministry issues a firm statement denying that any troops have been sent to Kinshasa.

The Real War

The real war is taking place hundreds of kilometres away under the canopy of the great forest. This war of killing and blood is coming closer, but we cannot yet see the killing for ourselves, we only hear of it.

We put up another map of Zaire in the BBC office in room 405 so we can all keep track of the rebels' advance and refer to it while we are editing. This map, too, stubbornly refuses to stay up on the wall, and it is lying on the floor every morning when we meet for coffee and a discussion about covering the day's events.

Further down the corridor a spirit medium has taken up residence. Every day somebody from Kinshasa's elite comes to consult him.

In watching their advance across the country, it is impossible to forget that Kabila and his forces are not only crushing Mobutu's cruel and absurd rabble before them; as they advance towards Kinshasa they are driving hundreds of thousands of starving Rwandan Hutu refugees deeper and deeper into the forest.

They are the 250 000 or so people who did not return to Rwanda and who fled west with the extremist Hutu militias. Many of the refugees, the hard men of the *interahamwe*, are battling the AFDL every step of the way and, along with isolated units of the DSP, are providing the only resistance in the towns; but most of the refugees have long since given up any idea of fighting. They are unable to go home, though. They are being dragged along by the militias and are trapped by the AFDL forces that lie between them and Rwanda.

The first reports of the AFDL committing human rights violations against these Hutu refugees began coming out in early March. The reports were careful and restrained. It was only with the fall of Kisangani that the first substantial evidence of real abuse began to come out. The bulk of the refugees were hiding out in the forests around Kisangani, dying at an estimated rate of ninety a day from starvation, exhaustion and disease.

Then there was the more horrific, but shadowy cause of death – Tutsi vengeance. It was denied over and over by Kabila and by the Rwandan government, but increasingly evidence was emerging of Tutsi death squads working in the wake of the AFDL victories, hunting down the Hutus and slaughtering them in revenge for what had happened in 1994.

After weeks of negotiation, the AFDL has finally authorized a UN-sponsored airlift of the refugees to Rwanda, but it is stalled by the Rwandans' refusal to allow the refugees to fly directly to Rwanda, claiming that to do so would be to risk cholera spreading among their people. So, for now, the refugees stay in their makeshift shelters in the forest, slowly starving and waiting for the next attack.

Despite the growing fear in Kinshasa, the people here cannot ignore the stories of the atrocities and the plight of the innocent among those refugees, hiding and dying in the forest. If anything, even among those who have allowed themselves to hope, the stories of the massacres make the people in Kinshasa more fearful of what might happen when their day of liberation from Mobutu Sese Seko finally dawns.

With the departure of so many of the rich and of the expatriates, and the closing of so many shops, the streets of Kinshasa are quieter than ever before. The market is still bustling, but prices are rising. 'They will shortly reach the threshold of unaffordability,' a diplomat tells me. Hunger and disease are growing in the city. An aid worker we interview tells us that there are at least 300 000 severely malnourished children in the slums and on the streets of Kinshasa, and the numbers are growing every day. No one has any figures for how many adults might be in the same predicament. The street children roaming the darkened streets at night are a reminder of the horror that lies underneath the burlesque of Mobutu's rule and which the war, drawing nearer every day, makes worse.

'These street kids are the casualties of Mobutu's economic disaster,' a UNICEF official tells me. 'Remember that Africans don't give up their children easily. To do so is like cutting off your arm when you have nothing left to give.'

Both in the city and in the forest, a massive human catastrophe looms for Zaire. A quick rebel victory is the only hope, as slim as it is, for conditions for the people to improve.

But what will a rebel victory really mean? Will it not lead to the break up of the country and to fractured civil wars taking place in two or three provinces of Zaire? Already many neighbouring countries are involved, could not the fall of Mobutu draw a vast swathe of African territory down into the vortex of war with it?

We have already heard the first stories of Angolan soldiers and units of the old Katanganese gendarmes appearing in Lubumbashi. There are further reports that more of them are waiting on the Angolan/Zaire border to come in.

Katanga. The very word conjures up the worst horrors of African civil war. Within a few days of independence on June 30 1960, the African soldiers of the colonial Force Publique in Leopoldville mutinied against their Belgian officers; it soon affected the whole country. Everywhere the message was the same: 'We are in charge now.'

Decades of anger and humiliation were unleashed in the space of a few days. Mob violence by the Congolese soldiers of the Force Publique broke out first in the capital and quickly spread across the country. Whites were beaten up and murdered, women were raped and tens of thousands of the remaining Belgians fled the country. At the same time, old political and ethnic rivalries within the country meant that riots broke out and thousands of Africans across the Congo were also murdered and beaten up.

The Belgian government sent in paratroops to protect their citizens. They secured Leopoldville, and began to move in on other parts of the country. It looked ominously like an invasion. Lumumba was furious. He denounced the Belgians as 'forces of aggression' and, backed by other independent African states, he requested the UN to send in a military force to counter the Belgians.

On July 11, Moise Tshombe, the provincial president of Katanga, grabbed his chance. He declared his province an independent state. Albert Kalonji, a former supporter of Lumumba, followed suit in the Baluba area of the province of Kasai.

The UN troops began arriving on July 15. The Belgians began to withdraw from the Congo, except from Katanga. The UN troops seemed incapable of crushing the rebellions in Katanga and Kasai and on August 15 Lumumba appealed to the Soviet Union for military aid. They sent aircraft and technicians to Leopoldville and Lumumba was able to advance on Kasai and its diamonds where his troops slaughtered at least 3 000 Baluba people.

At this point, the anti-communist Colonel Joseph Mobutu suspended the government and put Lumumba under house arrest. The communists and pro-Lumumbists withdrew to Stanleyville (now Kisangani) and, in open rebellion against Mobutu, declared themselves the only legitimate government in the Congo.

It was the nightmare scenario that most had hoped could be avoided. It was less than two months after independence. The elected Prime Minister had been arrested and then murdered and the central Congolese government, which was now run entirely by Colonel Mobutu and his 'Administrative College' of university graduates and students, was fighting three separate civil wars on three different fronts, in addition to having to deal with the seething violence and disorder in the parts of the country that had not declared themselves independent.

Finally, in 1962, the UN forces invaded Katanga and brought it under the control of the central government. Moise Tshombe retired to exile in Spain. The remnants of his forces scattered throughout the region, many of them disappearing into the growing liberation forces in neighbouring Angola. The province was renamed Shaba. There were two more unsuccessful uprisings in 1966 and 1967, and in 1977 and 1978 Katanganese rebels operating out of Angola attacked again, but failed to wrest control of the province from Mobutu who called in foreign troops and mercenaries to assist him.

The Katanganese gendarmes are not paunchy old soldiers waiting to ride in on the coat-tails of Kabila's troops. I remembered seeing a unit of them in action in Angola in February 1993 when the rebel UNITA forces had forced the MPLA government into near defeat. The government had been forced back into just holding on to the towns and almost none of the countryside. For weeks, UNITA had held the town of Caxito, just a little way north of the capital, Luanda. It was almost close enough for them to shell the city and finally a fresh military offensive had forced UNITA out of Caxito and the MPLA were driving forward, pushing the rebels as far as they could away from the capital.

I was one of a small group of journalists who had been given permission to accompany the MPLA forces into Caxito. We pulled up at an old Portuguese colonial church, *Boa Esperança*, on a hill south of Caxito. With its dirty stucco and tall European steeple, and the ground around it churned to mud, it looked vaguely reminiscent of a church somewhere behind the lines on the Western Front. A chunk had been blown out of the side of the church and MPLA officers with binoculars were at the top of the steeple using it as an observation post.

The young MPLA soldiers around the church were exhausted and burned out from the fighting. They mostly sat glassy-eyed on the steps of the church or in the few remaining patches of grass.

Nearby there was a truck crammed with heavily armed soldiers wearing camouflage uniforms and red berets. What struck me first about them was that they were all obviously so much older than the Angolan conscripts around them, and yet how lean and hard they still were. The second thing that struck me was that, unlike most of the troops around them, they were fired up; their postures were stiff and hard and their eyes were bright with battle-rage.

An officer was on the ground below the truck screaming at one of his troops, who was shouting back at him. They were yelling at each other in French, not Portuguese.

'Jesus,' said one of the journalists with me. 'They're Katanganese.' It was an eerie moment, seeing those men who were nothing more than armed refugees. Many of them must have been fighting for over twenty years, first for their own doomed cause, and now they were little better than perpetual mercenaries in the service of someone else's war.

The driver began to rev the engine of his truck. The officer was silent, his eyes hard, as he stood back and listened to the soldier harangue him. Suddenly, quick as a snake, the officer grabbed the solider by his lapels and headbutted him in the face. The soldier reeled backwards against the side of the truck. The other soldiers leaned down and pulled him up. The officer ran around and jumped into the cab. The driver revved the engine a few more times and they roared off towards Caxito in search of the enemy.

Now, at long last, they are back in their own land. They are a force to be reckoned with. Are they content to fight for Kabila's new Congo as they have done for the MPLA for twenty years, or do they still dream of their own independent Katanga?

The next couple of days are quiet. A violent downpour crashes out of the towering clouds one evening. Palms shake in the wind; people in the streets run for cover, their sodden clothes whipping around them. It goes on for an hour or more, heavy silver streaks of rain like mercury pouring out of the sky and filling the hot, steaming streets with water, turning the dirty buildings of the city for a few moments in the pale dusk light into shimmering fragments of insubstantial beauty.

That night in the hotel on the satellite channels, we watch, spellbound, along with the rest of the world, as the tapes in the studios in London, Atlanta, New York and Paris are played over and over again, and the ghostly figures on our screens storm and restorm the Japanese Embassy in Lima.

A Swirl of Leaves

What is the collective noun for butterflies? I cannot believe that it is a *swarm*. There must be a more poetic way of describing the vast, soaring, magnificence of snow white that swoops and tumbles through the humid tropical air, a fountain of colour that has come out of the forest and flies, darts and swirls through the grey crumbling concrete buildings of the city, streaked with black from the humidity and decay.

It is Wednesday, April 23. I open the curtains in my hotel room on to a slow, burning day in the tropics. It is the closest we have come to a normal day in the life of Kinshasa. Beyond the buildings and the butterflies, the river is flat and somnolent, gleaming like a mirror in the sun.

The rebels claim to have captured the towns of Ilebo, Tshikapa and Dowete. The claims are later confirmed by the Zairean army. They are now on the south and easternmost borders of Bas-Zaire province. Kinshasa lies on the river on the north-western border of Bas-Zaire. If Mobutu's army is to stop the rebel advance, they will have to make their stand here. It is now, or never.

UN Secretary General Kofi Annan says he is 'shocked and appalled by the inhumanity' of the rebels' refusal to allow aid to get to refugees around Kisangani and by their preventing Rwandan refugees from returning home.

Mobutu and Kabila were scheduled to meet in South Africa today, but the meeting is clearly not going to take place.

In the city, the streets are filled with the news of heavy fighting around Kisangani between units of the *interahamwe* and the AFDL rebels.

'The soldiers are nervous,' Clyde tells me. 'On the way in to work early this morning, I heard a gunshot and two of the soldiers outside the hotel just started running. Many of them are wearing civilian clothes under their uniforms, or they carry white rags to tie around their heads.'

Back at the hotel we hear that three Belgian journalists, who were on their way to pick up their accreditation from the Ministry of Information, were stopped by soldiers and robbed. 'Someone knew where they were going,' Clyde says. 'I think they were followed.'

Aid workers travel to Kasese camp in the East where there were 55 000 refugees. Rumours of mass killings have come out in the last few days. The aid workers find the camps empty. No one can say what has happened to the sickly, hungry refugees, many of whom had been too weak to walk only a few days ago.

We are still trying to look at life in the city beyond the obvious, so Clyde and I are at UNICEF, researching a story on the street children of Kinshasa. While we are waiting in the air-conditioned reception, Clyde asks if he can borrow my Telecell. He looks anxious.

'What's wrong?' I ask him.

'I have a problem,' he tells me. 'My passport has expired. I have a friend with contacts and he can get me a new one quickly, but it costs $140. I have to arrange to get the money to him. I need a passport in case things get nasty and I have to get out of here.'

The Belgian Embassy is saying off the record that they expect Kabila to be in Kinshasa in a month. The Americans say three weeks. The French say two.

'It'll happen on a weekend,' Ben says. 'The rebels always attack on Friday night when the FAZ is full of Primus beer.'

The UNHCR says that Biaro camp, also in the East, which had contained some 30 000 refugees, is now empty. Fifteen thousand refugees in other camps are also missing.

That night a story spreads like wildfire among the journalists that the wire services are reporting shooting in the streets of the city. It is only a Thursday night, but still we have to check it out. We are immediately on our Telecells, calling anyone who might be able to confirm or deny the story this late at night.

The story we manage to unravel is that a deserting FAZ soldier trying to escape the city tried to steal some petrol for his vehicle. He somehow managed to blow himself and three other people up with the hand grenade which he was using to threaten the petrol attendants.

The Angolan army and the rebels are reported to be holding joint 'exercises'. According to reports, the Angolans have sent both tanks and artillery to the border between Angola and Zaire.

It is time to repay old scores. For more than twenty years, Mobutu's Zaire has provided military and logistical support to the enemies of the MPLA. The memories of betrayal go deep. Battalions of Mobutu's army helped the Western and South African-backed FNLA besiege MPLA and Cuban-held Luanda only days after independence from Portugal in November 1975. The FNLA and the Cold War have long since faded away, but Mobutu's continuing support for UNITA has long been a source of rage for the MPLA government.

And if they are sending troops to support the rebels, then UNITA surely cannot be long in sending troops to help Mobutu, even if it is only to frustrate their old antagonists, the MPLA.

In Kisangani, Kabila announces that he is giving the UN sixty days to repatriate all Rwandan refugees. 'It is amply enough time,' he says. 'We hope that in sixty days they will all be gone. You should not prejudge. There are between 30 000 and 60 000 refugees.' He claims to know where the missing 50 000 are. Kabila also demands an apology from UN Secretary General Kofi Annan.

At noon on Monday we hear reports that Kikwit will fall in three days. The rebels, the reports say, are moving towards Bandundu. Bulungu is reported taken, but the reports are 'not confirmed'.

By evening, the story has grown. Kikwit will not fall in three days. Some are saying now that it has already fallen – but the government denies it. Other sources say it has definitely collapsed; still others say that it has not, but that the town is empty and waiting for the rebels to walk in.

A few hours later, the Kikwit story mutates yet again. One of Mobutu's circle has reportedly told one of the wire service journalists who called him to check the story: 'Yes, it's fallen. Our troops ran away as usual.'

Of the fate of Bulungu and Bandundu there is only silence.

The true horror in the East has at last begun to filter out. The stories are first: 5 000 refugees have been found in the forest near Kisangani, starving, wounded, more dead than alive. UNICEF is reporting that they have evidence that at least fifty children were abducted, tortured and killed.

Then there are the pictures of the people themselves. Here in Kinshasa we can see only what is broadcast to the rest of the world. There are the terrible pictures of the wounded, sickly refugees wandering out of the forest. Of a woman with her jaw shot off; a group of skinny men and boys dying, covered in their own excrement, flies buzzing around them . . .

That afternoon US envoy Bill Richardson arrives in Kinshasa. He drives through the streets of the city in a shining white Cadillac limousine and pulls up outside Mobutu's villa at Camp Tshatshi. They meet for a short while, and then come outside to shake hands in front of the cameras and for Richardson to make a short statement to the press: 'President Mobutu has assured me today that he is prepared to meet with Mr Kabila under UN and OAU auspices immediately with the goal of achieving an immediate ceasefire and an inclusive, transitional government leading to elections.'

Words again, loose and freefloating, like leaves spinning on the currents of the river. This jumble of sounds can be taken to mean almost anything, but deep within their deliberately vague resonances, one thing is clear: Mobutu has been told that the US wants him out.

For the first time, as he emerges with Mr Richardson, he seems small and frail. The imagery conveys more than the words can ever do. Mobutu appears, as always, in his trademark leopard-skin hat, but this time he is not alone, dominating the press conference as he has always done before. He appears together *with* Richardson and it is the American envoy's picture and words we use in our report.

Mobutu no longer defines Zaire. His image no longer rules the country. After today, he never again makes a statement to the international media.

Deep Background

Tuesday, April 29. At 6:00 am this morning the rebels walked into the empty streets of Kikwit. That is certain now. They are just over 500 kilometres from the city. The defence of Kinshasa is running before the wind.

American envoy Bill Richardson is meeting with Mobutu again this morning. The South African government offers one of their naval ships, the *SS Outeniqua*, as a venue for talks between Mobutu and Kabila. Richardson is engaged in shuttle diplomacy. After his meeting with Mobutu in Kinshasa he flies across the country to Lubumbashi to meet with Laurent Kabila. After the revelations of massacres of Rwandan Hutu refugees in the forest, Kabila no longer wears the bright shine of a liberator. He needs to improve his image, at least in the international community, and that will give Bill Richardson some leverage. Before Richardson sets off he tells us that he is still hoping for a 'transitional, inclusive government leading to elections'.

That afternoon Kabila agrees to meet under the chairmanship of Nelson Mandela on the South African ship that will anchor just off the Atlantic coast. But Mobutu, so far, has refused to agree to the meeting.

'When will he finally realize the game is up?' Clyde mutters in disgust from his chair behind the edit machines in room 405.

'Fight to the death!' That is now the official order that has been given to the army, and to the Presidential Guard in particular.

The city is quiet and sullen in the heat. The people are moving slowly on the streets, but the traffic is noticeably quieter. Tonight the restaurants in town are deserted. It seems that the last of the elite, with the exception of Mobutu's tightest circle, has finally fled. Perhaps it was the absurdity of the meeting on Sunday to begin the defence of Kinshasa that finally persuaded them, at least, that the game was, really and truly, up.

'This is all Deep Background,' an American colleague tells me cautiously over the phone that afternoon. Late today, Mobutu has finally agreed to meet Kabila for talks on the South African ship over the weekend. Now that Bill Richardson is in town, the Quiet American syndrome is beginning to manifest itself. Deep Background . . . The earnest, clean-cut figures of the young US diplomats and bodyguards now in Kinshasa are a disturbing reminder of how much the fate of first the Congo and then Zaire, and now perhaps the Congo again, has been first bungled and then mangled by these same square-jawed believers in the American Way.

There have been so many mistakes, and worse, so much duplicity from the Americans here in the past, that it is difficult for many Zaireans to trust their motives now. The ghost of Lumumba and of his mysterious, brutal death linger still in the memories of everyone here. Bill Richardson may have come as a peacemaker and an honest broker, but it will be difficult for him to shake off that legacy.

Still, this is the age of the single super-power, and if they are offering you Deep Background information, you would be a fool not to listen.

My colleague has been speaking to one of the US team in Kinshasa. 'The US thinks that Mobutu will agree to go,' she tells me. 'There's no way he can retire and stay in Gbadolite. The rebels will never agree to that.'

And what about the military situation? I want to know.

'They think the rebels could be in the city by Monday, but they probably won't. They are also worried about the possibility of looting. They think a pillage might start soon, in the next few days. Looting and chaos is in Kabila's favour, of course. If he comes in to the city and stops it, it makes him look like a liberator.'

The cold, calculating logic of politics. It is a universal language, and I wonder how much of it the Americans, or the French, or the Belgians themselves are suggesting to Kabila. Especially after the grim fiasco taking place in the forest. The Deep Background all makes a terrible, macabre sense. It is too late for Mobutu, nothing can save him now, but it is easy to see how the suffering and the bloodshed of people in the city can be turned to Kabila's advantage. And, consequently, to the advantage of those who are allied with him.

Fear, the very fear that now openly haunts the streets of the city, is the elusive philosopher's stone that will turn the rebel army's hot leaden bullets into golden hopes. By manipulating fear skilfully, Laurent Kabila can wipe out the memory of his cruelty in the forest and turn his soldiers, no matter what they might have done, into heroes, at least to the people of Kinshasa, so far away from events in the East. To be adored and venerated, it is very simple, all Kabila and his men have to do for the people of this city is to bring an end to their fear.

We hear now that the bridges between Kikwit and Kenge, the next major town on the main road into Kinshasa have been destroyed in an attempt to slow the rebel advance. Alain Likota, a friend of Clyde's and a new fixer we have added to our team, says carefully: 'Now Kinshasa will really have problems getting food. Now in the *cité* the people are saying that Kabila will be here in four days.'

Alain is a quiet, soft-spoken young man who is studying with Clyde at the same college. Alain's major is economics and when he is not out on the streets of the city with us, risking arrest by Mobutu's thugs, he sits quietly in a corner of room 405 working out actuarial models and doing differential calculus equations with nothing to help him but a ballpoint pen and the hotel stationery. I can't help thinking how Western students have calculators and computer spreadsheet programs to do these calculations for them. I wonder how many of them can still do what Alain is doing.

Alain also speaks fluent Lingala, French, Spanish and his English is impeccable. In fact, it is better than Clyde's and, every now and then, I sense the competition between them. Clyde is invaluable to us as a streetwise go-getter who can talk his way in and out of almost anything. He occasionally has a tendency to talk his way out of doing some of the more tedious tasks that his job entails, like summarizing the daily newspaper reports.

Alain succeeds in life by being unwaveringly, irreproachably competent. Unlike Clyde's often reluctantly scrawled notes, Alain's summaries of the newspaper reports are always neatly written with perfect grammar and punctuation. English is a fourth language for Alain. It really is an impressive performance for someone who is only in his mid-twenties, and who has never left Kinshasa in his life. He also has the remarkable ability that when he speaks, everyone falls silent, and listens.

There are stories – a mixture of *Radio Trottoir* and Deep Background – I have heard that trouble has already begun on the outskirts of the *cité*, that soldiers are tying people up, robbing them and shooting wildly – a mini-*pillage*.

'Is it really happening?' I ask.

'Not yet,' Alain says, his face grave. 'Not yet.'

I decide that the only practical response to Alain is to wait for him to finally pronounce: *'It is happening.'* Then I can be certain that it is, indeed, happening.

We go to film an interview with Juliana Lumumba, the daughter of Patrice Lumumba, at the Parliament building. She has no active role in politics but has returned from thirty-five years of exile and works now as a senior civil servant.

Her secretary ushers us into the wood-panelled office with tall ceilings and windows. Juliana gets up from behind her large desk and comes forward to greet us. She is smiling and welcoming. Tall and elegantly dressed, her eyes gleam in a way that carries just a hint of the photographs I have seen of her father's eyes behind his famous spectacles.

We sit in the armchairs in front of her desk and we begin to talk of the past, and of her memories of her father. She takes out some old photographs and we see images of her as a little girl holding her father's hand, of him addressing a rally somewhere in the interior in the days leading up to Independence, and then there are the sadder photographs – the pictures of her and her family in Egypt with the Sadat family, after they had fled the Congo following her father's murder . . .

'I don't think that revenge is a solution,' she tells us. 'For me, I don't hate Mobutu. For me what is important is to try and rebuild this society.'

Sitting in that office, listening to the measured, sympathetic voice of Juliana Lumumba, I feel that I am being shown a glimpse of another country. It might be called Zaire, it might be called the Congo, the name doesn't really matter. It is a country that exists beyond and in spite of Mobutu, and even Kabila. It is not even any more the country that Patrice Lumumba might have envisaged; nor is it the country that Tshisikedi or any of the other politicians promise the people.

It is a country not so much of geography and of politics – although they do have their place in it – it is, above everything, a country of people. It is the country that Juliana came back from exile to live in. The country she inhabits and believes in. It is the country that our fixers Clyde and Alain and Selemain and Peter and Didier, and the waiters and waitresses and the desk clerks at the hotel wish to inherit. It is the country that the angry protesters who fill the streets of the city are trying to find somewhere behind the clouds of tear gas smoke and beyond the pain and the fear of the soldiers' rifle butts.

It is the country of hope that exists only in the hearts of many of the people we have met. It survives despite everything that has happened to them, here, in the other country, in Zaire. It is still an invisible, hidden country, but maybe, just maybe, when the rebels come to town, somehow, someone will find a way to begin to make it real . . .

Juliana smiles and shrugs her shoulders. 'Let us see,' she says.

Outeniqua Blues

Tony Blair is the new Prime Minister of Britain. It bears remembering that Harold Macmillan was Prime Minister in the far-off days when Colonel Mobutu began his political career by being appointed Chief of Staff of the Congolese National Army. Since then, Britain has had seven different Prime Ministers, including Margaret Thatcher who served three terms.

The Leopard King has outlasted them all, even the Iron Lady, and now he is refusing to get on President Nelson Mandela's ship which has anchored off the coast near the port of Banana in the mouth of the river. The talks have been postponed for a while. But the captain of the ship, Fred Marais, has assured reporters that the ship has two luxury suites and that the food will be 'as good as they will get anywhere'.

There are reports that the town of Kenge has fallen, but they are not true, yet. According to our Deep Background sources, Angolan troops, mostly Katanganese gendarmes, backed by tanks and heavy artillery are now openly marching on the main road to Kinshasa along with the rebel alliance. Angolan troops are also gathering in the tiny Angolan enclave of Cabinda north west of Zaire's thin corridor to the sea.

It hardly seems possible, but yet another new Zairean banknote has been issued. It is blue and has a face value of 1 million new zaires, which is worth about 50 US cents. The city has already nicknamed it the '*Outeniqua*' in ironic honour of the South African ship that waits, less and less patiently, offshore. Some civil servants have already been paid with them, but with almost all the wealth-producing areas of the country in rebel hands, 1 million zaires is virtually worthless.

'They have no money,' Clyde says. 'The only way left for them to get it, is to print it.'

'The banks were closed yesterday. They have no credit left,' Alain adds. 'We don't know what's going to happen. The army hasn't been paid for months.'

Glenn, Clyde and I go out on to the streets to ask people what they think. The mood is angry, frightened.

'We're not going to have any food in the coming days,' one woman says.

'There could be a *pillage*,' another man tells us. 'It has happened in all the cities Kabila has taken.'

Aid workers have begun the process of relocating Rwandan refugees. Fifteen hundred were airlifted back to Rwanda. Thousands of others, exhausted and hungry, many of them with appalling wounds, are streaming back out of the forest, towards the camps in the East. At least one refugee staggered into one of the camps with a machete buried in his skull.

At 5:00 pm on the afternoon of Friday, May 2, President Mobutu finally arrives on the *SS Outeniqua*. But now Laurent Kabila is refusing to go on board, citing security worries. He says he will not attend if Bill Richardson is present at the talks.

Bill Richardson was summoned to Nelson Mandela's cabin in the early hours of Saturday morning. No one will say what took place, but the American envoy has now left the *SS Outeniqua* and the diplomacy to Nelson Mandela.

Nelson Mandela is still waiting on board the ship. President Mobutu is in Point-Noire in the neighbouring country of Congo-Brazzaville. Laurent Kabila is in Luanda in Angola. He says he will meet Mobutu in Kinshasa in 'two weeks'. He is also accusing France of sending fighter-bombers to defend Kinshasa.

Someone says to me in the hotel lobby that the strategic port city of Matadi has fallen.

More horror in the East. Nearly 100 refugees suffocated and were crushed to death when a train carrying them to Kisangani in preparation for being repatriated to Rwanda crashed. Journalists and aid workers found the mangled, bleeding bodies when the train came to a halt just across the Zaire river.

Reports are coming in that Mobutu's home village of Lissala has fallen to the rebels. They are now moving through the forest towards his palace at Gbadolite.

Kabila has finally agreed to board the ship that is docked at Pointe-Noire, but President Mobutu is refusing to board by helicopter as President Mandela had done. His officials also refuse to allow him to compromise his dignity by attempting to board the ship by climbing the thirty-one steps of the gangway. Someone suggested hauling him aboard by crane in a steel basket. Finally, we are presented with the fleeting image of Mobutu being driven in his limousine from the docks into the cargo door.

At 11:20 on the morning of Sunday, May 4, we in Kinshasa hear from the press pool on the boat that the engines of the *SS Outeniqua* are fired up and the ship is steaming due west into international waters.

The talks end after Nelson Mandela has called both Kabila and Mobutu 'two of the greatest sons of Africa'. Mobutu has finally agreed to step down, and Kabila has agreed to halt his advance on the capital for eight to ten days to give Mobutu time to negotiate his relinquishing of power. The two men agree to meet again after that time.

On the streets of the city the news is greeted happily. 'He must just go,' says one man standing in a small crowd of people gathered on a street corner, but his words are echoed ten thousand times across the city.

Interregnum

Now that our king's fate has been decided, we are entering the most dangerous phase in the life of our city. The Interregnum. What we, and the people around us, fear the most is the power vacuum that is rapidly developing as Mobutu's grasp on power slips away like a drowning man finally letting go of the straw he has been clutching.

Once he has let go completely, there will be some gap before Kabila and his AFDL rebels can secure the city. It is in this time of emptiness, which may last days, or just a handful of hours, that the worst mayhem will take place.

For now it is Mobutu's generals who still hold power, particularly General Likulia, the new Prime Minister, General Mahele Bolongo, the army Chief of Staff, and General Kpama Baramoto, Mobutu's brother-in-law. In a deliberate policy to prevent any opposition to him coalescing, Mobutu created no less than six different factions of the armed forces and there is no guarantee that they will work together either to defend or to control the city.

From the moment Mobutu stepped on to Nelson Mandela's navy ship, real power passed into the hands of the generals of this fractured army. It is they who now hold the fate of the city in their hands. If they decide to fight, and they can persuade their soldiers to follow, blood will run in the streets. On the other hand, if they decide to surrender, there is nothing Mobutu can do about it. The worst case scenario is if they decide to run and leave their soldiers alone and leaderless. An army in retreat is dangerous enough, a leaderless Zairean army in retreat is terrifying.

Late that afternoon we hear that Mobutu has decided to spend the night in Pointe-Noire. The man is seriously ill and the strain of the last few weeks is clearly beginning to tell. Laurent Kabila, on the other hand, has decided to rub salt into the ageing dictator's wounds. He has announced that he halted the advance only while the talks were going on. His next target will be 'Ndjili airport'.

The Realm of the Imagination

Where does it really begin? That final moment of a defeat when the last flickers of hope die out completely and you are left with nothing but the cold, empty realization that it is all over and you will be lucky if you escape with your life?

We journalists had no last flickers of hope for Mobutu, and that kept us partly aloof, but we were scared for our own skins, certainly, and so, as the last days unfolded, we could share the common human emotion of fear that the people around us felt.

A coward dies a thousand deaths, they say, and a hero but one. The rest of us, however, are fated to fall somewhere in between. We come near to death, real or imagined, on more than one occasion. There were no heroes among Mobutu's last defenders, but not all of them were cowards. There was something touching in watching Nzanga Mobutu angrily castigating journalists right until the very end for spreading what he claimed were lies and rumours about his father. There was something admirable in the reasoned loyalty of General Mahele, who stuck with his President to the bitter end, and tried to maintain order in the city even though he had understood for days, perhaps weeks, that he could not defend it against Kabila's soldiers and their allies. There was something compelling in the cruel and stubborn way that the bully boy Kongulu Mobutu refused, until the last moments, to accept the reality of his father's and his own imminent ruin.

So where does it begin, that final moment? For each of us it takes place at a different time and in a different way. Some of us never realize what is happening until it is too late to do anything; others can see it clearly, but lack the courage to act. The lucky ones see it and act, and so find a different way to live their lives.

When is it that you have stayed too long? For a few days the Old Man managed to stave off the answer to that question, for himself and for all of us in the city that he now no longer ruled.

'If *Mobutu resigns now we will be lenient to him and his family*,' Laurent Kabila is quoted as saying out of Lubumbashi this morning. If he does not, Kabila says his troops will be in the city in two to three days, and then '*We will hunt him down and humiliate him.*'

The cleaning staff in the hotel are suddenly nervous. They don't want to come to work for the rest of the week because they are scared of what might happen.

Journalists have seen units of DSP armed with missile launchers on trucks heading towards the airport. Salim, our Asian businessman contact, is now on the Telecell to George two or three times a day. 'The road to the airport from Kenge is in good condition,' he says. 'Kabila's troops could be here tonight.'

The sirens scream as his motorcade of air-conditioned limousines and armoured cars races down the potholed streets of the city past the shanty towns and the small clumps of refugees that are beginning to trickle into the city ahead of the rebel advance. No one can see inside the cars to be certain that Mobutu is inside, but his aides assure us it is true. He is back.

We will hunt him down and humiliate him . . . Je m'appelle Mobutu . . .

Defiant, the ageing, unwell tyrant has returned to the city after all. He is not welcome, but he is here all the same, brooding and plotting, and perhaps even still hoping inside the glittering recesses of his palace on the banks of the mighty river.

Mobutu Sese Seko Koko Ngbendu wa za Banga is at last trapped by his own creation: Zaire – an entire country whose inhabitants have shrunk from 40 million to a few thousand people at most, largely members of his family and his immediate clan. It is a country that already exists almost entirely in memory. A few pockets of illusion stubbornly remain. Still, there is no escape. In order for Kabila to complete the destruction of Zaire, he must destroy Mobutu. Many of the President's 20 000 soldiers still wear their uniforms for the moment, but almost all of them do so only because they are afraid not to. They wear their uniforms because they may be killed by the last Mobutu loyalists, especially the 15 000 or so soldiers in the DSP, for not doing so. The citizens do not yet openly defy the soldiers because the soldiers still wear their uniforms and carry their guns.

The balance of terror has not yet swung completely in Kabila's favour. Some desperate fighting is taking place 100 kilometres or so away from Kinshasa.

Matadi has not yet fallen. The palace in Gbadolite remains unscathed on its hill top above the forest. There are still a tiny number of places that have not yet reached the point where the rebels are able to kill the soldiers for wearing their uniforms. When that moment is reached, and the soldiers begin to change out of their uniforms, the end will have come.

What remains of Zaire is little more than the Emperor's Old Clothes – a leopard-skin hat and a few zips and buttons.

Under Cover of Darkness

Silence. The city of Brazzaville lies across the river from us. The capital of another Congo, the People's Republic of Congo. Its president, Pascal Lissouba, has been a staunch supporter of Mobutu. Brazzaville is linked to Kinshasa by ferries and riverboats that ply the stretch of brown water separating the two cities. From where we are, we can see the buildings set among the greenery on the other side of the bank, and behind them, the distant blue hills and the billowing white rain clouds that build up in the humidity almost every day.

Yesterday and last night, machine gun fire broke out in the streets of Brazzaville. It is apparently a protest by Congolese soldiers over a new law that affects their pay, and has nothing to do with the fighting taking place in Zaire. Most of the shooting was into the air, and it was concentrated near the Presidential Palace. Shops closed for the day and soldiers patrolled the streets in armoured cars.

We in Kinshasa heard nothing of the uproar, and it is over now. The only sign that things are not normal is that the ferry from Brazzaville hasn't come today. The rumours are that the shooting there yesterday made many people believe that Kabila has arrived in Kinshasa, and they are waiting to see what will happen.

The ripples of this war are spreading. What the people of Brazzaville fear more than Kabila and his troops, though, is the people of Kinshasa. The thought of tens of thousands of Zairean refugees pouring into their own fragile, poverty-stricken city terrifies them.

The wire services are reporting that the town of Gbadolite below the palace has been sacked – looted by government troops is probably more likely. Alain also says that the rebels are announcing over a clandestine radio channel that they are calling on all of Mobutu's soldiers to hand in their weapons and they won't be harmed.

A wild rumour is sweeping through the city, even some of the local newspapers are carrying reports of it. Mobutu has ordered that, before he finally goes, his loyalists must dismantle an experimental nuclear reactor at Kinshasa University, and then they will bomb the city with radioactive nuclear waste.

What am I to make of the fact that Alain does not smile his usual controlled, dismissive smile when he hears the news of this?

News from the shadowy front lines, pieced together from Deep Background and others – diplomats, aid workers and Salim's business contacts: The rebels and their MPLA and Katanganese gendarme allies are advancing down the main road to Kinshasa. The rebels apparently pushed through the town of Kenge and managed to get as far as the Kwango river where they met heavy resistance from a joint force of FAZ and UNITA. The rebels and the MPLA were pushed back to Kenge. As many as 200 people were killed in the bloody fighting. The UNITA troops have reportedly been told: 'Take no prisoners.'

UNITA is fighting not so much out of old loyalty to Mobutu, but partly because the MPLA has taken the rebel side and partly because they need to protect their diamond routes. They also need to buy time to remove their massive arms caches from Zaire before the country collapses.

Nuns in the city of Kenge have confirmed that soldiers on both sides of the conflict were speaking Portuguese. Rumour and reality are beginning to converge.

The next reports we hear are that the MPLA are massing with helicopters and tanks on the Angolan border near Matadi.

In my notebook: 11:14. Sounds of shelling at the airport!! . . . Rumour.

More sirens, flashing blue lights and a jet plane climbing high into the hazy tropical sky. Mobutu is leaving the city.

People in the streets are shouting 'PRESIDENT KABILA, PRESIDENT KABILA.' The *Maréchal* is going to Libreville, Gabon, for a meeting with five other African leaders. The presidents of Gabon, Congo, Equatorial Guinea, the Central African Republic and Chad and the foreign minister of Cameroon will meet with President Mobutu of Zaire to discuss the situation in the country. He will be back in Kinshasa on Friday, or so says the man on the television.

There are hardly any flights at the airport, but the very last people are leaving. These people who can afford to go are mostly expats and a few of the Zairean elite.

They have stayed longer than most, and the long queues in front of the check-in counters are reminiscent of the old black and white footage of people fleeing previous disasters in the Congo, but there is no panic. They have gambled and it has turned out all right. But to stay longer would be foolish. There won't be many more flights, and with what happened only a few days ago in Brazzaville and the ferries closing, even for a day or two, options for escaping the city are closing down rapidly.

We have been tipped off that some of Mobutu's family are on the Swissair flight early this evening, but we cannot find them. No doubt they have entered the plane through a discreet entrance. George and Glenn and I drive back to the hotel in the growing darkness. Later that evening while we are editing we hear that Air France have diverted their flight from Kinshasa to land in Brazzaville.

'They're going tonight,' Salim tells George on his Telecell late that night. 'Running like rats. Mobutu's clan. They're crossing the river in boats under cover of darkness.'

Staring Down the Barrel of a Loaded Gun

Byron, Clyde and I are at a small private local radio station doing a story on the possibility of developing democracy once Mobutu is gone. We are filming the DJ, interviewing the station manager, getting all the shots we need, when my Telecell rings. It is George. 'Come back to the hotel. Kenge has fallen to the rebels again. We need to do a piece.'

We politely make our excuses, but the manager understands the rapacious needs of the electronic news world. 'They put everything they had into Kenge,' he tells us. 'It's over now. The only place they'll fight is at Camp Tshatshi.'

We get back to the hotel to find that the real war is developing fast. There is no way of getting to the front line, but there is a fair bit of chaos in room 405. George, Martin, Milton, Allan and I, Clyde, Alain, Selemain – all of us are working the Telecells and the satphone. Information is coming in from all sides. Ironically, it is easier to get the wire service reports faxed in from London and Johannesburg than it is to get them directly from our colleagues who are frantically writing the stories only one or two floors above us, but we have to check them as far as possible with local sources: diplomats, aid workers, church groups, or with Gad Coen from Mobutu's office. Or even with Nzanga Mobutu himself.

As far as we can make out the situation is as follows: at least eighty-five rebels have been killed in Kenge. They are surrounded by UNITA and the government forces, but the FAZ is cut off in Kikwit. They are holding the rebels off for now. Further down the road the FAZ and UNITA are holding the bridges over the Kwango and the Bambo rivers, but there are reports that the rebels have gone around them and are besieging the town of Bukango-Lonzo further down the road. There is only one more town, Mbankana, on the 150 kilometre stretch of road that lies between them and Kinshasa.

Deep Background has this to say about the situation: 'If the government holds for two weeks it will be miraculous.'

A cameraman from WTN returns to the hotel that night. He and his Zairean colleagues were arrested by soldiers for filming at the port where the ferries to and from Brazzaville dock. They were beaten up, robbed of their watches, money and shoes and held for a number of hours before they were finally released. Somehow, they made their way back to the hotel barefoot, exhausted and shaken.

Parliament is sitting today, on a Saturday. In Libreville, Mobutu has announced through a statement made by the five African leaders he met with that he will resign in favour of a transitional government and a temporary president who will be the new Speaker elected by Parliament.

Bizima Karaha, spokesman for the rebels, has already announced the AFDL rejection of such a plan. 'Election of a President of the Parliament will be a sign of defiance,' he says.

At one point in the so-called democratization of Zaire, there were more than 450 political parties, many of them bankrolled by Mobutu to confuse and divide opposition to his rule. The chaos that this sowed is reflected in the proceedings today. With loud recriminations, much posturing and banging on tables, and the Opposition storming out, the Parliament finally elects Monsignor Laurent Monsengwo, the Archbishop of Kisangani, as Speaker of the Parliament. It is a meaningless farce. Why these people are going ahead with this play-acting, and not queuing at the Brazzaville ferry terminal it is impossible to tell. The ticket prices to Brazzaville have reportedly doubled already, and they are not going to get any cheaper.

We finish filming at the Parliament and return to the hotel. Down the road from the hotel is the French Embassy. Earlier today there was an anti-French demonstration and a Spanish TV crew were filming their correspondent talking to the camera. A soldier came up to them. There was a short argument. The soldier punched the cameraman and demanded that he hand over the camera. The cameraman refused. Enraged, the soldier took out a grenade and put his finger through the ring and shoved the grenade into the cameraman's face. He eventually resorted to pointing a pistol at them and took their tape.

'It's going to get nastier,' Clyde says from his armchair near the edit machines. 'They are building up this anti-press feeling.'

He has returned again from Libreville! Sirens, limousine, machine guns – the whole lot all came roaring back down the highway from Ndjili airport. Mobutu has surprised us all. Almost everyone had hoped that he would never return, and so save the city from bloodshed, but it is not to be. Whatever it is that Mobutu believes about himself will determine the fate of five million people. If he clings to the delusion that he can fight and win against Kabila, then there will be killing in the streets of Kinshasa. If he understands that his time is up, he can save perhaps thousands of lives by stepping down. Somehow, despite the absurd caricature of a tyrant that he has become, he has managed to retain enough of the mystery of power to determine the nature of his own end. He cannot win, but he can destroy much.

It seems almost incredible, but it is true: the fate of an entire city is a prisoner to one man's imagination.

That night, after editing the piece on Parliament, George and I sit up late, drinking whisky and talking. It is well after midnight when we hear some commotion below us. Trucks full of soldiers are driving slowly past the hotel. They are shouting in the darkness. Other soldiers are on the street, walking next to them. We watch helplessly as they shove young men through the streets ahead of them and finally disappear into the darkness.

Are they draft dodgers, looters, suspected rebels . . .? It is an inexplicable episode of menace. The atmosphere in the city is growing more and more sinister. Each day, the soldiers get just that little bit more out of control. The balance is beginning to shift.

We cannot go outside Kinshasa ourselves now. It is too dangerous. If the soldiers don't rob us, they won't let us past their roadblocks out of the city. We also have to stay near the hotel to feed the beast – the hungry maw of the satellite dish that constantly requires edited stories and live broadcasts.

But within these limits, we are searching always for pictures, scouring the city to find new stories or eyewitnesses who can tell us first-hand what they have seen. Today, there are five of us working together. Myself, Byron,

Clyde, Alain and Alphonse. We are looking for information on two things. The first is to find any sign of the 30 000 or so defeated FAZ troops that Deep Background estimates have drifted slowly into the city. We are particularly interested in finding any of the two barge loads of soldiers who came down the river after the battle for Kisangani. They finally arrived in Kinshasa, defeated, exhausted and angry. The army units based in Kinshasa tried to disarm them. The Kisangani troops refused to give up their arms and there was a near-mutiny before the issue was somehow resolved. Or so the story goes. We want to try and find some of these soldiers who came down the river on the barges to tell us their story.

The other thing we are looking for is stories from the port city of Matadi, which has reportedly fallen and been retaken so many times that it is difficult to keep up with its present status. Alain and Clyde suggest we go to the vegetable market in one of the suburbs of the *cité*. That is where any truckers who have brought goods from the port of Matadi will be offloading their cargoes.

'We might also find some soldiers there,' Alain says.

We don't find any soldiers, but the truckers are willing to talk. Their trucks are piled high with vegetables and other goods. They tell us that the port is in government hands, but the soldiers, they say, are particularly vicious these days. They stop the truckers at roadblocks every few kilometres along the road and demand money or even a portion of the cargo.

'They beat us if we refuse,' one of the truckers tells us.

'We are just waiting now for Kabila to come. That's all,' another says.

We shoot a sequence of them in their trucks, climbing into the cab, pulling off and driving down the road. We finish filming and climb into Alphonse's well-kept Mercedes Benz. He pulls off from the kerb and we enter the flow of traffic.

There is a battered white Volkswagen Beetle driving on the road next to us. I notice Alphonse looking at it, and then he looks over at Clyde and Alain. It seems strange that he should do this. I see there is a soldier in the car. He has a grizzled beard streaked with grey and he is wearing a red beret. He is also pointing a 9 mm pistol at us out of the window.

He gestures with the pistol to Alphonse to pull over. He stops the car a little way ahead, and the soldier pulls in next to us.

As we are stopping the car, I am frantically dialling on my Telecell, but the network is busy and I can't get through. Strangely, I don't feel nervous. What is happening seems almost unreal. The only thought going through my head is: *it's our turn now*.

The soldier is very quick. We are hardly out of the car when he is next to us.

He starts screaming. 'He wants to see your credentials,' Alain says to me, quietly and calmly as always, but I can see by his face that he is terrified.

I show the soldier the letter we have been given by the Ministry of Information. Still holding the gun, he glances at it and then makes a grab for my Telecell. Instinctively, I wrench it back from him and shove it deep into the pocket of the bush shorts I am wearing. I realize instantly this was the wrong thing to do, but the soldier has moved over to Byron. Byron pulls out his credentials that have been folded and refolded and stored in the back pocket of his jeans. They crumble into sweaty fragments of white paper as he hands them over to the soldier.

The soldier throws them on the ground and begins shouting even more loudly at Byron. There is something sinister about this pretence of officialdom that precedes the robbery.

'He says to put your camera in the back of his car,' Clyde says.

'No, please,' Byron says to the soldier, and then adds, by way of convincing him. 'It's my camera.'

The soldier cannot understand Byron, but he knows what he is trying to say. He roars with anger and motions with his gun for Byron to put it on the back seat.

'He says he wants to know who gave you permission to film here,' Alain translates quietly, out of the side of his mouth.

I take my press card out. The soldier waves it angrily away.

'He wants the camera. You'd better give it to him,' Clyde says to Byron.

Byron puts his camera gently down on the back seat of the car. I see there is an AK-47 also on the back seat.

I step forward and begin to speak to the soldier. 'Can't you just maybe take the tape and leave the camera –'

The soldier spins around, and shoves his gun at me. I notice that he has pulled the hammer back. The slightest movement will send a bullet smashing into my stomach.

I remember so clearly the muzzle of the cocked gun pointing at me – a dark, menacing circle like a worm hole in space. Suddenly time begins to slow. How many hours, days, weeks have we all wasted in our lives? Not enough to fill the moments when you are staring at the cocked hammer of a 9 mm pistol.

A vehicle full of aid workers drives past. One of them, a blonde woman, sees what is happening. She lifts her Telecell in the air and points at it to let me know she will call someone. She doesn't know who I am, but she will call someone. There is nothing else she can do.

I look at Alain; his face is drawn and tight. I look down again. The gun is still pointed at my stomach. I don't dare look at the soldier's eyes. I half-raise my hands and step back. The soldier shouts at us.

'He is ordering us to go,' Clyde says.

Alphonse is frightened too. His car, his only means of livelihood, is at terrible risk, but he calmly gets into the car and starts the engine. The rest of us climb in, one by one. We are not fast enough, and the soldier begins screaming again. He leans into his car and whips out the AK-47. He gestures with it for us to get going, to leave him.

Of all of us, only Alain has the presence of mind to write down the registration number of the Volkswagen.

I turn to the others. No one has been shot, that is the main thing.

'I know that fucking bastard,' Clyde says. 'It's Captain Castro.'

'He's notorious,' Alain adds.

'What was he shouting about?' I ask.

'It was very strange,' Alain says. 'He was shouting that you can film Mobutu and Kabila when they meet, but if you want to film the city you must wait until they have left the country. When Kabila is here, then, he said, you can film anything you like.'

I guess everyone wonders occasionally what it must feel like to be robbed at gunpoint. But driving back to the hotel it occurs to me that I'm not exactly sure how to convey the experience of being held up in translation.

The spiral of violence is getting tighter and tighter. It is coming closer to everyone. But it is our Zairean co-workers who are the real heroes of the day. Throughout the incident, Clyde, Alain and Alphonse were in greater danger than Byron or me. Captain Castro could have beaten or arrested any of them with impunity, and dragged them away to one of the anonymous prison cells hidden around the city. Their calm, courageous way of dealing with the situation – Alain and Clyde quietly explaining what was going on, Alphonse calmly waiting by the car and not panicking, driving away and leaving us stranded – were important reasons nobody got hurt.

Shaken, and feeling the exhausting after-effects of the adrenalin that has been coursing through our bodies, we go in to lunch at the hotel.

Nzanga Mobutu and Gad Coen from Mobutu's office are sitting at one of the tables on the far side of the room. Milton, the fixer extraordinary, goes up to them immediately and explains what happened. He beckons me and Alain over to join them.

'We don't know this officer who has robbed you,' Nzanga says, 'but we'll do our best to get your camera back.'

We go back to our table. Clyde is telling everyone what happened. 'This Captain Castro of the DSP,' he says firmly, 'everyone knows him. He is not mentally all right.'

We are having dessert when a man wanders into the dining room. He begins handing out leaflets to everyone. We get one. It is from the *Comité de Défense Civil l'AFDL*.

Clyde translates it roughly. 'It says we must prepare the way for Kabila to come.'

It doesn't seem possible, but the man calmly wanders over to the table where Gad and Nzanga are sitting. He clearly has no idea who they are, and assumes they are also journalists.

The whole dining room is watching agog as the man hands them the leaflets and wanders on to the next table. Gad looks at it, and smiles wryly before tossing it on the table in front of him, but Nzanga is clearly furious.

He does get Byron's camera back, though. Captain Castro made the mistake of trying to sell it to Zaire TV, but the word had already come down from Nzanga and the camera is returned to Byron that evening. It is one of the last acts of any functioning Mobutuist order.

Who Will Raise the First White Flag?

Deep Background has more information for us. The rebels are coming down the river in barges. They have reached Muluku at the eastern edge of Pool Malebo. Kinshasa lies at the western edge of the giant pool. A rebel motorized column is advancing down the road from Kenge. The commanders all have Telecells now. As soon as they are in range of the cell network, they will start calling their undercover contacts in the FAZ and the DSP. They also have the numbers of commanders who are not on their side. They plan to harass them with threatening phone calls, and also to confuse them by telling them first one thing and then another. If it looks like resistance is likely to be weak, the rebels might even tell the FAZ and DSP commanders their real plans, so that they can ensure their men are not there to fight them!

I cannot help wondering under whose name they signed all the contracts with Madame Pepe.

Soldiers dressed in camouflage and black SWAT gear are everywhere on our floor. They walk up and down in front of the elevator, stand guard on the stairs, and roam the corridor. Many of them are wearing sunglasses and all of them are heavily armed with folding stock AK-47s, 9 mm pistols on their belts and hand grenades strapped to their chests.

Confident, arrogant, these are the elite of the DSP, and they have taken over our floor. They are obviously used to being in charge wherever they go.

I look around, but I can see no sign of Captain Castro among their number. I push my way through to room 405. Inside I find the rest of the team gathering for our morning meeting. It is Monday, 12 May and we expect that this week will be the crunch week for the Mobutu regime. Negotiations have now all but failed, despite a last-minute attempt over the weekend by Nelson Mandela to keep them alive. There is no way back now.

'Kongulu Mobutu is in the room down the passage talking with the spirit medium,' Alain tells me. I should have guessed.

'I heard the soldiers talking about us,' Alain goes on. 'They say we want an interview with Kongulu.'

'Why not? That would be good,' I say.

'They were saying, "We'll watch them for a few days before we grant them an interview," ' Alain says and then he smiles wryly. 'So we are going to be spied on from now on.'

While Kongulu and his heavies are parading in the corridor outside, we are perusing yet another leaflet that has been handed out all over town and downstairs in the lobby, right under the noses of the most feared hard men of the Mobutu regime.

THE PRO-KABILA ARMED FORCES ARE READY HERE TO LIBERATE THE CENTRAL CONGO IN A SHORT TIME
DEAAR POPULATION
IN ORDER TO AVOID AN EVENTUAL BLOODBATH OBSERVE A DEAD CITY ON MAINLY DESERTED FROM WEDNESDAY 14TH THROUGH FRIDAY 16TH OF MAY
IMPORTANT
WAIT FOR A CHANGE AT HOME .. AVOID GOING TO THE HEART OF THE CITY AND THE FRONTIERS (AIRPORT ETC) FROM THE AFDL
1 THE FIRST DAY EVERYBODY MUST STAY AT HOME, IN ORDER TO AVOID STRAY BULLETS OR TO BE CONSIDERED A LOOTER
2 THE MILITARY AND THE FAZ ARE OBLIGED TO STAY IN THEIR RESPECTIVE CAMPS FROM WHICH THEY WILL BE ENLISTED INTO THE AFDL
3 AT THE ENTRANCES OF MILITARY CAMPS AS WELL AS IN MANY OTHER PLACES, THERE SHOULD BE WHITE FLAGS ON POLES AS A SIGN OF PEACE
4 THE ARMED SOLDIERS IN UNIFORMS WHO WILL BE WALKING AROUND WILL BE CONSIDERED AS OPPONENTS OF THE AFDL. CONSEQUENTLY THEY WILL BE DENOUNCED BY THE POPULATION AND TREATED UNCIVIC.
5 AS A SIGN OF JOY AND PEACE, THE POPULATION MUST SING SONGS OF JOY AND HAVE WHITE FLAGS ON POLES AT THEIR HOUSES

6 THE SECOND DAY. MARKET AND STALLS WILL BE OPENED IN ORDER TO ALLOW THE POPULATION TO SUPPLY THEMSELVES WITH FOOD. ONLY RADIO AND TELEVISION EMPLOYEES CAN GO TO WORK IN ORDER TO BROADCAST THE INSTRUCTIONS FROM THE AFDL.

Who will raise the first white flag? It will be a dilemma for the citizens and for the ordinary soldiers whose only desire now is to survive this unstable, violent interregnum. I find myself thinking of those tough, mean soldiers outside our door and the potential threat they represent. Will they attack those who do raise the white flags or, hidden in their camouflage uniforms or underneath their flak jackets, are they, too, carrying white emblems?

That afternoon we hear that the bridge over the Kwango river on the main road has fallen. Deep Background says it hasn't fallen yet, but it is about to. He says there is only one major front, the advance from the East. There are a few rebels on the river in pirogues, and a team is preparing to come from Angola to block the road from Matadi. There are, as far as he can ascertain, between 5 000 and 6 000 rebels gathered near Kenge. The plan seems to be that they will come in on the Kenge road and take Ndjili airport first and then be able to resupply their army with planes from Angola.

Normal life begins to deteriorate. The very first sign is that the power goes off frequently across the city. The generator in the hotel kicks in, so that we can operate our equipment, but at night there are huge swathes of darkness across the city, as if the neighbourhoods had suddenly ceased to exist.

Then fuel begins to run short. Long queues start forming at the petrol stations. The markets grow emptier and emptier every day, but the food never dries up completely. The rebels are letting many of the trucks through. This is not a war against the people of Kinshasa. They do not have to be starved into submission.

Clyde tells us that there is shooting in the *cité* every night – and Alain confirms it. The soldiers have begun looting and robbing almost systematically, and everyone is at risk from them. If either of them are working late, we arrange for them to sleep in the hotel now.

It is Tuesday evening, May 13. A curfew is announced. From 8:00 pm to 6:00 am, everyone must be off the streets. The soldiers are allowed to shoot anyone they catch looting, or even those who disobey their orders. It is, of course, the perfect cover for them to do their own looting.

We hear that a grenade has exploded on the ferry to Brazzaville, killing five and injuring others.

I am alone in my room just as evening is falling and the air is beginning to cool. Somewhere in the far distance of the city, I hear a muffled explosion. Could this be it? I wait for more, but there is nothing, only the sound of the dying traffic and of voices on the sidewalk below. What does that explosion mean? Where did it happen? Was anyone killed or injured? There is no way of knowing, and now no way of going to find out.

George and Glenn and Clyde go out to film Mobutu's motorcade speeding past for the final attempt at talks. An hour or so later, we get a call from George. He and Glenn have been briefly arrested for filming the motorcade but, as we all have feared for a long time now, it is Clyde who has received the worst of it.

The soldiers ran up to them and, with a kick, swept Clyde's feet away from underneath him. As he fell to the ground, they started beating him with rifle butts on his head and face. One of them shoved his foot on Clyde's chest as he was beating him.

Soldiers frogmarched Glenn and George off as the other soldiers were dragging Clyde away to jail.

Glenn and George call us on their Telecell when they are released. Clyde's whereabouts are unknown, but they are going to find him and negotiate his release.

An hour or so later Clyde arrives at the hotel. He is badly shaken, still shivering slightly with shock. He has bruises all over his face and an ugly lump on his head. Without his connections to the foreign press, it is unlikely that he would have been released. God knows how many people are languishing in prisons all over this city.

It is a shock to see how frightened and in how much pain Clyde is. He lies down on the bed in room 405 while we arrange for a doctor to see him. I try to speak to him, but he can hardly talk. He shakes constantly.

'Can I have some aspirin?' he asks finally. I get him some and a glass of water.

'Take it easy,' I tell him. I feel so inadequate. It is the brutality of what Clyde has been put through that underlies all the excitement of the Story. He has been there with us all the way, willingly coming along for the adrenalin ride, and he has enjoyed it, there is no doubt of that, but what shocks me is the horror beneath it.

Certainly, compared to what has happened to other people in this country, he has had only a light brush with it, and none of us have been immune either. I myself have only recently been staring down the barrel of a cocked 9 mm pistol, but it is Clyde and Alain who have to live with the threat of terror. When Mobutu falls and we leave, they will still be here. The hope they have allowed themselves to feel, and the fear that it may all turn out to be another ghastly illusion, is so poignant. This is their life, day in and day out, and it humbles me to see how courageous and cheerful they manage to be despite their knowing the terror that lies so closely under the surface of their world.

That evening Laurent Kabila announces that he is not coming to Pointe-Noire, and the proposed talks finally collapse. Mobutu is coming back to the city.

The days are confused. Nothing of importance seems to happen during the day. It is in the night hours that the true history of the last hours of this city is being decided. Every night now there are army trucks filled with heavily armed soldiers patrolling the streets.

The hotel chef, a Belgian national, was out after the curfew at night and the soldiers chased him through the streets, bursting into the lobby of the hotel. They dragged him out into the darkness and into one of their waiting vehicles. They took him to prison and are still keeping him there, barefoot and frightened.

'They want to show you,' Alain says, meaning us journalists.

You've Stayed Too Long

It is Thursday, May 15. Just after noon George gets a call from Salim.

'The rebels are 50 kilometres from the airport,' he says.

We hear a few minutes later that Mobutu's plane has landed at Ndjili airport. Unbelievably, he is coming back to Camp Tshatshi.

Cars are being turned away from General Likulia's house which is on the way to the British Embassy and the Intercontinental Hotel down by the river. Why this is happening no one can be sure, but it is likely that they are preparing for the final evacuation of the Mobutu loyalists to Brazzaville.

The Brazzaville ferry has been closed. No amount of money will buy you a ticket now. People with their bulging suitcases, women with babies in their arms, men waving their arms in the air and pleading desperately are being turned away, to drive or walk back into the city.

Some journalists are stopped five times on the road to the Intercontinental Hotel. Reuters and AP TN crews have been arrested on the airport road. It has become virtually impossible to film anything now.

The families of Mobutu's soldiers are streaming out of the barracks near the airport. They are carrying everything they can in bundles on their heads and jamming the road with pushcarts and wheelbarrows piled high with everything they own. Here and there, among the crowd, soldiers herd them along.

It must have happened late last night, or perhaps this morning at about the same time that George got the phone call from Salim saying the rebels were only 50 kilometres from the airport. Somebody, perhaps the wife of a senior commander in the barracks, must have suddenly said: 'It's time. We must go now.' At that moment, the individual decision transforms into a collective resolve. There is a hurried, anxious time of pulling open wardrobes, packing up shoes and T-shirts, gathering together some beans and a few stale loaves of bread – and then the flow of women and children on to the road outside becomes unstoppable.

The wheel has come full circle. The refugees are no longer strangers hidden in the faraway forest. They are neighbours and friends. They have nowhere to go, but deeper and deeper into the city. It is the greatest strength of the African tradition – to share in times of trouble – and somehow the squalid, rusting shacks and the crumbling concrete apartment blocks manage to absorb them.

On the streets, the soldiers stand and watch their families flee.

In the hotel there is a general mood of nervousness for the first time. Everywhere you go people are discussing what to do in the event of a *pillage*.

On the notice board in the lobby, someone has pinned up a hastily written advisory.

> ATTN: US/UK diplomats advise situation very tense and ask reporters to exercise utmost caution when moving around. They think it is particularly good sense to avoid the airport road. Reuters TV and AP TN were looted. Next time they may not be able to intervene.

We gather at the poolside to discuss the situation. If there is to be an evacuation of the city, when will it happen? Should we stay or should we go? If we go, what happens to the equipment? And, more importantly, if we go there will be no getting back into the city. If we decide to go, we will have to stop covering the story. But if we stay, what happens then?

Youssef, an Egyptian journalist, explains the security situation if the foreign troops do have to intervene.

'There is a rectangular block of the city that includes us at the Memling, the embassies and the Intercontinental that will be secured, but not permanently. It will be secured only for the duration of the evacuation. The evacuation will be triggered from the "bottom up". The decision to evacuate will be made by people on the ground in Kinshasa. It won't be taken by people based across the river in Brazzaville. The looting will be by chance. It will not be systematic.

'We are in the French and Belgian sector. If the *pillage* starts, their instructions are for us to stay in the hotel and not move. They will come and get us.'

The meeting breaks up. It is inconclusive, and none of us feels that anything has been done to make the hotel safer. The words of one of the British soldiers are still echoing in my head: 'You would be much better off at the Intercon.'

In the lobby I meet a Lebanese trader who was in Kinshasa in 1993. 'When the *pillage* starts,' he tells me, 'stash money in different places so when one guy comes in you give him that, but still have more for others. They come in waves. When you run out of money, get the fuck out of there, because then you've got problems!'

So the epicentre of our life and of the chaos in the city over the next forty-eight hours becomes the hotel. There is no particular moment when someone says: 'You cannot move,' but, from now on, we are trapped, nonetheless. We enter a parallel world where we hear things, and somewhere else in the city, they happen. The fall of the city depends on two things: the speed of the rebels' advance, and the time it takes for the city to hear about their next step. And anything can happen in between.

The Front Line

At 3:30 that afternoon, we hear the first reports of fighting at the airport. Milton comes in to room 405. 'The rebels have broken through the defence line,' he says. 'They're coming.'

The atmosphere in room 405 is electric. We are all fielding calls on our Telecells every two or three minutes. 'It's not the rebels yet,' someone says. 'The FAZ have abandoned the airport, and they are looting all around it now. The shooting is between different units of the FAZ.'

Rashid, the manager of South African Airways calls in: 'It's just all collapsing,' he says.

The FAZ are fleeing back into town away from the airport, looting as they go.

The Belgian Embassy staff are still looking for the chef who was dragged out of the hotel lobby late last night.

Confusion reigns. As the sun begins to set that evening, we can see on the roof of the French Embassy that they are preparing for the end. A bare-chested soldier is piling shredded documents into a large oil drum. He lights them and piles more and more on. The flames of the burning paper are red and orange against the darkening tropical sky.

At 7:00 pm we gather in the hotel conference room to wait for a press conference that we have been told is to be held shortly by General Mahele. We wait and wait, but the General never comes.

At 10:00 pm the ambassadors in the city are called together for an urgent meeting to discuss the possibility of calling an evacuation. There are more reports of fighting at the airport. Up on the roof of the hotel now, we can hear occasional bursts of automatic fire coming from the darkness of the *cité*.

The word goes out that there will be an announcement on the radio and on TV at 11:00 pm. We gather around the flickering screen in room 405, but there is nothing.

George's Telecell rings. He listens for a few minutes and then turns to the rest of us. 'A coup is going on,' he says. 'Mobutu is leaving tomorrow and General Mahele is taking over in order to hand over peacefully to the rebels.'

Finally at about 11:30 we hear that both the press conference and the announcement have been cancelled. 'Mahele was prevented from speaking tonight,' someone rushing down the corridor says.

No one can even think of sleeping. There is too much still going on; and too many stories flying around. It is impossible to keep track of them. There are perhaps 500 journalists in the Memling Hotel, each of them in contact with one or another of their sources. So much of it is confusion, chaos – the static of collective fear, but it *is* happening. You have only to go up on to the roof of the hotel and wait. The distant, sporadic bursts of gunfire in the darkness are proof enough of what you are hearing inside.

Well after midnight the news comes in that there will be no evacuation tonight. Off the record, the diplomats are hoping that the 'Mahele Option' will come through so that the army won't have to fight.

It is perhaps 12:30 or even 1:00 am when Kongulu Mobutu and a posse of armed soldiers pull up outside the Memling. He is dressed in a black T-shirt and combat fatigues and is carrying an AK-47 at his hip. His soldiers are similarly armed.

'We are going to the front line,' he announces in the lobby. There is a mad scramble of journalists to accompany him. They pile into the jeeps waiting outside the front of the hotel and Kongulu leads them off into the darkness.

It is a safari into absurdity. Kongulu and his band take them a few hundred metres up the road to the airport. Kongulu dismounts from his vehicle and steps out on the road in front of an armoured car, holding his rifle in a combat-ready position across his chest. The exhaust pipe of one of the antiquated armoured cars is dragging on the tarmac surface. The soldiers on the vehicles piled up behind Kongulu's solitary marching figure are clinging precariously to any surface they can find. They are utterly unprotected and they sway back and forward, trying to maintain their balance, as the vehicles move. They stare, wide-eyed, past the camera lights into the darkness of the city. Kongulu looks determinedly from left to right into the pitch blackness as he marches, apparently searching out the foe.

It is a meaningless hallucination. It is inconceivable that he can believe that this is going to convince anyone that he is embarking on a real military foray, or that he is going to defend the city. Tonight's pitiful sham is a long way from the hard, bully-boy attacks he led when I first arrived in the city against demonstrators armed only with leafy green branches.

A few hundred metres more down the road and the farce ends. The column halts and turns around. The journalists are rounded up and driven back to the hotel. By the next morning the world wakes to see the images of the Hector of Zaire preparing for his final, glorious stand.

The Final Departure

Friday morning, May 16. At 9:30 am George gets a call from Salim that Mobutu is on his way to the airport. There is no fanfare this time, no cavalcade. The news is a few hours late. He has already left this morning shortly after dawn. He slipped out unannounced. This time it is for ever. Deep Background says he is flying to Gbadolite for a final farewell, and from there, no one is quite certain where he will go. Last night was the end for Mobutu, that final moment when he saw, at last, that he was defeated, and that he would be lucky to escape with his life.

Three of the generals – Likulia and Nzimbi led by General Mahele – went to Mobutu late last night, while in our parallel world the confusion over press conferences and announcements was taking place, and told him that they could not defend the city. He should go, they advised. It would be best for everybody.

'One of my friends was given a call yesterday,' Salim tells us. 'He is a Hindu priest who does cremations. It was Mobutu's people. They needed him to cremate a body. It's unusual for Africans to cremate. They don't usually do it. But this was a special request. The Big Man himself wanted it done.

'It was Habyarimana's body. Mobutu had it brought from Gbadolite and cremated here in Kinshasa. He was scared that the rebels would desecrate it at the least, or use parts of it to make black magic.'

So the circle that began on April 4, 1994 when Habyarimana's plane was shot down has at last closed. The Big Men of the immediate post-colonial era in Central Africa are going. Mobutu was one of the last of their number. Millions of people have already died in the wake of their rule: in the genocide in Rwanda, in the mass movements of refugees across the borders of Rwanda and Zaire, and now in the civil war that marks the advance of the AFDL. The new era will be born in the coming hours.

At 1:00 pm we hear that all UNITA troops have withdrawn. They fled down a narrow corridor to Mbanza-Congo, one of the cities they hold in northern Angola. They have held up the rebel advance for as long as they could, and took as many of their weapons with them as they could, but there is no point now. Mobutu has gone and there is no Zaire left for them to hide their weapons in. Reportedly, they have had to leave big amounts of heavy artillery behind.

Despite the looting that began a few days ago and the indiscipline that is sweeping through what remains of the Zairean army, a few pockets of soldiers are sticking to their posts. Units of the DSP are still holding the junction of the Nsele and Zaire rivers where Mobutu's extravagant houseboat is moored. They have three tanks with them, and there are three tanks and some units of DSP still at the airport.

Most of the soldiers, however, are fleeing wherever they can. Some are crossing over into Brazzaville, others are refusing to report for duty and hiding in the *cité*. General Mahele has emerged as the only leader the city has. He is in contact with the rebels, trying to broker a deal to prevent any actual fighting over the city. It is his example that has kept the few loyal troops still on the streets patrolling, trying to make sure that the city does not degenerate into uncontrolled chaos and pillaging.

'I am not prepared,' he says off-the-record to George when he and Glenn go to interview him, 'to sacrifice an entire people in a battle over one man. That sort of thing is past. I don't want war for war's sake. Everything is being done to avoid a bloodbath.'

And then he added, hopefully, and perhaps it was an unwitting revelation of his attitude towards Laurent Kabila: 'In an era of democracy, it's impossible to see one side imposing its ideas by force of arms.'

The anger is at last being unleashed on the streets of the city. A crowd of civil servants are waiting outside the Ministry of Information to get paid. It is hopeless, but all the same the people are there. An official from the Finance Ministry drives past in a red hatchback. Somebody recognizes him, and shouts out. Somebody else throws a stone, and suddenly everybody is throwing stones. The rear windshield explodes into a glittering shower. Another rock bounces off the metalwork of the car. The man accelerates and escapes the mob.

At 3:30 this afternoon there is a press conference held by Kin-Kiey Mulumba, the Zairean Minister of Information. It is a ramble of words tortuously trying to explain that Mobutu has temporarily ceded power, but retains his title as President. At the same time, Kin-Kiey says, he has surrendered the powers of governance. 'The government will govern; the President will resign.'

It is the same thing General Likulia has been saying. In short, it means that while General Mahele might want to make a deal with the rebels, General Likulia and his followers intend to retain their hold on power.

'There's a split in the government,' Allan Little says. 'This is very dangerous.'

That night, at about 8:30, we hear the distant boom of mortar fire. Somebody says it is coming from the airport. We rush up on to the roof of the hotel to scan the darkness. There are no flashes, but we can hear the occasional crash somewhere in the direction beyond the airport. It is the direction the rebels are coming from. They must be encountering some last-minute resistance.

George calls Salim on his Telecell. Salim's contacts say that there are no rebels at the airport yet, but that the DSP abandoned the airport when they heard the mortar shelling. The rebels are not yet upon us, but the streets of the city below are deserted. For the first time since the curfew was declared, there are no soldiers patrolling the streets.

The Coming of the Whirlwind

Saturday morning, May 17. I am awake early. It is a sunny, almost optimistic day. From what I can see from my window, the city remains quiet. There is no one moving on the Boulevard 30 Juin. The buildings are stark and silent in the early morning light. I can see no one at the windows.

The atmosphere in room 405 is subdued and serious. We simply don't know what is going to happen. Martin fills me in on the news from last night. It is bleak. Some time after midnight, General Mahele was assassinated. He was shortly to fly to Lusaka, the capital of Zambia, to parley with the rebels. Before he left, though, he was touring the city, visiting the few remaining loyal units of the army, trying to reassure them that he had a plan. He was killed by the DSP when he arrived at Camp Tshatshi. Some people are even saying that Kongulu Mobutu himself pulled the trigger.

'Get some breakfast,' Martin says to me and Clyde and Alain. 'It's going to be a long day.'

We grab some coffee and a few croissants from the buffet downstairs and then rush back up to room 405.

We hear now from everywhere that the FAZ is utterly disintegrating, fleeing on all fronts. Laurent Kabila is claiming already at 8:00 am that his forces have entered the capital and have taken the airport. In the shanty towns on the outskirts of the city, we hear that people are beginning to line the streets with their white tokens, waiting for the rebels to march in.

It begins like a wind, small, spinning eddies of sound. A single, short burst of gunfire in the distance; then another. Closer by, echoing among the buildings is sustained shooting and a short burst of answering fire. It builds slowly, to a crescendo and, suddenly, from all over the city comes the sound of shooting.

A plume of black smoke rises up on the horizon, and then another. Soldiers are running through the streets. A red pickup truck driven by a soldier in camouflage wearing a riot helmet screams past the hotel. He is accompanied by a passenger in a black T-shirt waving a gun out of the window. Their car makes a tremendous noise as it thunders past. People are leaning out of windows and balconies all along the street to see what is happening.

The security guards in the hotel finally close the security grille across the glass doors, but they are forced to open it again because there are so many journalists who want to get out on to the street to see what is happening.

I go up to the roof. From there we can see the marketplace. People are milling about amid the empty stalls. Soldiers are running between them, shooting in the air. The legacy of the slain General Mahele has not been utterly in vain; there are some soldiers who are trying to carry out his orders to prevent looting.

The rebels control the airport now, and they are coming through the shanty towns with the population gathering behind them.

We hear that Kongulu and the rest of the Mobutu entourage will cross the river into Brazzaville as soon as they can. At about 9:15, two senior Mobutu men arrive at our hotel. What they are doing there nobody knows. They mill around in the lobby and then drive off again.

A few isolated shots ring out in front of the hotel, and then there is an uproar of shouting outside the hotel. It seems that the journalists filming on the roof are being ordered to stop.

A small crowd of Zaireans arrives at the hotel with their suitcases. The security guards prevent them from entering.

By 10:00 am pandemonium is spreading across the city. Everywhere there is random firing in the streets. Plumes of smoke dot the horizon. We hear that across town at the Intercontinental Kongulu Mobutu and a vast entourage of soldiers and their families have taken over the hotel. They have parked a tank and an armoured car at the entrance, and are now crossing the river to Brazzaville in a fleet of private speedboats. One of Kongulu's last acts was to turn and spray his Mercedes Benz with bullets, so that no one else could use it.

At about 11:00 am I go up to room 405 to make a quick phone call to my stepfather to let him know that so far everything is fine. We are talking when I see that outside on the Boulevard 30 Juin a troop of soldiers is walking slowly down the road.

'The rebels have arrived,' I tell him. 'I've got to go.' I get hold of Glenn and the two of us rush down on to the street to film them.

It is not the rebels. It is some of the last units of Mobutu's army retreating, most of them in their late teens. They wear ill-fitting, cast-off American uniforms, and they hardly seem able to carry the guns that are slung over their shoulders. One or two of them are carrying their boots around their necks. Their bullets have been taken away and some humane FAZ commander has ordered them away from the front line to return to their barracks. They are exhausted, dejected boys who would have been utterly crushed in any real battle. As I watch them stumble down the boulevard, I wonder if they know that they have been abandoned by the people who wanted to use them as their cannon fodder.

By midday the rebels are still not here. The sound of shooting has died down, and there are only the odd bursts in the streets around us. Then the firing tapers off and the entire city goes eerily quiet. For about thirty minutes, the city is absolutely still. It is a hot, bright afternoon and the rumours begin to flow, in some strange way filling the vacuum that the lull in the shooting has left. It is as if the city cannot stand the silence that makes it confront the enormity of what might happen to it. It is better, somehow, to talk, to fill the air with anything but the awful silence: *the rebels will be here in an hour, there is a plane landing at the airport, but no one knows who is on it, the French and the Americans are coming over, the evacuation is to begin . . .*

It is almost a relief when a sustained burst of fire opens up near the hotel, followed by the high-pitched sound of bullets ricocheting off the concrete walls. Then there is the distant boom of a mortar, and a single rifle shot nearby. All around us again the firing has started. It is exhausting, enervating, this constant barrage. Most of it is nonsense shooting – FAZ soldiers firing into the air, or taking potshots at some looters or even at one another, but a stray bullet will kill you just as easily as one aimed at you.

The afternoon wears on and the shooting continues. Still, there is no sign of the rebels, and I find myself smiling as I remember Ben Wilson's words of only ten days ago. *They always come in on a Friday night . . .*

The settling of scores has begun in the city. Amidst the chaos of the gunfire, people are taking the opportunity of seizing revenge where they can. Rumours come in that one of the first to be killed was the head of the secret police. Then we hear that the military governor of Kinshasa, and Foreign Minister Gerard Kamanda were killed at the airport as they were trying to leave. We find out later this is not true.

Fire

Three more plumes of thick black smoke appear on the horizon in the direction of the airport. At 3:00 pm we hear that the rebels have taken over the main radio station, the Voice of Zaire. At 4:30 somebody says 'the rebels are on the Boulevard'. Allan, Glenn and Alain and I go down on to the Boulevard 30 Juin. There is no sign of the rebels yet. Waiting with us are perhaps thirty or forty journalists and about 200 local people, a few of them with white headbands.

While we are waiting on the Boulevard for the rebels to come that afternoon, 1 000 miles away in Lubumbashi Laurent Kabila announces that he is taking over the powers of Head of State and that the country is now known as 'The Democratic Republic of Congo'.

Zaire no longer exists. Part of me says that it is only a name change, another part of me finds it eerie to be standing here witnessing the precise moment when history is made.

The shadows grow longer across the street, and still there is no sign of the rebels. The sounds of gunfire echo all around us. At 5:30, just as the sun is starting to go down, the first rebels are spotted near Wall Street which runs parallel to the Boulevard. The crowd runs across the Boulevard, cheering wildly, but it is only a small group of soldiers. They look exhausted and are very much on edge. They withdraw back down the street.

Darkness falls. The sound of shooting is unabated, but there is no mass movement of rebels taking over the streets. They are penetrating the city slowly, taking key positions, holding them and fanning out from there.

There is fighting at Camp Tshatshi. As the night grows we can see tracer lighting up the sky in the area around it. Judith Matloff, an American reporter, has been in the area nearby. 'It's growing more intense by the minute,' she tells us. We can hear mortars exploding. *Thump, thump, thump.*

Then a furious spray of green and red tracer bullets lights up the sky.

There are reports that this is not the only scene of battle. Some remnants of the DSP have fled to Matadi, and there is some sporadic fighting there.

At 8:00 pm that evening, surrounded by tracer and mortar fire, we hear from the British Embassy that the rebels have pulled back out of town because it is not secure yet. Remnants of the DSP are said to be trying to fight their way out of the city.

We are on the roof of the hotel when the ammunition dump of the *Garde Civile* in the centre of town suddenly explodes, huge sheets of white flame climbing into the night sky, and thousands of bullets shooting up beyond them. The gunfire ebbs and flows. It is becoming too dangerous to be up on the roof; with our camera lights we may draw fire, so we troop downstairs.

Every city at the end of its time produces moments like this. The juxtaposition of luxury and horror that has always been present in the everyday life of the city, but now is distilled into a single bizarre instant.

Outside the hotel, machine gun fire and mortar explosions rock the city; the main ammunition dump lights up the sky in a giant, deadly inferno. Inside, the band is playing quietly in the dining room. *Guantanamera, guantanmerrrra . . .*

And the evening's speciality is fillet steak with a creamy Bearnaise sauce. How the chefs have managed to achieve this, tonight of all nights, is beyond anyone's imagination.

Outside, renegade elements of the DSP are banging on doors in apartment blocks. 'Give us your keys,' they demand. Acts born of criminality and desperation.

'Mahele would have stopped it,' George says.

We sit up until late that night watching the incredible spectacle below us. Hundreds of thousands of rounds of ammunition are being shot off into the city. Some of them are nothing more than wild, drunken rampaging; others are deadly, directed fire.

From my window we can look down on to the Boulevard below. In the flashes of tracer fire and the bright, sudden flickers from the exploding ammo dump, we can see furtive, frightened bands of looters rushing to and fro across the street, carrying their plunder with them.

A strange, unreal sense of calm and fascination reigns throughout the hotel that night. There is always the risk that the renegade FAZ or DSP soldiers would storm in to attack and rob us, but we scarcely consider that any more. We are too engrossed in the drama unfolding before us, in trying to make sense of the chaos that is swirling in the darkness of the city around us.

For so long we have lived in the shadow of what might happen . . . now it *is* happening, and we are there, living in the very centre of it.

Morning

I hardly sleep that night and I wake up after a couple of hours to the sound of shooting. The dawn light is pink over the silver ribbon of the river. I rush down to room 405. We are all gathering there. Mobutu has arrived in Morocco, and Laurent Kabila says he will form a transitional government by Tuesday. I have forgotten that it is a Sunday. There is still sporadic gunfire going on.

7:17 shooting has stopped.

Ben Wilson and Clyde and cameraman Tim Facey and I drive out into the streets. The light coming through the buildings of the city is soft and golden. Broken glass lies everywhere. Everything is quiet and peaceful.

People are lining the streets, waiting to cheer the rebels into town. At 7:30 we see our first rebel column. My stomach gives a small lurch of excitement. There are about a hundred of them and they are marching steadily down the streets, looking neither to left nor to right. They are dressed in surplus US camouflage uniforms and they are heavily armed with mortar tubes, rocket grenades and machine guns. Many are wearing gumboots, others flip-flops, many are barefoot. They look tired, but they are disciplined as they march. There is no sense that they will break and turn on the city in a frenzy of looting.

The people lining the streets clap and cheer as the rebels march past them. They have come from the East and some of the people greet them in Swahili.

'*Habarigani*,' the shouts ring out.

Some of the soldiers turn and smile wearily. '*Mzuri*.' Good, they reply, and keep marching.

I speak to their commander. He is a young man from Rwanda. He seems pleased that I know his home country, but he smiles distantly, giving nothing away. The soldiers with him are Zairean, or I should say, Congolese, from Goma and Uvira on the edge of the Great Lakes. Some of them are Banyamulenge who have been fighting since the rebellion first broke out in September 1996.

They keep marching as we talk to them. The city is quiet, but they have an objective to reach, an area to be secured. They have little time to talk to journalists.

Further down the street are the smashed windows of a looted office. The photocopier lies upside down, powdery black toner scattered around the floor. Dozens of bottles have been smashed on the street outside and lie glinting next to a thick pool of blood. No one can tell us what happened. It was last night. Some say a looter was shot; others say the rebels caught him and beat him to death. A single pool of blood slowly drying in the streets of this city; it is one of hundreds scattered around.

More rebels come down the street. A hundred and fifty or so, wearing old East German army uniforms, marching in a long line through the shaded streets dappled with the morning light.

People begin clapping. *'Libération!'* they shout. *'Libération!'*

We stop the car to film. As we climb out and begin filming, people cheer and clap us.

Further down the street, another 300 or so rebels are coming. The cheering grows louder. We cannot help the electric feeling of excitement that runs up and down our spines.

'This is the beginning of the new Africa,' Clyde says happily, shaking his head from side to side as if he can hardly believe his eyes.

We've got enough footage here. We turn back to the hotel to drop the tapes off. We drive past two of the trucks that normally bring the vegetables to the city. They are crammed with rebel soldiers, people are running behind them shouting *'Viva Kabila'*.

Back at the hotel, it is nearly 10:00 am when we hear: 'Tshatshi fell to the rebels ten minutes ago.'

Within minutes, Allan, Alain, Clyde, Byron and I are downstairs piling into Alphonse's Mercedes.

Two words are all that is necessary. 'Camp Tshatshi.' Alphonse has heard the news too, through *Radio Trottoir*. He is as keen to go as we are.

We pull out on to the Boulevard 30 Juin. Four trucks full of rebel soldiers drive past. Crowds of people run alongside them, cheering, waving. 'Kabila, Kabila, Kabila!'

Three more trucks filled with soldiers drive down the Boulevard, going the other way, pushing their way through the crowds. The city is completely and utterly theirs.

'Can you believe it?' Allan says.

'It's like a dream,' Alain replies quietly, staring out the window of the car. 'It's no more Zaire.'

'There are a lot more rebels than I imagined,' I say.

Allan looks at me with his deadpan look that I have come to know is the herald of some witty insight. 'They're not the rebels any more,' he says.

We all break out laughing, even Alphonse, who hardly speaks English, understands and he is laughing too.

We are climbing the hills in the upmarket Mont Ngaliema district. The gates of the mansions of Mobutu's clique lie smashed and open, and people are running in and out, taking anything that they can with them. Everywhere we see people with chairs, tables, even refrigerators on their heads.

Here and there, like broken teeth, we can see the shattered, blackened remains of buildings that were hit by mortar fire yesterday and last night. But they are swallowed up by the crowds of people who are swarming through the streets, following the rebels towards Camp Tshatshi. There are just too many people, Alphonse can no longer push the car through. We will have to walk. We climb out of the car and make a vague arrangement for him to meet us later.

In front of us is a column of about 2 500 soldiers who are from Kalemie on the banks of Lake Tanganyika. They are young boys, many of them barefoot. Large numbers of them have been secretly airlifted by the Zimbabwean air force, but many of them have fought and walked miles through the forest. There is something fitting about the greed-besotted Mobutu, surrounded by luxury, being overthrown by barefoot soldiers.

It is a hot morning and we are all sweating as we march along with the soldiers, heading for the seat of power of the Mobutu regime – the real centre of this city. All along the road the weary soldiers are cheered by the people. To walk with a conquering army – for that is what this is – into the heart of a besieged, and now liberated, city is an extraordinary experience. It is why we became journalists, in the hope of being able to measure out our lives in moments exactly like this one.

Finally we reach the top of the hill. We can see down on to the river. The vanguard of the column is lining up in military order in front of the gates of the surreal compound. Two plaster leopards at the gate, their broken visages gleaming in the hot sun, gaze lopsidedly at the AFDL soldiers forming up. In the garden behind the elaborate security fence, a few zebra are grazing peacefully.

Somewhere in the distance a few shots ring out. They are probably to chase away looters, but it is a reminder that things are tense in the city.

We cannot enter Camp Tshatshi. The rebels have already sealed it off. We remonstrate with the commander for a while, but it is to no avail. He has his orders.

We wander down the hill for a kilometre or so. There is a compound of government offices that are being systematically looted. Young men are rushing in and out of the buildings, dragging anything they can out. Typewriters, armchairs, piles of copy paper – anything that they perceive to have the slightest value they are taking.

Two men ham it up for Byron's camera, sitting on an armchair and pretending to drink out of a coffee jug they have found. A group of about a dozen are dancing and yelling. They have found a Zairean flag and they are tearing it to pieces with their hands and even their teeth. One of the men has a cigarette lighter and he sets it aflame.

Beyond them three more are smashing a framed picture of Mobutu against a low garden wall. The image of the man who once floated as a godlike figure across the television screens of the nation has finally disintegrated, leaving nothing for our camera but broken glass and torn fragments of coloured paper.

One act of anger and violence leads to another, and the chaos begins to grow. The young men begin smashing windows with rocks, a typewriter comes flying out of an upper-storey window and thuds into the lawn below. There is more smashing glass; someone begins throwing telephones out the window.

I notice one young man sitting a little way apart, just watching the destruction. I go up to him and we begin chatting. His name is Enma and his English is excellent.

'This is madness,' he says, pointing to the orgy of destruction taking place in front of us. 'It won't be any different under Kabila. All I want to do is leave this country.'

A unit of AFDL soldiers arrives. They rush up the stairs and fire into the air. The looters begin to disperse. The soldiers chase them down the lawn, firing into the air with their AK-47s.

Somehow we link up again with Alphonse. He drives us past Camp Lufungola, one of the FAZ military barracks. It is surrounded by a cordon of AFDL soldiers. The soldiers and many of their families are still inside. They are chanting *'libéré, libéré'*. A large crowd of local Kinshasa people has gathered around the outside of the camp. They are staring through gaps in the fence at the spectacle in front of them. They point and laugh. The soldiers they feared only yesterday are now prisoners in their own camp. Someone has crossed out *'Zairois'* on the entrance sign at the front of the camp, and also *Maréchal Mobutu*.

We are not allowed in to film, so we drive back to the hotel. The city is still rejoicing. *Début Congolais! Liberté! Kabila!* they shout on every street corner. But back at the hotel we hear the news of the first lynching. Some journalists witnessed a man being beaten by a mob in the marketplace. When he was down on the ground they put tyres on top of him and burned him alive.

It is beginning to happen all over town. Mobutu's soldiers and obvious supporters are dragged out and set upon by mobs. Inside the military camps the soldiers are being disarmed. Many are cruelly tied up with their elbows behind their backs, others are beaten, some are threatened with knives.

The *Garde Civile* ammunition depot is still burning in the centre of town. It flares up sporadically, and then dies down. Glenn and I are cruising through town, looking for stories. We jump out to film the ammo dump. We approach cautiously, sheltering behind walls as we get nearer to the flames licking around the walls of the magazine.

All around us people are looting the shops, oblivious to the danger that the overheated explosives pose to them. Shattered glass from the explosion lies like a sheet of water for metres in the streets around.

We squeeze off a few shots. 'That's enough,' says Glenn. 'Let's go.' We duck down behind the walls and then drive back to the hotel. *Don't push your luck*, we are both thinking.

The End

It is getting late in the afternoon. Ampre, one of the young drivers whom Milton has hired, says he knows a back route into Camp Tshatshi. He has heard that the AFDL troops haven't started guarding it yet and so we can get into Mobutu's palace through there.

'Let's try,' I say to George. He and Glenn and Ampre and I roar off down the rapidly emptying streets towards Camp Tshatshi. It is already too late at the first gate we try. The AFDL have secured it, and no amount of persuasion will budge them. We are beginning to lose the light as we drive away.

'I know one more place,' Ampre says. He, too, has entered into the spirit of the never-ending journalistic chase for another story, and there is no doubt that he wants to get a look at Mobutu's palace as much as we do.

We drive down a hill, turn a sharp corner and then veer towards a patch of thick greenery. Ampre is right. There is a gate there and it is open. We hurtle through and drive up the winding roads through Mobutu's vast estate. We pass the barracks of the Presidential Guard, abandoned now. Further on there is a parade ground surrounded by rusting armoured cars and empty missile launchers. Beyond is the mansion and its well-appointed apartments.

The devastation that the looters have wrought is total. The neatly mowed lawns are littered with paper, broken glass, upturned beds, smashed TV sets and feathers from the plush mattresses. The strangest detritus is the piles and piles of worthless old Zairean banknotes scattered just everywhere. There are even whole sheets of banknotes dating back to the 1970s, straight off the printing machines and not even cut into separate notes. Every one of them has Mobutu's image on them. Hundreds of them have been deliberately trampled into the ground.

In front of the mansion itself are a number of cars with their windscreens smashed and the tyres ripped off. They must have been somehow disabled so that they could not be stolen and the looters have vented their rage on the cars themselves.

Ampre pulls up in front of the mansion, tyres crunching on the gravel, and the three of us jump out.

We walk into the mansion. It is silent and abandoned. Glenn begins filming immediately. The gutted mansion is a haunting, almost wondrously malignant sight. The crystal chandeliers have been pulled down from the ceiling and lie smashed on the white marble floor, a black marble table with gilt legs is bent and twisted and lying at a crazy angle in the corner. The closets have been ripped open, the pot plants tipped over. Water is dripping from the ornate ceiling.

The strangest detail is the hundreds of torn diapers spread out across the marble floor. They are evidence of Mobutu's incontinence due to his prostate cancer, and a poignant reminder of his humanity. He tried for so long to transcend it by creating his illusion of being the Big Man, the *Maréchal* of his people, of being Mobutu Sese Seko, the all-conquering warrior, but in the end it was to no avail. In the end, even Mobutu, the cruel buffoon, with his monstrous wealth and absolute power, was as human as any of us.

The sun is beginning to set outside, and as I wander through the darkening corners of this absurd, tasteless palace, I find myself wondering at this sickening lust for power and material things. At the foot of the gilt and marble spiral staircase lies a velvet jewellery case, forced open and the padding torn. Childish teddy bear prints are lying in a pool of water next to imitation Audubon bird prints. Further up the staircase a looter has abandoned a sledgehammer. At the top of the stairs, a few bedraggled peacock feathers lie on the stained carpet. In the marble bathroom on the upper floor, the mirrors are smashed and the golden faucets are bent and twisted, water dripping out of them and on to the floor.

What is it that created this monstrosity? I find myself thinking. At its root it is the desire of the simple village boy to escape the poverty of his childhood. It is fear that lies underneath this horror, that has gilded every inch of this palace. The fear of going back to a life where mothers die in childbirth, where infants die from the simplest of diseases, where children become blind and crippled from germs in the river water and parents die early from hunger and relentless toil.

I walk into Mobutu's ransacked bedroom. The huge bed with its enormous white panelled headrest has been broken and turned upside down. Empty gaping holes in the woodwork are where the looters have ripped out the costly electronic fittings that the Big Man could once control with a push of a button.

I step over the wreck of his bedroom and walk through the French doors on to the balcony. I stand at the railings thinking how Mobutu must have looked out over this same vista countless times. It is this that he carried with him always, through all the jungle wars and the gilded palaces. This is what lies outside the frame of every photograph ever taken of him.

The Congo river lies below, vast and magnificent in the bronze light of the setting sun. The forest comes right up to the edge of the river. Rafts of water hyacinth float, half-submerged, in the brown eddies of the currents. The roar of the rapids where the tons of water thunder through the sharp-edged rocks rises up in the cooling air of sunset. A delicate mist from the power of the flow hangs above the dangerous, swirling waters.

It is a beautiful, haunting sight, one of the most magnificent in all of Africa, and Joseph Désiré Mobutu must have thrilled to it as much as anyone. What a temptation it must have been to surrender to the belief that you could own that river, *nzere-nzadi, the river that swallows all rivers* . . .

A New World

The killing is over. The Red Cross estimates that at least 200 people were killed in Kinshasa over the weekend. By their count, fifty-two of the dead are civilians, the rest were soldiers. It is a small tally for the amount of firepower that was unleashed. It is a small tally for any city of five million people that has spent a weekend in chaos at the end of a civil war. It is a testament to the restraint of the AFDL, to the legacy of General Mahele and to the humanity of the majority of the Congolese people.

It is Monday morning and the city is almost entirely back to normal. The zaire has more than doubled in value overnight from 170 000 to the dollar to 40 000. People are going to work, the shops are open and there is a traffic jam on the Boulevard 30 Juin. There are no traffic police, so the street kids have donned the abandoned white gloves and helmets of the police and are standing in the little kiosks in the centre of the traffic circles. Onlookers stand and laugh good-humouredly as they watch the antics of these kids directing the traffic. They have spent hours, days, watching the police do it and they do a good job. The traffic moves slowly forward, amazed that it is the street kids who are keeping the city functioning.

Not everything remains peaceful. A plume of smoke rises up from the edge of the city. There are two attempted mob killings right outside the hotel. In one of them, the journalists manage to intervene and save the man's life.

But slowly things do calm down, and the new cycle of history begins. Laurent Kabila comes to town, and we are booked on flights out of Kinshasa.

On our last day, George and I go out for lunch with Salim. Without him, we would never have had such a good grasp of the story. George and I want to believe that Clyde was right, that the arrival of Laurent Kabila has meant the beginning of a new order in Central Africa. But already there is news that there is fighting between the AFDL factions and what are now Mobutuist rebels in Mbuji-Mayi. Three civilians have been shot overnight.

Salim has his Telecell with him. 'The whole town is closed,' he tells us. 'There is shooting everywhere.'

He looks at us. 'It lasted three days up there, that's all. Who knows how long it will last here? The people want a loose federation, but for now, Kabila's got the gun and he'll make the law.'

The roots of Laurent Kabila's uprising against Mobutu were a complex mix of political ambition, ideological fervour, economic conflict and struggles over ethnic identity. The Alliance that had tried to weld these together into some sort of coherent national movement did not last long. Within days of arriving in Kinshasa, Laurent Kabila banned public demonstrations and had suspended all political activity by May 26, less than a week after he had come to Kinshasa.

Less than a year after the Fall of Kinshasa, the AFDL coalition broke down and in August 1998 the Congo disintegrated into a second civil war.

On January 16, 2001, Laurent Kabila was shot dead by his own bodyguard. His son Joseph Kabila took over as president. In December 2002 his government and the main rebel groups signed a peace agreement. It was an important step forward for the country but, at the time of writing, there were still battles going on in the East of the country.

SUDAN

SEASON OF HUNGER

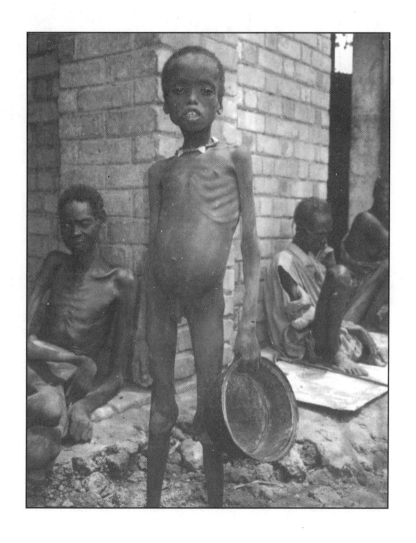

Dawn. Bird calls float in the cool air. A crimson hint of sunlight creeps up the hard, black edges of the mountain ranges. It spills out over the plains. The first rays catch the tops of the trees. They fill the fresh pools of water from the night rain with a still golden light.

The edge of the runway and a collection of small brick buildings that serve as a terminal are caught in the dark shadows of the hills. I can hear the sounds of the engines starting up – a clutter, a low-pitched whine and suddenly the roar of the C-130 Hercules transport planes explodes into the quiet African dawn.

It is April 1998. We are at the United Nations airbase at Lokichokio in northern Kenya. There is famine across the border in Sudan. The United Nations needs to fly in 40 000 tons of food to feed an estimated one million people who are at risk of starvation. The planes take off at dawn and the pilots fly sorties back and forth until sunset, when the darkness makes flying, and landing, too unpredictable and dangerous.

It is a massive effort. The pilots and aid workers face civil war between north and south, and a government based in the north of the country that has only just given permission for aid flights to resume. The Sudanese government has given the United Nations, and no other organization, permission for four C-130s and a Buffalo to fly over Southern Sudanese territory and make emergency food drops.

We are on a smaller plane that we have chartered ourselves. We've offered to take in a few bags of grain on our flight – it's not much, but it would be unthinkable these days to arrive in a plane in Southern Sudan and not bring in something.

Our flight is illegal. We do not have clearance from the Sudanese government to fly. We have filed no flight plan. If we appear on the radar in a cockpit of one of the government MiG fighters, there is a chance we could be shot down. The risk of it happening is small, but the government has threatened to shoot unauthorized planes out of the sky. The pilot himself has been clear. 'We don't stay on the ground for any longer than we have to in Southern Sudan. We drop you off and hopefully we will be able to come back and pick you up again.'

The plane takes off into the wide brightness of the morning sky. It is not long – a dozen minutes or so – before we cross the valleys and green scrub of the Didinga hills. Beyond the hills we leave Kenya and the last of the savannalands of East Africa behind. We are flying now over the Sahel, the ancient boundary between the fertile plains of Central and East Africa and the white dunes of the Sahara.

Below us is a vast, empty landscape – the most remote and inaccessible in all of Africa. There are almost no roads here, the landscape is made up of layers of rocky mountains, ochre and black against a wide blue sky.

Between the mountains runs a green flood plain. It gleams in the morning sun. The countless tributaries of the Nile are silver ribbons far below, threading their way through papyrus swamps. In the main channels where the water runs clear and deep, settlements of huts are dotted along the banks.

Here the Dinka and Nuer people live with their cattle, their crops, their hunting and their fishing. The same scenes are carved in stone on the pyramids and monuments of the Pharoahs far to the north, but here, in Southern Sudan, a way of life survives that stretches back further into time than even humanity's oldest monuments can record.

But the war here is a modern war. The people who live in the land below us are surrounded, embroiled and fighting within the context of the most contemporary political events. Politics that are influenced both by African conflicts and by those that exist in the wider world.

The civil war that has led yet again to widespread famine among the people in the south is fought with machine guns, bombs and aeroplanes. Its roots are complex, filled with all the angry ambiguities of our age. It is partly a conflict between the government led by Arabized Muslims from the north and Christian and African animists of the Sudanese People's Liberation Army (SPLA) in the south. But, like so many conflicts in Africa, it is also about resources, about who will control the oil and the other minerals that lie beneath these stark mountains.

At the heart of the war is the Nile. Here, in this harsh, dry land of the Sahel, control of the water means survival. The Nile's immemorial seasons of flooding and ebbing direct the traditional cycle of life. Since long before living memory, the 'Hungry Months' have come. From July to October the food from the last harvest runs out and there is nothing yet from the next harvest. In those months people have always lived off wild fruits and what game they can find – many trek across the shimmering plains with their cattle to the swamp waters of the Sudd on the banks of the Nile where they camp on the islands in the swamps, living off fish and the milk from their cows.

But now, with the disruption caused by nearly two decades of fighting, hundreds of thousands of people rely on regular food aid from the UN when the 'Hungry Months' come. The traditional season of shortages and drought has not even properly begun, but already the situation has reached crisis proportions with widespread hunger on the edge of slipping into mass starvation.

High in the cool, blue layers of the morning sky my thoughts are jumbled, confused. Such immense physical beauty defines the land around us, but so much horror exists within it too. I cannot deny a small nagging sense of fear – the thought of the predatory jet fighters somewhere in the emptiness of the sky, or of being caught on the ground in one of the government's bombing runs sits uncomfortably in the back of my mind.

But the most disturbing thoughts are of what lies ahead of us when we land. We are heading for Panthou, a tiny village deep in rebel territory. Aid workers have told us that this is one of the worst-afflicted areas. It will not be the first time I have witnessed starvation. In Mozambique in 1992 I saw famine. It affected me terribly. People lose all dignity when they are dying of hunger. I remembered seeing women so exhausted and famished they were crawling on all fours out of the bush, stick-like children scrabbling in the dust for grains of corn, babies dying with flies clustered around the last of the moisture in their eyes.

It seems almost impossibly far away in Britain that there is a growing debate raging over whether what is happening now in Sudan really can be called a 'famine' or whether it is just an 'emergency'. Sitting in the plane, I reflect that I don't have the skills, the experience or the capacity to judge when a 'famine' finally can be officially termed a 'famine'.

But I do know that the images of the starving human beings we, and the other TV crews in the region, are about to film will have a huge impact on this debate among the politicians, the media and the aid community.

I also know that the aid workers who are taking us to Panthou are decent, dedicated human beings who want a world where children do not die of starvation. I know, too, that each one of them will have his or her own position on whether what is happening in Sudan is a 'famine' or an 'emergency', and that we will be largely subject to their agenda in what we see. We, as journalists, will be asked to judge them and their understanding of how serious the situation really is.

I don't want to judge them. And I don't want to witness starvation ever again. But I and the others in our crew are here, on this plane, to do both of these things.

The most important thing, though – the thing that ultimately overrides all our judgement and analysis – is to get our pictures back in time to be broadcast on the evening news in London.

Faced this first clear morning with the reality of what lies ahead of me, I find myself uneasy. I am not particularly afraid of any physical danger – the risks are small.

What I feel is a personal, inner anxiety. I know what famine means, what it does to people, how extreme hunger is an obscene cancer eating away at the bodies and lives of tens of thousands of people.

The images of hunger that appear periodically in the West, from Biafra, Bangladesh, Ethiopia, hold some kind of deep, subconscious fascination. These photographs and TV shots underline an instance where pictures are infinitely more powerful than words. It doesn't really matter how many newspaper stories are printed with the correct statistics of hunger, malnutrition, disease – they all blur into a fog of abstract numbers. It is only the pictures that create powerful reactions.

It is almost as if these terrible icons of human beings in the most dire of circumstances, human beings at the very edge of life itself, hold up a mirror to the well-fed and largely contented people in the West. In the images of starvation from faraway lands, they see some distant premonition of their own mortality. Buried within this fascination is the danger that the images themselves become more important than the real humans they represent. This is not true for everyone, but there can be no doubt that the West's reaction to famine is partly a kind of ghoulish voyeurism.

But at the same time these images unleash a powerful, and deeply felt, impulse towards compassion. Money pours in to help the victims, activists mobilize public opinion and politicians are forced to act. The choices they make may influence the situation, for better or worse, for years, decades, to come. The stakes are high, and our pictures play a crucial role.

The truth is that I am apprehensive about my own reactions. I worry that I will find myself paralysed by my own doubts coupled with the sheer horror of the plight of those who are starving.

Inside me, I know there is the danger that I will slide into a kind of inert cynicism. An empty, burned-out place, where I simply work to get the pictures out, and refuse to confront the power the images hold within them.

Our focus was the massive hunger that the civil war had left in its wake. We had two main difficulties: the first was getting into Sudan and the second was finding a place that was representative of the 'situation'.

The first morning we flew up to Lokichokio we had been given a briefing by two UN officials, Claude and Jason. Claude was from West Africa, Jason from the US; both of them were passionate and committed to Sudan and its people.

'We have a feeding centre in Panthou that is exclusively for malnourished children,' Claude said. 'Two weeks ago we were feeding 350 children. Now we are feeding more than 800, and every day more children arrive with their mothers.'

Jason pointed to the map I spread out on the table in front of us. 'Many people have fled because of insecurity in the area. Some of them are beginning to come back to Panthou, and they have nothing to eat. Any cattle or grain they did have will have been looted. There was an attack in the area by the pro-government militia last week. The government troops are heading for this area on the train. They send the militia ahead on horseback to clear the way. The train travels very slowly and they come down in front to protect the line. The government made a push to take the area. But they were pushed back by the SPLA.'

'These people are really a threat,' Claude said, referring to the militia. 'They are accountable to no one.'

'The old traditional slave trading routes are still active,' Jason said. 'It's one of their main motivations for fighting.'

'The militia is our main fear,' Claude added. 'We've never been confronted by government troops. There are also the power struggles within the rebels. Two of the commanders met last week. But the alliances can shift overnight. The whole area is very unpredictable. The SPLA has not always been clean and they are paying the price for it now.'

'Until now we had only one C-130 that could drop food. We delivered some food to Panthou a month ago, but no one has been back since. Early this month we got clearance for one more C-130, so we're planning to go back soon. It would be a good time for you to go and see the situation for yourselves.'

'We estimate that we now need food for 700 000 in Southern Sudan. We're getting permission from the government in the North for one more C-130. That doubles our capacity, but it still doesn't cover a month's need.'

'The rains have come,' Claude said. 'Usually rain in Africa is a blessing, but for us now it's a curse. We can't use the roads because of the rain, so we have to make up the capacity lost with the planes. But now the runways get wet too, and that can put them out of action for days.'

'People are starting to slaughter their cattle. They are eating the seed grain they had been saving to plant for next season. So next year will be worse, because nothing will be planted.'

Claude looked at me across the map. 'We have reached the disaster point. If we had been given permission for more planes by the government last August, we could have acted to avoid this. They have only given us permission now because they are feeling pressure from the world's press.'

The UN compound at Lokichokio is compact and well guarded. Even in the days of British rule Northern Kenya was always largely beyond the reach of the colonial police and army forces. Today, it remains wild and largely beyond the reach of the Kenyan police and army. It is stunningly beautiful country, with red soil plains and wide green spreading acacia trees that lead up from the flat lands into the rocky hills. It's one of the few places left in Africa where lions and other game still roam wild, outside of game parks. Every now and then you will come across a Turkana or Turposa warrior in traditional cape, mud-packed hairstyle and jewellery, carrying a carved walking stick or a G-3 rifle. Cattle raiding is still a common activity in the area, and today the traditional spears that the warriors carried have been traded for modern assault rifles. The convoys of UN trucks bringing supplies from the port at Mombasa on the coast are often ambushed and the drivers killed or wounded. There is very little the police and army can do about it.

Lokichokio is a frontier town – no, a frontier village. You have the sense when you are there that it is a place not only remote and at the end of the world, but a place that exists between worlds. It acts firstly as a border post between the political worlds of relatively peaceful Kenya and war-torn Sudan; it stands at the very edge of the savanna and the Sahel. But most of all it exists as a gateway between the conscience of the rich world and the starvation that has gripped Southern Sudan.

This fine tarmac runway that can accommodate the largest of transport planes gleams oddly in the hot sun of the African bush. Lokichokio exists only because the UN has run Operation Lifeline Sudan out of here since 1989. There is something unreal about getting in a plane in Nairobi and two hours later floating down out of a cool blue sky and landing in Lokichokio. And it is even more disorientating to fly out of here deep into the sun-baked heartland of South Sudan and return again before dusk. In a single day you may easily travel more than 1 000 kilometres over the African plains. But it's not the physical distance that matters as much as the distance you travel between worlds. There are a few driveable roads in the extreme south of Sudan, near the border with Uganda, but for the rest of the country, it is only the aeroplane that brings outsiders in. And so few outsiders ever do go in.

My head was spinning after my briefing with Claude and Jason. Such unfamiliar names, such vast spaces of land, and so much war and turmoil seething across the land. I had to keep on checking the map I carried with me to remind myself where we would be going.

I walked over to the SRRA compound. SRRA stands for Sudan Relief and Rehabilitation Association. It is the humanitarian branch of the Sudanese People's Liberation Movement (SPLM). Without a pass issued by them, we would not be able to work on the ground in Panthou.

Dark rain clouds hung in the sky. A C-130 roared overhead as it came down to land. Along the perimeter fence that surrounded the airstrip, a Turkana woman and her daughter were collecting firewood. A gentle breeze carried the smell of rain across the grasslands.

While I waited for our passes to be stamped and properly registered, I spoke to Malul and Diong. They were tall, grave young Dinka men who had just come back from Panthou and the nearby village of Malualkon. 'From the field,' they called it.

'The situation is bad, very bad. In Panthou there are at least 20 000 people gathered near the airstrip waiting for food,' Malul told me. 'They are coming in every day in very bad condition. They are very hungry. Seven children died at the feeding centre last week. There are at least two or three times as many dying in the bush where we can't reach them.'

'In Malualkon we found bodies from the fighting,' Diong said. 'They were still lying on the ground. We got news that a militia attack into Malualkon was driven back only yesterday. They came in on horses, and they are still somewhere in the area.'

Sudan is a land that has been cursed by war. It is the largest country in Africa, larger than Western Europe. The population is only 30 million, but it is made up of over 600 different ethnic groups who speak, between them, over 200 languages and dialects.

But the most fundamental division in the country remains that between Arab Islamists in the north and the Africans in the south. The present war has been fought, off and on, since 1956.

This war in Sudan seems utterly remote from events in Europe and the West, but it is worth remembering that its origins are deeply intertwined with both the defeats and the victories of the high Victorian Imperial era.

'If the expeditionary force – and I ask for no more than two hundred men – does not come in ten days, the town may fall, and I have done my best for the honour of my country.'

So wrote General Charles George Gordon in his personal diary in January 1885, only days before he and the last of his Anglo-Egyptian troops were overwhelmed by the army of the Mahdi in their *jihad* to rid Sudan of both Egyptian and proxy British rule. The truth of Gordon's last stand will never be known. Some accounts have him waiting in a 'dignified manner' at the head of the stairs in his palace for the Mahdi's soldiers' spears to pierce his body. Other versions of the story claim that he made a desperate, last-ditch stand, going down fighting at the last.

Whatever the reality of Gordon's death, the relief force arrived two days too late, to find 50 000 angry and victorious Arabs in control of Khartoum. The men of the town had largely been slaughtered, and the women raped and enslaved. Gordon's head was cut off and stuck in a tree for the victors to throw stones at. The steamships turned and fled back down the Nile, harried for days from the banks by the Mahdi's men.

Of course, it was lost on a grieving and angered British public that the

Mahdi and his army had been fighting for the honour of *their* country. The Mahdi and his successor, the Khalifa, set out to create a Sudan ruled by their interpretation of Islam and of *sharia*, Islamic law.

For well over a decade, they expanded their rule into the south of the country. They took over the Bahr-el-Ghazal region where the Dinka and Nuer lived. They pushed north against Egypt and east to the Red Sea coast. Soon, the Khalifa's realm was almost the size of Western Europe. He even wrote to Queen Victoria demanding that she become a Muslim, or be 'crushed by the power of God ... by reason of thy Satanic presumption'. Both the Mahdi and the Khalifa renewed the violent slaving raids and the subsequent trade in chained and brutalized Dinkas, Nuer and other south Sudanese peoples – acts of cruelty and inhumanity that shocked Victorian Britain and which remain a source of bitterness within Sudan to this day.

But despite the steady growth of a powerful Islamic state in Sudan, Britain had not forgotten Gordon and his last stand. In an eerily similar parallel to the relationship between the West and countries like Iran, Iraq and Afghanistan in the last two decades of the twentieth century, the Khalifa's Islamic state was perceived as a threat to Christian and Western civilization.

For over a decade, the British public waited for their revenge. Finally, in April 1896, General Kitchener and his army of 25 000 British and Egyptian infantry embarked on the Nile. They fought battles with the commanders of the Khalifa all down the twists and bends of Africa's greatest river. At Firket, Dongola, Berber and Atbara, the Anglo-Egyptian army with their modern rifles, artillery and steamboats drove the Arab armies back. At Berber, General Kitchener, mounted on a white charger, led a victory parade through the streets of the town. Here he indulged in cruelty of his own. The defeated Mahdist commander was chained and bound at the neck, wrists and ankles and forced to stumble along at the head of the column while he was pelted with rubbish.

It took nearly two years for the expeditionary force to make its way down the Nile. Finally, at dawn on September 2, 1898 Kitchener's army lined up on the empty plain that lay west of the Nile and north of the mud ramparts of the city of Omdurman.

A young officer of the 21st Lancers, Winston Churchill watched partly in awe and partly in horror as 50 000 Arab warriors armed with spears, swords and antiquated rifles marched towards the British forces. The 'Dervish line' as Churchill called it, was a magnificent sight. It was the last mustering of a medieval host ever witnessed in our world. In the very centre of the army, the Khalifa's enormous black banner swelled and rippled over the lines of his soldiers. The white and green flags of the lesser emirs and chieftains spread out among the troops to left and right.

Many of the warriors carried emblazoned shields and were dressed in chain mail under their colourful *jibbas*. They marched in steady, imperturbable rows, shoulder-to-shoulder in serried ranks under the golden light of the morning sun.

Many, perhaps most, were certain in their massive advance of impending triumph. The Khalifa had decreed it, based on an old prophecy that predicted Allah would grant them victory here, at Omdurman, over the infidel.

Two shots rang out from the middle of the Khalifa's forces. The British field batteries, gunboats and revolving Maxim guns roared back with unimaginable power. Churchill recorded: 'About twenty shells struck them in the first minute. Some burst high in the air, others exactly in their faces. Others, again, plunged into the sand and, exploding, dashed clouds of red dust, splinters and bullets amid their ranks. The white banners toppled in all directions. Yet they rose again immediately, as other men pressed forward to die for the Mahdi's sacred cause and in defence of the successor of the True Prophet. It was a terrible sight, for as yet they had not hurt us at all, and it seemed an unfair advantage to strike thus cruelly when they could not reply.'

So, in a murderous hail of steel, hot lead and fire, died the last of the old world – by the end of the day, Khartoum had fallen to the British. It was estimated that 10 800 Dervishes were killed and 16 000 wounded. The British and Egyptian losses were 48 killed and 382 wounded. The bones of the Mahdi were tossed into the waters of the Nile. England, and Queen Victoria herself, were shocked when the news leaked out that Kitchener had taken the skull of the Mahdi as a trophy of war to use as an inkstand or a drinking cup. He was forced to apologize to the Queen and the skull was buried at night in the Muslim cemetery at Wadi Halfa.

The battle of Omdurman was the end, for well over half a century, of any dreams of an independent, Islamic state in Sudan. Sudan became a British colony. North and South Sudan were run under separate colonial administrations. After World War II, the British decided to withdraw from the country gradually and grant independence to a united Sudan. In 1953, the first elections were held and a year later British administrators were replaced by Sudanese. Most of the new officials were Arabized northerners. The process was resented by southerners and in, 1955, a mutiny broke out in the army. It was crushed, but the feelings of unfairness and under-representation remained. Shortly before independence in 1956, the Sudanese parliament voted that the ultimate future of the relationship between North and South should be agreed by a referendum.

It never happened. On 1 January 1956 the independent Republic of Sudan was created. Elections were held, but in 1958 General Abbud led a military coup against the elected government. In 1962 the Anya-Nya movement, consisting mostly of Christian southerners, began a war for independence. Hundreds of Christian missionaries were expelled from the south and hundreds of thousands of Southern Sudanese people tried to escape the Northern crackdown and growing civil war by fleeing to Uganda, Congo, and Ethiopia.

In 1969 Colonel Mohammed el-Nimeiri took power in a coup. His was a regime marked by abrupt and, ultimately, hopeless shifts in ideology and direction. First, he declared Sudan a Socialist State. In 1972, under the Addis Ababa agreement, he allowed the South regional autonomy on almost all its own affairs except defence and foreign affairs.

It almost worked. For over a decade, Nimeiri held the Islamists at bay. From 1972 to 1982 the South had its own parliament in Juba, separate from the government of the North based in Khartoum. The economy began to pick up, there was some foreign investment, agriculture improved, there was even some growth in tourism. In 1978, oil was discovered in the South.

For a while, it seemed as if things would be all right. The same year Nimeiri released a number of political prisoners. Many of them were radical Islamists. One of them was Sadiq al Mahdi, a descendant of the original Mahdi. In retrospect, it seems as if three conflicting forces were at play against Nimeiri. The first was the resurgence of the powerful Islamist sentiment that had been in existence in the North since the days of Anglo-Egyptian rule. The second was the Southerners' own desire for independence. The third was the question of who was to control the resources of the South – both the water of the Nile and the oil that had recently been discovered.

Then, in 1983, almost out of the blue, Nimeiri abandoned his socialist doctrine and declared *sharia*, Islamic law, over the whole country. Over one hundred public amputations were carried out for stealing by the end of the year.

At the same time, he released a new map of Sudan showing vast areas of the South, including the oil-rich areas, to be placed under Northern control. He also recommended completing the Jonglei canal which was designed to divert huge amounts of water from the swamps of the Sudd to irrigate the fields of the North.

In May 1983 there was a mutiny of troops in the South and the civil war started again. John Garang, a colonel in the Sudanese army and a Southern Dinka, was dispatched to help put down the uprising. He defected and became the founder of the Sudanese People's Liberation Movement and the leader of its armed wing, the Sudanese People's Liberation Army.

The devastation and unrest of the war created the first of the serious food shortages in the South that would put hundreds of thousands of lives at risk from starvation. In addition, the SPLA itself began to fracture, and internal faction fighting made the situation worse.

In 1989 radical Islamists led by Colonel Omar al Bashir took control of the North in a coup. In the midst of the civil war and growing cycles of displacement and starvation in the South, a campaign was launched to Islamize the entire country. *Jihad* was declared in the South and the government handed out weapons to the Arab tribes who traditionally lived in the remote border regions between North and South. This militia became known as the Popular Defence Force (PDF) or the *murahaleen*. Their incentive to fight was largely the booty they could take from their raids into the lands of the Dinka and Nuer. Grain, cattle and, most prized of all, slaves were their rewards; at the same time, the government hoped they would help to clear the South of the troublesome Christian and animist African tribes. Those who were not massacred or captured as slaves were sent to camps in the North of the country.

The civil war was, and remains, brutal. Groups like Amnesty International have documented frequent serious human rights violations committed by both sides in the conflict. They have submitted countless reports outlining deliberate attacks on civilians, executions of both civilians and prisoners of war, forced relocation of communities in the South to so-called 'peace villages', the abduction of women and children into slavery, the forcible recruitment of child soldiers, torture, rape. The list goes on, and on, and all sides, including rebel factions and the government army and its militias, are implicated.

By 1998, well over 1.5 million people, the vast majority of them Southern Sudanese, had died in the fighting and in the waves of starvation that had followed in its wake.

At the same time that the Islamic government declared *jihad* in the South, they made Khartoum a centre for the export of Islamic *jihad* around the world. Many experts suspect Sudan to have been behind an attempt on President Hosni Mubarak's life in Ethiopia in 1995. In 1998, after the bombing of the American Embassy in Nairobi by Islamic extremists, the US launched a missile strike on a pharmaceuticals plant outside Khartoum. The US claimed it was a chemical weapons production facility linked to Osama Bin Laden. This claim has never been properly substantiated.

That night the stars were bright in a black sky. I could hear the high-pitched 'chip-chip' of insects. The heat of the night pressed down on me inside the tent where I lay on my bed. The shadows of the trees fell on the ground beneath the starlight. Before I went to sleep, I found myself thinking of something a Kenyan aid worker had told me at dinner. 'The women we give food to in the day; but what happens to that food at night? You never see a starving soldier.'

The next morning I awoke before dawn. As I was dressing, I could hear the distant sound of a muezzin. The call to morning prayer drifted across the bush through the cool layers of the morning air. I stepped out of the tent. The first bird calls were clear and hard under an indigo sky.

Arkanjelo's Warning

For over two hours we flew north into the vastness of the continent. Slowly the landscape below us changed. We left behind the swampy Sudd and its bright blue ribbons of water surrounded by green. In front of us the land became flat and arid. The colours turned to yellows and blacks. The soil was arid and unshaded, the growing heat of the sun flaring off the land below. There was not a single road that cut through the vast empty plains.

With a sudden dip we began the descent into Panthou. We could see the huts of the villagers, known in Sudan as *tukuls*, spread out among trees and bushes parched grey and brown from the drought. A few young men were herding cattle through the dust and dry bush. The few crops in the fields were devastated by drought. The desiccated stalks were bleached pale as bone. They lay scattered at crazy, jumbled angles in the dusty soil. The grass was thin and brittle, its broken edges glinting and sharp as old glass. The heat from the baking earth came up at us through the thin metal skin of the plane.

The runway was a white shimmer in the sand – and then we were down. The engines screaming. The fuselage bumping and yawing across the rutted landing strip. The propellers threw up a cloud of dust. Through its swirling haze we could see the people lined up to greet the plane.

As the plane came to a halt, we jumped out. The heat swept over us in a wave, instantly bringing sweat to my face and pushing hard against the inside of my lungs.

The villagers were already crowding around the gangway. They were the tallest people I have ever seen. Many, both men and women, had rows or patterns of ritual scars on their faces. Many of the men carried walking sticks or light, delicately balanced hunting or fishing spears. Some were virtually naked, others wore some scrap of clothing. A few of the women wore neat, brightly coloured dresses.

The warmth and friendliness of the welcome they offered us was almost overwhelming. The surrounding evidence of the crippling drought was stark and hard. I had expected to find the villagers listless, defeated by hunger and exhaustion. I remembered so well the terrible combination of anger and fear that I had seen in the faces of the people at the feeding centres in Mozambique.

But here the people crowded around us joyfully, reaching out to shake our hands, calling out '*chibak*', the traditional greeting in Dinka.

We had only an hour on the ground to get the pictures we needed. We had to work fast. The feeding centre was being run jointly by MSF and the SRRA. Arkanjelo was the local village official delegated to work with us. He adroitly steered us through the crowd and across the blazing sands towards the feeding centre.

'There have been *murahaleen* raids all along the railway line these last weeks,' Arkanjelo told us. 'Villages were burned, and people killed all around this area. The instability means that the last food distribution was early March. The situation is getting worse. Somebody died just last night from hunger.'

Martin Dawes, the correspondent, went ahead with Arkanjelo to the feeding centre, while the cameraman, Byron Blunt, and I followed more slowly, filming whatever we could.

A short distance away from the runway, we came across a woman and her small child. The woman was picking leaves off a small thorn bush. The leaves were unusually bright and green against the grey of the surrounding dust. Her child was holding a small calabash. Every now and then she bent to fill it with handfuls of leaves. The tree I learned later was called *lalob*. It is one of the traditional wild foods that people have turned to for generations during the 'Hungry Months'. In truth, the woman and her child were not that badly off. They both looked fairly healthy and robust.

While Byron filmed the two of them, I couldn't help thinking that this woman and her child epitomized the difficulty of the debate surrounding the notion of a famine here in Southern Sudan. Our pictures of them would definitely go out on the air in Britain that same night. To a Western audience, the images of a woman and her child picking leaves of a scraggly – albeit quite green – thorn tree to eat would be incomprehensibly shocking.

But these two people were not starving. Not yet, anyway. The Hungry Months were part of the cycle of life here, and had been since time immemorial. This mother and her child were turning to the environment around them for sustenance. They were using ancient knowledge and wisdom that sprung from the deepest and most vital part of their culture; a knowledge of their land and its ways that had been handed down from their ancestors, generation after generation.

At the same time, one had to be careful. There could be no question of getting sentimental about this. That woman would certainly have been far better off if there was no drought and especially no war to disrupt and destroy the crops and the cattle. The leaves from the *lalob* tree were a survival mechanism, not a real alternative source of food.

Making a judgement about the situation was perilously difficult. One could understand the aid workers' reluctance to go off half-cocked, to declare a 'famine in Southern Sudan' when, in fact, it might be that the present emergency feeding schemes were sufficient to get the population through the Hungry Months, this year at least. It was dangerous to cry wolf. If the aid workers called it wrong, they had to face all the dangers of compassion fatigue in the West. If it turned out that they had overstated their case, then the next time, when there really was a famine, public and media cynicism might prevent the aid being sent when it was most needed.

Further along the hot dusty path, a mother came up to us. She smiled and thrust her child at me. The baby had a rash that had spread on its face. The woman obviously assumed I was a doctor or health worker. There was nothing I could do for the child. She was certainly ill with some minor infection, but again, neither she nor her mother were starving. Nor were many of the people who greeted us as we moved along the dusty pathway.

The evidence of the drought was clear. Also, all the aid workers I had talked to in Lokichokio had been quite emphatic that the situation – especially the situation here in Panthou – was indeed very serious, if not critical. But the people I had seen, from the first enthusiastic group who had greeted us as we got off the plane, to these individuals we came across as we walked along the village pathways were not starving. It was so different from what I had seen some years back in Mozambique.

I began to realize that we were entering into the life of the village and of the famine layer by layer. What I had done in Mozambique was fly by plane directly into the centre of the famine. We had seen only the worst cases, because that was what the TV cameras needed to show on the screens back in the West. It had given me a distorted understanding of famine. It had seemed to me to be a mighty, implacable force that swept through a community like some grotesque Angel of Death – an explosion of hunger that felled its victims with the rapid movement of an epidemic.

What I was seeing here in Panthou was the reality of famine which existed in the real village, in the lives of the people outside the images that the TV screens demanded. Hunger, I saw here, affects communities in layers. It descends slowly on a village, or a town, or even a province, in concentric circles. Unlike other disasters – a flood, an epidemic, a bomb blast – there is no element of luck. There is a slow, inevitable logic to the progress of a famine. The poorest and the weakest suffer and die first, the richest and the strongest die last.

Walking down the hot, dry path into the village of Panthou, we were following the course of that pitiless certainty, step by step.

In front of us was a large green tree. It must have been hundreds of years old. Its trunk was metres thick and its leafy canopy towered into the blue sky. The shade it cast was a cool refuge from the heat. Two or three dozen people were gathered underneath it – mostly women, small children and sick men. Alongside the tree were a couple of neatly thatched shelters that served as the MSF emergency feeding centre.

Here was evidence of real hunger and the disease that comes with it. At the entrance to the feeding centre, a desperately thin adult man was begging to be allowed in for treatment.

He was only eighteen years old. All he was wearing was a pair of black shorts. His arms were as thin as sticks, the skin was stretched tight over his hips. His face was tight and shrunken. He looked like a man of seventy. His eyes gleamed with fear and desperation as he pleaded with the aid workers to be allowed in. He had walked for days to reach the feeding centre, he said. He had to leave his mother behind. She did not have the strength to walk to the feeding centre.

Both the Sudanese and foreign aid workers had to be firm. Finally he gave up. He turned away and walked a few steps with his stick to help him. He was trembling with the effort as he slowly lowered his wrinkled, emaciated body on to the hot white sand. He sat silently, staring into the distance.

The feeding centre had been set up for treating malnourished children under five. That was all the aid workers had the resources for. In order to save the lives of the youngest, most vulnerable children they had to refuse treatment to older children and adults. If they allowed everyone who was in need to come into the feeding centre, they would have been swamped.

The aid workers were frantically busy. They let us film what we wanted to, but they had little time to speak to us, and even less time to explain how they felt deep down inside.

The French nurse who had turned away the eighteen-year-old, picked up a tiny baby. 'She's very small and very weak. I can feel it. I can feel her heart beating. It's not normal.'

'Are the children dying?' Martin asked. She turned to look at him. 'So far, two died last week. But if they are dying here, then many more are dying in the bush where we cannot reach them.'

The children here were tiny, emaciated. Some of them could barely eat or drink the special emergency feeding rations that had been prepared for them.

'The situation is getting worse,' Arkanjelo told us. 'Somebody died in the village last night. Three people died last week. All from hunger.'

The biggest problem that Arkanjelo and the other aid workers faced was that everybody in the surrounding district knew that at Panthou there was food and medicines. Mostly, where they lived there was nothing. Many had walked for miles to come to Panthou. The people of Panthou had not driven them away; they had shared what they had with the people who had come. Now there was very little left for anyone.

Sitting on the ground nearby was Alek Bol and her three children. The day before, her daughter had died. When Alek spoke to us, she was angry. That was something I had seen before – the anger, the deep-rooted, but helpless fury that famine produces in its victims. It is the rage of life. It is the last gateway of normal existence. When people can still be angry, there is still hope. Beyond the anger lies debilitating sickness and possibly death. When they are no longer angry, they have begun the slide into the abyss.

'She was eating leaves,' Alek told us. 'She got diarrhoea and died. These others are suffering from the same thing now. They have only leaves to eat.' She narrowed her eyes and spoke to us in a harsh, barely controlled voice. 'It was hunger that killed her, nothing else.'

We stumbled out of the feeding centre with our camera to film the rest of the village. I felt half-dazed with the horror of what we had just filmed. We walked along a path outside the feeding centre. We were moving away from the centre of the famine back into the layers of normality that surrounded it.

One of the village elders came up to me. He was a tall man dressed in a dark blue robe. Unlike the people in and around the feeding centre, he was in good health. I guessed he was in his late forties. He had a gentle face with deep traditional scars carved in a V on his forehead.

He carried a long thin white stick and another shorter, carved ebony stick. I had been told by Claude back in Lokichokio that Dinka elders carried such ebony sticks as a symbol of authority. The man walked up to me on the pathway. He smiled and handed me the short ebony stick.

I wasn't sure what to do. It was clear that this was a greeting, an honour bestowed on a visitor, but I wasn't sure whether it was right to take the stick, his symbol of authority. At the same time, I didn't want to offend him by not accepting his gift. I hesitated, looking at him and back at the stick. We couldn't speak a word of each other's language.

The elder was still smiling as he watched me. He waved the back of his hand at me. The gesture was clear. The stick was mine; it was his gift to me.

He turned and began walking away. I ran after him through the dust. The only thing I had to give him was my plastic water bottle. He seemed almost bemused when I pressed it into his hand. I knew that it probably would be useful to him, but it seemed such a shoddy commercialized offering compared to his courteous gesture that was filled with tradition and meaning. He smiled and turned again, the water bottle in his hand.

We were rushing against a deadline. The plane would take off in half an hour at most. We were broadcasting our story on the news that night. My head was spinning both with the powerful conflicting emotions and with the need to make sure that we did not miss our deadline.

Further down the path six young men were sitting on the dusty ground under a tree. They were strong and healthy. An AK-47 was leaning upright against a tree trunk. Next to it were half a dozen slender hunting spears. As Byron and I approached with the camera, one of the men deftly took the gun and slid it underneath his white cotton robe. With a single movement, the gun had become invisible to us and to our camera. It seemed an apt metaphor for the war and its constantly shifting factions, loyalties and front lines. The fighting was hidden from us, but the results were in the terrible sights of the feeding centre only a few hundred metres away.

Beyond the men with the gun we came across a group of uniformed rebels. Their commander was standing against the open door of a 4x4. It was the only vehicle for miles around. He was wearing a camouflage uniform with the bright red insignia of rank on his shoulders.

We put to him the question that the government in the North had been putting to the aid agencies. How could we be sure that the food aid was not going to his troops?

'We started this war without any relief aid,' he said. 'We are fighting for our people. We cannot divert food while we see our people are suffering.' A denial, on camera, it was the most we would get. But I couldn't help feeling frustrated. We had no evidence ourselves, either way, whether or not the rebels were diverting food. To have found such evidence would have meant spending days on the ground, perhaps weeks, before we could have been sure either way. The only thing we could be sure of were the images we had filmed of the starving children inside the feeding centre and of the desperate adults outside it.

It was time to go. The pilot was already revving his engines. We rushed back to the plane, sweat pouring freely off us. A hot wind swept across the dry plain, picking up whirling dust devils as it went. Long lines of people stood in the sun waiting patiently for the food that the UN was handing out.

'This food is not going to help much,' Arkanjelo said. 'It's not nearly enough. This time we are calling the warning that people – many of them – are going to die. We can only hope that something will be done.'

We flew for nearly four hours back to Nairobi, high over the lowering light that fell across the rocky tan-coloured mountains and the flat sands of the Sahel. Once, near a government-controlled town, we saw the tiny shape of a single truck moving in a cloud of dust along a straight road that cut through the landscape. Further along was a fortified government army outpost. Its back was against the silver waters of the Nile. The front of the post curved out into the semi-desert scrub. Trenches had been dug into the dry soil; barbed wire ringed the perimeter. The soldiers below were the descendants of the army of the Mahdi, but their fortifications had been learned from Kitchener. It was a desolate and terrifying place. A place built in the expectation of violent death. There was a good chance that it would come. The roles had been reversed. The SPLA now was fighting for their people's freedom not with spears and gleaming swords, but with mortars and rocket grenades. They would tear into the flimsy outpost bringing death in a surge of explosives and molten steel.

We stopped only briefly in Lokichokio to refuel. Kenya spread out lush and green below us as we flew south and east. The sun was setting in a blaze of orange behind the Ngong hills when we came down to land at Wilson airport.

We rushed back through the flickering darkness of Nairobi's ill-lit streets to the office where we edited our story. Panthou and its path of hunger was the lead story on the news that night. We weren't the only journalists in Southern Sudan. The story was growing on the networks and in the newspapers of the world. There was still furious, even bitter debate in the press, amongst the aid agencies and even in the British parliament on whether the emergency had become a 'famine' or not. But only a few days later, the government of Sudan upped the quota of planes allowed to fly food into Sudan. Despite all the layers of debate and political manoeuvring, the pictures had done their work. More food would get to Panthou. Someone at last was heeding Arkanjelo's warning.

A Memory of the Dead

'No one has been there for months,' the missionary said to us in the flickering candlelight at the table in Lokichokio. 'The situation in Tonj is desperate. Three people died of hunger yesterday. You must go there and see for yourselves.'

The famine in Sudan had become big international news. TV crews and journalists from all over the world were flying into Bahr-el-Ghazal to cover the story. At last the food was beginning to get in. It was coming very late, but at least it was coming. But even with the new quota of five C-130s the UN couldn't fly food in everywhere. There were places in Southern Sudan that were slipping through the safety net. Tonj, the missionary told us, was one of the forgotten places of South Sudan.

That night correspondent George Alagiah and cameraman Alistair Lyne and I gathered around a map of South Sudan with a flashlight. Martin Seemungal from Canadian TV was with us. He had been the first of us to speak to the missionary. Tonj was almost in the very centre of Bahr-el-Ghazal. It seemed incomprehensible that a town that was directly on the flight path to places like Panthou further north would have been forgotten. On the map, at least, Tonj was on one of the few roads through the Sahel. It was on the way to Wau, a regional capital. Tonj had been taken from the government by the SPLA in May the previous year, and there was still a tremendous amount of instability in the area.

The rains had begun so the airstrips were only usable if there were at least eight hours of dry weather before we landed. That night, in the humid darkness, we decided to go to Tonj – it was a risk, we couldn't be sure the strip would be dry enough for us to land. In the end, it was the catch of fear in the missionary's voice that convinced us we had to go.

The dawn sky was filled with towering banks of cumulus. Tonj was just over an hour's flight away. It was close enough for the weather there to be too rough for us to land. We decided to go anyway.

We took off into the fluffy white cloud. Within moments raindrops were streaking wildly across the windscreen covering the cockpit. The pilot could see nothing in front of him. He had to rely entirely on his instruments. Over the swamplands of the Sudd the sky cleared a little to dull grey, but the river was green and silver through a patchwork of tiny clouds.

We left the river behind and flew on into the rains. The sky was overcast. The bush below was thick with waving grasslands. As we came down to land rain fell in dark swathes on the horizon.

We passed low over the town. An avenue of mango trees was bright green against the red soil of the road. The buildings of the town were mostly roofless. Patches of water gleamed on the ground. Our pilot had once flown for the French Foreign Legion. He brought the plane around in a wide arc and roared just a few feet above the runway to check the surface. It was damp. A large flock of sacred ibis took off from the runway. They rose in fluttering, anxious, snow-white layers into the grey sky.

The pilot decided to risk a landing. We turned again and headed for the strip. Two children were standing at the edge of the runway. As we touched down, perhaps sixty or seventy people had gathered. A 4x4 was nosing its way towards us through a track in the long grass.

As the plane came to a halt, the group of people collected around us. They all looked well. There was no evidence of starvation among them. They shook our hands. George introduced himself and shook hands with one of the men. They laughed delightedly when George made the effort to repeat his name.

A man emerged from the crowd. He was wearing a clean white shirt and a pair of trousers that an office worker would wear. He looked carefully at our press passes and then he introduced himself as Moses. He was the senior SRRA representative in the town. There were no foreign aid workers in Tonj.

'The situation is bad,' he told us. 'Four people died yesterday.'

Moses and the people around him were healthy and well fed. This time I was not surprised. I had learned about the layers of hunger that exist in a village when famine comes.

Moses and the other villagers led us down a road towards the town. The town of Tonj normally had a population of about 900, but with the influx of refugees the numbers had swollen. 'The people came to escape the fighting in Wau,' Moses said as we walked alongside him. 'Now there are some 5 400 people living here. Ninety per cent of them are suffering seriously from famine.'

It seemed hard to fathom. The grass around us was green. The rains had come, but I knew that all over Southern Sudan the rains had come too late. The fighting last year meant that no crops would have been planted. The continued raids by the *murahaleen* around Wau would have meant that no crops were planted there either.

There was a gentle, measured courteousness about Moses which might have seemed at odds with the situation he was describing. In fact, there was something utterly decent and compelling about his manner. It was his way of greeting strangers even in times like this. It reminded me of the hospitable gesture of the village elder who had given me his ebony staff. Some Westerners might have interpreted his restraint as apathy for the fate of his village. I had heard so often the absolutely incorrect cliché that Africans do not value life as highly as other cultures. I guessed it was this outward stoicism of people like Moses that had led people to think that way. I had learned enough about Africa to know how untrue this was. I had seen, and filmed, so many times the bitter, impassioned grieving of Africans to know how deeply they valued human life and the lives of those they loved. Moses' quiet, dignified reserve was a sign of his courage, not of his indifference.

We passed a shattered mud brick house. The walls had been blown out and the jagged edges of destruction stood against the empty sky. It was the first sign of the war that had swept through this village during the previous planting season. In front of us was a wide avenue of towering green trees. They arched up towards the rain-filled sky, their shade dappled and cool.

Underneath the trees we came across the first of the dying. Men, women and children stood in a silent arc, waiting for us. Everywhere I looked, people were showing signs of desperate, near-fatal malnutrition. Their wrinkled, dried-out skin hung loose over their bones. A woman held her tiny infant. The child was too exhausted even to look at us. Her head hung down against her tiny, emaciated chest. Her hair was a coppery brown and her delicate skull seemed grotesquely huge in comparison to her body.

Two desperately thin youths came through the trees. They were carrying a woman in her mid-forties. Her body was shrunken, devoid of any strength.

They put her down gently on the ground. She sat there, dazed and uncomprehending. Her name was Ador, and all four of her children had already died from starvation. Somehow, she had survived, but it was not clear how long she would live. She was already too weak to speak to us.

'So many mothers here have already lost their children,' Moses said. Listening to him, I understood in a way that I had not before the courageous choices I had seen the aid workers make in Panthou only a few days before. It was the little children who died first. To save them, the aid workers had turned away the adults. Here, in Tonj, there was nothing at all, so often the children died first and the adults had to watch and wait for their own deaths.

'April was the last time anyone came to help us,' Moses said. 'They brought 200 bags of sorghum. It lasted one day, and then there was nothing. If you have no means to get food what can you do but eat leaves? So many of them have died of diarrhoea.'

We could do nothing to help. Our plane was small and we had had no room to bring extra food. No one asked for anything, but we all felt our helplessness. We could only film and promise that we would show the world or, at least, the people of Britain what we had found here at Tonj. We took refuge behind the glass and plastic and electronic circuitry of our cameras. We felt the human shame of not being able to do anything then and there. The machines hid it for us, giving us an excuse to carry on. And yet we knew it wasn't a meaningless promise. The story of the famine in Sudan was big news in Britain, and in the world. People would listen to what we had to say about Tonj. I think we all felt the same way as we walked through that terrible silent avenue, strangely balanced in a moral limbo between not being able to act, but having the power to speak, to bear witness in the knowledge that somebody, at least, would be listening.

Moses led us further into the layers of desolation and suffering that made up this town. We passed an old factory that had once provided jobs and an income for the people who lived here. The factory made sacks to store and transport the sorghum crop that once had been plentiful in Tonj. It had been set up with British money in the early seventies. 'In the 1980s, it was destroyed,' Moses told us. 'By the fighting. Everything is destroyed here. Even the school is no longer functioning now.'

The greatest irony was the heavy rainclouds that hung in the air above us. It was mid-morning. The air was humid and warm with the promise of growth, but there was nothing to plant. Without help from outside, the people of Tonj could do nothing to improve their lives for at least the cycle of an entire harvest. They had reached the end. In one year the war had brought an end to agriculture here. Without outside help, the concentric circles of hunger's logic would slowly strangle the people of the town to death.

A little way beyond the factory a woman and her four children were walking towards us through the trees. She had a basket balanced on top of her head, and her children were spread out on either side of her.

As a shot for the camera, it looked idyllic – an almost clichéd scene of rural African beauty. Moses took us over to speak to her. Her name was Adut. She took the basket off her head and put it on the ground for Alistair to film. The basket was half-full of small green fruits about the size and shape of unripe plums.

'These are called *rak* in our language,' Moses said. '*Lulu* in Arabic. We can eat these, but they must be mixed with sorghum. You get diarrhoea if you eat them on their own.'

'How long has she been out collecting them?' George asked.

Moses spoke to Adut for a few moments. 'She left Tonj yesterday,' he told us as we filmed him and Adut. 'She spent the night in the bush and came back with this half basket. It is all the food she has found, and it must feed twelve people. These fruits will be finished today. In the evening she will go back again.'

As we walked deeper into the bush, we saw a small movement through the vegetation. As we drew closer, we could see that it was a teenage girl crawling on her knees along the hard, sandy pathway. Her mother was walking alongside. Ajak was the girl's name. Her mother was Abul. Ajak had come down with polio some ten months before. The disease had crippled her. In all other ways, she was healthy, but she had lost the use of her legs. In Tonj there were no wheelchairs and there were no adults in her family strong enough to carry her. Ajak had to crawl.

'We heard the plane,' her mother said. 'We came because we thought you were bringing food.'

Between the thick bush surrounding the airstrip and the factory there was a open stretch of savanna. Moses led us past the shattered remnants of buildings that had been strongholds of the government troops during the battle for Tonj. They showed signs of having been hit with mortars and rocket grenades. There were a few abandoned trenches and rusting vehicle parts lying alongside.

'A lot of people have died in Tonj. People have been dying since November. We don't know when anyone will come to help us,' Moses said as we passed the evidence of war.

It was only a few hundred metres on that we saw the first white bones of a human skeleton. More evidence of war. Further along there were two skulls and a small pile of jumbled bones. It had been scarcely a year since the fighting.

In front of us, on a wide open plain blasted by heat was a large collection of human bones. Femurs, vertebrae, and hip bones were bleached white against the dry brown soil. A white skull lay smooth and peaceful in the shadow of a bush. Nearby lay a skull on its side, a large hole gaping darkly in the fragile white bone. Beyond it lay five skulls, clustered together on top of a thick pile of bones.

'These are all people who have died of hunger,' Moses told us. George, Alistair and I exchanged sharp glances. This was hard to believe. The fighting had been a year ago. That was plenty of time for the bones to have become so bleached. The deaths from hunger, Moses himself had told us, had only begun some five months before, in November. It was difficult to believe that the bones would have become so clean and bleached in the space of five months.

We found ourselves in a terrible quandary. The suffering of the people of Tonj was cruelly evident. There was no doubt that people were dying of hunger here. Moses and the other men who led us into their town had behaved towards us with such dignity and courtesy. It was difficult, now, to say in effect: 'We don't believe you. Prove what you are saying about these skeletons.' At the same time, we both knew that death in African societies is something that affects the whole community. In a small society like Tonj, every family would be intricately tied to another. They would know each other well, and many would be related. Such significant numbers of dead people would have affected everyone in the town. Also, while many Dinkas, such as Moses, were Christians, the older beliefs of Africa had by no means died out and the connections between this world and the afterlife were strong. Those who had died had not lost their place in the minds of the community. The memory of the dead existed as a tangible force in the daily affairs of the living. We knew we risked causing both pain and offence by questioning what Moses had told us.

In situations like this, journalists usually have access to some kind of evidence collected by organizations like Human Rights Watch or Amnesty International. Often, aid agencies or the UN have reports that we can refer to. But here in Tonj there was no written word we could turn to, to back up the truth, or otherwise, of the images that we were filming. We would have to decide for ourselves what we would say about these piles of bleached bones spread out on the grasslands in front of us.

George was talking to Moses. Alistair started moving carefully around the perimeter of the bones, choosing the best shots. I walked behind Alistair, trying to find some clue that would help us decide what we thought about this pile of bones. Firstly, I counted the skulls. I don't quite know why I did this, but it seemed to me that I had to start somewhere. I have no knowledge of forensics at all, but I needed something concrete to start trying to unravel the truth of what had happened here.

I turned to my notebook to begin this process. I bent my head and in the margin I scribbled *(±) 15 skulls* in a nervous, uncertain scrawl.

'How many are there?' I heard George asking Moses. 'We don't know exactly,' Moses said. 'These bones are from January. Already we have buried 120, but many others are not buried.'

'But why are they not buried?' George asked. 'In Africa it is very unusual for people not to be buried properly when they die.'

'Because nobody was strong enough to bury the bodies. Every day people are dying. Even today somebody has died.'

It was awful to have to question people like this. It was insensitive, even disrespectful. We both felt embarrassed. But we couldn't avoid doing it. The political pressure back in London regarding the nature of the 'famine' was immense. We couldn't film the skeletons of the dead and say they were famine victims without having done our best to make sure that they really were.

'But the bones are so white and clean,' George persisted.

'There are still hyenas and vultures here,' Moses told us. 'They have been eating the bones.'

I found myself wandering down a ghoulish but necessary corridor of thought. What Moses said was entirely possible. There wouldn't have been many hyenas left in the area as the human population density was too great. The few remaining hyenas could have crunched some of the bones without being able to finish them all off. The passage of people moving around the bones would also have done much to deter the hyenas. And, of course, there was the awful fact that there were so many bones. Perhaps the remains of the fifteen or so humans we could see scattered around were the ones the hyenas had not been able to finish.

There was a much greater number of vultures and birds of prey left. I had seen some of them circling in the sky myself. The birds would have definitely picked the flesh off the bones, making it likely that the remaining bones would have become bleached by the sun and rain. I looked at the skull with the smashed hole in it. I had been sure, when I first saw it, that it represented a bullet hole. Here again, I turned to the only other experience I had with mass death: the churchyard at Nyarubuye in Rwanda. The hole in the skull looked remarkably like that of an exit wound from a high-velocity rifle bullet. It was only when I looked again, more carefully, that I began to doubt my initial analysis. The hole was in the very top of the skull. To have made such a wound, the bullet would have had to come from directly below. It would have to have been an execution-style killing with the barrel of the gun placed directly under the chin. It was an unlikely wound for a soldier to sustain in a firefight, although it could have been from a victorious soldier finishing off one of the wounded.

But there was no damage to the soft bones in the roof of the mouth, to the bones that would have been hard for a hyena's teeth to gain access to. On the other hand, there were no *discernible* tooth marks around the shattered edges of the skull. I had to leave it at 50-50 whether I believed the hole in the skull had been caused by a bullet or by a hyena's powerful teeth and jaws. Still, in my mind, the odds in favour of Moses' version were growing.

Then, underneath the corner of a pile of bones, I noticed it – a torn fragment of a cloth. It was a small, tattered piece of a camouflage uniform.

My heart started beating just a little faster. My mouth felt dry.

'What about this, Moses?' I asked, pointing to the piece of camouflage cloth.

'Yes,' George said. I could see he was angry, and upset at the same time. 'What about that?'

Moses looked at us. 'It is the uniform of a policeman. Not a soldier. Eighteen policemen have died from hunger here. Four of them were not buried.'

George and I looked at each other. We had both visited other villages controlled by the SPLA. I had seen more than one young man wearing a pair of camouflage pants and a T-shirt. Now that I thought about it, most of them I had seen had been carrying light, thin sticks. I couldn't remember seeing any of them carrying a gun. I had assumed that they were rebel soldiers who had been assigned to help with non-combatant duties and to keep order during the handouts of food.

There was nothing more to say. Either we believed Moses or we didn't.

Moses took us down an overgrown track into the town of Tonj proper. It was a tiny place, a relic of a colonial outpost. There were only two or three streets in the town. The shops and houses were mostly mud or brick-walled. They were roofed with rusted corrugated iron. A few had small verandas that stuck out on to the dirt road that served as the main street.

The signs of battle were everywhere. Abandoned bunkers half-overgrown with elephant grass lay at the edge of the road. Empty machine gun cartridges gleamed in the dull overcast light. The walls of one of the houses had been daubed with graffiti in Arabic.

The starving and the desperately ill had gathered on the edges of the pathetic main street. A group of emaciated children sat listlessly on the cement floor of a veranda. A grandfather lay stretched out, unmoving, across the steps. An old woman was led out by a younger woman. Both were starving. The old woman was blind from the filarial worm that attacks the optic nerve and causes what is known as river blindness. A few women were crouched over pots of *rak*, the wild fruits that Adut had been collecting. The green mess bubbled slowly over smoky fires. There was no corn or sorghum to go with it.

George and Moses and Alistair were filming on the main street. I went off down one of the side streets with another man from the SRRA called Thomas. It was growing late in the day and we were getting pushed for time. I wanted to make sure we were not missing anything for our story. We passed through the market square. It was a desolate, silent place. Here, the people were not starving, not quite, but they were very close to it. There was almost nothing for sale. Men sat behind pitifully small piles of tamarind and other wild fruits. Thomas pointed them out to me. '*Cui*,' he said, pointing to one minute, withered collection of vegetable matter. '*Ardep*', he said about another. I had no idea what these fruits were, but I wrote the names down in my notebook. There was nothing else for sale, and it struck me that I saw nobody buying.

We passed through the market and Thomas took me to the outskirts of town. We stood at the top of a sloping, dusty patch of ground that led down to the curve of a small river. The water flowed slow and muddy in the sticky heat.

Out of the corner of my eye, I saw another two skulls lying in the dust. I walked closer to them. One of them had been badly smashed. The other had a hole in it that had been clearly chipped out by the clean, destructive power of a bullet.

The doubts began to rise inside my head again. I didn't know what to think. The starvation in the town was clear. People were dying. But all these skulls told a macabre and confusing story. While I was unsure about the fifteen or so people who had died on the savanna on the other side of town, I was absolutely convinced that these people had been killed by bullets.

I decided to voice my doubts openly again.

'More people who died in the famine?' I asked, being deliberately disingenuous.

'No,' Thomas said. 'These were killed in the battle.'

The light was just beginning to sink as we moved away from the river. Heavy rainclouds were gathering in the sky. The pilot came across town to warn us that we would have to be leaving soon. At the end of the main street was a small collection point that had been set up by the SRRA for the worst cases. Here the suffering was acute. The men, women and children gathered in the shadows of the dilapidated brick buildings were soundless, gaunt shadows. Here, at last, was all the morbid imagery of famine. Here the anger of life had faded. There was nothing left for these people but the slow descent into death. Sister Maria Latissia was one of the few people who had the strength to help the others. She was a Dinka who had been sent by the Catholic church to help her own people.

Sister Maria said little as she led us into the room where the body of Theresa Achol lay. Theresa had died that very morning. Some time while we were battling our way through the heavy rainclouds above the Sahel, Theresa had slid into oblivion in the cramped, fly-spattered confines of this room. Sister Maria had found some minor way to grant dignity to her death. Theresa had died privately, under a roof, away from the frightened, desperate eyes of the others who still somehow clung to life.

Theresa's body was covered with a blanket when we arrived. Her children, Gai and Athony, were sitting nearby. Someone, probably Sister Maria, had given them a small helping of cooked maize meal. They ate in silence. They were too young to understand the significance of what had happened, but they were subdued by hunger and the fear that filled the room around them. The window was open. Outside we could hear the thud of a pick and the scrape of a shovel as someone began to dig a grave for Theresa. That, at least, was something Theresa would find in death. Unlike the others whose bones were scattered among the dust.

No one knew what had happened to Gai and Athony's father. The children's future was entirely in the hands of people like Sister Maria. 'I cannot run away from here,' she told us, her face sombre but filled with a deep certainty. 'We hope for someone to come to help us.'

We decided to believe Moses and the others about the skulls. Not that, in the end, it would have mattered much. The suffering of Tonj was so overwhelming that it was enough to tell a thousand stories of famine. For in Tonj there could be no doubt that it was famine we had witnessed. The story of our journey into Tonj ran as a long special on what was then the Nine O'Clock News. We were back in Lokichokio preparing for another trip into Southern Sudan when we heard that after our story had run UNICEF decided to relaunch their Sudan famine appeal.

Peace talks are under way, but at the beginning of 2003 the war still rages in Sudan. The threat of famine that the fighting leaves in its wake has not ended. In the last few years, the government of Sudan has shown an increasing resolve to end its isolation in the world community. It has also shown a greater readiness to end the war in the South. Some of the blame for the war must be shared by the SPLA who seem to have chosen to continue the war in spite of the government's professed willingness to find a solution.

How events in the increasingly fractured relationship between the West and radicalized elements of the Islamic world will affect the outcome of the longest civil war in Africa remains to be seen.

Since the terrible season of 1998 I have been back to Southern Sudan a number of times. I have been lucky enough to see the country at times when it is not struck by famine, or, at least, not so badly afflicted as it was that year. Beyond the war and famine and suffering, an ancient way of living survives despite the devastation.

Many of the men in the village are carrying fishing and hunting spears; even while discreetly in the background uniformed rebels carry their Kalashnikovs. In the blazing sun of noon the village elders gather under an enormous tree. It stands alone on the flat, parched earth. Its leaves cast a shade that is deep and cool as water. Women and small children join them. We can hear the sound of laughter and the rhythm of unhurried conversation.

We meet Akod in the tiny marketplace where men are selling grain, tamarind seeds, dried fish and hot sweet tea brewed on thornwood fires. Two teenage boys are playing with a pet monkey, agile and affectionate as any household cat. The young soldiers nearby have their foreheads marked with long horizontal scars. They are from another village. 'Each generation has a different pattern,' Akod says. 'Their grandfathers had six, but now some men have eight or ten.'

In the huts around us women begin pounding what grain they have to prepare for the evening meal. In the marketplace the tea fires burn down and the people begin to drift homewards.

As the sun sinks below the horizon, huge-winged marabou storks come to roost on the conical roofs of the huts. The village paths are filled with a low, contented murmur as people come in from the day's tasks – men tending the cattle and women the dry, meagre fields. There is the aromatic smell of the woodsmoke from the cooking fires drifting up against the sunset.

The stars come out first. Akod points to the Milky Way, vast and swirling in the clear, black night. 'We believe it is the boundary that divides the dry season and the rainy season,' he tells me.

Then the full moon emerges above the horizon. Slowly at first, and then rapidly, the sound of hard, calloused palms beating the skin of drums rises from the huts all around us. Akod explains that for three nights around every full moon the people celebrate. They eat well of the grain stored from the harvest and they drink the beer they have brewed. We can hear laughter, rhythmic clapping and singing emerging from the huts.

For tonight, at least, the modern war is far away and an older Africa emerges. The sand is cool and white in the moonlight; the broad ancient trees are dark, haunting silhouettes in the silver glow. Deep into the night the drums reverberate and snatches of song drift over the bush.

KUWAIT

DESERT SUNSETS

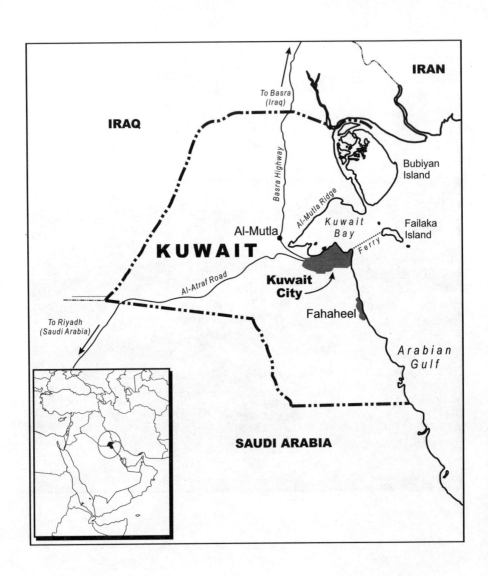

I never covered the Gulf War. I wasn't even a journalist when it began. I was living in New York, working on a novel and teaching English in order to survive.

I was sitting in the SideWalk Café in the East Village on the evening of January 17, 1991. That day was the deadline for Saddam Hussein to begin pulling his troops out of Kuwait, or the coalition troops would start the bombing campaign. My sister Candace was working as a waitress at the restaurant and I had gone to have a few drinks with her and her friends that evening. It was my habit when I visited her to relax at a table on my own, reading a book, ordering a beer or two and chatting to her when she came over between serving customers.

The television was on in the corner of the restaurant. Usually we ignored the images flashing across its screen, but that evening everyone was watching as events began to unfold live on television. I was reading a book about Zaire at the time, and I had brought it along with me. After I had skimmed through a few pages, I stopped reading and started watching the TV along with everyone else.

As the deadline drew closer in faraway Kuwait, the tension in the restaurant grew. Nobody seemed to be ordering any longer, all their attention was taken up by what they were seeing on the screen. Candace and a few of her friends stopped waiting tables and came to sit down with me.

I can't even remember which country the reporter who was appearing live on screen was in. All any of us knew was that he was somewhere in the Middle East in a country close to, or bordering, Iraq. I can remember very little of what he said. The main message he was conveying to us in that restaurant in Manhattan was that he was scared. For that hour or so before the deadline expired, he had dropped his confident, extrovert TV-presenter manner. I don't know whether he intended it consciously or not, but his face and his voice showed his emotions clearly and honestly.

The crew were invisible to us watching him on the screen, but the reporter kept referring to them. In doing so, he broke the usual rules of television in which the vast and complex technology used to carry his message is assumed not to exist. By keeping the equipment and the support crews out of sight and hearing, an illusion is created where we, the audience, agree to believe that the reporter is somehow talking directly to us – almost as if by a kind of magic.

By breaking that illusion, the reporter gave us a vivid impression of what it was like to be there, waiting for war to break out. He told us that the thing they all feared most was that Saddam Hussein would unleash chemical or biological warheads against his enemies in the Middle East. They were terrified that in the next hour or so they would find themselves caught in a series of huge explosions, followed by clouds of poison or germ-laden gas.

It was a sickening thought. He made us understand exactly how frightening and dangerous this new type of war was. We in that restaurant began to share his emotions and that of the TV crew and of the Arab hotel staff around him. As the minutes towards the deadline ticked away, we too became more and more afraid. We began to share their reality.

I opened my book at the very last page. On the blank flyleaf at the end of the book, I began making notes. I didn't quite understand why I was doing it, but it seemed important to record what was happening around me. We were living, moment by moment, through those images on the TV screen. But for memory, somehow, I needed to write, to put something in words.

They are still there, those few words I scribbled down. The edges of the pages have begun to yellow slightly. The blue ink of the ballpoint pen is still scrawled vividly, reflecting my own fear as I wrote.

6:50 – war starts. I'm watching CNN.

8:30 – Rumour – bombs found in Houston and Broadway subway stations.

Besides the expression of fear on the TV correspondent's face, I remember so clearly something that happened a little while after that. One of Candace's fellow waitresses, a pretty young woman in her early twenties, came up to our table. Her soft brown hair was in disarray. Her face was twisted with fear. She leaned over the table anxiously and spoke in a staccato, breathless rush.

'It's impossible,' I told her. 'It can't be.'

'Just relax,' Candace said to her quietly. 'That's not happening. It's going to be okay.'

'No,' the woman said. 'It's not. It's not going to be okay.'

8:56, I wrote. *Rumour – Don't drink water in New York city – it may be poisoned.*

Such a thing did seem absurd then. Now, since September 11, 2001 we know that anything is possible.

Shortly after that evening, while the bombing campaign was still going on, I decided to return to live in South Africa. Nelson Mandela had been released from prison the year before. The continent was alive with change and hope.

From the far southern end of the African continent, the Gulf War seemed remote, almost irrelevant to people's daily lives.

For weeks afterwards, the world witnessed on its TV screens the bombing runs, the explosions, the anti-aircraft fire arcing over the Baghdad sky, the tanks and troops in the desert, and finally the exhausted Iraqi soldiers surrendering in whole regiments.

As we watched, and victory for the West and its Arab allies became certain, the fear soon faded away. But still, none of us will ever forget how week after week, twenty-four hours a day, the images of war played themselves out on our TV screens.

The urgency and the vibrancy of events in Africa soon persuaded me to take up journalism instead of teaching as a way of earning a living. Soon I was travelling and working as a journalist all over the continent. I had missed the Gulf War, but I would never forget those moments of fear that we had felt in Manhattan.

Then seven years later, in January 1998, Saddam Hussein began questioning the right of UN weapons inspectors to have unlimited access to sites where they suspected chemical or biological weapons were being produced. The main point of contention was that the weapons inspectors were dominated by American interests. By January 13, the UN arms inspectors were effectively barred from doing their work. Three days later the American members of the team left Iraq. By the end of the month, US Secretary of State Madeleine Albright left for Europe and the Middle East to begin the long process of finding support for the US stance against Iraq.

By early February, it was clear that Saddam Hussein was again challenging the West and America, in particular, to do its worst. Martin Turner, the BBC bureau chief in Johannesburg, called me on my cellphone. 'They are getting crews ready to go to the Gulf. I want to suggest to London that your name be on the list.'

I accepted his offer, but I couldn't help the small involuntary flash of fear that surged through me. I had seen enough on the news and in the papers to know that there was evidence that Saddam had been building up his chemical and biological warfare capabilities. If war broke out again with Iraq, who knew how many of those weapons might be launched?

Claustrophobia

'The komodo dragon is the first example of biological warfare. Sure it bites you, but it's the bacteria on its filthy teeth that kill you.'

Steve, our instructor on the Nuclear, Biological and Chemical (NBC)

Warfare course, grimaced at us. The BBC and other networks had sent a group of journalists to the spacious grounds of an old country house that had been converted into a conference centre. The room we were sitting in had once been an elegant, panelled drawing room. Now it was filled with rows of formica desks, plastic chairs and a TV and video machine.

Steve, ex-British army, and an expert in NBC warfare, shook his head. 'I don't want to go anywhere near where you are going.' He lifted the clear plastic ruler he had been using as a pointer.

'Don't get depressed now,' he said, shaking the ruler in our direction. 'It's just that you have to know one thing. With chemical warfare, the agents that attack your nerves or blood cells are incredibly virulent. The filters in the respirator on your gas mask will protect you for about twenty minutes. After that, they become saturated and the blood agents leak into your lungs. In other words, if there is a chemical attack, don't believe you can stay in the area and do your work. You've got to do one thing – just get out of there!'

Steve pushed the button on the remote control for the video screen. We sat in silence as the tape fast forwarded. The vast mushroom cloud of a nuclear explosion grew in jerks and starts as the tape sped through the images. Steve looked at us while the tape wound through the machine. 'It's a bloody joke – trying to teach you how to survive a nuclear attack. With the explosion, you've got blow out and then the shock wave of blow back.' Steve slapped the ruler in his palm, and then held it there.

'There's no point in teaching you anything. You're not going to survive being nuked.'

With a click, he shut off the machine. It was nearly 11:30 in the morning. The neatly typed programme on the formica desks read:

1030/1100 Lecture Room: Biological Agents. Definition/bacteria/viruses/toxins
1100/1130 Lecture Room: Chemical Agents. Blister/blood/nerve/phosgene
1130/1145 Reception Hall: Break. Coffee/tea/biscuits

After the break we moved on to: *1145/1245 Lecture Room: Wearing of NBC IPE. Unpacking – wearing mask and equipment.*

Steve watched, plastic ruler in hand, as we struggled with the unwieldy NBC IPE suits. NBC IPE stood for Nuclear, Biological, Chemical Individual Protection Equipment.

Glenn Middleton and I had been sent from Johannesburg as a team. We helped each other force our legs and arms into the tight, ill-fitting suits. It was February in Britain, but even in the chill air we were sweating with the effort of trying to get into the suits.

I tried not to think about what it might be like trying to get into them in 45°C heat in the desert somewhere. I knew, too, from places like Kinshasa, how in the event of an impending attack, the spiral of fear would be steadily rising within each one of us. That would make it even more difficult to get into the suits properly.

'Make sure you pull those rubber gloves right up over the sleeves,' Steve admonished one pair of journalists wrestling with their suits. 'Remember, it takes a drop smaller than a pinhead of blood agent to kill you. You've got to make sure there are no leaks anywhere in your suit.'

Finally the dozen or so of us were suited up. The last step in the procedure was to pull the close-fitting rubber mask over your face. It felt weirdly like being a scuba diver. As the mask came down over my head and pulled hard against the skin of my face, it felt like I was cutting myself off from the outside world. The helmet of the suit cut down my ability to hear by at least 50 per cent. The heavy gloves and boots severely limited the feeling in my hands and feet. The round eyeglasses of the mask allowed me almost no peripheral vision. I could see only a narrow tunnel in front of me.

Steve waved his ruler, and we set off behind him in a long line. We had to cross a wide green lawn towards a thicket of three-hundred-year-old pines. The idea was to get us accustomed to wearing the suits, and to the difficulties of moving around in them. I am an experienced scuba diver, so at first I had no problems in adjusting to the suit. But as we tramped under the pines the oppressive feeling of the suit began to weigh on my mind. Even in the coolness of a sunny winter day in Britain, we started to get unbearably hot and sweaty inside the suits. Glenn and the other people around me flitted in and out of my vision like frustrating, annoying puppets, disappearing and reappearing unexpectedly. I began to wonder what it would be like if we were under a chemical attack. How would I keep track of my colleagues? Would I lose them in the fear and alarm? Or would they lose me?

A wave of claustrophobia swept over me. It was totally unexpected. In years of scuba diving I had never felt such a panic. My heart started pounding wildly. My temples throbbed, my palms were instantly wet. The only thing I was conscious of was how hard it was to breathe. I could hear the air sawing through the gas filter on my mask. It was a hollow, rasping sound that cut off everything else.

I had to stop myself grabbing at the cloying rubber mask and tearing it off my face. *What, I thought, will I be like in a real attack?* Slowly, I brought my mind under control. My scuba diving experience helped. I let go of the panic, feeling it dissolve out of my mind and then, slowly, out of my hands, my arms, my chest and finally my temples and forehead.

The branches of the pine trees slapped against my mask and suit. It was okay. I would just have to get used to a different way of breathing. If we did get caught in an attack, it would be okay – for twenty minutes. But surely, I told myself, it will never come to that. We would get out long before then.

BA 157, Saturday, February 14, to Kuwait City was delayed by more than two hours. It was not leaving from the passenger terminal. We were bused a long way across the tarmac to the air cargo terminal. The plane was filled with US military personnel – young men and women both – fit and looking ready for action. A few of the soldiers were in civilian clothes, but most were in camouflage uniform. There was none of the usual carefree American banter. The rows of soldiers crammed into the seats were silent and thoughtful.

There was real, and frightening, substance to the US accusations against Saddam Hussein, particularly with regard to his developing chemical and biological weapons. He had started such a progamme as far back as the 1970s. In the Iran-Iraq war of the early 1980s numbers of chemical warheads had been fired by Iraqi forces. Saddam had put his cousin, Ali Hassan al-Majid, in command of crushing a Kurdish uprising in 1988. Ali Hassan authorized the use of chemical weapons. The clouds of poison gas killed mostly women and children and refugees.

The Gulf War of 1991 had not destroyed Saddam Hussein's chemical and biological capabilities. The UN weapons inspectors uncovered a vast arsenal of chemical and biological weapons in Iraq. They had destroyed nearly 500 000 litres of live chemical agents. They had found nearly two million litres of raw ingredients used in the making of chemical weapons. In addition to the chemical weapons, they uncovered 20 000 litres of botulism bacteria and nearly 8 400 litres of anthrax. Iraq was also known in the past to have produced spores for gangrene and cancer-causing agents and the plague bacteria.

The amount that the weapons inspectors had uncovered so far was already enough to kill off the entire population of the world many times over. The biggest fear was what remained hidden from the UN inspectors. This was especially true of the biological weapons. Unlike chemical weapons, they could be produced relatively easily in small, secret laboratories. The most horrifying aspect of these biological weapons is that, once released, they can become even more deadly as the spores and bacteria multiply and mutate into drug-resistant forms.

The US and its closest ally, Britain, had now decided to draw a line in the sand. Unless Saddam Hussein allowed the UN weapons inspectors back and gave them free, unfettered access to the sites, they would attack Iraq.

There were already 1 500 US ground troops in Kuwait, and 3 000 more were on their way. We were sitting amongst the first wave of those reinforcements.

The US had already deployed six of its ultra hi-tech stealth bombers in Kuwait, and Britain had sent eight Tornado bombers. All in all, the US had about 450 aircraft, 15 warships, including 3 aircraft carriers, and 13 support vessels in the Gulf region. There were an estimated 25 000 troops at bases across the Gulf. At least 250 cruise missiles were ready to be fired at Iraq. The British were steaming *HMS Invincible*, another aircraft carrier, towards the region.

The British cabinet had backed Tony Blair on the use of force if no diplomatic solution to the crisis could be found. Later the following week he would seek backing from the House of Commons. Tony Benn, a senior Labour MP, gave voice to the doubts of many on the Left in both Britain and America and elsewhere in the world about the rapid deployment of troops, planes and warships. 'I'm afraid,' he said, 'the war has been agreed on already by London and Washington.'

Many people across the world concurred. Few thought that bombing Iraq would prevent the development of chemical and biological weapons. It seemed to many people that nothing other than killing innocent Iraqi civilians would be achieved. Whatever happened, Clinton and Blair were never going to assemble the coalition that George Bush senior did in the Gulf War. Russia and China were vehemently opposed to military action. Close allies Turkey, France and Japan were furious at what they saw as the US's lack of consultation over their war plans. Unlike August 1990, when an aggressive and uncompromising Iraq invaded Kuwait, this time Iraq was using more moderate language. The Deputy Prime Minister of Iraq, Tariq Aziz, had already stated that his country had no plans to attack either Kuwait or Israel if it were attacked by a US-led force. Whether Saddam Hussein planned to stick to that remained to be seen. Nonetheless, the rhetoric was very different in tone to that of 1990.

Arab opinion was deeply opposed to military action against Iraq. Most Arabs no longer saw Saddam Hussein as a threat to them and the stability of their countries. They saw him and, more importantly, the people of Iraq, now as victims of US aggression and US-led sanctions. In addition, seven years after the Gulf War, little had been done by the US or its Western allies to secure peace in the Middle East. To many Arabs, the continuing Palestinian-Israeli conflict remained the most obvious and bitter symbol of broken promises by the West.

The situation had all the makings of a giant mess. There was no doubt Saddam Hussein was a brutal dictator who not only oppressed his own people, but whose growing arsenal of chemical and biological weapons threatened world stability. On the other hand, America and Britain could not act against him without alienating huge numbers of people all over the world.

Still, war seemed imminent. Anthony Zinni, a four-star Marine general and US Commander-in-Chief, had told reporters a few days before: 'We are within a week or so.'

The luggage carousel ground to a halt. There was no doubt about it. My luggage was missing. I had been issued an NBC protective suit in London and it was in my suitcase. There were no spare suits. I had landed in a potential chemical or biological war zone without protection. I filed a lost baggage report and tried not to think too hard about what might happen.

As we drove on to the wide, multilane freeway that led into Kuwait City our driver began to talk to us. 'People are not just worried here,' he said. 'They are scared. We don't know what Saddam will do. Many people are leaving Kuwait. From today, British Airways crew will not sleep in Kuwait any more.'

As we approached the outskirts of the city I thought of reports I had read in the newspapers on the plane. The government of Kuwait was seeking to reassure its people. There were rumours circulating in the city that schools and even the airport was soon to be closed. While Kuwait remained a staunch ally of America, and would certainly act as a crucial launching pad for any US-led strikes against Iraq, the government was at pains to point out that Kuwait was not directly involved.

It was eerie to be driving into Kuwait City. There was no visible damage left over from the Iraqi invasion and the war that followed. We passed rows of flat-roofed concrete houses. Most of them were ugly, but adequate – far better than the sort of housing one saw in most African cities, and an indication of the wealth of Kuwait. In between the simpler concrete houses were luxurious mansions built in a variety of styles. Some had tasteful, curved Arabic archways, others had wide balconies with rows of freshly painted colonnades.

Kuwait is a tiny country, about the size of Wales, with a population of about two million of whom less than 20 per cent are native-born Kuwaitis, although, with naturalized citizens, Kuwaitis make up about 32 per cent of the population. It was they who enjoyed the prosperity. The per capita income in Kuwait before the invasion by Iraq was over $10 000 a year. (This compared favourably with Britain's at just over $14 000.) Tiny Kuwait has 20 per cent of the world's known oil reserves. It was the world's second largest oil exporter, earning a staggering $20.5 billion dollars a year in exports.

Voting rights were restricted to the 70 000 or so Kuwaiti men who were 'first class' citizens. They were members of the families whose ancestors had been living in Kuwait before the 1920s when the British negotiated a formal treaty with the rulers of Saudi Arabia recognizing Kuwait's existence as a separate kingdom ruled by Sheikh Mubarak al-Sabah.

For native Kuwaitis and their families, housing, education and medical care were free. Jobs were reserved for them and many Kuwaitis were sent overseas at the government's expense to study at international universities. Even phones were free and income tax was zero. Like many of the Gulf States, an army of immigrants worked as cleaners and construction crews, and manned the oil rigs.

But the good life was under threat again, and people in Kuwait were scared.

'Everybody is shopping today,' our driver told us. 'I went to buy bread this morning. I waited forty minutes to get one packet.'

Our luxury hotel in Kuwait City had been a bombed and burned-out ruin in 1991, but it had been completely reconstructed. The lobby was floored in green marble. Columns and pointed arches of ivory marble soared to the roof high above. Crystal chandeliers and gilt finishes gleamed from the ceiling.

The rooms were huge. The floors were covered with thick, plush carpets. The spacious bathrooms were filled with gleaming taps and marble sinks. The walls were mirrored and rows of toiletries were lined up on the sink. A thick towelling robe and slippers had been laid out on the bed. There was a personal TV, video player, sound system and fax machine placed in various corners of the room. A huge bowl of exotic, colourful fruit stood on the polished table alongside the armchair.

As I stood in my room without my luggage, in just the clothes I had been wearing on the plane, I couldn't help thinking that this was going to be the strangest war I had ever covered. None of this luxury would mean anything if the missiles with their chemical warheads started falling on Kuwait City. But you couldn't think that way. I went over to the sound system. There was a note above it telling guests to contact the reception desk to request whichever CDs they wanted.

Next to it was another neatly typed sheet of paper:

The Management and staff wish you a pleasant and comfortable stay at our hotel.
We would like to inform you that due to the present situation, the following plan has been devised to be followed in the event of an emergency.

There were a number of instructions about how to evacuate the hotel in an air raid. The notice exhorted us to keep calm and to follow instructions. Towards the end of the paper was written:

In case of chemical attack. Keep wet towel around your mouth and nose and replace every 15 minutes. Do not breathe during replacement.

The window of my room overlooked a small souk. Many of the city's immigrant underclass gathered in the open space in front of it. I watched as the crowds of Pakistanis, Bangladeshis and Filipinos chatted in small groups.

Occasionally, they browsed through the stalls selling Adidas sneakers, Seiko watches, Coke and glasses of mint tea. There were also stalls selling gold necklaces, rings and other trinkets. The workers seldom bought anything. Sometimes groups of young women would gather and buy ice-cream cones. Once I saw a young man buy one for his girlfriend. She held it carefully out in front of her so that it did not drip on her clean dress while he pocketed his change without counting it.

I watched them from behind the solid glass window that separated the surreal zone of luxury of the hotel from their lonely world of economic exile. The sound of their conversation and occasional laughter drifted up to me. It murmured constantly through the airtight window.

Before the Gulf War, the majority of expatriate workers in Kuwait had been Arabs, especially Palestinians. But the vocal support given to Saddam Hussein after the invasion of Kuwait by Palestinians in the West Bank and Gaza meant that they became deeply unpopular in liberated Kuwait. After the war, most of them were expelled from the country. The Kuwaiti government policy since the Gulf War had been to encourage immigrant workers from Asia rather than poor and semi-skilled Arabs. A large population of angry, disaffected Arabs from countries all over the Arab world could be potentially troublesome in the event of future conflicts. The Asians, however, were seen as unconnected to events in the immediate region, and could, in the last event, be easily deported.

The Asian workers seemed a sad and forgotten group of people. I suppose many of them could have gone home if they had chosen, but I was sure that an equal number of them could not have afforded the air ticket. Not without wiping out their savings. Most of all, they could not afford to risk losing their jobs if they went.

If war came, these people would be the worst off. They had no gas masks or chemical suits. The suits cost nearly £300 each, well out of reach of these people, even if they had been available. They lived mostly in crowded flats or rented rooms, sharing accommodation in order to save money. Even if it was only conventional missiles that were fired at the city, they would be at terrible risk.

That first weekend was quiet. An air of unreality hung over the city. No one could quite believe that the countdown to war had begun. Every day a blue sky hung over the motionless turquoise sea. Ships, fishing trawlers and freighters moved across the flat water, sparkling in the winter sun. The aircraft carriers and battleships stayed invisible beyond the horizon. Whether that was their intention, or whether it was coincidence, no one knew. Certainly, the outline of a warship on the horizon would have been ominous and frightening to the citizens of Kuwait City.

Cold air swept through the buildings and streets of Kuwait. Driving on the multilane highways we could get glimpses of the desert between the tall buildings.

If there was to be war, it would be fought in the desert. There seemed little chance of another invasion of Kuwait, but if there was to be an attack on Iraq by the Americans, the flat dunes of Kuwait would almost certainly be one of the places from where the tanks would begin to roll.

'The truth is,' General Henry Shelton, chairman of the Joint Chiefs of Staff, told journalists in Washington, 'war is a dirty thing. We will lose some people, and that weighs heavily.'

UN Secretary General Kofi Annan was still in New York, trying to broker peace within the corridors of the UN offices. But all over the world there was talk of war. The *New York Times* ran a piece on when war might start. There were all sorts of things to be considered. The sensitivities of Washington and London's Arab and other allies were crucial to when the bombing might begin. But then, the article said, the cycle of Muslim holy days had to be considered, as did the timing of the President's trip to Africa.

For the American and British pilots, though, the most important thing was the moon. They needed dark, moonless nights to help hide them from Iraqi anti-aircraft fire. There were few moonless nights left in February and in March President Clinton was scheduled to go on his long-planned trip to Africa. So just when could the war begin?

The only person who seemed to know was, as always, a taxi driver. 'The shooting will start on Friday.'

'Why do you think that?' I asked.

He looked at me in the rear-view mirror. 'I *know*,' he said, tapping his earlobe. 'I hear.'

My bag was found. With it, came my gas mask and NBC kit. I was pleased to get my luggage back, but the truth was that I had mixed feelings.

There was also the threat of nerve gas. In order to protect yourself against nerve poison, you had to decide a considerable time beforehand that you were likely to be attacked with nerve agent. The only way to protect yourself was to begin taking tablets called NAPS (Nerve Agent Pre-Treatment Set). The tablets had to be taken at eight-hourly intervals. The theory was that the NAPS tablets would create some sort of protective coating around the nerve tissue and synapses. This layer would, it was claimed, help to prevent the poison from penetrating the nerve tissue. NAPS, though, were not enough on their own. If you were exposed to nerve gas, you had to inject yourself immediately with a device called a Combopen. You were supposed to do this by slamming the point of the Combopen into the thigh muscle 'midway between knee and hip', the manual said, and then push the top of the Combopen until a chemical known as atropine had been injected into your muscle. You were not supposed to inject yourself with atropine more than 'once every 15 minutes'. And if the 'symptoms of nerve agent poisoning' still remained, well then, you were to seek further treatment from qualified medical personnel.

There was an added catch. If you had not been exposed to nerve agent and you injected yourself with atropine then that might be harmful too. The manual advised that you learn the symptoms both of nerve gas poisoning and of atropine poisoning. Nerve gas was initially supposed to cause things like running nose, increased saliva, tightness of breathing rapidly leading to nausea, involuntary defecation, twitching and jerking of muscles, stoppage of breathing. The manual ended its list of symptoms there.

You could tell if you had atropine poisoning apparently by noticing a rapid pulse rate, a very dry mouth and throat, and hot dry skin. How you would tell the difference between atropine poisoning and real terror in a desert city while you were under threat of a nerve gas attack was anybody's guess.

The manual was clear on one point. You could tell the difference between atropine poisoning and nerve gas by looking at the pupils. Nerve gas pinpointed the pupils, while atropine enlarged them.

I was willing to take my chances. I had no NAPS tablets and no Combopen – both of them were implicated in the mysterious Gulf War Syndrome that many veterans claimed to be suffering from. It had been my choice to come to Kuwait, and I wanted to see the story through to wherever it led. If a chemical or biological attack did come, it would be so horrifying that it didn't really bear thinking about. There was something abstract and unreal about the prospect, so I mostly just put it out of my mind.

In my private moments, I had to admit that I was in a strange state of mind. I didn't want war to come. When I allowed my mind to wander I did fear what the bombs and missiles might do. I didn't want to die or, worse, to be crippled with wounds, but I didn't want to leave for a safe place either. I wanted to see what would happen.

There was a parallel to my state of mind a year earlier in Kinshasa. There, we had lived in a city under siege. But here we were living with the possibility that if a war started, it could escalate into a nuclear conflict, especially if the existence of the state of Israel came under real threat.

We were very far from that point, but it was not an impossibility.

The hotel became a vast, teeming media centre. The American networks had taken over the ballrooms and the conference halls. They had set up temporary cubicles with desks and computers, turning their sections into open-plan offices. An enormous bundle of cables tumbled out of the windows and snaked up to the roof where they were connected to communications satellites. A friend from one of the networks showed me their twenty-four hour internet, fax and email connectivity. In addition, they had round-the-clock satellite feeds for their television pictures.

The BBC had a much smaller operation. We, too, had a permanent satellite dish and satphones with internet connections. But the entire BBC operation was crammed into a small suite at the end of the corridor on the eighth floor of the hotel. Whenever we went into the 'office', we had to fight our way past piled boxes of television equipment, flak jackets, emergency food and water.

Glenn and I had flown from the Johannesburg office to Kuwait. Our friends George Alagiah and Milton Nkosi had flown from Johannesburg to Baghdad. Glenn and I called them on the satphone. We took turns chatting to George and Milton. The line was echoing and hollow. It was hard to have a proper conversation, but it was good to hear their voices and know that we would be sharing this experience, whatever came of it.

The greatest skill in producing television news is to balance the twin demands of cost and the constant need to find new images. The screen can never be allowed to go black – there must always be something for somebody, watching somewhere, to see.

If there are no new pictures to flash on the screen, then the correspondent must appear. He or she must talk to the camera, and keep talking for as long as anyone is watching, or is presumed to be watching. This means that even the most experienced correspondents are often tied to the satellite dish.

They must be ready to go live and appear on screen at a moment's notice. Quite often on a breaking story, they don't get the opportunity to leave the hotel for days at a time. If they are lucky, they get to quickly whip down to the nearest street corner where the cameraman records what is called a 'standupper' or 'piece to camera'. This is what viewers at home see when they watch a correspondent talking into a microphone. That is sometimes the nearest the reporter on screen gets to personally witnessing any of the events that he or she talks about in the report. This is not always the case, but for the best journalists it is the most frustrating aspect of the increasing demands of twenty-four hour news. Most of them hate being so hamstrung, and try to get out whenever they can, but the insatiable demands of just putting something on the air mean that far too often they do get caught up in just that cycle. They are forced, many times, to experience the events by reading wire service news reports on their laptop computers and by seeing the images on the tapes that the camera crews bring in from the field.

Glenn and I were one of those crews. We were to be a roaming crew. We were doing specials for the Nine O'Clock News. Our job was to drive off into the desert and find whatever extra pictures we could. It was real, old-fashioned reporting, where you get out of the office and look for stories.

Abdul Rahman was hired to help us work our way around Kuwait. We met him in the lobby of the hotel. He was a smallish, wiry man of about thirty-two. He was dressed traditionally in a long black *dishdasha* and wore a red and white checkered *gutra*, or headscarf, on his head with a double black silk rope to hold it in place. Underneath his *gutra* he had dark, smiling eyes and a thin moustache.

Abdul Rahman worked as a journalist on one of the local Kuwaiti papers, but he was clearly looking forward to working with the BBC. I was sure it was not the money that had enticed Abdul Rahman. He was a young, single man. It was obvious from his clothes, his level of education reflected in his extremely good English, and from his confident bearing that Abdul Rahman was somebody of privilege and wealth in his own society. It seemed to me that he was intrigued with the idea of being part of the enormous electronic broadcast team that had invaded his city.

Abdul Rahman, traditionalist as he was, still had the irreverent sense of humour that marks out most journalists. We were standing on the marble floor of our luxury hotel. It was clear that many of the precious artefacts had been carefully chosen to highlight Arab and, in particular, Kuwaiti culture. Hanging on the walls were daggers and swords, hand-worked in silver and semi-precious stones; there were antique copper trays and drinking vessels that had been painstakingly hammered out in the sun-drenched souks and marketplaces long before crude oil had come to dominate life in Kuwait. The artefacts were really quite lovely and had been tastefully arranged, but there was a hint of cloying nationalism about the display. There was something about it that was both a little self-satisfied and artificial.

The centrepiece of the display was an exquisite silk carpet that hung on the wall in the centre of the gleaming foyer.

Abdul Rahman pointed up to where it hung proudly. 'You see that carpet,' he said. 'It is hand-woven. The knots are very fine. They say the weave can only be tied by the delicate fingers of the most beautiful virgins.'

Abdul Rahman shook his head sadly. 'Sometimes,' he said, 'I wish I were a carpet.'

Dune Buggies

The rows of mangled tanks, trucks and armoured cars stretched out as far as we could see. We had come to film the Iraqi tanks and vehicles that had been destroyed in the Gulf War. The enormous size of this graveyard of devastated military hardware was testimony to the destructive power of the American and coalition forces. Crushed and dented trucks lay on top of one another in piles. Rusted tank barrels stood up against the blue desert sky. Many of the thick armour-plated turrets had been torn open by the fearsome magnesium and titanium-tipped bullets fired from the Allied jets. Steel plate, several inches thick, had been ripped open by these bullets, turning the interiors of the tanks into death traps of searing, white-hot fire.

One of the tanks had 'Diana' written in blue spray paint across its rounded turret. Rotting rubber wheels and corroded tracks were slowly disappearing under waves of white sand. The desert wind whistled softly through the gaps in the jagged edges of the broken machines. The rusting steel carcasses stretched for miles across the desert, silent under the wide blue sky. The vastness of the destruction was a kind of grotesque monument to a post-industrial Ozymandias – a testimony to the mighty despair of war itself.

While Glenn and I filmed, Abdul Rahman wandered through the silent rows of wrecked tanks. We were all mostly silent. There was something frightening about these acres of destruction. They were the ghosts of the war that had started in 1991 and had not ended. It lasted only forty-three days. No one knows exactly how many Iraqis were killed in the Gulf War. The figure could be as high as 85 000 killed and wounded. Out of 500 000 soldiers deployed against Iraq, the Allies had less than 300 casualties, only half of them in combat.

Despite the overwhelming military victory of the Allied forces in the Gulf War, Saddam Hussein remained in power; Arab nations were increasingly suspicious of the West, and of America in particular; and the volatile Palestinian-Israeli conflict was no nearer being solved than it had been before the Gulf War.

For seven years the memory of that war had echoed back and forth across the world. Now we were being dragged to the edge of war again. There was a bitter irony in the fact that a single brutal man, Saddam Hussein, could determine the fate of so much of the world. There was a ghastly genius in his ability to stay in power and it was mirrored by the inability of either the West or the Arab world to do anything about him.

The destruction that lay around us had not achieved it. All the 'smart' bombs, all the titanium-tipped bullets, all the Patriot missiles had failed to remove Saddam Hussein from power. They had liberated Kuwait, but they had failed to improve the lives of the people of Iraq, or to bring peace to the Middle East. Seven years on, and the prospect of a world war – of a dreadful 'clash of civilizations' between the West and Islam – remained a possibility.

For now, the tank graveyard was silent. But 'Operation Desert Thunder' was being carefully planned. President Clinton knew that this time his options were far more limited. Already, it was an open secret that Clinton realized that he couldn't remove Saddam Hussein. The limited goal of Operation Desert Thunder would be to damage the Iraqi infrastructure so badly that they would be unable to make chemical and biological weapons. Then, when the Iraqis had rebuilt their weapons factories, the plan was to bomb them again – a year or so later. There was widespread scepticism as to whether even this regular bombing would do anything meaningful to prevent Saddam Hussein from developing his horrific weapons of mass destruction.

There was a perverse illogic to this campaign. The vast arsenal of the United States and its allies could be used to destroy a country, but not to win a war.

It occurred to me that there was something monstrous hidden within the depths of this new kind of conflict. The politics of the West would not allow their governments to declare war as they had done in the past, and then send the troops out to win it. Public opinion, quite rightly, at the end of the twentieth century was horrified by both the body bags of their own troops coming home and by seeing in the living rooms of their homes the television images of 'collateral damage' – the deaths of innocent civilians caused by the bombs.

But there was an inescapable dilemma contained within the real compassion and horror people felt towards witnessing the death and maiming of the victims of war. It seemed to me that this new kind of limited conflict had ironically added another layer of suffering to the people who found themselves trapped within it.

War has always been horrible. At least, though, in the old way there was the dim knowledge that one day the battles would be over, and there would be peace.

But in this new war, the Iraqi people had been and would be subject to bombing, and to the psychological threat of more bombing, for years, perhaps even for decades. Children were growing up so that the only world they could remember was one where they were caught between the vicious cruelty of Saddam Hussein, and the mercilessness of the sophisticated weapons of the West.

On the road back to Kuwait City we passed a group of SAS soldiers riding in one of their dune buggies, specially adapted for desert warfare. They were heading down the road towards the Iraqi border. Glenn sprang out of the 4x4 with his camera and tripod. I helped him as he scrambled to set up his camera on the side of the road. The SAS soldiers saw us and our camera. The driver lifted his hand and waved angrily at us to stop filming. Glenn kept the camera rolling. The SAS vehicle turned off the tarmac highway and disappeared behind one of the low desert dunes.

Glenn and I breathed a small sigh of relief. 'We got them on tape,' Glenn said cheerfully. We discovered when we got back to the hotel that our pictures were a minor scoop. They were the first visual evidence anybody had of the special forces being deployed in the region. There was even something of a sensitive situation with the British military censors. They sat in their camouflage uniforms and peered glumly at our shots on the monitors in the BBC office on the eighth floor. Glenn and I kept a low profile at the back of the room where the edit machines and video monitors were. We didn't want to be identified as the people who had taken the shots. Neither of us wanted to be seen by the censors as potential troublemakers – not quite so soon after we had arrived in Kuwait, anyway.

But in the end the officers decided not to be heavy-handed. It was impossible to tell from our pictures where the SAS soldiers were actually going, or even exactly which unit they belonged to. They agreed to allow our shots to appear on the news.

It was a small incident, but one which illustrated a crucial point about Operation Desert Thunder and the images that would be allowed to come out of it. Because we were working with the BBC, our focus was naturally on the British rather than the US troop build-up. But both armies were determined to control the footage that the public back home would see. There was a genuinely delicate balance to be struck between the public's right to know what their troops were doing, and between endangering the lives of British or American soldiers by carelessly revealing information about troop movements or deployments.

Even the few seconds of footage of SAS soldiers we had filmed was of extreme interest to the military authorities. If war did break out, they would be even more determined to keep our images under their control.

It's a difficult issue. I believe it is our job to keep the public informed. We're not soldiers. I know from speaking to a former SAS officer a year or so later that the military knows too that we're not soldiers. Their attitude is to let us get on with what we are doing, unless they judge that by filming we will genuinely threaten the lives of their troops or the success of their operations. Then, as he said. 'We'll ask you to leave the area. And if you don't, then we'll hold you until you are decontaminated.'

To be decontaminated is to be held incommunicado until the knowledge you have of the operation in question is useless – until the operation is over, and that, of course, could be weeks.

The approach Glenn and I took for the next couple of weeks as the crisis unfolded was to film what we could, as and when we could. Luckily, we never had to be 'decontaminated'.

That main news of the day was that President Clinton had warned that he was moving closer to ordering air strikes. 'Force can never be the first answer,' he said. 'But sometimes it's the only answer.'

UN Secretary General Kofi Annan announced that he would be leaving at the end of the week for Baghdad in a last-ditch effort to persuade Saddam Hussein to compromise and to avoid air strikes.

That evening Glenn and I went out for dinner. We teamed up with Vincent Magwenya, a friend and colleague from South Africa. The three of us drove first through the wide streets that ran near the coast. We turned on to the wide double highway of Arabian Gulf Street. Large American cars flowed at high speed back and forth along the road. The lights of the city gleamed on one side; the dark expanse of the Gulf lay silent on the other. All along the waterfront were a series of American franchise joints. We pulled into the parking lot of a burger joint with its blinking neon lights above the glass doorway. The place was packed. There was something that was both comforting and deeply unfamiliar about the scene. As we walked in and headed towards a table, just about every person in the restaurant turned to watch us, two white men with short-cropped hair and a tall black African. Even we could tell that we must have looked very much like a group of American soldiers, and our presence in the restaurant could only have inspired the kind of endless speculation that the rapid build-up of forces in Kuwait was leading to. Even if some people realized we were journalists, we would have inspired exactly the same level of speculation. Kuwait was crawling with soldiers and journalists. And we were there for one reason only: their country was heading yet again towards the edge of war.

Only a few days before, the Information Minister of Kuwait, Sheikh Saud al-Nasser al-Sabah, had tried to calm the fears that were steadily rising in this small country. 'You will witness more troops arriving,' he had announced. 'They are not coming to harm you, but to protect Kuwait and its land.'

The interior of the restaurant had been copied, or imported, in exact detail from the States. Hanging on the walls were the framed pictures of sports stars, old ice hockey sticks and baseball bats. The booths were lined with oak and green leather. The bar had a long brass rail and a shiny row of pumps to dispense draught beer – only here there was no beer, the pumps dispensed fizzy drinks and fruit juice cocktails. It made me think, though, of what one of the Kuwaiti liaison officers at the press centre in the hotel had told me the day before. 'You can get anything you want in Kuwait. But it must just be under the table.'

American rock music was playing out of speakers artfully concealed in the ceiling and the atmosphere was one of excited chatter and laughter.

We ordered steaks and non-alcoholic daiquiris. I found the place strangely disquieting – there was something hollow about sitting on the edge of the Arabian Gulf (or the Persian Gulf, depending on your perspective) in a faux American setting. Of course, I hadn't expected camels or fragrant hardwood fires under the stars in the desert, but I couldn't help feeling that something was forced and artificial about the whole place.

But no one around me cared what I thought. Everyone was clearly having a good time. At first sight, it seemed a perfect example of the intrusion of Western culture. There were very few women who had covered their heads and all the young women were wearing jeans and Western blouses. The men too were wearing jeans and T-shirts. Many were smoking Marlboro and drinking fizzy drinks and milkshakes through straws.

It was only when I looked closer that I saw the pattern of seating that reflected a cultural certainty much deeper than the watery bottom of a Coke glass. Husbands and wives sat with their children, but nowhere else did men and women sit together. The young men in their T-shirts were grouped around one table, while nearby sat a group of pretty young women, often with an older woman discreetly seated among them. There were no dating couples, not even any flirting.

My steak, when it came, was tasteless. It had been frozen somewhere and shipped in. It seemed to me that there was a kind of schizophrenia frozen in the air for everyone in that restaurant – both us outsiders and the Kuwaitis. The force of the shiny, brass-railed and neon new could no longer be denied, but the old ways were still powerful. This world was filled with new *things*: air-conditioned cars, stereo-systems, and sweet, non-alcoholic daiquiris, but they had not replaced the old beliefs and customs. Within living memory Kuwait had been little more than a small collection of mud houses and a fishing fleet of dhows.

It was the money from the oil that had brought all these new things. But it was war and the threat of another war that was bringing so many new and uncertain fears.

Alone in my hotel room that night, I read in the *Arab Times* that Martha Gellhorn had died at the age of eighty-nine. Martha Gellhorn was often called the 'first' female war correspondent. Whether she was actually the first or not mattered little to me. It was the power of her insights and the clarity of her writing that had inspired me.

What a life she had. In 1930, at the age of twenty-one, she had arrived in Europe determined to become a foreign correspondent. In the years that followed she covered every major war of her time, from the Spanish Civil War, World War II, the Arab-Israeli War, to Vietnam and Central America. She was married three times, and bore one child, a son, George. One of her husbands was Ernest Hemingway, but she became a successful novelist as well as a famous journalist in her own right.

For some years now, I had owned a copy of her classic work *The Face of War*. I would dip into it often, just to remind myself of how the world had been and of how it was possible to write so clearly and so bravely about the things one had witnessed.

The introduction she wrote to the 1959 edition of *The Face of War* is to me the finest description of what war journalism is, or should be. I read it often, and every time it gives me some new insight.

In the space of a few hundred words, she charts the course of every journalist's moral life. We all begin, as she did, very young, believing in 'the perfectability of man, and in progress'. So many of us think, as she did, of 'journalism as a guiding light'. We hope that if 'people were told the truth, if dishonor and injustice were clearly shown to them, they would at once demand the saving action, punishment of wrongdoers, and care for the innocent'. Like her, we tend to imagine 'public opinion as a solid force, something like a tornado, always ready to blow on the side of the angels'.

It is the destruction of that 'energetic hope' that is damaging to the souls of many journalists. Soon we discover that our words or images have little effect. It is when, after having witnessed so many wars and so much destruction, we learn that the 'guiding light of journalism was no stronger than a glow-worm' that many of us slide into cynicism, even bitterness.

Martha Gellhorn never allowed that to happen to her, and that is why her writing remains so powerful today. 'War,' she wrote, 'is a malignant disease, an idiocy, a prison, and the pain it causes is beyond telling or imagining; but war was our condition and our history, the place we had to live in.'

But it was in her closing words that I found much of my own inspiration as a writer and a journalist. 'The point,' she wrote, 'of these articles is that they are true; they tell what I saw. Perhaps they will remind others, as they remind me, of the face of war. We can hardly be reminded too much or too often. I believe that memory and imagination, not nuclear weapons, are the great deterrents.'

The Enemy in the Desert

Angry shouts. Accusations. An embarrassed silence from the men up on stage behind the microphones. The cameras panned wildly, the images on the screen became slightly confused as the protesters began to chant. 'One, two, three, four, we don't want your racist war.'

Top officials in the Clinton administration were being harassed at Ohio State University. Secretary of State Madeleine Albright, Defence Secretary William Cohen and national security adviser Sandy Berger were being lambasted live on CNN. Out of an audience of some 6 000 Americans, there were perhaps 200 or so protesters, but their message was being carried across the world. There were deep divisions even in the conservative heartland of the United States concerning a new war against Iraq. The images flashed on the TV screens in the hotel all day. They were being shown on TV screens in the souks and kebab restaurants of Kuwait City, and no doubt all over the Middle East and Gulf region.

Anger, and doubts about the war for the whole world to see. It was an admirable display of the open society that Americans so value. But nothing could have been worse for the Clinton administration's aims. If we could see his officials being publicly taken to task then so, too, could Saddam Hussein. What would he make of it? was the question many people were asking. Would he conclude, like so many other dictators have done in the past, that Americans were somehow 'soft'? Would he confuse the ability to tolerate open debate with uncertainty and an inability to act?

It was only a day or two before Kofi Annan was to head for Baghdad for his last-ditch attempt at persuading Saddam Hussein to back down peacefully. The images were out now, and everybody had seen them, over and over again. How they would be interpreted was unclear. There was a deep and potentially bitter irony contained within the images. The protesters had no doubt chosen to make their mark in front of the TV cameras to gain maximum exposure for their cause. But it was entirely possible that the very same pictures of their vocal demonstration would embolden Saddam Hussein.

Television images are difficult enough to control, but their impact is impossible to predict. It could well turn out that in demanding peace, the protesters had now, paradoxically, made war certain.

Saddam Hussein could be sure of one thing. No matter what devastation was wreaked on his country by American and British bombers, he would remain in power.

President Clinton had made it clear that his aim was limited to being able to 'substantially reduce or delay' Iraq's potential to produce chemical and biological weapons. But there was a report in *The Times* of London that as many as fifty leading Iraqi scientists and technicians had already been moved out of the country in anticipation of American air strikes.

Many had gone to Libya, Algeria or other North African countries. According to the report, the families of the scientists had been forced to stay behind in Iraq to prevent them from defecting.

Intelligence on the exact size and location of the production sites for weapons of mass destruction was limited. One of the biggest problems in identifying such sites was the fact that much of the equipment used to develop germ warfare weapons in particular could also be used for legitimate industries. The ordinary tools of any agricultural or medical laboratory could just as easily be used to make deadly payloads of anthrax or plague bacteria. It would be difficult to isolate sites as solely dedicated to the manufacture of chemical or biological weapons. The risks of bombing factories or sites that were used for genuine chemical or medical manufacture were great. World opinion, especially Arab opinion, would soon turn against America and Britain when the new TV pictures of destroyed baby-milk factories started coming out.

In the meantime, while President Clinton and Tony Blair were making their plans for a series of air strikes against Iraq, the Iraqi armed forces were busily hiding their tanks and missile launchers. The Iraqi air force had about 300 planes that could be used to hit back at Allied aircraft. Many of those were carefully hidden in bomb-proof bunkers.

At the same time, Saddam Hussein himself was reportedly taking no chances. He routinely used doubles to confuse anyone who might try to assassinate him. He had a number of safe houses scattered around the country. He would choose one of them to sleep in at the last minute, and he never slept in the same place twice. Even if one of the unstated American or British aims was to assassinate him with a smart bomb, it would be almost impossible for them to know for sure where he was at any one time.

Every day the airwaves swarmed with pictures of President Clinton, Tony Blair, Madeleine Albright, Sandy Berger, Kofi Annan – talking, explaining their thoughts, artfully revealing pieces of their strategy that might scare Saddam Hussein into doing what they wanted him to. But from Saddam Hussein himself there was almost nothing. Silence and invisibility seemed to be his strategy. His opponents could talk and explain all they wanted. He would watch, and wait, giving them no clue as to what his true intentions were.

He seemed to understand instinctively how, in a world of images, it is also what we do *not* see that tantalizes us and leads us on, deeper and deeper into the endless labyrinth of what we hope to see.

The winter sun glimmered on the desert sand. Glenn and I and Abdul Rahman were heading north up the Basra highway towards the border with Iraq. We were simply cruising with the camera. Correspondent Ben

Brown had asked us to try and get as close as we could to the Iraqi border. 'If you can find a way to get shots of the border that would be perfect,' he told us back at the hotel. 'If not, just get whatever pictures you can. We need something different for the Nine.'

On the eastern horizon, oil wells sent up columns of black smoke into the clear sky. Towering power lines ran across the wide expanses of flat desert. It was only about 80 kilometres between Kuwait City and the Iraqi border. There was hardly anyone in sight for miles around. It was easy to understand how quickly the Iraqis had taken Kuwait. It was the perfect terrain for a land invasion, the highway itself was a wide, perfect strip of tarmac. A spearhead force could come rolling down this road at lightning speed. The rearguard could spread out rapidly across the flat desert meeting little or no resistance as they came. That was exactly the way it happened on August 2, 1990. At 2 am, the first Iraqi tanks crashed through the border. They reached Kuwait City before sunrise, and by midday they had overrun the whole country to the Saudi border.

Traditionally, the Arabs knew the desert the way ancient sailors knew the sea. The limitless expanses and the shifting, waterless dunes had provided the perfect cover for Arab guerrilla war for well over a thousand years. The lightning speed of their attacks and their fleet-footed retreat into the desert had brought Arab armies victory over dozens of enemies – from their defeats of the Byzantines to their final winning of independence from the Turks in the early twentieth century.

But the desert brought no safety to tiny Kuwait. Abdul Rahman seemed to be reading my thoughts. 'You can see how easy it was for the Iraqi tanks,' he said, looking out over the flatness of the terrain. 'We could do nothing to stop them.' Abdul Rahman, like many Kuwaitis who had the means, had fled into exile when the Iraqis invaded. He didn't like to talk about it. I guessed he had the mixed feelings of all exiles – a volatile mixture of relief at having escaped the worst and guilt at not having shared it with those who stayed behind.

But he was back now, and this time he would face whatever it was that the future held. I didn't know much about Abdul Rahman, but I could tell that he had the ability to hide his thoughts. His expression, as he stared out over the desert, was surprisingly revealing. Abdul Rahman was worried. It was as if this drive up the highway was bringing back many memories and setting off new fears. Once you were outside Kuwait City, beyond the hotel, the immaculate ring roads, and the American-style restaurants on Arabian Gulf Street, you could see how little there was to Kuwait. Oil wells and a tiny patch of desert – that was all there was. There were no mountain ranges for partisans to hide out in. The country was open for the taking. It was only the presence of American and British troops that guaranteed the existence of Kuwait. It was a geography of perfect vulnerability – the same vulnerability that was reflected in Abdul Rahman's face.

We were still some distance from the Iraqi frontier when we came across the first layer of defences. A vast ditch had been dug in the desert and tons of sand piled up in front of it. It stretched east and west across the desert as far as the eye could see. The piles of bulldozed sand formed a massive defensive berm against the advance of an Iraqi army.

We stopped. Glenn took the camera out. We weren't sure if we were allowed to film the berm, but there was no one about to see us. Abdul Rahman and I watched while he set up the camera and began taking a few shots.

'If the Iraqis come,' Abdul Rahman said, 'they will fill the ditch with oil and set it alight.'

It seemed an extraordinary irony that in a world of AWACS, smart bombs and laser-guided missiles, such a medieval strategy would be employed. Abdul Rahman seemed comforted by seeing this ditch and the berm in front of it. Here was something concrete that he could see that would be used to defend him and his family. I could see that in its own way it made a kind of sense. Kuwait would be deploying the only meaningful weapon at its disposal – oil. An enormous fire of crude oil blazing across the desert would be a formidable, terrifying barrier.

A little further down the road we saw in the distance a row of tank barrels standing at an angle against the horizon. They were all pointing north, towards Iraq. Glenn turned the 4x4 off the road. We headed across the desert towards the tanks.

'It is a Kuwaiti regiment,' Abdul Rahman said. 'The tanks are Yugoslavian.'

Yugoslavian. It must have been close on a decade since the former Yugoslavia exported any armaments. I'm no expert on weapons, but I couldn't help wondering why the Kuwaitis would be using virtually obsolete tanks. Later, I asked around about it. No one seemed to know the answer, but it underscored to me the fragility of the Kuwaiti defences.

There were perhaps half a dozen tanks parked in deep pits dug into the desert. The sand had been piled in front of the pits as an extra defensive measure. The whole position was semi-permanent. I supposed that in the event of an attack, these tanks would hold the line against the Iraqi advance for as long as they could. Perhaps for as long as it took to flood the ditch behind the long desert berm with oil. The soldiers in this position ran the risk of being trapped between an advancing Iraqi army and the blazing oil behind them.

There was a tent pitched in the centre of the formation of tanks. A few soldiers gathered around as we drove up.

'See if you can get permission for us to film them,' Glenn said quietly to

Abdul Rahman.

We were greeted by a sergeant major. '*Salaam-aleikum*,' he said, putting out his hand.

'*Wa aleikum as-salaam*,' I replied, exhausting my Arabic immediately. The sergeant major seemed pleased, all the same. We shook hands. He lightly touched his heart with the palm of his right hand and then turned to greet Glenn. It was the first time I had seen the traditional Arabic handshake. It was a gesture that stopped everything else. For that brief moment you felt the ancient courtesies of guest-friendship in a way that has been lost in Western culture. It was a deliberate pause in the order of business. It lasted no longer than a single heartbeat, but it was a sacrosanct moment of gentleness that was honoured between you, no matter what might happen in the future.

We shook hands all around, but he didn't speak English, and Glenn and I didn't speak any Arabic. We smiled awkwardly.

'He is inviting us inside to drink tea,' Abdul Rahman told us. The soldiers ushered us towards the tent. We bent down at the entrance to take off our hiking boots. The outside of the tent had been carefully pegged down and sealed against wind and sand. The floor inside was covered with a variety of handwoven rugs. Large embroidered cushions had been arranged in a horseshoe shape around the walls of the tent. In one corner a soldier was leaning against the cushions smoking a bubbling brass water pipe known in Arabic as *argileh*.

We stepped inside in our stockinged feet. The sergeant major gestured for us to sit down. Some of the other soldiers hastily brought more cushions and bolsters for us to sit against.

Abdul Rahman and the sergeant major sat at one end of the horseshoe. Glenn and I and the soldiers arranged ourselves beneath them.

At the back of the tent was a large ammunition box. Sugar, tea and a kettle stood on top of it. In the opposite corner stood an enormous communal *argileh*. It was as tall as a man and had ten or so pipes curling out of its central rounded water bowl. Beside it stood a small TV set. The aerial poked out of a corner of the tent.

A soldier handed out small glasses of tea on a brass tray. The tea was dark and strong. It was sweet and flavoured with cardamom.

Abdul Rahman and the sergeant major did most of the talking. Every now and then, the sergeant major would ask us a question and Abdul Rahman would translate.

The problem was that there were no senior officers present. The sergeant major was polite, hospitable but absolutely firm. We could not film his tanks or his men without clearance from a senior officer. In the end, we gave up. It was clear that we were never going to get permission to film them.

Abdul Rahman rocked his tea glass gently back and forth. 'You should do the same,' he told Glenn and me. 'It shows we have had enough tea.'

The soldiers waved at us as we drove off into the desert and headed back for the highway.

As we drove north the light was beginning to fade. Further south, nearer the city, the Kuwaiti police had simply waved us through their checkpoints. But as we drew closer to the Iraqi border, the checkpoints grew more frequent. We had scarcely passed through one and left it out of sight behind us when another loomed up in front of us. I guessed they were probably planned that way. At these checkpoints our reception varied. At one or two of them we were stopped. The policemen demanded our press cards and then let us carry on.

We had still not seen a single American or British tank, jeep or soldier. They were deliberately keeping a low profile. As we drove we passed through layer upon layer of the Kuwaiti defences. The psychology of the people we met changed as we passed through each layer. The closer to the Iraqi border we got, the more suspicious our reception was. The friendliness of the soldiers at the tank outpost had been left behind in the lengthening shadows of the desert. Now we were greeted curtly by the policemen on the road. They demanded our identification and stared in at the back windows to see what we were carrying in our car.

We reached the final layer. A checkpoint somewhere close to the border. 'Don't try and film here,' Abdul Rahman said.

The policemen looked at our press cards. Abdul Rahman rolled down the window. He talked for a long time to the two officers. Then he turned back to us.

'We should go now. We cannot go any further.'

Glenn shrugged. We had been expecting it. He turned the car around and we headed back down the highway. The policemen stood in the middle of the tarmac, watching us until they disappeared out of sight behind a low ridge.

The shadows on the gravelly desert began to stretch across the sand. We came to an old gas station about halfway between the border and Kuwait City. We had hardly noticed it in our eagerness to press forward on the way up towards the border. Now we stopped. The gas station had been utterly destroyed during the Gulf War. The walls were shattered. The concrete columns hung suspended macabrely in the air, their rusting steel reinforcing rods twisted and mangled. Artillery shells had smashed through what had once been offices and rooms. Heavy calibre bullet holes had punched into the walls. There was no evidence of small arms fire. The battle over this gas station had been fought with heavy weapons. The defenders had abandoned it without hand to hand fighting.

It was clear that this gas station was one of the buildings that had been hit by Allied planes during the Gulf War.

Glenn stopped the car and took out the camera. We had no worthwhile pictures from a day out in the desert, so he wanted to get some shots of this bomb-damaged building.

In the soft light of the late afternoon a single steel helmet lay on the ground. It was rusting and cracked at the rim. It was the only evidence of the Iraqi soldiers who had taken over and manned this lonely building. It was the only evidence of the men who had been here when the missiles struck.

An eerie sense of déjà vu crept over me. I felt like I had been here, at this place, before. Then in a sweeping moment of comprehension, I understood. For every single one of the forty-three days of the Gulf War, starting with that first afternoon at the restaurant in Manhattan, I had watched on television as Kuwait and Iraq had been pounded by Allied bombers.

I had been safely living in the US and in South Africa at the time, but I *remembered* the Gulf War. The grainy black and white images from the bombers' cameras had become a part of my memories. Somewhere amongst that enormous flow of images that had flashed past me on the TV screen thousands of kilometres away had been the image of this building being destroyed. Or, at least, the images of dozens of other buildings just like it. I could see those images now. The cross hairs of the bomb sight swooping over the target. The sudden zooming in as the plane dived closer. The white streaks of the missiles on the screen and then the grey dust cloud as the warheads exploded.

This shattered wreck of a building and the empty, abandoned helmet were the stark reality at the other end of those television images. I had never been here, but the power of those images in my mind could not be denied. I, like millions of people across the globe, had witnessed the Gulf War on my television screen; it was an integral part of my experience of the world I lived in.

Or so I had thought; in fact, it was the *imagining* of the Gulf War that had been my experience. Now I found myself standing on the shifting border between memory and imagination. Television had given me tangible, concrete memories of a war I had never been to, of a war I had never even *seen*.

'The light is great,' Glenn said. 'The pictures will be fantastic.'

I picked up the tripod and followed him. He squeezed off a few shots of the ruined building. Then he turned and pointed. On the far horizon a line of tanks was moving against the skyline. The tanks were moving north towards Iraq, silhouetted against the red ball of the sinking sun. It was an exquisite panorama.

These were exactly the kind of shots the Nine O'Clock News was looking for. The pictures would show perfectly the military build-up that was happening in the desert of Kuwait. There was the potential of a new war here, and the shots of these tanks were proof of it.

We knew, as we filmed, that these pictures would make the evening news. These were real tanks moving in a real desert sunset. The images were beautiful and compelling. These tanks were what people wanted to see. They were the way people *imagined* the build-up towards war in the desert to be. Later, when the bombing started, they would demand to see the heavily censored grainy black and white images from the bombers' cameras. It wouldn't just be ghoulishness – although there would be some of that too. No matter which side of the war they stood on, the world would want to see what was happening. It was part of their lives now, part of their experience. Television had made the world that way. Without seeing the pictures on their screens, it would be hard for them to believe in the reality of the war.

We wanted to drive closer, but we couldn't. We weren't supposed to be filming tanks. The real desert, too, was dangerous. It was filled with land mines from the Gulf War which had been lost among the shifting dunes.

The Souk of Weapons

Kofi Annan was on his way to Baghdad. He was to present a final offer to Saddam Hussein. To avoid war, Saddam Hussein would have to agree to allow weapons inspectors to all the major sites of contention, the so-called 'presidential sites'. At the same time, the inspectors would have to be accompanied by diplomats from the permanent members of the UN Security Council. The US reserved the right to reject any limits on what the inspectors were allowed to see.

The French were strongly behind this deal. It was a hard one, but if anyone could get Saddam Hussein to agree to it, then Kofi Annan would be the man.

Opposition to US and British air strikes was growing all over the Arab and Muslim world. China and Russia had already condemned the idea of air strikes against Iraq.

That evening after coming back from the desert, Glenn and I set off by foot from our hotel. Immediately beyond the gold souk was a maze of streets. Street crime was scarcely heard of in Kuwait City, so Glenn and I were content to wander in the maze of streets and trust our sense of direction to get us back to the hotel.

Development in the second half of the twentieth century had come rapidly to Kuwait. That, and the destruction caused by the Iraqis in the

Gulf War meant that there was nothing of the old city left. There are some beautiful mosques, but even they are of modern construction. Kuwait City today is all concrete, steel and neon sandwiched between the gleaming multilane freeways.

Alexander's Greeks had come this way. He died in Babylon in 323 BC, only days before what he had planned as his final campaign – the conquest of Arabia. Almost immediately, his empire began to collapse. His generals and viceroys began warring amongst themselves. Somehow, within that chaos, a Greek colony was set up on the island of Failaka. It was a strategic point for shipping then as it still is today. A small but prosperous community set itself up and lived for centuries on Failaka.

It was the coming of the al-Sabah family that began the history of modern Kuwait. They arrived some time in the late seventeenth or early eighteenth century. The name Kuwait derives from the diminutive for Kut, a small fort or walled village. Before the invention of the internal combustion engine and the need for oil, there was little change in Kuwait. For centuries, people traded, fished and dived for pearls, much as they had done since the days of the ancient Greeks.

But Kuwait and Failaka island had strategic value. The Ottomans claimed Kuwait as part of their empire, but they had little strength left to enforce their claim. Still, they persisted. In 1899, the ruler of Kuwait, Sheikh Mubarak Al Sabah Al Sabah or Mubarak the Great, signed a treaty with Britain. It served the interests of both countries. The Kuwaitis promised not to negotiate with any foreign power without consulting Britain first. Britain promised to guarantee the territorial integrity of Kuwait. That stopped both the Germans and the Turks from extending their territory and railways into the headwaters of the Persian Gulf and so threatening the outer boundaries of Britain's Indian empire.

In the 1920s, Britain and its promises were put to the test. Abdul Aziz Bin Abdul Rahman Al-Saud had set out to reconquer the land of his ancestors, Saudi Arabia. As his conquests and his power grew, Abdul Aziz tried to conquer Kuwait. The *ikhwan*, his army of Islamist warriors, were set loose on the people of Kuwait. The tiny kingdom would certainly have been brutally absorbed into modern Saudi Arabia if it hadn't been for the British. They managed to negotiate a treaty with Abdul Aziz that recognized the independence of Kuwait, in return for taking much of the land that Kuwait had claimed for itself.

After World War II, when it was discovered that Kuwait held nearly 20 per cent of the world's oil reserves, the country changed forever. By the late 1970s what had been little more than a fishing village in 1940 had an income of nearly $10 billion. It was no wonder there was nothing left now of the old mud-walled town that travellers like Freya Stark had visited less than a generation before.

Such enormous wealth did nothing to enhance Kuwait's security. In 1961, when Kuwait became a fully independent state, the Emir of Iraq claimed Kuwait as part of his territory. The British came to the rescue again. A small detachment of soldiers deterred the Iraqis from invading Kuwait. In 1973 Iraq invaded again, but they were persuaded by the Arab League to pull out. The Iraqi invasion of Kuwait was detracting from their bigger goal – an invasion of Israel.

Then there was August 2, 1990.

The map we had of the city was not much use. It showed the English names of many of the streets as Street No 12, or Street No 17. Most of the signs were in Arabic, so we simply walked, taking in the atmosphere of the streets around us. People seemed subdued, but they were friendly towards us. Often men would raise their hand in a casual greeting, or shout out 'hello' as we walked past. We saw very few women on the streets, but many of those we did see were wearing Western clothes. They never greeted us like the men. Instead, they pretended not to notice that we were there at all.

The coffee shops and kebab restaurants were filled with men. They were playing backgammon, smoking *argileh*, reading newspapers and drinking coffee or tea. Almost every one of these gathering places had a large TV screen placed at the far end of the room. All of them were tuned to news programmes and well over three-quarters of the men were watching. They sat in their plastic chairs staring at the screen. The images were a disturbing rerun of the first stages of the last war: planes taking off from aircraft carriers, Arab leaders in dressed in expensive *dishdasha* and *gutra* emerging from black limousines, White House press briefings, tanks in the desert.

There had been mixed feelings about the invasion of Kuwait. The truth was, Kuwaitis had a bad reputation amongst many in the Gulf region. Their wealth, their coddled lifestyle where everything was taken care of, the fact that they were so reliant on America to protect them – all of these things counted against them in the public opinion of many Arab states.

Kuwaitis were accused by many of being lazy, arrogant and spoiled. What their detractors seldom mentioned was that despite some serious disputes between the liberals and the ruling al-Sabah family over how far democracy should be extended, there was not one *single* Kuwaiti who had been willing to serve in the sham government imposed by Saddam Hussein after his invasion. It was a record any nation could be justly proud of.

Still, I wondered how many people had painful memories of the past. During the Gulf War, nearly 6 000 Kuwaitis were dragged off to captivity in Iraq. Now, seven years later, over 600 of them were still being detained in Iraq. During the Iraqi occupation of Kuwait, hundreds of homes, shops and businesses were ransacked and destroyed. Many public buildings were systematically looted and destroyed, including the National Museum, the National Assembly Building and the Emir's palace, parts of which dated back a hundred years.

Much worse, though, was the treatment of the Kuwaiti people. Hundreds of women were raped. Random beatings were meted out on the streets and hundreds of Kuwaiti men were tortured and humiliated during interrogation. Around one thousand Kuwaitis were murdered by the Iraqis. Their deaths were never recorded. Their families were never told what happened. The bodies lie in unmarked graves.

At the end of the war, a man-made apocalypse swept across Kuwait. The Iraqis intentionally opened the valves at a number of Kuwait's oilfields. Crude oil spilled out into the seas around Kuwait, creating a vast poisonous slick half the size of Kuwait itself. As the war raged, they also systematically began setting the Kuwaiti oil wells alight. By the end of the war, nearly 100 oil wells were pouring toxic smoke and fumes into the air. The black cloud from the burning oil was so large that it literally blotted out the sun.

But there was a largely untold story too, and it was one of Kuwaiti guilt. After the war ended hundreds of arbitrary arrests, instances of torture and killings were made by the Kuwaiti resistance and the newly returned Kuwaiti police and security services. Most of the victims were Palestinians. They had stayed on in the country after the Iraqi invasion when the Palestinian leadership had endorsed Saddam Hussein's invasion. Many, no doubt, had collaborated with the Iraqis, but just as many had stayed on because they had nowhere else to go.

After the war, they were brutally treated. There were reports, too, of Iraqi and Sudanese citizens being tortured. Amnesty International recorded at least ten extra-judicial killings but they suspected that 'scores' more had occurred. Their investigators were hampered at almost every turn in trying to investigate the reports of abduction, torture and killing.

As Glenn and I walked past the teeming shops and coffee houses, I knew that there were still many untold stories of suffering and of hate locked up inside the brooding silence that stared at the TV screens. But tonight it was not memory that occupied most minds, it was the anxious wondering about what might happen next. Around us was the silent fear that the destruction and killing would begin again.

The winter weather was beginning to lift. The air was the warmest it had been since we had arrived, and Glenn and I walked for a long time through the streets of the city. We came to a souk where weapons were being sold. It was already dark, but people were still working. Dozens of men were sewing leather holsters and ornate gun cases. Shotguns and other weapons were for sale behind carefully locked cabinets. Rows of colourful 12 bore and other cartridges were lined up on the shelves.

Further along was the street of the metal workers. Here a gleaming array of pots and pans and coffee urns spilled out from the stores on to the streets. In this street in another age we would have been surrounded by the sound of tiny hammers beating out the shapes of these utensils, but the kitchenware now on display had been imported from China and the other mass markets of Asia.

We walked past a shop selling cosmetics. There were three women inside, all of them covered in expensive silk cloaks. They were completely veiled. They were buying incense. The shop owner had lit a number of different cones and the women were leaning over to smell the different scents. The shopkeeper gestured to us to come inside. We hesitated, but he held up one of the cones for us to smell. The women moved aside and watched as we lumbered into the shop. We worried that we might be causing offence, but their dark eyes flashed with amusement at the sight of first Glenn, and then me, leaning with our noses pointed over the cones of incense.

'Hmmn,' Glenn said. 'Very good, very good.'

'You buy?'

'No, not tonight,' Glenn said. There was a muffled laugh from the corner of the shop where the women were clustered. We went back out on to the street, leaving them to conclude their business with the shopkeeper.

Finally we stopped at the Café Walima. It was one of the few places to have retained something of the atmosphere of old Kuwait. The walls were made of what looked like mud, but was probably tinted cement. Wooden doorways with iron hinges were set into the walls.

Benches had been arranged around an open square. They were covered in traditional cushions and bolsters just like the ones we had sat against in the Kuwaiti army tent.

We ordered *argileh* and tea. The waiters bustled around, showing us how to use the steel tongs to light the sweet, cherry-flavoured tobacco with a glowing piece of charcoal. I had given up smoking years before, but I wanted to give the *argileh* a try. I soon became light-headed with the nicotine and the effort of pulling the smoke through the water.

'It is very clean, this smoke,' one of the men sitting nearby said. 'Much better than cigarettes. The water takes everything bad out of the smoke. It is cool in your mouth.'

I felt a mild dizziness, which, I had to admit, was extremely calming. There was even a barely detectable narcotic effect which allowed me to float slightly, at peace with everything around me.

'Very relaxing,' I mumbled, exhaling a mouthful of sweet, cloying smoke.

The man smiled. 'We keep our traditions, but you can also see how things are changing in Arabic culture. The religious people are trying to keep certain things on the one hand, but the liberals are gaining on the other.'

I thought of the women we had just seen in the cosmetics shop. There were none of them here tonight, I observed. Only men.

The man took a drag on his *argileh*. 'In Kuwait there is no rule against women – it is only custom that prevents them from coming here. On the Arabian Gulf Street you can see more modern restaurants and coffee shops. There you can see women smoking.'

I knew that, on the one hand, even in Kuwait's limited version of democracy women could not vote. On the other, nearly half of its university students were women. They were allowed to drive themselves and well over a third of the Kuwaiti professional workforce was made up of women.

We smoked for a while in silence. The men had not introduced themselves and we had not felt any pressure to do so. There was a comfortable atmosphere around us, but we could feel the same curiosity that we had encountered at the burger restaurant.

To understand Kuwait, one had to see the patterns of conquest that had defined its history. This tiny chunk of desert had been subject to claim and counter-claim for centuries. Kuwait would never be powerful enough to protect itself. It had always relied on bigger powers to protect it and to guarantee its existence. Even within living memory, Kuwaiti history was a palimpsest of fear. For the whole of the twentieth century they had been threatened by their neighbours. First it had been the Turks, then the Saudis, and now the Iraqis who had tried to swallow up both their land and whatever sense of identity they had managed to forge from their uncertain history.

For all that time it was the British and now the Americans who were guaranteeing their nationhood. Everyone we had met had been extremely, almost overwhelmingly, polite and friendly, but I doubted whether I would ever know what the Kuwaitis truly thought of Westerners. It must, I thought, have been a strange kind of pride in the self that relied so utterly on the strength of outsiders, and on cutting deals with whoever could provide protection.

My thoughts were interrupted by my neighbour. 'Saddam blew up this place in the war,' he said. 'It is very old, a part of our culture. So we had to rebuild it.'

'You should see something else of our city,' his companion said, leaning forward on his bench. 'There is another place like this near the Souk Mayi – the Water Market.'

The cold night wind came out of the desert and swept between the buildings. Glenn and I walked back to the hotel through the darkened streets. Prides of tiny feral cats yowled and crawled through drains, gathering on the rubbish dumpsters that lay on the sidewalks waiting to be taken away.

The only other people walking on the streets so late were Asian workers. Police cars roared along the wide streets, darting suddenly into the smaller side streets. They had searchlights that the cop in the passenger seat controlled. The harsh white beams arced along the sides of the tall buildings as the cops roamed the streets. They let us go, but every time they saw one of the Asians, they pinned him down in the light and jumped out to search him.

It was an ugly thing to see. It had echoes of the treatment of Palestinians and others after the end of the Gulf War. It was one more layer in the state of war that was building up around us.

Saddam's Chips

Not everyone was taking the growing threat of war seriously. The hotel was crawling with bored tabloid hacks, desperate for a story.

In the mirrored confines of the lift early one morning two of the British broadsheet journalists were earnestly discussing the prospects for peace emerging out of Kofi Annan's last visit to Saddam Hussein.

Towering above us all was one of the tabloid reporters. He was definitely of the old school. He was a huge man, with greying hair and an enormous pot belly from frequent visits to the local pub.

'Anyone for breakfast, then?' he bellowed at the two much younger broadsheet writers. 'I'll have a coffee and a *naan*.'

One of his colleagues had accompanied an official Ministry of Defence tour to one of the British army bases. The reporters had been allowed to photograph the planes and the troops marching, but they had been given very little opportunity to have any real contact with the troops.

The tabloid hack had little interest in the planes and the official statistics. He couldn't find a story that would suit him. He was almost in despair until one of the senior visitors decided to put on something of a public relations show for the press.

'Any problems?' he asked the assembled troops.

'Well, sir,' one of them replied, 'we're getting tired of the food. We want chips, but every day it's just rice, rice, and more rice.'

The headlines on the London streets the next day were predictable.

'SADDAM'S HAD HIS CHIPS, BUT OUR BOYS HAVEN'T.'

Out in the desert we could hear the stealth bombers now. They flew so high that when we looked up we could see only the empty blue sky. The noise of their engines was a distant booming roar that echoed down towards us in layers of sound.

We were filming at the Al-Mutla ridge. It was a low range of desert hills a few miles north of Kuwait City. Here, in the very last hours of the Gulf War, the Allied bombers had trapped the vast fleeing column of Iraqis. The US Marines had secured the ridge the day before, destroying Iraqi tanks, dugouts and anti-aircraft positions. Throughout that day and the previous night, Allied aircraft had destroyed all vehicles leaving Kuwait City.

When the Iraqi defences finally collapsed, hundreds of vehicles carrying Iraqi soldiers streamed on to the highway heading towards Iraq. They found themselves trapped by the Marine outposts on the ridge and by the fact that the road narrowed here. There was no way for that vast, panicked convoy to spread out into the desert. The Allied pilots pounded them unmercifully. The road became known as the 'Highway of Death'. Hundreds of military and civilian vehicles were left burning on the tarmac as those Iraqis who could fled into the desert to surrender to the waiting Allied troops.

The desert around us now was silent. Rusting coils of barbed wire, rotting tyres and a few rusting scraps of metal were all that remained.

It was a sobering reminder of what might lie ahead. The war, if it came, would arrive step by step. President Clinton had announced that he would begin with an initial heavy four-day round-the-clock bombardment of Iraq. It was already estimated that these raids would entail 300 bombing flights a day.

The first targets would be Iraq's air defence systems, then they would attack the suspected chemical and biological warfare sites. Finally, the bombers would try to destroy Saddam Hussein's military capabilities so that he would be less of a threat to countries around him, like Kuwait.

Those initial attacks would come from cruise missiles on warships and submarines hundreds of miles away. Then would come the next layer of the attack, the stealth bombers we could hear cruising high, high above us. Only then, once the Iraqi air defences were down would the F-14s and F-15s come screaming off the flight decks of the aircraft carriers; they would be followed by the fighter bombers.

The firepower available to President Clinton was astounding, but the real question the world was asking was what would be achieved by unleashing it?

Glenn and I finished filming at the Al-Mutla ridge. We continued north on the road to the border. Kofi Annan had just begun meeting Saddam Hussein. They were expected to continue for two more days at least. But the plans for war were continuing. The US government had ordered all 'non-essential' staff to leave their embassies in Kuwait, Israel and the

Palestinian territories.

We were still looking for pictures, anything different that would tell the story of the tension that was building here, while talks began in Baghdad. A single shepherd stood in the emptiness of the desert. His *gutra* was wrapped tight around his head to protect him against the chill wind. He was a solitary, lonely figure in this landscape. His sheep were white against the patchy green of the desert scrub. They bleated as they hesitated to cross the fresh, deep tank tracks that had been scored into the soft sand overnight.

Further down the road we saw our first US troops. A small column of them were travelling in Humvees down the road to Iraq. There were more Kuwaiti tanks in the desert where we had filmed a few days before.

We were stopped long before the border. As we drove back again the sun was setting. Three shepherds were prostrating themselves on their prayer rugs spread out on the desert sand. The US column was parked along the edge of the road nearby. One of the soldiers gave us a lazy wave as we drove past.

We had dinner at the hotel that night. We couldn't go out because we had to be nearby in case anything happened. After dinner we went up to the BBC office. On the satellite screens Kofi Annan was just emerging from a long meeting with Tariq Aziz, the Deputy Prime Minister of Iraq. He announced that he would meet Saddam Hussein on Sunday.

'Looks like peace in our time,' the senior producer Julia Williams said. 'The word from Baghdad is that it's a done deal.'

A Deal

The next morning I wrote in my notebook:

Sunday February 22. Kofi Annan emerges looking tired and less confident. The word at breakfast is that peace looks less likely.

Overnight the mood had changed. Kofi Annan remained openly confident that he would reach an agreement with Saddam Hussein, but the mood in Kuwait suddenly dipped. Now that the crucial moments had been reached, the fear that had been held down began to surface.

Many Kuwaitis had left the country on 'holiday' or 'business'. The announcement from the US Embassy hadn't helped people's frame of mind either. There was no visible tension in the streets, people seemed to be going about their daily business as best they could. But there were telltale signs that all was not normal. The police had stepped up their patrols all around the city.

On the TV screens in the hotel came reports of heightened unrest across the Middle East as the possibility of a US strike grew closer. At least one person was killed in a protest in Jordan.

One of the journalists in the hotel turned away from the screen. 'I reckon it will be war before the Haj.'

All morning Kofi Annan was meeting Saddam Hussein in Baghdad.

12:00: Clinton has approved air strikes. US has advised its citizens to get out of Iraq ASAP. US military preparations continue.

Late that afternoon Kofi Annan was still meeting with Saddam Hussein. The longer the meeting continued, the worse the prospects for peace were. The sun was just beginning to grow low in the sky when we saw the first convoy. A long chain of eighteen-wheeler flatbed trucks was moving up the highway towards Iraq.

This was the real thing. The trucks were carrying tanks and missile launchers. These were not the obsolete Yugoslavian tanks of the Kuwaiti army, but the most sophisticated hardware the US army had at its disposal. Humvees with heavy machine guns guarded the convoy. Busloads of US soldiers were scattered amongst the trucks. The line of trucks stretched all the way back to the outskirts of Kuwait City. I counted at least seventy-five vehicles moving up the highway before I stopped.

It was an awesome sight, seeing that convoy moving through the golden light of late afternoon. The shadows of the tanks stretched long and angular over the white desert sand. The roar of engines, and the clash of gears was deafening.

'Let's get up on the bridge,' Glenn yelled at me.

We clambered up the sand slope of the highway overpass. I was carrying the tripod. Glenn was rushing ahead of me with his camera. I raised the tripod legs and Glenn hurriedly slammed the camera on top of it. He bent over the eyepiece and began filming.

We hadn't been set up for more than a minute before I heard the squeal of a siren. The police car screeched to a halt beside us. Two Kuwaiti cops jumped out. There was a routine to deal with this. I left Glenn to continue filming, while I deliberately walked forward, away from the camera, to meet the cops. All I had to do was keep them talking for thirty seconds, even fifteen seconds, and we would have enough pictures for the evening news.

We knew they would stop us filming. The trick was to create enough time for Glenn to squeeze off a couple of usable shots. And then try to persuade them not to take the tape.

'Good afternoon,' I said jauntily, putting out my hand.

The police glowered at me. 'Speak Arabic?'

I shook my head.

'We are FBI,' one of them said menacingly. I took it to mean that they were from the Kuwaiti special branch. But they didn't speak much more English. The cop pointed at Glenn.

'Go!' he said waving the back of his hand at us.

'Yes, sir,' Glenn said, smiling politely. I knew that smile. He had the shots he needed.

The news came through at 10 o'clock that night. We had just finished an interview with the Kuwaiti Defence Minister. Glenn and I were outside in the driveway packing the gear away. The driveway was filled with limousines and luxury cars. They were the cars of the Kuwaiti governing elite who had come to meet with the minister in case of war breaking out at dawn the next day. The drivers were gathered in an anxious huddle.

The radio in our car was tuned to the US armed services network. There were, the announcer said, 'reports out of Baghdad of a possible deal'.

One of the drivers came up to us. 'Saddam cancel war,' he said. He looked grim. I was surprised. I had expected him to be happy.

'War is good business,' he went on. 'CNN, NBC, BBC. They hire by the day, not by the hour.'

ISRAEL

THE INVISIBLE CITY

There is a famous story about Jerusalem. It goes something like this: an Israeli is away on business in one or other foreign city. He wants to phone home, so he asks the hotel switchboard operator to connect him to Jerusalem. There is a puzzled silence on the other end of the line. 'Jerusalem?' the operator says. 'You can't call Jerusalem. That's where God lives. It doesn't exist on earth.'

The story is surely apocryphal. It certainly has all the attributes of what today are called 'urban myths'. However, as with all myths, it contains within it a deeper and more resonant truth. Jerusalem is as much a real, geographical place as it is a state of mind.

There is no other region in the world that has produced so many television pictures, so many images of violence for so long as the Middle East. The conflict there ebbs and flows in horrible, predictable cycles.

For decades, ever since the founding of Israel in 1948, the modern media has reported on this spiral of violence. But no one ever gets numb to the killing and the horror of the Middle East. There is too much at stake, for billions of people all around the world.

Jerusalem, and everything it represents for Jews, Muslims and Christians, stands at the centre of it all. There is no middle ground in Jerusalem. Most people who come to Jerusalem see only the city they believe in. The city that others believe in is invisible.

I first visited Jerusalem in 1998 shortly after I had been in Kuwait. It was a typical flying visit for television news. All week we had rushed from one place to the other, interviewing people about the Middle East, and about the anger and uncertainty they felt in the wake of how close things had come to US and Britain bombing Iraq again.

I had heard every important opinion on the current situation imaginable. I have forgotten most of it now, but then I could have quoted almost every major politician in the Middle East chapter and verse as to what he, or she, thought about the past, the present and the future of the growing violence in the region.

What I hadn't had time to see, or feel, for myself was Jerusalem. We had sped back and forth past the major landmarks in taxis, but there had not been a moment to get out and walk through the city.

My chance came at the end of the trip. The rest of the crew were flying on to Europe, but I was returning to Johannesburg. The flight I was on left late the following evening, so I found myself unexpectedly with a couple of days to walk on my own through the city.

I have never used guidebooks much. I understand that they have a practical purpose and that, without one, you are likely to miss seeing all sorts of things. Still, I find myself chafing at the need to follow instructions of any sort. *Walk down the hill and you will see on the right, just beyond the northern edge* . . . well, yes, no doubt the writer knows what he is talking about, but I want to stumble across the wonders beyond the northern edge all by myself, or perhaps ignore it altogether and spend the day wandering along the southern prospect if that is what seems to me to be worth doing.

I usually set out with a guidebook of some sort, intending to see, and learn about, all the fascinating things that a city has to offer. Inevitably, though, after a couple of hours, I find myself wandering through the streets with the guidebook long forgotten at the bottom of my backpack.

I don't quite know why this always happens. It's not that I am not curious about all the things around me. I am, and I love reading guidebooks in the comfort of my hotel room. It's just that when I get out and about in any city, I soon find myself absorbed by the bustle of the streets and by the people I meet.

There is one thing I am obdurate about. I will not take a guided tour. I long ago decided that having the freedom to make your own mistakes is the difference between travel and tourism.

The tour guide handed me a white paper yarmulke. 'You must keep it on all the time you are inside the tunnel,' he said.

In my wanderings around the old city, I had come across the entrance to the Western Wall tunnels. The tunnels had been dug by Israeli archaeologists to uncover the Western Wall of the Second Temple built by Herod and destroyed by the Romans. The first Temple was built by Solomon in 950 BC and destroyed by Nebuchadnezzar in 586 BC. Both Temples were built on the same ancient stone platform known as the Temple Mount. The diggings of the Western Wall tunnel had revealed large sections of these historic foundations.

I knew that the excavations were deeply controversial. For Jews, the tunnels were a fascinating look at their holiest origins. For Muslims, however, the Western Wall tunnels were a flagrant insult to their religion. The Temple Mount complex was known to Muslims as Haram al-Sharif, the Noble Sanctuary. Here were located the Dome of the Rock and al-Aqsa Mosque. The rock under the Dome is, according to Muslim belief, the place where the Prophet Mohammed ascended to heaven after his night ride from Mecca to Jerusalem. (Jews believe it is where Abraham was ready to sacrifice his son Isaac at the command of God.) Haram al-Sharif is also the site of the third mosque built after Mecca and Medina.

For many Muslims, the tunnels were not only sacrilegious, but represented an attempt to destroy the Haram al-Sharif complex by undermining its foundations.

The only way to get to see the tunnels was by going on a guided tour. It was usually booked up days, or even weeks in advance, but because of the uncertainty surrounding events in the Middle East, there were very few tourists around. At the barred entrance to the tunnels I was told that there was space on the next tour.

'Come back at two o'clock,' the woman selling the tickets told me.

Just before two I arrived to find a group of Canadian and American tourists waiting to enter the tunnel. I was the only non-Jewish person in the group. The other men had all brought yarmulkes of one kind or another. I felt conspicuous with the paper yarmulke balanced precariously on the top of my head.

From the moment we entered the tunnel, I could feel the change that came over the group. Outside, they had been a typical group of wealthy, middle-aged North Americans who talked in loud, friendly voices. As we stepped inside, they fell silent. A quiet, respectful mood came over everyone.

We came first to a cool stone corridor of vaulted archways. This was once a passageway attributed to King David, mentioned also by the Islamic historian Mujir al-Din. Some of the arches had been part of an aqueduct carrying water from Solomon's Pools.

But, most importantly for the people on the tour, this was where the Jewish defenders had torn down the causeway to defend the Second Temple against the Romans. This cramped corridor stood for so much to the people with me. I could sense how the history of these old stones was flowing out into their consciousness.

So we went deeper into the tunnel following the course of the old Temple Mount. It was a short, cramped, even claustrophobic walk, but it was an extraordinary journey into the mind and soul of the people I was with. I had entered the tunnel as a tourist, but soon I felt the full weight of the privilege it was to witness this unfolding of history amongst people to whom it meant the world.

A narrow row of electric lights lit the way for us. We passed a wall of enormous dressed stones. These were the very foundations of both the ancient temples of the Jews. One of the stones was extraordinary. It was over thirteen metres long and nearly four metres high and wide.

'This stone,' the guide said, 'was quarried nearby. But no one knows how they managed to fit it into its place here. Today we cannot imagine what tools or levers they could have used to lay this stone. It is a mystery.'

At some point in the tour we came to a small niche in the wall. A tiny flame was burning inside the niche.

'This,' said the tour guide, 'is the nearest point we can come today to the Holy of Holies.'

For a few moments an absolute silence reigned over the group. In this damp stone chasm it was suddenly hard to imagine the real city above: the crowded streets, the armed soldiers and police, the barricades and metal detectors. The entire meaning of Jerusalem for these people was subsumed within this single point, and in that moment – for each one of them alone in thought – of the fact that they were there, alive, to witness it.

Slowly, after some moments of reflection, people began to move on through the tunnel. I was caught at the back of the group and so had to wait while the others took their time. The last person to leave was a young woman who I guessed was in her early thirties. She stood for a long time in front of that tiny, flickering flame. I didn't want to intrude, so I stood patiently to one side and waited.

There was a part of me that couldn't help remembering what lay on the ground almost directly above this subterranean memorial. The day before I had visited the Dome of the Rock. I had stood under the magnificent golden dome and stared at the dark, folded contours of the rock. I was surrounded by the calm reverence of Muslim pilgrims who peered at this site that had stood as an unshakeable symbol of their faith for centuries.

In a parallel state of reverence, the Jewish woman never closed her eyes once. She simply stared at the flame as if to fix it in her memory. Her quiet, dignified silence was deeply significant. The day before I had seen how much the Dome of the Rock meant to Muslims. Watching this young woman, it was easy to see the magnitude of this place, and of this city, to the Jewish psyche. The Roman conquest, the diaspora, the Holocaust – all that and more must have been brimming in her soul in those few silent moments.

I wanted to get something special to remember Jerusalem by. There were so many cheap souvenirs for sale that I was beginning to despair. Finally, I wandered into the narrow stone alleyways of the Christian Quarter street in the Old City.

There were a number of carpet shops along the street, and all of them were hustling for the few tourist dollars that were available. Carpets are a weakness of mine and of my wife's so I thought that a carpet from the Old City of Jerusalem would be a worthwhile thing to take home. I was prepared to spend a decent sum of money on a carpet that I liked.

I came to the first shop just off the Via Dolorosa. It was a large emporium piled high with rugs from all over the Middle East and Central Asia. There were 'Welcome' signs in English, French, German and Japanese dotted around the walls and pillars of the shop.

It was clearly a tourist trap, but even from outside I could see that some of the carpets were of good quality. Against my better judgement, I found myself wandering inside. There were a few other tourists inside the store, and all of them were flipping through the piles of carpets.

I began to look by myself. I picked up the corner of a carpet here, inspected the colour or the weave of another there. Some of the carpets were really quite good, but the prices were high, and there was nothing that caught my eye as really special or unusual. The piles of stock might just have easily been in a store in New York, or London, or even Johannesburg.

Finally, one of the owners of the shop brought me an Afghan rug. It was one of the rugs that had been made there during the fighting against the Russians. It had helicopters and tanks woven into the design.

'This one is special,' the man said to me. 'You won't find them easily now.' I knew he was right. Since the Taliban had taken over most of Afghanistan, they had banned the creation of any images, so rugs like this were not being woven any longer. There was a finite stock of them, and one day they could even become valuable.

But this was a poor quality rug. The knots were uneven, the designs were crude and ill-shaped. To crown it all, part of the rug had been gnawed away by moth larvae. They had left a network of tracks all along the bottom edge.

The man was watching me carefully as I inspected the rug.

'Five hundred dollars,' he barked at me.

It was all I could do not to laugh out loud. 'But it's been eaten by insects.'

'Pffh,' he scoffed. 'That's easy to fix.'

I walked along the street. It was growing late and I was beginning to give up hope of finding anything worthwhile. I had to catch my plane late that evening, so this was my last chance.

Finally, deep in the old stone souk built by the Ottomans, I came across a tiny shop that was filled with tasteful things. Old brass coffee pots, antique tiles, and beautiful rugs. The shop was hardly bigger than a normal-sized living room. Much of the merchandise had tumbled out on to the ancient cobbled street.

I liked the place immediately. It was obvious that the owner had taste. I stepped in and peered around.

'Can I help you?' Yusuf, the owner of the shop, was a small man, much the same height as me. He was slightly balding and had green eyes. He wore an open-necked shirt and a pair of polyester slacks.

I hadn't formed any clear idea of what I was looking for, but the flawed

Afghan rug I had seen in the first shop had stuck in my mind.

'I'm looking for an Afghan rug,' I said, on impulse. 'One of those with the tanks and the aeroplanes.'

Yusuf shook his head thoughtfully. 'They are rare now. I don't have any.'

I turned to go.

'Wait,' Yusuf said. 'I will see if I can find one.' I stood in one corner of the shop while he picked up the telephone. He dialled one number, and then another. I heard the words 'tanks', 'aeroplanes'. He put down the receiver and began searching through a tiny address book. He dialled another number holding the receiver against his ear with his shoulder and reading the numbers from his address book.

I saw him nodding. Then he put the phone down. 'My wife's cousin has one. A very good one. But they are in Ramallah. They will bring it here, and you can see it tomorrow.'

'It's a pity,' I said. 'But I won't be here tomorrow. I fly tonight.'

Yusuf looked at me for a moment. 'I can take you there, to Ramallah.'

'But – '

He smiled and raised his hand to forestall further argument. He reached behind the telephone and brought out a large padlock. 'Just a few moments.'

Yusuf ushered me out of the shop. He closed the door and reached up to pull down a heavy iron shutter. It clattered as he brought it down on to the stone floor. He locked it with the padlock.

He was closing the store early. One or two of the other storekeepers shouted out at him in Arabic. He laughed good-naturedly and pointed at me.

He led me through the narrow streets of the Old City to where his car was parked just inside the Jaffa Gate. It was a battered Toyota. He opened the door for me and the two of us climbed in.

It was late in the afternoon and the traffic was beginning to build up rapidly. Yusuf pulled out into the roar of modern Jerusalem, smoke pouring from his exhaust. We were heading for Ramallah, where few tourists venture.

We hadn't gone far before we came to the first Israeli roadblock. The young soldiers, men and women in their late teens and early twenties, stopped the cars and peered inside. They were nonchalant, but their M-16 assault rifles hung ready over their shoulders. Yusuf looked at me across the steering wheel.

'Don't be angry or nervous,' he said. 'They'll stop us for hours then. I know them – you can never win.'

We pulled up at the roadblock. Yusuf spoke to them in Hebrew. He reached into his pocket and pulled out his driver's licence. One of the soldiers looked at it for a few seconds and then handed it back. They hardly even glanced at me before waving us on.

The traffic on the road to Ramallah was awful. We sat for long minutes while the cars ahead of us slowly inched their way towards the next Israeli roadblock. In this slow, agonizing procession of vehicles, we were moving from one Jerusalem to another. Almost everyone in the cars around us was a Palestinian. As the day ended, the worlds of Arab and Jew drew apart. They never saw each other's worlds.

'I have three children and my wife at home,' Yusuf told me as we waited in the traffic. 'They are all girls. It is easier for me to have girls. If I had boys I would have to find the money to build them each a house. The Jews tell their children to leave the house at eighteen. With us it is different. We stay with our mother and father until we are married.'

We came to another roadblock, and soon after another. The soldiers seemed fairly relaxed. 'It is easier with you in the car. If I am alone, then they might think I am a suicide bomber. But they can tell that you are not Arab. They think I am a taxi driver.'

There were perhaps half a dozen roadblocks on the way to Yusuf's wife's cousin's house. The roadblocks were a fact of life here. In many ways, they were the primary fact of life. They were a constant and intentional reminder of who was in control of the city. With each roadblock we passed, we were shutting behind one world and entering deeper into the heart of another.

'I am not religious,' Yusuf said. 'But I will never cheat anyone. I believe God is watching me.' He laughed. 'I never go to mosque – maybe I will when I am old, but for now I have three children to raise.'

Finally the roadblocks ended. The traffic eased and we found ourselves on a narrow street running along a steep hillside. A few rows of olive trees clung to the soil amongst the white boulders on the slopes.

We came to the house. It was a large stone house, newly built. Yusuf parked the car and his cousin came out on to the street to greet us.

He was wearing a *dishdasha*. We shook hands. 'My name is Khalid. Welcome.' He ushered me into the tiny yard in front of the house. A few carpets had been hung on the low stone wall that overlooked a steep valley. The modern townhouses and high walls of a Jewish settlement were on the opposite slope of the valley. The walls of the settlement were perhaps 250 yards away from Khalid's house.

We sat outside on plastic chairs around a cheap garden table. A woman brought coffee. She was wearing a headscarf and traditional robes. She smiled when she put the coffee down, and then disappeared back into the house.

Khalid poured the coffee and Yusuf handed me a tiny brass coffee cup. It was strong and sweet.

'That settlement has caused us problems,' Khalid said. 'They want to take some of my land for a road that will go to it. They say they will pay us the value of the land as it was in 1948. I will fight them in court if they come to take my land.'

We talked of a few other things, but mostly the talk was of politics, the past and the future. Finally, Khalid looked at me.

'Which one do you like?'

There was only one that I was interested in. The beautiful dark blue Afghan rug with the fine well-tied knots, the clear, intricate designs of tanks and planes and trucks so cleverly worked that they looked at first sight like traditional geometric designs. It was a very fine rug and we all knew it.

'The Afghan,' I told him. Yusuf stood up and pulled the others to one side.

Khalid gestured at the Afghan. 'Please take a look. Feel free.' I knelt down to where the rug had been spread out on the ground. It was every bit as good as I had thought. This design and this quality would not be found again easily.

'How much do you want?' I asked.

'It is a good carpet,' Khalid said. 'But we have no business these days. I can give it to you at a good price – $1100.'

I hesitated for a moment. 'I can only afford $400.'

Khalid smiled. 'Let us drink some coffee. It is our hospitality.'

'We will drink coffee and then we can go back to your hotel,' Yusuf said.

The last of the sunlight glowed on the hillside. A shadow crept up towards the crest of the hill, covering the rows of olive trees.

'How much is your top price?' Khalid asked.

It was a good rug. I knew what I would pay for it anywhere else. I doubled my offer. 'Eight hundred dollars.' It was a mistake. I should have gone up by less. He had given me no idea of how much he was prepared to come down, but now he knew how much I was prepared to go up.

'This is the first time you visit my house,' he said. 'Give me 900 and we have a deal.'

Khalid had outwitted me and we both knew it. 'I can't,' I protested feebly.

'How much can you give me in cash?'

In the end, I got the rug. I didn't get it cheap, but I didn't get ripped off either. I knew that much from the prices I had seen elsewhere in the world. It was a good buy for me and Khalid got a fair price. We shook hands warmly on the street outside. Yusuf and I climbed into his ancient car. Khalid had rolled up the rug carefully and put it on the back seat.

'We like cash,' Yusuf said. 'Then we don't have to pay tax to the Israelis.'

It was dark by the time I set out for the airport. We were slightly late, so the taxi driver sped along the highway. I was tired and slightly anxious about the long flight ahead of me, so I didn't say much.

We were just taking the turn-off to Ben Gurion airport when the taxi driver's cellphone rang. It was his wife. I couldn't understand what she was saying, but I could hear that her voice was frightened.

The driver closed the flap on the phone. 'The soldiers have shot three Palestinians at a roadblock in Ramallah.'

A cold wave of shock washed over me. It was only hours since I had been through those same roadblocks with Yusuf. I had a strange, claustrophobic sense of being trapped. I wanted to know what had happened, who had been shot. I assumed that Yusuf had got home safely after dropping me off at my hotel, but I couldn't know for certain.

Already we were turning into the airport, leaving the city. I turned to look back, hoping to see the city one last time. But there were only the lights of the cars on the highway as they flashed past in the darkness.

The soldiers from the first security checkpoint were coming up to the car. Their guns were hanging off their shoulders. They were like all the other Israeli soldiers, young kids barely out of high school. Their faces were blank, professional. They were neither hostile, nor welcoming. It was just another late night on duty.

As they approached, the taxi driver shook his head. 'Our life in this place, it is like a lock without a key.'

AFGHANISTAN

A HIDDEN WAR

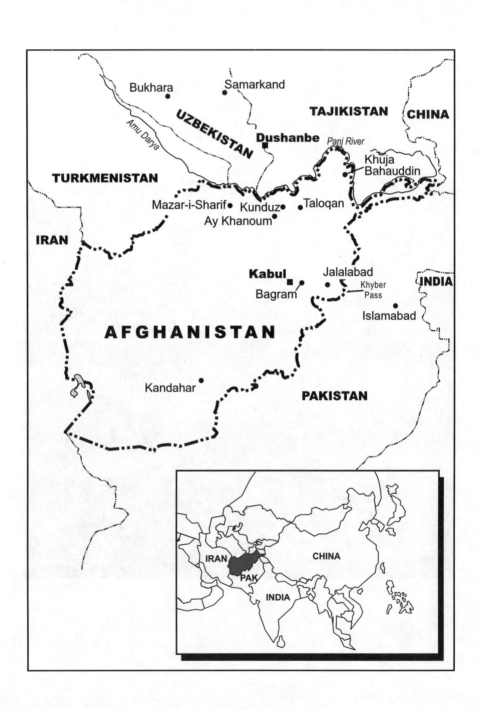

Every evening you could hear the distant gunfire in the hills around the city. As the darkness of the tropical night fell, the bats came out and circled over the Hotel Burundi Palace on the main street of Bujumbura. The gunfire began to slow then. It seldom came into the centre of town anyway, so the expatriates and the elite of Burundi would park their 4x4s along the old colonial boulevards outside one of the fine restaurants. They always reopened when there were peace talks or a lull in the fighting.

'This is a war without a front,' a colonel in the army told us. 'There is hardly a night when you don't hear shooting in the suburbs.'

At the beginning of September of 2001, the ongoing civil war in Burundi was as far away from the concerns of the developed world as it was possible to get. It epitomized the apparently senseless small wars that raged on the outermost borders of the vast Imperium of the industrialized world. To people in the US, Japan and Europe these wars were unconnected to the everyday events of their lives. These wars and the people who fought and died in them existed in the forgotten shadowlands of the world. It seemed that was how the twenty-first century was going to be – the End of History for the rich world and permanent exclusion, the Edge of History for the poor world. It was difficult to get stories like the war in Burundi on to the screen.

I was back in Nairobi when I turned on the TV set in my hotel room. There was a vague news item from another shadowy war going on somewhere in a remote corner of Afghanistan. Two men, posing as television journalists, had tried to assassinate the leader of the Northern Alliance, Ahmad Shah Massoud. The killers had hidden a bomb in a televison camera and had detonated it when Massoud sat down for the interview. Massoud was reportedly in a critical condition.

I knew very little about the war in Afghanistan, but I remember how much the report disturbed me. Years ago, on one of the first stories I had worked on in television, we had been filming Jonas Savimbi of UNITA at his base in Jamba in southern Angola. I remember one of the older journalists saying how easy it would be for terrorists to smuggle a bomb into a press conference inside a camera. 'It'll happen one day,' he said grimly. And now it had. It was an ominous portent for those of us who worked in TV news. We could now be regarded as potential assassins. It would make our jobs even more difficult and dangerous.

Two days later, on September 11, 2001, we were at the BBC bureau in Nairobi editing our story on Burundi when the first pictures of the flaming twin towers of the World Trade Center appeared on the TV screens in the office. The story we were working on seemed pointless now, but we couldn't abandon it. We kept working throughout the day and deep into the night, alternately editing our story on the civil war in Burundi and watching, along with the rest of the world, as the events of the atrocity unfolded.

Back at the hotel, I tried for hours to get through on the phone to my cousins and my uncle in the States. My wife's brother lived in New York. His apartment was just below 14th Street – the exact line where the police cordon was drawn, dividing Manhattan into a safe zone above and an unsafe zone below.

The lines out of Kenya were jammed solid. Of all African countries, it has probably the closest links to the West. Kenyans, too, had their own memories of terror. In 1998 there was the bombing of the US Embassy in Nairobi by associates of Osama Bin Laden when 213 people, mostly Kenyans, were killed. Finally, near dawn, I managed to get through. When I heard my uncle's voice on the other end, I suddenly found myself unable to speak. I was afraid of what I would hear. But we were lucky, no one we knew had been killed.

From the moment the planes crashed into the World Trade Center buildings it was clear that a new type of war had begun. The distant, barely understood conflicts of the shadowlands, and the hatreds that fuelled them, had struck at the heart of the new Imperium. At the same time, it was a monstrous act of cruelty against innocent people. Because of it, our world would never be the same again.

President George W Bush in his September 20 address to the Joint Session of Congress made it clear that this war against terror would be a long and difficult struggle. 'Americans,' he said, 'should not expect one battle, but a lengthy campaign, unlike any we have ever seen. It may include dramatic strikes, visible on TV, and covert operations, secret even in success.'

Two weeks later I was sitting alone in the departure lounge at Johannesburg International Airport. The high glass windows of the restaurant stood open to the African night. The lights of the planes gleamed on the darkness of the tarmac. Somebody on the television above the bar was predicting war 'within days'.

At dawn the next morning I saw the first clouds over the Mediterranean coast of France. But the sunrise gleamed pink and beautiful over Paris.

In London the Serpentine sparkled in the morning sun. Joggers were out along the pathways of Hyde Park. The first fallen leaves of autumn lay golden on the soft green lawns.

The talk in the streets was all of war. 'They skin them alive over there, don't they?' the taxi driver asked when he heard I was on my way to Afghanistan. 'I believe they teach them in the schools how to put poison in the water.'

I was in London to join a crew from NBC television news. There were hundreds of journalists in Pakistan. We were to head for the north, to Central Asia and Northern Afghanistan. I met Justin Balding, a senior producer, in the NBC office in Hammersmith. He had studied Russian literature at university and worked as a journalist in Moscow for many years. He spoke Russian fluently and had covered stories all over the former Soviet Union.

'Our plans are like the war at this stage,' he told me. 'Characterized by clandestine uncertainty. We're trying to charter into Dushanbe, in Tajikistan. The problem is that the only place we can get Tajik visas from is in Berlin. It looks like I'm going to have to go to Germany over the weekend.'

He spread out a map on his desk and pointed to a tiny dot on the map in the far north-eastern corner of Afghanistan. 'Once we're in Dushanbe somehow, we don't know how yet, we plan eventually to get to Khuja Bahauddin, the military headquarters of the Northern Alliance. NBC already has a satellite dish set up, so we can broadcast from there.' He looked at me through his glasses. 'Khuja Bahauddin was where General Massoud was blown up.'

The visa hold-up was an unexpected delay. That weekend was cool and wet in London. I stayed with my brother and his wife. I read the papers and watched the rain dripping from the trees outside. The chimney pots stood out against the grey sky that stretched over the city.

'Special Forces in Afghanistan Seek Out Targets' read one headline. 'Teams Paving The Way For Strikes' was another. *Perhaps*, I wrote in my notebook, *I am wondering, the first casualties*.

'Make no mistake about it,' George W Bush was saying. 'We're in hot pursuit.'

This was the beginning of the hidden war. The pictures on the television showed almost nothing of what might really be happening. There were the same shots of fighter jets on aircraft carriers that the world had seen so many times since the Gulf War and a few shots of troops gathering in the Gulf and at home in bases in America.

The real fighting was hard to follow. A British SAS patrol had reportedly already traded fire with the Taliban. Two thousand US special forces like Delta Force and the 75th Rangers were being deployed in Central Asia, in Uzbekistan, Tajikistan and in Pakistan. Other units were gathering in Northern Afghanistan, preparing themselves for a campaign that would last months. When they went out on operations they were to hide during the day and come out at night. They would use night vision goggles and the intelligence gleaned from hi-tech satellites, U-2 spy planes, radar-equipped JSTARS and unmanned drones like the Predator.

Despite all this surveillance equipment, the reports that were coming out of Afghanistan were vague and unclear. It was obvious that this was deliberate. In this war we would see only what we were allowed to see.

Heading East

It was dark by the time our Antonov 26 finally took off from Stanstead airport heading east for Prague, Odessa, Baku, and finally Dushanbe. To be taking off from London in a Russian transport plane to cover a war in Afghanistan and events in the former Soviet Union was a post-Cold War irony that Le Carré might have appreciated. There were eight of us on the plane. Myself, Justin, cameraman Richard Burr, correspondents Dennis Murphy and Kerry Sanders, assistant producer Ian Wenger. With us were two satellite engineers, John Kranz and Paul Stimson. We had three tonnes of equipment crammed into the hold of the cargo plane. Much of it was the satellite transmission dish, but a lot was for our team. We had brought extra food, tents, flak jackets, helmets, biological and chemical warfare suits packed tightly into heavy plastic cases. In addition, we had two satellite phones and all our filming and sound gear. It took up twenty-four separate cases and weighed about 800 kilograms. That was before we had taken into account our personal baggage. We had each packed two suitcases of both summer and winter clothes because we were travelling at the turn of the season. Now, in early October, the weather in central Asia and – if we got there – in Afghanistan would be warm, even hot. But within weeks we could expect icy weather to set in.

'We're taking too much bloody stuff,' Richard groaned. He and I had found a small niche at the back of the plane. It was behind all the piles of equipment, right beside the large cargo door that opened up on to the tarmac. It would be cold, but at least we had space to lie down. To reach the others in the tiny passenger cabin we had to crawl on our hands and knees across the piles of hard silver boxes. The gear was piled so high we had to be careful not to bang our heads on the roof of the plane.

There was a small round porthole at the back. I arranged one of the hard cases to form a makeshift seat so that I could stare out of it as we flew. The thrum of the engines lifted us into the night sky over London. The golden spray of the city's lights stretched out behind us. They were cut here and there by the dark streams of the Thames.

We flew at a much lower altitude than a commercial airliner. The lights of the city and the surrounding countryside spun out below us until, suddenly, they were gone and we were thrusting through the inky blackness of the Channel. A few ships sailed through the darkness below us, their own lights dimly incandescent on the water. In less than twenty minutes we had crossed the Channel and the towns and cities of Europe stood out like islands of light in the night. I was already cold and uncomfortable in the freezing draught of the rattling cargo hold, but I didn't mind.

Flying at such low altitude gave me a completely different perspective than I had ever experienced in the bleak, anonymous experience of modern jet travel. It transformed the claustrophobic boredom of a 'flight' into a journey. Each landmark below was a tangible connection to the land we were travelling over.

For the war we were going to cover, the land of Afghanistan would be transformed into the virtual reality of glowing patterns on a computer screen. For the laser-guided smart bombs of the B-2 and the F-18s and the JDAMS, targets were numbers and coordinates from a Global Positioning System. Once the numbers came up, the bombs were released on the earth from altitudes so high the planes were cruising at the outer edge of the atmosphere.

But from my seat in the freezing cargo hold it was worth trying to think of how it might have been for the pilots in the aerial wars of the past, in the Battle of Britain, and in the terrible bombing runs over Cologne and Berlin. The airfields of Britain were less than an hour behind us. Within thirty minutes of taking off, the pilots would have hit the first flak barrages and the Luftwaffe squadrons over occupied Europe. They would have struggled to hold their course with the steel and high explosive shells exploding in the air all around them. They had maps and compasses, even radar, but the reality of their war was the constant danger of the flak, and the need to follow the roads and the cities and the mountains unfolding beneath them through the curve of a porthole.

Midnight on the Old Town square of Prague. We had to be back on the plane at six the next morning for the next leg of our journey, but a few of us had decided to catch the last round at one of the cafés on the square. The famous astronomical clock seemed to be shut up for the night, but it was a warm early autumn evening. The last of the late-night couples and tourists were strolling across the cobbled square.

We finished our beers and strolled through the tiny, darkened streets of the Old Town. Prostitutes emerged from almost every doorway. 'Sex,' they hissed intimidatingly. 'Blow job!'

'Funny how they always know what language to use,' Kerry said. We walked up the main road towards the train station. A bronze statue of a knight stood on an island in the centre of the road. Bouquets of flowers stood beneath its plinth. Candles flickered in glass jars in the middle of them. There was a picture of a US flag and a large banner that read *Obětem Terorizmu*. We didn't know what the words meant exactly, but the sentiments were obvious.

It had been a long and often bitter journey for the Czechs away from Communist rule. I thought of the Prague Spring of 1968, the revolution of 1989, the split with Slovakia, the moves towards EU membership. Now the Czechs were members of NATO and the world had been turned on its head. The brutality of the Communist decades seemed a distant memory. With the attacks on New York and Washington, NATO had invoked its mutual defence clause for the first time in its history – an attack on one member state was considered an attack against them all. These flowers and candles were an expression of sympathy for Americans, but they were also a statement of identity by Czechs. They were affirming that, at long last, they belonged to the West.

Just after midnight we strolled along one of Prague's most famous monuments, the Karluv Most, or Charles Bridge. Six hundred years old, it had been built originally for tournaments by jousting knights. The lights of the old city of Prague lay in huge fire-orange sheets over the Vltava river. A statue of a single knight with a shield and lance stood in a sharp silhouette.

Dawn was grey and still. The reception on the TV in my hotel room was blurred and distorted. But the shapes of Israeli tanks moving through the white stone buildings of Gaza and the West Bank were unmistakable. Another hidden war being fought under cover of the war that was rapidly building in Afghanistan.

Soon we were heading east into a bright sun. The fields below us were a bright emerald green. Small pockets of forest nestled between the rolling meadows and the towns. The countryside was flat as far as the eye could see. We were flying over the gateway to the vast steppe country that flowed for thousands of miles from the vastness of central Asia. Here Hitler's tanks had ground up the harvests under their tracks and Mongol horsemen had galloped in their hundreds of thousands.

A single schloss stood on a small rise of wooded ground above a winding river. Beyond it factories and gleaming white towns spread north and south. Barely three weeks before I had been in Burundi, in the heart of central Africa. Now I was flying above the wide plains of central Europe. I had travelled from one far edge of the Imperium to here, where I was crossing another – beyond Slovakia and Hungary lay another civilization, that of Russia with its double-headed eagle that looked both east and west.

In one single day, the familiar borders of our world had imploded in on themselves. I was here to witness and record a world that was changing so fast now that no one knew for certain what might happen next. All over the world people were trying to see where they fitted into this new order of things. An order that was still unclear but which was rapidly emerging out of the smoking rubble of Manhattan.

The truth was, part of me was a little scared of what lay ahead. Just before I left London, I phoned a friend who had been to Afghanistan several times before. 'Be careful,' he told me. 'It's a very dangerous place. If the Northern Alliance say a road is safe, don't necessarily believe them. You can't trust them with your safety. You have to make your own decisions.'

Below us was the geographic patchwork of Soviet illusions. The map showed the borders: Ukraine, Romania, Moldova, Ukraine again. All of these countries were in the midst of a new, post-Soviet nationalism. A decade after the break-up of the Soviet Union, they were trying to salvage some kind of identity from the crushing conformity that had ruled their societies for most of the twentieth century.

From the air, their tragedy was stark. It was impossible to tell where one country ended and another began. They were united by the fact that they were all part of Europe's Third World. Town after town looked exactly the same – a conglomeration of utterly undistinctive square boxes, gathered erratically into a settlement of some sort, or placed in unforgiving straight lines. They were like the townships planned by the racial dreamers of apartheid. I was observing from high up in the air, and, for as far as I could see, these grim concrete settlements sprawled across the landscape. There were no farmhouses or quaint, isolated villages. The scars of collectivization defined the geography of these countries. The fields were large and cut into severe shapes. There were barns and silos in the countryside, but no place that anyone might think of as a home.

The roads in the countryside were mostly unpaved. When a tractor or truck moved on them, they threw up thin trails of pale dust the colour of chalk or bone into the morning air. Factories with tall chimneys and dismal concrete apartment blocks lined the banks of the rivers or were stuck somehow on to the checkerboard of square box houses. For hours we flew over this grim, unrelieved landscape of semi-squalor.

Seeing it from the air, what struck me so forcibly was the enormity of what the Soviet system had destroyed, and of what it had imposed on its people. Western cities had their slums, but here there was no escape from the bleakness, either in the towns or the countryside. It seemed little wonder to me that in these countries poverty, alcoholism, prostitution, violent crime and political fascism were on the rise. People here were trapped by the geography of a failed dream.

For a moment, I might have thought I had gone back in time nearly ten years when I was covering the war in Angola. As we came down to land, I saw the same Soviet radar trucks and the same layout of bunkers for the MiG fighter jets. Only there were no baobab trees and red dust plains. Here vineyards were laid out in neat lines and the surface of the Black Sea glittered in the afternoon sun as the plane banked on its final approach. The plane taxied and stopped on a distant section of the runway. Through the porthole I could see the Ukrainian soldiers and customs officials moving towards the plane. They were carrying a dirty rope that had been knotted together in various places. We had no visas for Ukraine, and were in transit for Azerbaijan, but they were taking no chances – this was the military airfield near Odessa and they wanted us sealed off from the rest of the airfield.

Richard and I clambered across the piled baggage, grateful for the chance to stretch our legs. The weather was warm outside, but a cool breeze was blowing. On either side of the tarmac, the hardy steppe grass was a luxuriant bronze colour. Autumn had come, but the cold weather was still weeks away. We had been in the air for nearly twenty hours.

Dennis put his hand on my shoulder as I climbed stiffly on to the tarmac. 'We're not even halfway there yet.'

'They've told me we have to change planes here,' Justin said.

'Why?' Richard wanted to know.

'I don't know,' Justin said. 'It's something to do with insurances and the charter company. We need a different plane for Azerbaijan and Tajikistan.'

'But they told us when we left London that we're not covered by any insurance policy anyway.'

Justin smiled. 'It's not us they're worried about. It's the plane.'

'I'm not unloading and reloading three tonnes of gear,' Richard barked.

'Don't worry. The charter company say they'll do it.'

The customs officials took our passports and walked a little way off into the grass where they sat down to examine them.

We sat on the tarmac near the plane. One of the officials climbed up to the cockpit. The pilot was a Hungarian who spoke Russian. Justin translated their exchange for us.

'May we look inside?' the official asked.

The pilot ushered them in graciously. 'My home is your home. My wife is your wife.'

We sat for hours watching as the ground crew transferred our cargo and baggage to another Antonov. The heavy silver cases containing the satellite dish were the largest items. Everything had been neatly packed on to wooden pallets. The whole operation could have been completed in less than half an hour with a good loadmaster and a forklift truck. But they had only one hand-cranked wheeled dolly. Each heavy pallet had to be pushed to the edge of the cargo hold and held there while the dolly was ratcheted up underneath it. Then half a dozen or more soldiers and ground crew would push it across the tarmac to the cargo hold of the new plane. The wheels of the dolly squealed and juddered on the rough surface of the tarmac and the load swayed precipitously with each tiny obstacle that the wheels hit. It was a miracle that none of the sensitive electronic gear came tumbling off.

The light grew rich and filtered. The breeze came up and whistled softly through the low grass. The shadows of the planes poured out over the ground. The officials had removed the string barricade. They gave us our passports back. Finally our new plane was loaded.

'A toast,' Justin said. 'They are proposing a toast.' Someone had a bottle of whisky stored away in the plane. He dug into his baggage and brought it out. Justin found some plastic glasses. He poured everyone a tot of whisky. The Ukrainian officers raised their glasses above their heads.

'Na Zdorovya!'

We all downed our whisky in one slug. The Ukrainians looked anxiously at the bottoms of their plastic cups. There was a little more whisky in the bottle. John, the satellite engineer, shared it out. Everyone smiled.

'Na Zdorovya!'

There were a few moments of silence. One of the Ukrainians muttered something in Justin's ear.

'They say it is their turn now. They want to toast us in their way. With vodka.'

'Oh no,' Richard groaned quietly.

'Patience,' Dennis murmured. 'It's like the thirteen stations of the cross.'

Someone came running up with two bottles of vodka. They had red plastic tops fashioned in the shape of a cossack's head.

The plastic glasses came out again. One of the Ukrainians went around the circle. He poured each of us a large, suitably hospitable, slug.

The vodka fumes wavered in the plastic glass like methylated spirits. It was a tad rude, but I could only sip at mine.

'They are wishing us a good journey,' Justin said. 'And a safe time in Afghanistan.'

'Na Zdorovya!'

Finally we took off at about 5:00 pm. The first pink tinges of sunset were on the horizon. A forest of birches caught the last of the light on its yellowing leaves. An enormous tractor shuddered through a field below us. The Black Sea loomed out of the steppes, a single blue curve separating it from the land and then a shimmering immensity of water.

I looked back and caught a glimpse of the city of Odessa. The docks of the port stuck out into the dark blue sea. The wake of a single ship cut across the distance and then the bronze of sunset began to surround the plane.

It was freezing in the cargo hold. I had wrapped a blanket around me, over my anorak and fleece-lined jacket. Richard had gone to sleep on top of some of the boxes. We were flying above a low bank of clouds. Above us was the darkness of night and the clear, bright stars. My breath frosted on the cold surface of the porthole. The clouds rippled and glowed in the moonlight beneath us. We soared over them, a giant surreal sleigh ride, with the lights of the towns on the coast of the Black Sea glittering far below.

A single bright star shone in a purple sky above the wing. The navigation light pulsed its orange rhythms into the darkness. The engines flowed and hummed. White clouds lay in the valleys below the first shadowy foothills of the Caucasus and the Georgian republic. We left the lights of the Black Sea behind us. The Caucasus rose up in dark layers in front of us, mist-shrouded valleys lay in the moonlight below us. The folds of the narrowest valleys grabbed at the mist like fingers. The moonlight shifted as we flew. We passed over the western slopes first, opaque and smooth as water, then, as we crossed the jagged peaks, the eastern slopes burst into a shimmer of moonlight, the rock faces clear and etched, gleaming almost as bright as snow.

In the distance there was the dim orange glow of a faraway city. Our flight path was close enough that it might have been Grozny in the tiny republic of Chechnya, where fighting between Russian forces and Chechen separatists was still going on. In the valleys below us there was the almost complete darkness of wilderness, only the occasional glimmer of single isolated lights, or the tiniest cluster, deep in the valleys.

I remembered speaking to a friend in Nairobi on the subject of Africa and the gap that was growing between Africa and the West. He had recently spent a number of years based in Moscow. 'It's not only Africa,' he told me. 'In the mountains of Georgia you come across villages that have not changed since the twelfth century.' I could imagine what he meant now. The darkness below us, and the lack of electric light it implied, was a world as far away as it was possible to get from the world that contemplated Britney Spears' navel and believed in the paradise offered by the dot-com boom.

I saw that just as one can never understand America until one has seen the plains of the Midwest, the psychology of Europe would never be truly revealed until one had seen these vast hinterlands that lay beyond its fertile tip. For Europeans there would always be the fear, and the wonder, of the glowering immensity of the land that lay in the East.

The sky turned a deep velvety green above the tip of the wing – a deep green of countless shades, the moonlight and darkness layered into the sky like the hammered metalwork of a Damascus blade.

I shivered even with the blanket wrapped tightly around my shoulders. My feet turned numb with the cold air rushing in from around the edges of the cargo door. But I wouldn't have missed those moments beside the porthole for anything. I stared for hours while, in a sea of moonlight and shadow, we crossed over the last ramparts of Europe and floated into the skies of Asia.

Ahead of us the Caspian Sea gleamed like iron against the rugged blackness of the land. There was a shift in the noise of the engines. The angle of the plane changed and suddenly we were coming down to land. The ground below us was bleak and arid in the moonlight. The wing dipped as we turned over a flat expanse of water. A burning string of oil terminals flamed in the darkness. Then below us glimmered the lights of the city of Baku, capital of Azerbaijan.

Baku was one of the first cities Marco Polo mentioned in his *Travels*. 'There is a spring from which gushes a stream of oil, in such abundance that a hundred ships may load there at once. This oil is not good to eat; but it is good for burning and as a salve for men and camels affected with itch or scab.'

We, too, had come for the oil. Our Antonov needed refuelling. It was one in the morning local time. I had long since lost track of what time it might have been in London, or even Prague.

We clambered out on to the tarmac. A cold mist was creeping in off the water. I could smell the crude oil hanging in the heavy, dank atmosphere. The pilots and the ground crew scurried around, clamping hoses to the wing, testing the fuel tanks for water and sediment.

A small knot of customs officials and soldiers gathered around us. They were curious about a plane that arrived in the middle of the night, full of Western journalists.

'Are any of you Americans?'

Most of the crew were Americans, Justin told them.

They peered at us through the darkness. One man gently touched his heart with his hand. 'I'm sorry for what happened in New York,' he said in a quiet voice.

'Did any of you see the attack?' Justin asked.

'It was live on TV here, about twenty minutes after the planes hit the buildings,' one man told us. 'It was a tragedy. A terrible tragedy.'

'Some people we know here were meant to be in the buildings,' another man added. 'But they were late for work that day.'

The conversation went forward in fits and starts. Justin had to translate anything complicated for us, but we managed to communicate simple things in gestures and a few shared words. I found someone, for example, who spoke a smattering of German.

'Where are you going?' one man wanted to know.

'Dushanbe,' I told him.

'And then?'

'Afghanistan.'

The man nodded. It was the answer he had been expecting.

Another, older man was listening to our conversation. He was wearing the old Soviet-style police uniform with the wide-brimmed officer's cap. The same uniform the police in Prague and Ukraine had been wearing – only the badges and the colour of the cloth were different.

'I was a soldier in Afghanistan in 1979.'

'What was it like there?' I asked.

He shook his head slowly. 'It was hard. Very hard.'

I woke, freezing inside my blanket, to the morning sun glinting on the steel curve of the engine. We were flying just above a range of black mountain peaks looming through white clouds and an ochre haze below. A line of pink separated the blue sky from the dust storm beneath us. Somewhere in the night we had flown over the Karakum desert, Samarkand and Bukhara, the ancient caravanserai of the old Silk Road lay just to the north.

The plane descended into a pale haze. There were fields, the artificial lines of a canal, and a neighbourhood of low, dust-covered houses. A narrow riverbed wound its way listlessly through the houses. We came down in a screech of tyres. The pilots revved the engines to turn the plane. Huge clouds of cement-coloured dust erupted around us. The view from the porthole was blotted out. 'This is awful,' Richard muttered in the semi-darkness of the cargo hold. 'Absolutely desperate.'

Genghis Khan Soup

The sun was a white ball in the hazy sky. Thomas, the NBC fixer in Dushanbe, had brought a truck to meet us. On the tarmac, the ground crew offloaded the heavy silver boxes and manhandled them into the rickety back of the truck. We watched as the camera gear, chemical warfare suits, tents and camping equipment were shoved into growing piles on the truck. We had been travelling for forty hours and were dirty and exhausted.

While we waited for the unloading and loading to finish, Justin tuned into the BBC World Service on his shortwave radio. We heard the headlines wavering faintly through a sea of static. 'Military action against the Taliban by the US now seems inevitable.'

Thomas took our passports to have them stamped. Later he would take them to the Ministry of Foreign Affairs to get our *dokumenti* – press ID.

Dushanbe was as ugly and soulless on the ground as I had imagined a Soviet town to be from the air. The houses and apartment blocks were shoddily constructed. Ugly rusting pipes and rough concrete walls sprouted everywhere. Windows were often cracked and shored up with layers of cardboard, rusting barbed wire had been coiled along the tops of the walls. The roofs of the houses were made of fraying asbestos and rusting tin sheets.

The main road into town was prospekt Rudaki, once prospekt Lenin, but renamed now after Farid-eddin Mahommed Abdallah Rudaki, the 'Adam of Poets' – the first of the great post-classical Persian poets. Legend has it that Rudaki was blind from birth. What is known is that he was born in about 870 in a village in what was then Transoxiana and which today roughly approximates the territories of Turkmenistan, Uzbekistan and Tajikistan. Where Lenin had once stood for the international revolution of the proletariat, Rudaki symbolized a reawakening of the greater Persian roots of Tajik nationalism.

Prospekt Rudaki was a dual carriageway with grassy islands and benches. It was lined with tall trees, still green in the last warmth of summer. There were a few blonde Russians walking along the streets, but most of the people were dark-skinned Tajiks. The men wore colourful embroidered skullcaps. Some of the women wore scarves over their hair, knotted under the chin Russian *babushka*-style, not wrapped around their heads in the style of the Muslim *chador*. The streets were bustling, but not crowded.

Closer to town some of the buildings had a kind of faded Orientalist glory. The public buildings from the early Soviet days had pointed arches and exotic pillars that hinted at a tenuous strain of Asian culture allowed to exist within the orbit of the greater Soviet dream.

Our hotel, the Hotel Tajikistan, was just off prospekt Rudaki, across from Lenin Park. It was a monument to Soviet dullness. Taxi drivers and porters lounged on the wide steps, chewing green tobacco. They spat the juice out on to the sidewalk with loud 'splats', leaving frothing pools of watery green saliva.

The grey marble entrance and square pillars were cracked, revealing the concrete and rusting pipes underneath. The floor of the foyer was covered with a dirty red carpet. The front desk was crammed into one corner, and a small kiosk selling chocolates and cigarettes was at the other. There were so many journalists staying in the hotel that the owner of the kiosk, a diminutive Tajik woman, had added notebooks, ballpoint pens and maps of Tajikistan and Central Asia to her shelves.

The foyer was filled with journalists scurrying to and fro. They were all wearing the unofficial uniform for this story: hiking boots, jeans and colourful fleece tops. Heavy steel cases were piled everywhere as the porters struggled to fit them into the impossibly narrow lifts.

Thomas had reserved us rooms on the sixth floor. One of the old Soviet 'floor ladies' faced me sternly as I exited the lift. She had dyed orange hair and wide bands of purple eyeshadow on her eyelids.

'Key? For room 642?' I asked hopefully.

She frowned and shoved a piece of paper across the desk at me. I wrote '642' on the paper. She nodded and reached down into a drawer at her side and handed me the key.

It took us over an hour of pushing and shoving and hauling to fit our twenty-four cases into the rooms that had been assigned to us. At the end of it, we were covered in sweat which mingled unpleasantly with the grime of our forty-hour flight.

The rooms were tiny, but clean, with narrow wooden beds. The bathrooms were cramped. Small electric hot water tanks had been screwed to the walls. There were no separate cubicles. The water from the shower sprayed out over the toilet which barely worked. To flush, I had to fill a plastic wastepaper basket with water from the shower and pour it down the toilet. The taps for the hot water gave me a juddering electric shock when I turned them on.

After my varied and extraordinary ablutions, I found myself crammed into the tiny lift with a Russian journalist, down here from Moscow. He was friendly, wanting to help.

He stared intently at me through his spectacles, his blue eyes wide with seriousness.

'Don't eat in the Mafia restaurants,' he said. 'Never.'

'Why not?'

'There is nothing to be afraid of about the Mafia, but the food. It will make you sick.'

We couldn't do anything until our *dokumenti* had been issued. We were also eager to avoid the fatal mistake of collapsing into a deep sleep in the afternoon and then waking up at two in the morning. We needed to be fresh the next day. Thomas had warned us that transport into Afghanistan was erratic; we could be stuck here for days, or we could suddenly have to leave tomorrow.

In order to keep us awake, Thomas suggested that Timur, one of the local drivers he had hired, take us to an old caravanserai and fortress called Hissar, a little way out of the city.

Dushanbe was a frontier town. Everywhere you looked was evidence of Russian, specifically Soviet, colonization. The trees were a different species, but the wide tree-lined boulevards were the same European colonial blueprint that I had seen everywhere from the humid acacia-lined *avenidas* of Portuguese Macao to the crumbling ruins of colonial English or Belgian towns in Sudan or Congo. Like all colonial settlements, Dushanbe stood poised uncertainly between cultures. It was both Russian and Asian. It was caught in time, too, between the certainties of Soviet rule and the fragility of the unrest that had followed its collapse.

'Zaire with snow' was a favourite nickname among foreign correspondents for the Soviet Union. I could see now what they meant. The Russian need to expand their frontiers southwards into Central Asia arose out of a more complex psychological need than Western European colonialism. Domination, and the desire for territory were part of it, certainly; but there was something deeper than this in Russian colonialism. It arose out of the double workings of historical anger, and of fear.

For centuries following the conquests of Genghis Khan, Russia was divided into a number of small dukedoms and principalities. The rulers all owed unquestioning allegiance to the Golden Horde. The Russian dukes had to pay the Mongols large sums of tribute every year. If the demands were not met, the Mongol horsemen were sent to exact brutal retribution. For centuries, generations of Russian girls and boys grew up dominated by the fear of being slaughtered or taken as slaves.

In the two decades of the 1480s and 1490s, Western European colonialism was taking its first confident steps. In 1483 the Portuguese mariner Diogo Cão planted a stone cross at the mouth of the Congo river. In 1487 his compatriot Bartolomeu Dias rounded the Cape of Good Hope in a storm. By 1492 Christopher Columbus was making for America.

It was in these same two decades that Russians liberated themselves from the tyranny of the Mongols. It began in 1480 when Ivan III, subsequently known as Ivan the Great, the Grand Duke of Moscow, refused to cooperate any longer. In a moment of rage, he declined to pay the customary tribute to the great Ahmed Khan, supreme lord of the Golden Horde. Ivan also put to death a number of the Khan's envoys. Seething, the Khan mustered an army and marched on Moscow. Ivan at first was intimidated by this, but his Bishop, Vassian, urged him on. The two armies met at the waters of the Ugra river. For months, they faced each other indecisively. Finally, on November 11, Ahmed Khan and his army retired back into the steppes. It was scarcely a moment of great victory for the irresolute Ivan, but it was a moment of unavoidable psychological truth for the Russians. Their mighty oppressors had retreated. After two centuries, the Russians had learned that they, too, could be feared. Within two years, the Great Khan himself was slaughtered in battle and the power of the Golden Horde broken forever.

Never again would Russians allow themselves to be surrounded by the feared Asiatic hordes. The psychology of Western Colonialism was largely one of unquestioning superiority made possible by the ferocious power of their technology – by their swift ships and their iron cannons. The Russian fixation with conquering Central Asia was driven by an added dimension, the centuries of humiliation buried within the need to say 'never again'.

Russian power came late to this part of Central Asia. This region was inhabited from the earliest times by the ancient Bactrians and Sogdanians. Herodotus writes that they marched with Xerxes when he invaded Greece in 480 BC '. . . Armed with bows of cane, after the custom of their country, and with short spears.' The Arab invasions of the seventh century brought Islam to the region, but Arab rule was soon supplanted by the Persian Samanids. It was under the Samanids that poets like Rudaki and Avicenna, the great Persian philosopher and physician, were able to flourish. The Turkish invasions of the tenth century brought an end to Persian domination but not to Persian influence. The two Muslim cultures were able to exist side by side. 'Tajik' referred to the people who were settled traders, as opposed to the widespread nomadism of many of Central Asia's peoples. They survived with many of their essential features intact despite the invasions of the Mongols and the later bloodsoaked conquests of Timur the Lame, or Tamerlane, in the fourteenth century.

For centuries these parts of Central Asia and Northern Afghanistan were ruled by a succession of warring emirates and khanates. The high Pamir mountains prevented the Czars from exercising any effective control over Tajikistan which was nominally ruled by the corrupt and collapsing Emirate of Bokhara. It was only in the chaotic years after the Bolshevik revolution of 1917 that the early Soviet Union managed to firm up its control of this region. The first Tajik autonomous region was set up in 1924, and only became a full republic as late as 1929. Despite their international rhetoric of anti-colonialism, the Russian Soviets ruled supreme here.

Islam was effectively banned and the mosques shut down. Tajik children were taught Marxism-Leninism and to write their language in a specially adapted Cyrillic alphabet. Dissent was crushed, and most government positions were filled by Russians from Moscow. It was as unrelenting and brutal a form of colonialism as anything practised by the Western powers.

But things were changing fast. With the collapse of the Soviet Union, many ethnic Russians had found themselves stranded in Tajikistan. There was little room for them in this new society. They were almost entirely excluded from government and the sweeping Tajik nationalism left no place for them either. The only Russians who were present in force were soldiers. They were there at the invitation of the Tajik government to protect the border with Afghanistan. The Russian civilians I saw on the streets and in the hotel had been mostly relegated to doing menial jobs. The management and the pretty young women at the front desk were all Tajiks; the 'floor ladies', the cleaning staff and the janitors were all ageing Russians. There seemed hardly any young Russians on the streets. Centuries of outward expansion were being reversed, the young were all leaving, heading northwards, returning 'home' to Russia – a country most of them had never seen.

We drove out of town heading west. We stopped for a few moments at the Haji Yakoub Mosque and madrasa. The ceramic tiles that covered its minaret and arched gateway were a brilliant splash of turquoise, gold and azure against the dull grey of the city and the dust-filled sky. Building on the mosque began in 1990 with funds from Pakistan and the Middle East. A pair of workmen smiled down at us from an upper-storey window where they were plastering. A few teenage male students wandered in at the gates. A young man was selling Islamic tracts and books spread out along the sidewalk. Timur ushered us into the courtyard. Work was still going on in one corner. A large ditch was being dug in the ash-coloured earth and piles of broken concrete lay in another.

Timur asked somebody if we could take a photograph. He shrugged and walked on.

'It is okay,' Timur said. This unfinished mosque seemed to represent the state of mind of the 95 per cent of Tajikistan's citizens who were nominally Muslims. There was an allure to the mosque, the work on it was genuinely fine. I found myself wanting to take in the beauty of the tile work and the curves of the archways that represented a long-lost heritage. Looking at this mosque while surrounded by the combination of extreme poverty and the deadening conformity of the Soviet city, uplifted the spirit. And yet there was something too new, too uncertain about it. Most Tajiks were not observant. They drank vodka and few women even wore headscarves. There was, too, the uncomfortable reality of the extremists of the Taliban only a couple of hundred kilometres across the border in Afghanistan.

The civil war that had followed independence in 1992 had died down. But the country was still unstable. Estimates put the numbers of dead in the civil war at 60 000. The roots of the war were complex, and had their origins in Tajik factional politics. A significant faction, though, had been the Islamic fundamentalist guerrillas of the PDA or Popular Democratic Army. The government of Imamali Rakhmanov had finally defeated the PDA and a formal truce had been signed in 1997. But it had taken the intervention of 25 000 to 30 000 Russian troops to ensure the government's victory. Guerrillas were still operating out of Taliban-controlled Afghanistan. A Christian church had been bombed by internal extremists only a year ago. Ten people were killed and 200 wounded in the attack.

The government, too, was deeply suspicious of religion. In the peace deal of 1997, the Islamic Revival Party had been given 30 per cent of the seats in a power-sharing government, but the Rakhmanov faction tolerated little in the way of Islamic religious activity. Six decades of Soviet Atheism and a decade of unrest and civil war had left people insecure and exhausted.

On the outskirts of the city two young boys were leading a donkey; behind them a group of schoolgirls with pigtails and satchels on their backs straggled along the edge of the road. Women with headscarves and the long colourful dresses called *kurta* stood at the doorways of the low mud houses with their dilapidated roofs and tiny vegetable gardens.

A feckless, desperate market economy had taken grip of the roadside. Petrol, for example, was being sold in tiny quantities – in one or two litre plastic bottles. How much profit could one make off the sale of one litre of petrol? And how far could anybody travel on a single bottle of petrol? It was a tragic indicator of how little wealth was being generated in this economy.

A young man sat under a large, leafy plane tree. He was selling grapes in a bucket – a single bucket. Next to him somebody had half a dozen watermelons piled up in the dust. An old man hoeing a field was wearing the black embroidered cap known as *tupi* and the heavy quilted jacket known as *chapan*.

Dust filled the air. It spread an unearthly atmosphere over the landscape. All day the sun was the same translucent white disc.

A huge willow tree was a splash of bright green against the dull sky. It was so large it hung over the middle of the road. Someone had cut the long drooping branches straight across like a giant fringe, so the trucks had enough room to drive underneath. Beyond it was a police roadblock. Timur stopped for a moment. The police looked in the windows and waved us through.

We passed through a tiny village. The flat platform of a teahouse or *chaikhana* stood overlooking the road. But there was no one in it. The wooden planks of the floor stood shadowed and empty, waiting for a traveller who might have the time, and the money, to take his leisure with tea or, as likely, with vodka.

A small stream burbled alongside the road beyond the village. There was a patch of long green grass in one of its bends. A tethered donkey was grazing on the long stalks. In a scene that might have been out of Tolstoy, a small girl in a white blouse was kneeling in the grass in front of the donkey. She was clutching her schoolbooks to her breast with one hand. With the other, she was stroking the donkey's nose and talking to it as sweetly as any Western child might talk to a dog or a cat.

Timur drove fast, roaring along the uneven surface of the tarmac in the

4x4 that he rented out, along with his own services as a driver. He was a good driver and spoke a little English, two qualities that had made him suddenly indispensable in Dushanbe. The growing possibility of war in Afghanistan had brought hundreds of Western journalists to the city. With them came dollars and the first chance in years for something of a mini-boom to flood the city. Not much would reach the countryside, though, and it was here that conditions were bad. The worst drought in seventy-four years had gripped the country and the Red Cross estimated that a million people were in danger of suffering from famine, and a further two million of suffering 'severely'. This massive risk of famine was yet another legacy of Soviet rule. Traditionally, Tajik farmers had grown a wide variety of crops – everything from wheat, to corn, to apricots, grapes and other fruits. The Communists had systematically destroyed individual agriculture. Like they had done all over their empire, they forced farmers and villagers into collective farms and diverted the rivers from their natural watercourses using a system of canals. Tajikistan became a cotton-producing region with its quotas of cotton determined by bureaucrats in Moscow.

Now even that system had collapsed. Tajikistan was always the poorest Soviet republic, but since the civil war its GDP had declined by a massive 50 per cent. The environmental damage done by the canals and the huge amounts of pesticides and agrichemicals that had been dumped on the fields meant that when the cycle of drought hit this time its effects were magnified. The government could provide little help. It was still paying for the five-year civil war that had racked the country. According to the World Bank, some 80 per cent of Tajikistan lived below the poverty line. The GDP per capita was $330, making it one of the poorest countries in the world.

Timur was one of the lucky ones. His foresight in learning English had served him well. His brother was even luckier. 'He works for the United Nations,' Timur told me. 'It is a good job.' Timur spoke in the oddly formal way of many people unfamiliar with English. 'The situation is very bad in Tajikistan. Before there was war. Now the country is very poor. It was better before, under the Soviets. I was only a boy, but then no one was hungry like today. There was no war. There were many Russians here then, but most of them have gone now.'

And what about the Russians that had stayed, I wanted to know.

'We have no problem with them. I have many Russian friends. My sister has married a Russian.' I knew that not everybody felt that way. Life was hard in Tajikistan, and it was certain to get even harder for the Russians who chose to stay.

Timur slowed the car. Ahead of us a procession of men in dark clothes had filled the road.

'A funeral,' Timur said. Half a dozen of the men were carrying the body shoulder-high on an open bier. The body was covered in a red cloth with a low scarlet awning above. Timur covered his face with his hands briefly in the Muslim way and then put his hands back on the steering wheel.

'Where are the women?' I asked.

'They are at home, preparing the food. They do not come out for this.'

We came to a bend in the road. The landscape around us was semi-desert. Tiny scrub-like bushes grew in the mustard-coloured dust. Goat tracks crossed the dry, empty patches of land. A small village lay on one side of the road. A group of children played in the rusting skeleton of a car. A man in flannels and a windbreaker used a pitchfork to spread hay out across the road to dry. This was the road to Uzbekistan, but there was not much traffic on it since the civil war, and the relationship between the two countries had deteriorated.

On one side of the road was an ancient caravanserai with its arched compartments for travellers to spend the night. On the other lay a collection of mounds of earth. Brick towers stood between two of them. This was the fortress of Hissar. It had been an important watering point along the Silk Road, and the fortress was built in the eighteenth century. In the 1920s it was a stronghold for the basmachi forces of Enver Pasha and his vision of driving the Russian infidels out of Central Asia and creating a unified pan-Turkic state. The Bolsheviks annihilated that dream with 100 000 troops, machine guns and cannon. In 1922, Enver Pasha was slain in a final headlong charge against the Bolsheviks – or so the legend goes. It took until 1924, though, for the Red Army to destroy Hissar. These mounds and the reconstructed towers were all that was left.

There was not much else to see. We climbed up on top of the mounds that had been city walls. You could see how they had stretched in a wide circle across the plain. Broken shards of tiles glinted in the dusty earth.

A sense of desolation hung over these windswept mounds. At the foot of one of the mounds a copse of mulberry trees stood around a well. Small pieces of bright cloth had been tied to the tiniest branches of the trees. They reminded me, eerily and tantalizingly, of another Asian culture more than a thousand miles away. I thought of the *omikuji* tied to the branches of cherry trees planted in the gardens of Shinto temples in Japan. I wondered if there could be a connection.

Timur shrugged when I asked him about these tiny votive offerings. 'I don't know why people do it. Maybe for good luck.' He paused for a moment. 'The trees are old, very old. Maybe 500 years. And the well is 2 000 years old. Always people came here for water, that is why they built a fort here.'

So much history buried and forgotten in this desolate place. It reminded me somehow of the sadness underlying *Dr Zhivago* – so many lives and so many memories disappeared forever, swallowed up in the vortex of Revolution.

Back at the Hotel Tajikistan we had mutton soup with fresh green parsley and clear pools of fat floating on the surface. We tore at roundels of bread called *lepyoshka* in Russian, and dipped them into the soup.

'I suspect this is exactly what Genghis Khan would have eaten,' Dennis said.

'It's been boiled,' Justin pointed out. 'You probably won't get sick.'

'I had a group of Italian journalists here the other day,' Thomas said. 'They kept on asking me: where we can get soup *without* grease? I told them they were lucky to be getting soup.'

When we had finished eating Justin brought out his map. The terrain we had to cross was rugged. The contours showed high mountains and steep valleys. Many of the roads shown as lines on the map scarcely existed in reality. Others had small notices in red printing. *Danger! Roadmines.*

We looked at the distance between Dushanbe and Khuja Bahauddin.

'There's no doubt about it, the best way into Afghanistan is by helicopter,' Justin said.

Thomas raised his eyebrows. 'Helicopters haven't flown for two days because of the dust. Anyway, the Northern Alliance controls the helicopters. The tickets cost $500 a person.'

'One way?'

'No,' Thomas said. 'They are return tickets. Not that your seat is guaranteed either way. Everything depends on the Afghans. The Northern Alliance military has absolute first priority for the choppers. Sometimes they have casualties, or they want to move crates of ammo, whatever. The army gets the chopper. It's quite common for journalists to sit on the tarmac until it gets dark at around 5:00 pm, and then the Northern Alliance says: "No flights today."

'And you can't charter your own helicopter and just arrive in Afghanistan. To get permission to cross the border you have to deal with the Tajik Foreign Ministry, the Tajik Internal Security Ministry – which is really the former KGB. Then you have to get permission from the Russian army who have been invited in by the Tajiks, and finally, the Northern Alliance have to give you permission to land. You're dealing with three governments and five different agencies. It gets to be a mess. There are at least 200 journalists already on the waiting list for helicopter flights, and 85 more arrived on the flight from Munich today. The Tajiks have been overwhelmed. They are only allowing five people in at a time to the Foreign Ministry building. And that's only the first step in getting your permission.'

'What are our other options?' Dennis wanted to know.

Thomas smiled. 'You can drive south to the Panj river. And get a barge across. But then you've got to arrange for someone to meet you on the Afghanistan side. Then it's a long ride bumping over rocky ground all the way.'

'But it can be done?'

'It can be done, but let's work on getting your permissions first.'

The air became chilly as night descended. There was not much of a sunset. The dust in the sky grew dark and faded into night. There were no stars, they were hidden by the dust. I sat alone in my hotel room. Below me in the concrete and marble courtyard, groups of journalists were hunched over their shots of vodka and bowls of what had quickly become known as 'Genghis Khan soup'. There was a wedding in the ballroom of the hotel. The disco thudded out 'Unchain My Heart'.

Waves of tiredness welled up from deep inside me. *'God knows what time zone I'm in,'* I wrote in my notebook. *'God knows what century I'm in!'*

A Snapshot

At breakfast the next morning the news was that Donald Rumsfeld had completed his alliance-building tour of Central Asia. He left neighbouring Uzbekistan the previous night. Thirty thousand US troops and 350 planes were said to be ready to move. There was fighting reported between the Taliban and the Northern Alliance at Kunduz and Taloqan. Bagram, a town just north of Kabul had reportedly been taken by the Northern Alliance.

'Did you hear that the Ukrainians shot down a plane en route to the north?'

I hadn't. I remembered vaguely seeing a graphic of a plane over what looked like a map of the Black Sea on Russian television before I went to sleep the night before. I hadn't understood a word of the report, so I hadn't paid much attention.

'They said it was an exercise,' Justin said. 'It was on its way from Tel Aviv to Novosibirsk. No one is sure of the details, but it seems a stray missile hit it. Everyone on board is missing. The Ukrainians first said it might be terrorism but the US monitored the firing of a missile. It happened very near our flight path. It couldn't have been more than an hour or so from when we took off from Odessa.'

We had shopping to do. We had been issued with our *dokumenti* – laminated press identity cards with a colour photograph of us on one side and an impressive coloured crest of the Republic of Tajikistan on the other. We were now free to move around the city.

Thomas was dealing with our permissions for getting into Afghanistan. In the meantime, we had to stock up on supplies for the trip. The most likely scenario was that Ian would go with the truck convoy by land. The rest of us would try and get seats on a Northern Alliance chopper.

We set off with a long and varied list. Cups, kettle, tea, coffee, batteries, salami, cooking oil, two small fridges, ketchup, mustard, tins of sausage (beef, no pork), instant noodles, matches, washing powder, shovel, onions, biscuits, bottled water, tins of peas and corn, toothpaste, blankets, a microwave oven.

The last stop of the day was the bazaar. We intended to buy some fresh vegetables there and perhaps a few odds and ends like candles and matches. The bazaar was a fascinating sight. Here some of the heart of Central Asia had survived. Women in their colourful *kurta* were selling fresh corn and other vegetables. Men were selling small trade goods, from razor blades from China to kerosene stoves from Iran. In one corner were rows of shoes on display, in another someone was selling bread and fresh, deep-fried doughnuts.

I pulled out my camera and took a snapshot of one of the tables of merchandise; then there was an attractive young woman selling corn, an old couple dressed in colourful *kurta* and *chapan* . . . suddenly two policemen descended on me. One of them was huge, and his front teeth were made of solid gold. I hardly understood what was happening when he grabbed my hand and reached into my waist pouch and fished out my camera. His hands were enormous and powerful. I could sense immediately that he was a man accustomed to violence and to using it to control people.

'*Dokumenti?*' he yelled. '*Dokumenti!*' I was suddenly grateful for the bright plastic cards Thomas had obtained for us only hours before. I pulled my card out of my top pocket with my free hand and gave it to him. He took it with a grunt, glanced at it briefly and held on to it. It was not a good sign. I knew from having been arrested in Africa by countless rebel groups and ragtag government forces that if your credentials were handed back to you, the soldiers would probably not bother you for long.

The policeman held my camera and press pass in one hand, and started calling on his walkie-talkie with the other. The only reply was a buzz of static.

Justin and Akram, our Tajik translator – a small, softly spoken man who was prematurely balding – saw what was happening and came over immediately. Timur deftly slipped over to the second, less aggressive, policeman and began negotiating for my release with him.

It was to no avail. No matter what Justin or Akram said to the gold-toothed giant, he only grunted angrily in response. The biggest problem seemed to be that he couldn't raise anyone on his battered walkie-talkie. I had learned that often what was needed to get out of these situations was something that would allow the soldier or policeman to save face. Sometimes it could be an extra piece of paper, a letter of recommendation written by a local commander; other times it would be the arrival of a senior officer who could take responsibility. This time, I sensed that it would be the walkie-talkie. But the damned thing stayed silent. I found myself inwardly cursing Soviet technology as I watched the policeman's huge thumb press down on the talk button and his face screw up in frustration as he got no reply.

The other policeman brought up the battered Lada that served as their patrol car. The giant started manhandling me towards the back seat. This was suddenly getting serious. He brushed Timur away with the back of his thick forearm.

'I'm getting in the car too,' Justin said. He and Akram squeezed in next to me. The situation had been mildly annoying. Now it was thoroughly unpleasant; even a little frightening. I couldn't understand a word of what was being said, but it was obvious they were taking us to the police station. I was terribly grateful to Justin, and to Akram, for coming with me. There was a possibility that things could go wrong, and that I or perhaps all three of us would end up in jail. Spending even a few hours in a former Soviet jail was not something I wanted to happen to me, or to the others. I knew, though, that whatever happened, Akram would get the worst of it. He would also still be living here when I was long gone. It was very brave of him to insist on coming along to help me.

'This kind of thing happens all the time here,' Akram said quietly. 'They just want to show their power. At the end of this, I'm sure there will somehow be money. I was carrying an amplifier for my guitar once. I had the paper to prove that I had bought it, but they made all kinds of stories – in the end, I bought it again.'

'It'll be okay,' Justin said.

The giant glowered at us from the front seat. My camera stood accusingly on the dashboard.

'We'd better stop talking,' Akram said.

A few minutes later we arrived at the October Region police headquarters. There was a police guard at the gate. The giant yelled at him to open up.

The car pulled to a halt inside a dilapidated courtyard. The two policemen ushered Akram and me into the charge office. Justin somehow managed to sidle off to one side and take out his cellphone. The giant lunged for it but Justin whipped his hand away and jumped back. The giant was in a quandary now. Akram and I were already in the charge office; Justin was tempting quarry, but he was free. *Better a bird in the hand* . . . He left Justin alone and lumbered into the charge office. He slammed the door behind him. It was a cold concrete room with bare walls. A window to one side looked out on to the courtyard. Out of the corner of my eye, I could see Justin calling on his cellphone. Across the room was a low counter with a sliding glass window. Three or four policemen were crammed at its edges, peering at Akram and me. Their curious faces were pressed against the glass.

A plainclothes policeman was sitting at a rough wooden desk. The giant strode up to him and triumphantly placed my tiny camera on the desk. Next to it he slapped down my press card. Then he moved to stand behind us. He towered over us. The atmosphere in the room was extremely threatening. It was clear that these men were a team who had done this kind of thing to countless other people before. I was glad Justin was outside with the cellphone. Without him, both Akram and I would have felt terribly isolated – which, no doubt, was exactly how we were meant to feel.

'*Dokumenti!*' the plainclothes cop yelled at Akram. He was visibly shaken as he searched inside his jacket for his identity card. I admired him all the more for having come with me; but it also made me aware how close he felt we might be to the edge where they would turn on us in earnest.

We were now crossing the border into the Republic of Absurdistan. The situation was frightening, but in many ways the whole thing was comic. It felt like a real-life version of Kafka meets *Stir Crazy* – with my own personal version of Grossburger standing in uniform behind me. All I had done was take a tourist shot of a woman selling corn and some old people in traditional dress. Now my pocket camera stood like some sort of murder weapon dripping blood on the desk in front of me. Outside, Justin was hunched over his cellphone talking furiously *sotto voce* like a character in Mad Magazine's *Spy vs Spy*.

'Do you want me to say anything?' I asked Akram.

He shook his head slightly. 'No. It's better not.' His eyes were scared.

Within seconds, a whirlwind of shouting erupted around us. The only word I could understand, and which kept being repeated, was '*bazaar, bazaar, bazaar*'.

First the plainclothes cop yelled at Akram. Then the giant strode over and banged his fist on the table. It was a strange thing, being an observer at my own interrogation. I felt sorry for Akram who taking the brunt of the situation, and guilty because I had got him involved in this preposterous but frightening charade.

Then the door opened behind us, and two more policemen marched into the room. The cops peering through the charge office window grew visibly animated. I couldn't help noticing Justin's worried face popping up above the window sill.

Now there were four policemen standing over us, haranguing Akram. It was obviously a practised technique, this ganging up. They were yelling at him, and pointing at me and at him in relays. It was clear that something had shifted in the accusations. The focus was shifting away from me and on to Akram.

In the midst of the cacophony of shouting and accusations, I saw Justin pushing his way through the observers. He said something to the senior plainclothes cop. He scrunched his head sideways through the charge office window. He stuck his arm out and handed his cellphone to the plainclothes cop.

The voice on the other end of the phone was abrupt and clipped. The plainclothes cop nodded several times and handed the phone to the policeman who had arrested me. It disappeared into his meaty paw. He nodded several times too, and then closed up the phone.

The plainclothes cop went back to the table. He stood in front of Akram and me and slowly picked up my *dokumenti*. He handed me the card and shook my hand. Then, in turn, the other two cops solemnly shook my hand. The giant picked up my camera and ushered me out of the charge office. In the courtyard he turned and ceremoniously handed me the camera. Then he put out his hand again. Akram was still inside, so I thought I'd better take it.

'Who was on the phone?' I asked Justin

'That was the Ministry of Foreign Affairs. I was lucky to get someone on the line. They close for the day in a couple of minutes.'

'What do we do about Akram?'

'I've made some calls. It'll take a while, but I think they'll let him go.'

We sat down to wait on a wooden bench in the courtyard. Now that I was no longer a suspected spy, I became a guest. Two or three of the other cops came over to sit near us. Justin handed around some American cigarettes. There was a tall plane tree above us and a small garden of cherry trees alongside. The cops were polite and inquisitive now. What did we think of what was happening in the world, they wanted to know? Had we been there when the planes crashed into the towers?

No, Justin told them. But we had seen it on television.

'So did we,' one of the cops said.

'Bin Laden is a snake,' another added. 'He was fed by the Americans and now he has come to bite them.'

One man puffed gloomily at his Marlboro. 'I think there will be a war between Muslims and Christians.'

Justin exhaled and shook his head. 'No, there are Muslims in America too.'

The man held up three fingers. 'But few, very few.'

The first cop rounded on his colleague angrily. 'You can't say these things, about war. It's just terrorists who do these things – against Muslims or Christians.'

We waited a long time for Akram. Finally Timur came in through the gate of the police station. He had found Akram's backpack with his passport in it, and he brought it hoping that it might help. Justin went inside to the charge office with the passport. A few minutes later he and Akram emerged.

'It's okay,' Justin said. 'We can go.'

Back at the hotel, we ordered some beers and laughed about what had happened. It turned out that Kerry had taken a photo of me being arrested for taking a photo. It was stored on his digital camera and he took great pleasure in showing it to the assembled group.

'They asked me, "Why did he want to take a picture of old people?" ' Justin said. 'I told them you've never been here before. For you the bazaar is exotic. They all laughed at that.'

I noticed Akram was not laughing much, though. A little later, I found a moment when were alone. I thanked him for standing by me, but I could see that he was still upset and shaken by the incident. I don't know what they said to him inside after they had released me, but it was something about his documents not being in order. No doubt they had wanted money from him after being forced to let me go, but Timur's quick thinking in bringing in the passport had given them no further excuses. He hadn't been roughed up inside, but Akram was still hurt, and angered, by the way he had been treated.

'This kind of thing is very common here,' he said bitterly. 'This is how we live.'

A Whirlwind of Dust

'The word is,' said Justin at breakfast two days later, 'that the call could come at any time now. The Northern Alliance claim to have taken five villages near Mazar-i-Sharif, so they're on a roll. The choppers could free up any minute. We have to be ready to go at a moment's notice.'

The plan was that Ian would go with the majority of our supplies on the convoy. The four of us, Dennis, Justin, Richard and I, would get on the chopper and fly directly to Khuja Bahauddin.

We were keen to get going. We were becoming frustrated hanging around in Dushanbe. In addition, there were serious signs that the US and Britain were getting ready to launch an attack against Afghanistan. The Taliban had offered to release eight foreign aid workers if America would back down on its threats to attack Afghanistan. The White House rejected the offer out of hand. 'Full warning has been given,' President Bush said. 'For those nations that stand with the terrorists, there will be a heavy price.'

US intelligence sources were saying that there was a '100 per cent chance' of terrorist attacks being launched inside the US after military strikes began against Afghanistan.

An outbreak of anti-aircraft fire had been reported over Kabul. The Northern Alliance claimed that the Taliban were strengthening their ground defences in expectation of an attack.

Tony Blair had just finished a rapid tour of Russia, Pakistan and India. 'We are ready to go,' he told journalists. 'Everything is in place.'

By lunchtime we were on the tarmac at Dushanbe airport waiting to get on one of the choppers.

Each of us held a sheet of paper printed off a word processor. It read:

Embassy of the Islamic State of Afghanistan.
Office of the Military Attaché, Dushanb.

Received the amount of US$ 500- as fare for ~~one way~~/round trip to Afghanistan.

Note: The flights to Afghanistan are not scheduled and therefore this receipt does not necessarily guarantee the availability of the flights on specific dates or times.

At the bottom of the printed page someone had added, in ballpoint pen:
This ticket is not valid for domestic flight.

There were nearly a dozen other journalists who held the same pieces of paper. Most of them were TV crews who had as much equipment as we did. Tempers were rising fast. Already one woman journalist from a British network was using her considerable powers of self-confidence and persuasion to get herself and her crew on the chopper ahead of us. She was no rookie, and it was obvious that she was very good at getting her way.

'We have held these tickets for two days now,' she was haranguing the Afghan man who was in charge of allocating seats. '*Why* are we not on the helicopter?' He shook his head and muttered. It was impossible to accommodate everybody, so he tried to ignore those who hadn't been given seats.

The trick was, of course, to get your names on the flight manifest. Once the flight manifest had been written out, and your name was on it, you would be almost certain to take off – if the chopper was going to take passengers after all.

We had Justin, who could speak Russian, and a calm, unassuming Japanese TV crew had a Tajik fixer. While the British woman was loudly importuning whomever she could, Justin and the Tajik fixer were quietly talking to the man with the flight manifest.

After about half an hour of uncertainty he read out the names on the manifest.

'Why? *I demand to know*,' the British woman roared. 'We have held these tickets . . .' It was too late. Our names and those of the Japanese crew were on the list. A lone Irish journalist had quietly managed to finagle her way on too. 'It was pure deceit and guile,' she gloated.

We loaded the chopper in a mad rush. We were taking as little as we could, but between the lot of us, the hold of the ageing Russian chopper was filled up. Hydraulic oil was leaking out of some pipes in the back of the chopper.

We hadn't filmed a frame of video footage since we left London. New York was interested in a story of our journey, so we filmed the loading of the helicopter. Tokyo had obviously asked their crew for a story of the journey. So we filmed them and they filmed us getting on the chopper. Dennis and the Japanese correspondent each did a piece to camera. The rotor blades kicked into life and we scrambled, sweating and excited, up the rickety ladder at the side of the helicopter into the hold.

The noise of the engine was terrific. We couldn't hear each other speak. The whole machine juddered and squealed as the rotors built up speed.

The pilot opened the door to look back into the hold. Between him and the co-pilot was the frayed crimson remnant of a prayer rug. He stared for a long moment at the mountain of silver boxes, bottled water and personal luggage piled up at the back of his craft. Then he shrugged his shoulders and slammed the door shut. The tattered prayer rug somehow seemed a good motif for this flight.

The engine accelerated. As the helicopter lifted off the tarmac we were still filming the Japanese and they were still filming us.

The nose of the chopper dipped and we began to move forward. We scudded rapidly over the grey, amorphous buildings of Dushanbe. Suddenly we were into the steep hills and valleys of a brown range of mountains. Dry grass covered the barren slopes. Sheer rock faces loomed unexpectedly up in front of us. The thin glittering ribbon of a stream cut through the desolate landscape. Richard and the Japanese cameraman had opened the portholes and were filming the mountains sliding past below us.

We crossed the wide silver arc of a river that meandered through a deep valley. Fields lay on its banks; a single dirt road had been carved out along the contours below the mountain peaks. The river was the Vaksh, the northernmost arm of the Amu Darya or the ancient Oxus river that had seen the long-forgotten cities and realms of Persians, Zoroastrians, and Buddhists along its banks. A short way downstream from here the army of Alexander the Great had floated across the Oxus in a great flotilla of animal hides stuffed with dry grass.

Beyond the river the landscape altered. The mountains were sharp peaks carved out by ancient glaciers. The few acacia-like trees that had been scattered across the slopes disappeared. There were no more large cultivated fields; the villages grew sparse and tiny. Roads ceased and only footpaths followed the steep contours of the slopes. We came to a wide, empty plain where a giant river meandered and flowed in a dozen different courses through the bone-dry land. It was the Panj, the southern arm of the Amu Darya.

We had crossed into Afghanistan. It was mid-afternoon, but at this altitude the sun was already low against the horizon. The peaks of the next mountain range loomed dark and menacing in the dust-filled sky. The harshness of the terrain was breathtaking. It was beautiful, but I couldn't help thinking what it might be like to have to fight a war there.

On the other side of the mountains we came to a lush valley with flat green fields, mud houses and the brown gentle curve of a river. They were paddy fields. My eye caught the glint of sunlight reflected among the emerald green rows as the chopper turned and banked in the sky. Donkeys wandered along white sand paths. A row of poplars stood at the edge of the gleaming paddy fields. In the bleak, concrete remnants of the Soviet Union in Dushanbe I had forgotten something essential. *This is, after all, Asia*, I scribbled in my notebook.

We landed in Khuja Bahauddin in a whirlwind of dust. I was aware of the curve of the river, and a row of flat-roofed, mud houses breaking the skyline on a ridge above us. We tumbled out of the chopper while the engines were still throbbing. We doubled up under the whirling blades dragging our boxes of equipment along the dry ground. The power of the rotor rippled against our clothes and shoved us half-stumbling against the ground. Once we had unloaded everything we ran to the perimeter of the landing site and closed our eyes and turned our backs on the chopper. There was a roar and a furious wind whipped around us. Somebody's hat went rolling across the ground. The chopper lifted off with a thudding clatter. It turned against the sky and headed back for the distant brown peaks of the mountains.

A silence filled the valley. I could hear the laughter of children. Heat shimmered off the dry, stony ground. Donkeys walked in a slow, diagonal line up the barren hillside towards the cluster of houses. The animals were laden with piles of hay so large that only their hooves were visible beneath a fringe of yellow stalks. They were led by two young boys and a woman in a dark *burqa*.

A man in a camouflage uniform came up to us. An AK-47 was slung upside down over his shoulder. With him was an official of the Northern Alliance. He was wearing the traditional flat-topped *pakol* cap and a black and white checked scarf hung over his shoulders.

He took our passports away. 'Wait here,' he said. 'We will bring transport.'

The river formed a fragile, narrow green band through the pale dust of the valley floor. A low bridge of logs and mud connected the two halves of the valley. Beneath our feet was a thin white scum. It was the residue of agrichemicals, or – worse – of pesticides. Where it covered the ground, nothing grew.

'It's blown over from Tajikistan probably,' Justin said.

At the edge of the river men and boys gathered to stare at us. Some were wearing turbans and riding donkeys; others had bright, embroidered skullcaps. They all wore traditional *shalwar kameez*, a long shirt-like garment with a colourful waistcoat over it.

They must have seen scores of chopper loads of journalists being dropped off here in the last weeks, but the children, especially, were friendly. Some of them had learned a few words of English, and every now and then we would hear: 'Hello, how are you?' followed by peals of delighted laughter.

Our passports were nowhere to be seen, but the Afghans brought pickups for us. We loaded them. There was not enough room for everyone in the cab, so Justin and I climbed on the back and stood among the luggage. The trucks climbed up the steep dusty hillside to the village on its crest. We entered the narrow streets bounded by high mud walls on either side. The women flipped their long veils back over their faces when they heard the sound of our vehicle coming up behind them.

The NBC villa was a large stucco house on the top of a ridge above the village. It overlooked a valley with a river and rice fields stretching out for some miles. It had a wide cement porch where all the laptop computers, camera gear, and satphones vied with the electric cooker, kettle, plates, cups, knives and forks for space.

We had two generators to run all the cooking and communications equipment and the enormous satellite dish that had been erected in front of the porch. The generators also had to run all the television lights. If you turned on the kettle to make tea while one of the correspondents was going live, the whole set would go dark as the kettle tripped the lights.

It was a cluttered, inconvenient arrangement, but we were far better off than most of the other journalists who were crammed into a tiny mud-walled compound nearby. At least we had toilets that you could throw a bucket of water down to flush. The others had to make do with a pit toilet that was rapidly filling up.

One edge of the house was boarded up and black smears of oily smoke residue climbed up the walls. Jean Chu, the senior producer running the operation, pointed at the room. 'That was where Massoud was blown up. You have to be very careful around it. The Northern Alliance don't like anyone walking too close to it. We can't even set up any cameras on that side of the house. It's a kind of shrine for them.'

Richard and I took one look at the crowded rooms where people were sleeping crammed together on the floor.

'I think it's tents,' he said. The two of us wandered around to the back of the house. We chose a location at the edge of the high ground that was far enough away from the room where Massoud had been killed.

Two enormous stone capitals stood half-buried in the sand. One of the Northern Alliance guards came up to us. He slapped his hand on top of one of them. Then he began to count out with the fingers of his left hand. 'One, two, three, four, five.' Then he brought up the other hand and counted. Then he put up two hands together. 'Two thousand,' he said.

It took me a moment before I understood what he was trying to say. These were not, as I had assumed, the relics of some half-forgotten British colonial embassy or outpost. These stone capitals, with their simple Doric lines, were much older than that. They were the remains of a town built by the Bactrian Greeks – the descendants of Alexander's soldiers who had stayed on and built a kingdom that had lasted until shortly before the birth of Christ.

The ground next to the columns was littered with shattered glass and pieces of camera from the explosion. For a moment, I was hesitant. It seemed macabre to be pitching a tent here among the residue of the explosion that had killed a man. But the truth was, there was no other place where we could pitch our tents without being in someone's way.

As we were pitching our tents I could hear the occasional distant cough of an artillery round in the distance. We were closer than I had realized to the front lines. It was difficult, at this distance, to tell the difference between incoming and outgoing fire. Sometimes there were two or three shells and, a little while later, an answering volley.

So many layers of war buried in the dust of this tiny village. And the latest one was about to begin. Things were beginning to get tense around the laptops and cellphones on the porch. We could watch a hazy version of MSNBC, the NBC cable channel on the return feed from our satellite transmitting dish.

President Bush was warning that the attack would be soon. All around us people were on the satellite phones to contacts in the Pentagon trying to get confirmation of whether the strikes would begin tonight or not. No one could get anything definite.

'It looks like it's really going to happen tonight,' Justin said. We had arrived in Afghanistan just in time. Ours had been the last Northern Alliance helicopter to take off from Dushanbe for the next few days at least, maybe longer. The Northern Alliance were clearing the skies of Afghanistan in anticipation of American and British action. But what would it be?

'And where the hell,' somebody asked, 'is Osama Bin Laden?'

Things were beginning to build up quickly. I felt utterly disorientated. We had just arrived in Afghanistan and now we were on the brink of war. No one around us was particularly worried. Khuja Bahauddin was the military capital of the Northern Alliance and had been secure for a number of years. It seemed certain that the Taliban would not be able to advance towards it when the air strikes began. But what would happen in their aftermath? What kind of confusion would they unleash?

I suddenly found myself thinking of the grim policeman we had met in the middle of the night in Baku. He and thousands of his fellow Soviet soldiers had been driven out of Afghanistan by the determination of the mujahedin fighters, many of whom were now on the sides of both the Taliban and the Northern Alliance. At least 15 000 of them had been killed and 400 000 wounded. Many people said the true figures were even higher, perhaps as much as 40 000 or 50 000 Soviet soldiers had been killed. Half a million Afghans were estimated to have been killed in the war, and four million had fled the country as refugees.

The air began to cool as the last of the light slipped away. In the river below us men were washing trucks. A group of boys had brought some donkeys down to drink. Someone else was washing clothes in the river. Women in *burqas* collected water in terracotta jars and carried them back up the slopes towards the village. A line of camels tied together walked slowly and undulatingly across the plain.

The call to prayer rang out somewhere from the village behind us. The sun disappeared rapidly behind the dusty horizon.

It looked like it was going to be a long night. I grabbed an MRE (Meal Ready to Eat) from the store in the basement of the house. It was meatballs and ketchup. I tore open the silver packet and ate it cold with a plastic spoon. There was no time to bother about heating it up. In the basement, too, was the satellite transmission control room. The two engineers, Tom and Julian, were frantically switching buttons and testing channels as calls came in from New York and London to get correspondents on the air.

It was a strange atmosphere to be working in. We could see nothing of what was happening, but we were in Afghanistan and the correspondents were expected to have something to tell the world. It was our job as the support crews to make sure that they got on air and had something worthwhile to say. But all our information was downloaded from laptop computers connected to satellite phones. The anchorperson in New York or London would ask the correspondent in Khuja Bahauddin a question live on the screen; and the correspondent would answer it based on information he had read and downloaded from the database in New York or London.

There was something uncanny about the whole operation. Somewhere out there in the world there was real information – not much, but there were things that happened, or things that we were told, that we could report on. This real information was coming from dozens, perhaps even a hundred, different places.

Decisions were being made in the White House, in Downing Street, in Islamabad, Kabul, Jalalabad, on the flight decks of the carriers in the ocean. It was all being fed into this vast matrix of colour and sound of which we here in Khuja Bahauddin were a tiny node. As events progressed that night we downloaded information and spewed it out again at a dizzying pace. We were at the centre of reporting the start of the biggest war on the globe. The newsdesk was crossing live to Khuja Bahauddin every thirty minutes or more and yet we could not see a single shot being fired.

Only a couple of hours ago, in the daylight, I had been watching people living their lives in a way that had not changed since the tenth century. Now, in the darkness, the electronic world and the confusion of its new war had swept in.

*

8:00 pm: MSNBC is reporting that US troops are in position and 'ready to strike'. They are waiting only for the go-ahead from President Bush. Still, the situation is unclear. There is talk of the 1 000 or so soldiers standing by in Uzbekistan. Surely they couldn't be sent in now?

9:00 pm: 'The word is,' says Justin, 'that something – probably air strikes – could happen within the hour. MSNBC sources say the US is likely to take out some of the Taliban air defences in this first wave of attacks.'

Some of the Northern Alliance fighters come rushing downstairs in their camouflage uniforms. They have left their AK-47s in the room they share upstairs, but they are very excited and gleeful. They seem to think that because Tom and Julian control the technical aspects of the satellite transmission, they have access to all the information coming in as well.

'What happen, Mr Tom?' they ask. 'Attack?'
'I think so, but from here I can't see anything more than you guys.'

9:20 pm: I call my brother Steve on the satellite phone. He is working on the newsdesk of Reuters TV in London. He, in turn, has heard by satellite phone from his crews south of us in the Panjshir valley. They are saying that they have seen flashes over the night sky in Kabul. Soon MSNBC is reporting flashes over the night sky in Kabul.

9:35 pm: A report comes in that 8 000 Taliban are heading towards nearby Mazar-i-Sharif. MSNBC is reporting flashes of anti-aircraft fire near Bagram airport. And then four or five big explosions near Kabul.

Some of the fighters have put on their canvas ammunition pouches and are carrying their AK-47s. I suppose they're doing it in case something happens. Most of them, though, are gathered in the room they share. In keeping with their custom, they have taken off their combat boots and are sitting barefoot in their camouflage uniforms on the carpet. They are gathered around a crackling shortwave radio.

One of them looks up as we come in. 'Thank you, America,' he says.

Another grins, and draws his hand across his throat. 'Osama Bin Laden,' he says. Of course it's for our benefit, but certainly these guys are ecstatic that they now, essentially, have the most powerful air force in the world.

10:00 pm: The situation is still unclear. The only thing that has been confirmed is flashes in the sky over Kabul. But there has been anti-aircraft fire over Kabul quite frequently the last couple of weeks. The Taliban are jittery and likely to fire at anything.

A French journalist comes over from the compound where many of the other journalists are staying. 'You know it's really happening?' he asks. 'There are live images on CNN.'

The Northern Alliance command has the only TV in the village and it is based in the compound where the journalists are housed. At one time or another, some of the dozen or more technicians based in Khuja Bahauddin have been asked to fix the reception on the satellite dish. Invariably, they find the memory of the decoder has stored the numbers of pornographic channels.

But tonight there are more exciting things to watch. The Northern Alliance soldiers are crowded around the tiny screen. Somehow CNN has managed to get a videophone with a nightscope up about 40 kilometres from Kabul. Tiny green flashes pulse and throb on the bluish tinged screen.

In an insert at the bottom of the screen, Christiane Amanpour is providing commentary on the bombing from miles away, across the border in Pakistan.

It seems almost ridiculous. And yet, it is the real thing. Under those blurred pulsing flashes, buildings are collapsing and people are dying.

A half moon hangs in the sky outside. Its cold light gives the dust in the air a glowing luminescence. Everywhere in the compound I can see the dark shadows of journalists and soldiers moving excitedly about.

'Kandahar *and* Kabul,' one of the soldiers watching the TV says gleefully.

Bursts of illumination light up the horizon. For a moment, there is a flurry of excitement that they may be the flashes from the bombing runs. But they are not. The lights we can see faintly sweeping over the horizon are the headlamps of trucks and 4x4 vehicles on the road heading towards the front line. For that many vehicles to be moving on the road at this time of night means that the Northern Alliance must be moving reinforcements up to the front line where they are facing the Taliban.

President Bush is on the screen now. '*On my orders, the United States military has begun strikes against Al Qaeda terrorist training camps and military installations of the Taliban regime in Afghanistan . . .*'

The layers of information overlap and feed on one another – lots of crews and photographers are taking pictures of the Northern Alliance soldiers watching the bombing and President Bush's announcement on TV. Some of the soldiers don't want to be filmed for either religious or personal reasons. They have wrapped their scarves around their heads so that they can't be identified. Of course, that only makes a more fascinating picture for Western audiences. In one corner of the compound a photographer is sending his pictures of the soldiers watching TV out from his laptop by satellite phone. The soldiers he photographed are leaning over his shoulder watching their images being beamed across the world. Half a dozen photographers are taking pictures of the soldiers watching their picture on the screen.

12:05 am, Monday 8 October: The wire services are reporting that fifty cruise missiles have been launched against targets in Afghanistan. Osama Bin Laden has reportedly issued a *fatwa* to kill Americans and their allies.

1:15 am: Finally we get a chance to sleep. Dennis has done a number of live crossings on the satellite dish, but eventually New York has stood us down. I am more tired than I realized. All night the camera lights blaze into the darkness as one correspondent after another gets up to go live on the satellite channels. My last memory before I go to sleep is of the beauty of the river in the valley below us, gleaming calm and silver in the moonlight. I realize that it is exactly this clear moonlight that the military planners must have been waiting for.

The Front Lines

The dust rose in fine choking clouds. The battered Niva jeep we were in careened wildly over the ruts and deep potholes in the road. I could see hardly anything through the dark plastic glareproof sheeting that had been stuck on to the windows. We passed men riding camels and donkeys along the edge of the road. In the dust and the glare of the sun their images were blurred by the dipping and rearing of the car. In front of us a goatherd hurried his flock across the road. The dust their hooves kicked up met the dust our car raised. They disappeared into a swirl of choking, hot powder.

The high mud walls of the villages we passed enclosed tantalizing glimpses of gardens: poplars and willows with dust-covered leaves, a row of apricot or mulberry trees drooping in the heat, children squatting in the cool mud around a water furrow. Afghanistan was always known for its gardens. In ancient times, the mosques and shrines of cities like Balkh, Herat and Kabul were famous for their architecture and for the poetry, art and philosophy that their gardens of roses and lilies inspired. When he entered the region which is now Afghanistan in the mid-1270s, Marco Polo found 'rich herbage, fine pasturage, fruit in plenty and no lack of anything'. Twentieth-century travellers like Robert Byron, Eric Newby and Bruce Chatwin, who came here before the Soviet invasion of 1979, all write of the beauty and peace of Afghan homes and gardens. The poet Peter Levi called his book on Afghanistan *The Light Garden of the Angel King* after a description of Afghanistan over the tomb of its greatest king Babur, the founder of the Mogul dynasty.

But to us, as we passed in our screeching, rattling jeep, the gates of the gardens stood firmly closed. No one waved at us as we drove past. The memories and fears of over twenty years of war seemed shut up inside those gardens, too, hidden behind the silence of the heavy wooden doors with their iron rings and hinges.

We were on the road to the front line at a place near the Tajik border called Ay Khanoum. The American and British bombing was pounding the Taliban positions all across the country. No planes had been reported over the Ay Khanoum front yet, but since the bombing had started, the pace of the fighting had quickened.

Zamuruddin, our translator, sat in the front seat. Dennis, Justin and

Richard were crammed into the back seat. I was the smallest member of the group. Somehow a space had been found for me behind them. The car lurched over the bumps in the road with the speed and suddenness of a roller-coaster. I clung on to a canvas strap that had been hung across the back of the car. Richard had a bad back. Every time the car hit a bump it wrenched his spine painfully. He was genuinely suffering and when the worst bumps came he could not suppress a cry of pain. '*Fuuuck*,' he would roar as the chassis jack-knifed upwards into the air.

The road was so bad and the car lurched so violently that it was dangerous. None of us could relax for a single moment, or we risked hurting ourselves. If I didn't hold on to the canvas strap with all my strength, I was likely to smash my head hard against the steel sides of the jeep. It was an exhausting journey. Zamuruddin and the driver had the best time of it, by far.

'The Americans bombed near the front line last night,' Zamuruddin said. 'Near Taloqan and Kunduz. They hit some pockets of Taliban, and I heard that eight Taliban officers were killed in Mazar-i-Sharif.'

A village emerged from the dust in front of us. 'This village used to be on the front line,' Zamuruddin told us. 'Just beyond here was the Taliban. But we drove them back some months ago.'

The driver stopped the car in the shade of a tree. 'We have to wait here for permission from the commander to proceed to the front lines.' He and Justin set off in search of the local commander while Richard, Dennis and I got out of the car to stretch our legs.

Shade from trees in the walled gardens fell over the road. A camel tethered to a stake stretched up his long neck and crunched the leaves off one of the trees. Women in long white *burqas* hurried past us with their faces averted and hidden behind a grid sewn into the mask that covered them.

A truckload of soldiers was parked on the opposite side of the road. Most of them were dressed in camouflage uniforms. A few of them wore turbans or *pakol* caps. They stared fiercely at me when I lifted my camera to take a picture. The flash went off and they laughed when I took a second.

A group of children had gathered to watch the excitement of the soldiers and the journalists heading for the front. Their brightly coloured clothes were refreshing splashes of colour against the dun-coloured mud walls. Royal blue, pink, scarlet, purple, but when I got my camera out to take a photograph, one of the soldiers wagged his finger at me.

There were five other 4x4s carrying journalists parked in the road, waiting for their translators to come back from the local commander's office with permission to 'proceed to the front lines'. There was the familiar feeling of paranoia in the air that always happens when groups of journalists aggregate around a story. Most of them tacitly refused to acknowledge the presence of the others.

These big groups of journalists were called – in our own charming and sensitive argot – 'clusterfucks' or 'gangbangs'. They were the worst aspect of what we did. There was something absurd in the way the herd mentality would take hold in situations like this. Before you knew it, two or three dozen people would be scurrying about wildly brandishing cameras and tape recorders in every direction. The levels of desperation would feed on themselves as each individual tried to get something, just *something*, different from everyone else. Inevitably, the clusterfuck would gravitate mindlessly and headlessly, swirling like an amoeba in a Petri dish, into the most dangerous situations.

The danger on the front line was real, though; and so was the war we were covering. It seemed the Northern Alliance had experience in managing journalists. One by one, the translators appeared with permissions to proceed, and none of us saw each other again for the rest of the day.

We came to a high mountain peak. On either side we could see where trenches had been dug. A rusting, abandoned Russian armoured troop carrier had been incorporated into the defences at one point. Empty artillery shells lay in a heap on the ground.

This side of the mountain was safe from the Taliban shelling. Zamuruddin led us up a pathway to a shelter dug into the mountainside. The path was neatly lined with stones, and a small garden of bright flowers had been planted outside the entrance to the dugout.

Some soldiers were lounging in the shade of the dugout. A small fire burned at the back. A pot with beans was bubbling on the flames. Someone was boiling water in a spent tank shell. Steam swirled out of its narrow, upright neck. Nearby lay a pile of dusty potatoes and a watermelon.

There was hot tea and flat, cold *naan* bread. I could hear the sporadic thud of a shell landing far away; then there was the heavy, unmistakable rhythm of a 50 mm machine gun echoing across the lines.

We walked up to the top of the mountain. The hard ground was covered in twisted, deadly fragments of shrapnel from exploded shells fired across the valley by the Taliban.

The trenches were deserted. Rags, an abandoned boot, and small heaps of human shit baked in the sun on their cracked mud floors. On the other side of the crest of the mountain a Russian tank was dug into the earth. Its turret was covered in sandbags. The commander of this tank wore a camouflage uniform and a straw cowboy hat. His deputy wore civilian clothes, a long dark green *shalwar kameez* and turban.

At the edge of the mountain an observer in a turban squatted with a pair of binoculars in his hands and an AK-47 slung over his shoulder. He had a dark angular face with a neatly trimmed beard.

Zamuruddin came up to us. 'There,' he pointed, 'are the Taliban. Across the valley. You see that line of trees. They are on that ridge behind them.'

We looked out over a wide flat valley. On one side lay an abandoned mud-walled town. I could see a solitary old man leading a straw-laden donkey through the maze of empty streets.

'Some weeks back the town was shelled by the Taliban,' Zamuruddin said. 'The people fled, but some of them come back in the day to cultivate the fields.'

Lying between us and the Taliban lines was an enormous meandering watercourse of curving sapphire channels and white, sandy gravel. Below us the Kokcha river flowed into the Amu Darya. A long trench ran across the front of the mountain slope parallel to the direction of the river. It was empty now, but if the Taliban attacked across the valley, the Northern Alliance would hold them back at this point.

The noise of shelling and machine gun fire was sporadic. Between volleys, silence filled the hill top, and there was only the sound of the wind whistling past our ears.

We were waiting for General Bharylai, the local commander, to come up to meet us. While we were standing there, one of the soldiers came up to me. He waved his arm in wide arc in front of him. 'Iskander,' he said. 'Iskander.'

I knew what he was trying to say. That Alexander had been here, too. What I didn't know, and found out months later, was that Ay Khanoum meant Lady of the Moon in the Uzbek language. It had been a Greek city 2 300 years ago, and possibly a Persian city before that. It was almost certainly the site of Alexandria-On-The-Oxus founded, perhaps, in the lost year of his campaign, 327 BC. The ancient sources cannot agree on what he did that year, but he was almost certainly in this region of Afghanistan. Whoever founded the city, located it for the same reason the Northern Alliance had chosen to place their tanks here: it was a superb defensive site.

It must once have been a wealthy city. The Kokcha river led east into the Afghan province of Badakshan which in Roman times, and before, had been the world's richest source of the fabled lapis lazuli. French archaeologists had discovered the Greek ruins in the early 1960s and had been carefully excavating the site. But now, after so many years of war, the ancient relics had been plundered. The only things left here were the rusting armoured cars and the piles of shit drying in the cold wind that blew in from the river valley.

'The General says the Taliban know you are here,' Zamuruddin told us. 'They can see you through their binoculars.'

General Bharylai and his fellow commanders had between 10 000 and 15 000 men to call on. They had hardly any tanks or guns, except these old relics dug into position on strategic hilltops along the front line. The Taliban had as many as 45 000 troops and militia, plus the ability to bring in 200 000 to 300 000 conscripts. They also had hundreds of tanks, heavy guns and armoured personnel carriers. They claimed to have forty jets at their disposal, but the real number of fighter jets able to fly, and shoot, was estimated to be about six or eight. The Northern Alliance had no aircraft except a few antiquated helicopter gunships.

The General was wearing neatly pressed camouflage fatigues and wrap-around sunglasses. He ordered the tank to fire at the Taliban. Richard set up the camera a safe distance from the tank. I put my fingers in my ears. White smoke and an enormous orange flame flashed out from the barrel. The ground shook. The sound wave rolled over us. Then there was the long, echoing whistle of the shell, layers of sound building up across the emptiness of the valley.

A few seconds later, a huge shower of white dust billowed up on the low hills across the valley. Then there was a faraway *crummmppp*, like the sheets of steel in a car accident collapsing into one another.

Richard zoomed in as a tall plume of black smoke rose up on the horizon, mingling with the dust suspended in the air.

I wondered what had happened as that shell landed. Who might have been beneath its thundering explosion? The General and his men probably had a good idea of exactly who and what lay across the valley. They were shelling the Taliban every day now that the American and British bombers had started their campaign. The Taliban were shelling them back frequently. The jagged shrapnel we had seen lying around was evidence of that.

The reality of the explosion and who lay beneath it was hidden from us and from our camera. We could only see, and report on, what we had filmed – the column of smoke rising up into the air and the white dust hanging in the distant haze on the horizon.

I watched the Northern Alliance soldiers eject the empty cartridge and throw it smoking on the dry ground next to the turret. As they loaded another shell into the breech, I wondered how much in this war would remain hidden from us, and from our cameras.

The General ordered another shell to be fired. A flash. The ground around us shook. Huge clouds of smoke and dust rose in the air and hung there in the golden afternoon light.

The sound of machine gun fire broke out across the valley. Then some isolated rifle shots. One. Then three or four in quick succession.

'The Taliban sneaks across sometimes,' Zamuruddin said. 'It is a relatively unstable area. They come in quite often.'

We all knew the dangers. I thought of the old rule in war reporting that I had learned in Rwanda and the Congo. *Outgoing attracts incoming.* These positions were dug in. The Taliban must have known exactly where they were. They were likely to fire back after a few minutes.

But we still had work to do. We had to interview the General and some of his soldiers.

'The front line is static. When will you advance?' Dennis asked the General.

The General looked at the camera through his sunglasses. 'We are waiting for the Americans to finish their work, and then we will attack.'

We moved over to one of the soldiers manning the tank. 'Why are you fighting this war? Why do you want to destroy the Taliban?' Dennis asked.

The man hesitated for a moment. 'Because the Taliban are Pushtun. They come here from elsewhere to attack us.'

Sunset layered the sky. Black, crimson, ochre and, high above, where the Stealth bombers and the B-52s cruised, were the last violet hues of the afternoon light. Thousands of Northern Alliance troops were heading for the Panjshir valley and then Kabul. They had no vehicles to spare, so they were walking the whole way. Tonight they were camped behind the front lines on the banks of the Kokcha river.

Their tents made silhouettes against the setting sun. The smell of smoke from the cooking fires rose into the cool air. Voices drifted across the flat plain, the sounds of metal striking metal, the bleating of tethered goats, the thud of firewood being chopped.

I thought of that soldier on the hill near the tank, and his urgent, insistent voice. 'Iskander, Iskander.' Some time in that lost year, Alexander's soldiers must have passed very near this place. Their encampment would have sounded exactly the same as this one.

Sandstorms

A lone grey heron winged its way down the river in front of my tent. Across the valley three men were threshing rice by driving two cows in a circle of beaten earth. They used pitchforks to winnow it. The chaff flew up into the air, catching the first still light of morning before the breeze swirled it away.

The heron's slow flight. The morning sun. Dark furrowed earth and rows of broken yellow stalks. Harvested paddy fields and stacks of sweet-smelling rice hay. I remembered another lifetime – an autumn in Japan when I fell in love with my wife.

In the house nearby I could hear the soldiers starting their morning chores. The radio crackled with news in Dari. One could hear, almost feel, the ancient Indo-European roots of the language as the soldiers discussed the articles of news amongst themselves. They sat barefooted and cross-legged on the cheap scarlet and mustard carpet. A battered kettle of tea was being passed around. Their black and white checked scarves wrapped around their head to ward off dust and flies. '*Ast*' – 'it is'; '*khub ast*' – 'it is good;' '*nist*' – it isn't.'

A teenage boy brought canisters of water on the back of a donkey. The sound of the fresh water echoed as the soldiers poured it into the empty galvanized tank. One of the soldiers was lighting a kerosene stove to boil water for tea. Another carried plates of rice and beans and freshly baked whole-grain *naan* across from the compound. The soldiers were grim-faced usually, even when we shared food with them. When we thanked them for it, they sometimes smiled then, but even those who didn't would bow their heads and put their hands across their chests to touch their hearts.

This place and its people entering memory in an almost physical accretion of sight, sound, distance and time, all layered on top of one another.

Two men in turbans and long flowing robes walked along the still edges of the river. One had his hands clasped behind his back, both had their heads bowed as they talked intently. They looked like two philosophers from an older Afghanistan, before the tanks and the helicopters and the mines. The country of gardens and couplets of Sufi poetry recited over cups of green tea.

Every night now, we followed the virtual war on the blurred return channel on the satellite. There was bombing in Kabul, Kandahar, Jalalabad, and nearer to us, the Taliban defences in Mazar-i-Sharif, Kunduz and Taloqan were being hit nightly. Far away in the Pacific ocean, the *USS Kitty Hawk* had left Yokohama and was moving into position somewhere off the coast of Pakistan in the Arabian Sea.

The Taliban claimed that a stray US bomb had hit a village, killing 200 people, mostly women and children.

In Florida and New York, anthrax had been discovered in people's mail. One of the letters had been sent to NBC's headquarters at Rockefeller Plaza in New York. The offices of Nightly News were hastily evacuated because of the possibility of contamination. The reports of the bombing got lost under the fear that this strange, untraceable new threat had forced into the minds of Americans.

Hakim was hired as the chief fixer and organizer for the NBC operation. He was a young man in his early twenties. He grew up in Kabul and had been studying to be a doctor before the Taliban had driven him out. His English was excellent. 'Hakim' means 'doctor' in Arabic, so I suspected, although I never asked, that Hakim was a nom de guerre.

'South Africa?' he said delightedly when I told him I lived in Johannesburg. 'When I was in exile in Pakistan, we always supported the South African cricket team. We Afghans liked them more than the Pakistani team.'

Hakim told me something of his story. 'I was a medical student in Kabul when the Taliban came. They first made life very hard for women. Here in the countryside, for women to wear *burqa* is the rule, but it was not that way in Kabul. The Taliban closed all the schools for women. They must just stay in the house.

'We moved first to another house in the city to hide from them. But then things got bad, so we moved out of the city to Bagram. The Taliban are torturing people there who are not Pushtun. I am Tajik, I speak Dari, so they didn't like me. My family was also threatened by them. My cousins and I, four of us, we came here to the Northern Alliance territory one and a half years ago, just some weeks after the Taliban took over. Since I left Kabul I haven't seen my family. I don't know where they are now.'

Hakim's eyes grew serious as he said this. It was clear that he had told his story many times before, but now, since the Americans had got involved, his emotions were conflicting. I could sense a certain hope within in him that things would change, that the Taliban would be driven out and that he could pick up his life again from where he had been forced to stop. But there was also fear underlying what he had left out: the fact that his family were still in Kabul living under the American bombardment.

'I don't like fighting at all,' Hakim said. 'I want to be a doctor, an educated man, that is very important for me.'

It had been a long journey for Hakim, at twenty-three, to reach even this point. After leaving Kabul and his studies he had first gone to Pakistan. From there, he had somehow found his way to Tajikistan where, being an ethnic Tajik from Afghanistan, he had managed to make his way back to university. 'I was studying medicine in Dushanbe, but after the attack on America, the KGB came to me and to my friend. They arrested us. We spent seven days in jail. Every day the KGB said to us, "You are an Afghan. You are just like Osama Bin Laden – a terrorist." I said to them: "No I am a student." But nothing helped. Eventually I said to them: "Take me to my country."

'Two KGB men came with us. They brought us to the border. There was a big Russian guard there. He said to them: "Why are you sending them away? They are students. They have a visa." '

Hakim smiled. 'The KGB were shaking in front of the Russian, but when he went away they said: "Now we will kill you. Why did you tell the Russian that?"

'It was no good. We went back to the Russian and said to him: "Please let us go to our country. We will never go back to Tajikistan." So, now I am here.'

That had been only four days before. He had come through the border while it was officially closed during the start of the American air strikes. Somehow, he had found his way here, to Khuja Bahauddin and to a good job with an American network paying dollars. I had to admire his resourcefulness. Already he was planning his next move. He wanted to go to Kabul now and see his family.

'If you want,' he said, 'I will go to Kabul with a camera. There are many secret ways to go. I speak Pushtun. I look like a Pushtun. My family can help me. They know many secret ways. I will go, why not?'

Three men in the hospital had been wounded in an ambush by the Taliban near Ay Khanoum. They had been patrolling the wide strip of no-man's-land between the two front lines and were caught in a hail of gunfire. One of them was wounded in the shoulder, another in the toe, and the third had his chest ripped apart by an AK-47 round.

In the bed next to them lay a teenage boy who had stepped on a land mine. He was lucky not to have lost his leg.

The hospital was critically short of medicines, bandages and equipment. But they were better off than people who had been wounded on the Taliban side. The Taliban had declared it a sin for doctors to be trained by dissecting human corpses. Very few doctors had remained in Taliban-held areas; those who had stayed had been forced to train new doctors with plastic models of the human anatomy. They never practised real operations.

The hospital in Khuja Bahauddin had been built with funds from Iran. It was a simple concrete and brick structure with open windows instead of air conditioning. The operating theatre was clean with new white tiles. The operating table was old. Some of the hinges and wheels were rusty, but the surface was wiped smooth and clean. There was very little equipment, but somehow the Afghans managed to operate and save limbs, and lives, in this makeshift operating theatre.

The doctors and male nurses kept the corridors and the wards clean. The windows looked out over an improvised garden where a few tufts of grass and flowers had been planted over the new rubble from the building. Beyond the walls of the hospital you could see the peaks of a mountain range etched against the wide sky. The sound of birds came in through the open windows.

Blood seeped through the white cloth of the bandage on the wounded man's shoulder. 'We will fight for our country,' he told us. 'Whatever America does or does not.'

There was a hand pump in the centre of town. Men, women and children gathered around it all day, waiting their turn. Along the edge of the road that served the pump, a line of wooden stalls had been set up. A lively market existed in this row of wooden stalls. Money changers sat cross-legged in front of tin trunks stuffed with *afghanis*, the name of the local currency. The notes came in 1 *lakh* bundles; 1 *lakh* was 100 000 *afghanis*, which was worth about $2 now. Piles of *lakhs* tied in bundles with string stood in front of them on the carpets in their stalls. Next to the money stood a pair of scales. Justin wanted to change $250 to cover various expenses. The money changer offered him 10 million *afghanis*. It was a bad rate – he should have been offering 12.5 million, but since the influx of journalists into Khuja Bahauddin, the dollar had been losing value to the *afghani*.

Near the money changers were stalls selling almost anything imaginable: bags of corn and bales of hay, 'Moon Rabbit' batteries from China, almonds, sweet biscuits, tinned food, enamel mugs, tapes of Afghan and Pakistani pop music. A man in a dark turban was selling pomegranates, peanuts, chillies and apples. On the edge of the street alongside him two small boys climbed on their father's motorbike. The seat was covered with a pair of woven-saddlebags that were designed to be spread over a camel's hump.

One of the wooden and mud stalls was a medical diagnosis centre. The owner sat behind a rickety wooden table with an old microscope in the centre of it. For a few *afghanis*, he would take a blood sample and peer at it through the microscope, searching among the corpuscles for telltale evidence of the malaria parasite or other diseases. There was a chemist nearby, but they had few medicines for sale even if the man found something in your blood.

Latif was five years old. He and his brother Sandek worked the central area around the hand pump. They both begged for money, or anything they could get, but Latif was more successful than Sandek. He was younger, and cuter, and he didn't have a huge, scablike infection covering his lower lip and chin.

Once he had chosen someone, Latif would never give up. He followed them everywhere they went in the market, whining, wheedling, reaching up his hand whenever they stopped to talk to a shopkeeper. If they tried to ignore him, Latif would tug at their clothes. When they looked down, he would smile at them and put out his hand. If they brushed him away in irritation, Latif would disappear into the crowd. But, a few minutes later, he was back again, tugging at their clothes, whining, wheedling, putting out his hand.

We watched and filmed as Latif followed a Western aid worker all through the market. The aid worker was used to the ways of Afghan beggar children and calmly ignored Latif until she reached her 4x4. When she opened the door, she handed him a few crumpled *afghanis* and a handful of sweets before her driver kicked the engine into life and drove off in a cloud of dust. Sandek came up to Latif and eagerly put out his hand. Latif gave him one of the candies and unwrapped one for himself.

Sandek was not popular among the people of the market. They seemed to hate his wheedling and his scab-ridden face. At the fruit market, a stall-owner's son shouted at him and pushed him on the shoulder. Sandek snapped back. The other boy slapped Sandek. Sandek grabbed his shirt and a tussle broke out. A group of boys gathered around Sandek, punching and kicking him and trying to pull him down into the muddy ground covered in rotting fruit peels. The adults roared with laughter at Sandek's torments.

There was nothing Latif could do, he was too small. His face was twisted into a tight mask of unhappiness as he cowered in one of the stalls and watched his older brother fight to maintain his dignity. Sandek wrestled and punched, while the tears fell down his face and mingled with the blood dripping from the scabs on his lip.

The scuffle lasted only a few seconds before the father of one of the boys stepped in to stop it. Our translator, Faizel, couldn't stand it any longer. He stepped in, too, and shooed the bullies away.

Somewhere along the line in the last few days, we had lost Zamuruddin. Faizel was our new translator. He was a gentle, soft-spoken man who dressed in traditional Afghan *shalwar kameez* and carried a string of prayer beads. He had a shock of greying hair that was brushed straight over his forehead.

Faizel patted Sandek on the shoulder for a moment, but the boy twisted angrily away from him and disappeared into the crowd. Faizel asked Latif how it was that he and his brother had come to beg in the marketplace.

'My mother died from sickness,' Latif told him. 'My father was killed when a bullet came in through the window.'

Latif was too young to remember where this had happened, or even where he had come from. All he knew was that after it had happened he and Sandek had come to Khuja Bahauddin with their grandmother. They lived in the refugee camp a little way out of town. Their sister stayed with their grandmother, but they came to the market every day to beg.

At the end of the day, before they started walking back to the refugee camp, Latif and Sandek stood at the edge of the clearing near the hand pump and compared earnings. Sandek had almost nothing. Latif had a few thousand *afghanis*. The filthy, crumpled notes sat in his tiny hand.

Latif would not give up. He tugged at Dennis's sweater and put his hand out. Faizel had told him we would give him money but, at five years old, Latif had heard that line once too many times before.

The refugee camp lay on a wide dust plain beneath the mountains. Nothing grew on the plain at all. The drought had destroyed everything. The camp housed perhaps 700 families who had fled from the fighting and from the Taliban. They lived in small shacks made of straw and mud and plastic sheeting. A few cows and goats grazed among piles of rubbish.

There were hardly any young men here. It was mostly women and children who squatted around the stones of the cooking fires in their colourful robes. A few old men wandered among them. A bearded older man was organizing some youths who were building a shelter of mud and long curved sticks. He pointed authoritatively at the walls, and the youths obediently bent the wooden supports as he directed. They giggled when he cursed them.

There were rumours that the Americans intended dropping food parcels over this camp, but so far none of the promised food had come tumbling out of the sky. The people here had very little to eat – a few handfuls of beans, some wheat and rice, that was all.

It was about three kilometres from the centre of town to the refugee camp – a very long walk for a five-year-old child – and Latif and Sandek did it together every day, all the way through the hot, choking dust plain to town and back again. We followed the two brothers through the narrow alleyways and the ramshackle shelters that served as people's homes.

We came to a hut partly dug out of the ground and roofed with straw. Latif and Sandek's sister Amina came to see what her brothers had brought home. Amina was a little older than her brothers. She was about ten and had green eyes and red hair under her headscarf. She had a few chickens that she tended and kept penned under a wicker basket.

Latif pulled open the torn plastic sheet that served as a door to their shack. A woman in her late thirties lay, exhausted and ill, on the dirt floor. Her head was covered in a bright scarf but her face was thin and lined. She coughed continuously into her bony hand.

Latif knelt down at her side and pulled out the money he and Sandek had earned.

'What can she buy with this?' Dennis asked.

Faizel shook his head. 'She says this is not enough even to buy bread.'

'But what will they do?'

'She says they will save it, perhaps tomorrow the boys will get enough.'

A Night Journey

We could hear the gunfire from the front lines all day now. If the Taliban broke through, they could overrun the village in a couple of hours.

'What's going on?' I asked Faizel.

'I don't know,' he frowned. 'I ask many times, but all the officers say they don't know. They won't tell us anything.'

'There is shelling, but no movement at the front lines,' Faizel told us. 'I don't understand why not. We have no idea when the attack will begin. We just have to wait.'

Later in the day I saw a message from New York that flashed up on Justin's computer screen. '"*The US army is making it up as they go along*" – *and that's a quote from one of my Pentagon sources. They don't know what they are going to do next. Some special forces are probably in Uzbekistan already, but they haven't had enough time to get a lot of them in yet. The CIA is trying to do something with the tribes in the south, but the information is unclear and uncertain – everybody is guessing and waiting.*'

The time had come for us to make a decision. Our job was not to follow the daily grind of news events, but to try and find something different, to find unusual angles. There was nothing more for us to do in Khuja Bahauddin. One significant new development was that the Uzbek government was willing to allow US troops to be stationed on its soil. That alone would have been unthinkable only two weeks before. They wanted guarantees, though, that the US would protect them. They were scared of a scenario where the US launched a few strikes against Afghanistan and then departed, leaving the Uzbeks at the mercy of Taliban revenge and their own extremist groups inside the country.

The helicopters were not flying because of the increased American air strikes. We decided to go by land back to Dushanbe. From there we would go on to Uzbekistan to see if we could find a different angle to the war there.

Layers of bright light hung over the Panj river. Each one was a slightly different shade, from the gleaming silver surface of the river to the brown and jade of the mountains and the empty blue of the sky.

A crumbling watchtower stood on the hill behind us. It had been built some time in the nineteenth century to defend the borders of Afghanistan from the armies of the Czar during the years of the Great Game. One wall had completely caved in, and its mudbrick loopholes had long since disintegrated. Beside it stood a pair of cypress trees, like dark green clouds against the empty horizon.

A glittering, emerald-feathered kingfisher darted down towards the rushing water of the river. The smoke from the soldiers' tea fire drew a thin white line up towards the sky. We were not far from the front lines at Ay Khanoum. In the clear, cool air we could hear the distant sounds of shelling.

The commander of the border crossing and his troops were sitting cross-legged on a carpet that had been spread out on the concrete barge jetty. They invited us to join them for tea, *naan* and beans. We sat down with them.

Across the river lay Tajikistan. The barge lay at anchor on the opposite bank. We could see no one there.

'The commander says today is Sunday,' Faizel told us. 'For the Russians it is their day off.'

'We need to get across,' Justin said. 'Ask him if he can try again to raise them on the radio.'

The commander nodded. He put his teacup down. He picked up the walkie-talkie off the carpet, pressed the button and barked into it. There was a crackle and a hiss, but no reply.

Someone brought a short wave radio to listen to the news. We sat on the carpet listening to the fading waves of static. After one news item had been announced, Faizel looked up at us. 'Osama Bin Laden is warning Americans and British not to live in tall buildings or to fly in planes.'

There was nothing to be done until the Russians were contacted. I sat down to read. The only shade I could find was that of our vehicles, so I put my back against one of the wheels and opened up Rudyard Kipling's *Kim*. Justin and Faizel were sitting above me in the passenger seat of the cab smoking cigarettes.

A young soldier came and squatted close by me. He must have been perhaps seventeen or eighteen years old. He stared at me for a while, watching my face while I read. Then he shifted on his haunches and leaned closer in towards me. I held out the book for him while he stared at the print on the page. Then I smiled at him and shifted the book back so I could read. The youth smiled back at me, but he squatted there beside me for a long while, staring at me while I read.

The commander stood up and wandered down to the riverbank. He faced across the river and tried again with the walkie-talkie.

Faizel had seen the interaction between me and the young soldier. Justin and he climbed out of the car and stood near me while they watched the commander on the walkie-talkie. Faizel lifted his prayer beads and started shuffling them with his fingers.

'There is no order here,' he said. 'There is no one really in command. That man has no education. He doesn't understand anything. His soldiers cannot read, and he cannot read or write, but he is a general.'

Faizel shook his head slowly. 'What are we going to build out of all this mess?'

Somehow, in the end, we got permission to cross. A Russian officer named

Viktor agreed that, even though it was Sunday, he would allow us to cross. There were a few shouts across the river; a splash of cables and the tractor engine on the deck of the barge coughed into life.

The sun was low by the time the barge chugged across the river to meet us on the Afghan side of the border. We had our twenty-four boxes of television equipment and our personal luggage. It first had to be unpacked from the 4x4s we had brought with us from Khuja Bahauddin. Then we had to open each box and case for the commander and his soldiers to inspect. What they thought we might be smuggling out of the country I couldn't imagine. We never felt threatened, or that we were being asked for a bribe. It soon became clear that they were motivated as much by curiosity as by anything else. The amount of *stuff* we were carrying was unimaginable. Cellphones, satphones, lenses, tapes, batteries, video recorders, extra cameras, two pairs of boots each, extra shoes, fleece-tops, down jackets, T-shirts, socks, flashlights, books, even bottles of *water* that we were carefully carrying across the biggest river in the whole region . . . it must have been astonishing to people who owned hardly anything.

The search was thorough and time-consuming, but finally it was finished. Our boxes were loaded on the barge and the commander was anxious for us to get moving. We said goodbye to Faizel. He hugged us, his prayer beads clacking as he gently put his arms around us.

'When you come back to Afghanistan, bring a TV,' he said. 'A colour TV that works on batteries. I'll pay you for it, but I want to see what is happening in the world.'

Viktor was waiting for us as the barge ground to a halt on the gravel bank in Tajikistan. He was somewhat amused by the amount of luggage we had with us, and the precipitate haste with which we were determined to continue our journey to Dushanbe.

Viktor and his soldiers checked one or two of our boxes at random and then allowed us to proceed. Somehow Justin with his Russian managed to get a car and a small Niva jeep to carry us to the border town of Moskva.

It was dark by the time our ride to Dushanbe began. I remember fragments of a journey. A Russian soldier patrolling the barbed wire border fence riding on a donkey. His AK-47 strapped to his chest and his combat boots almost touching the ground beneath the tiny donkey.

I felt like an impenetrable but transparent wall was descending between me and the world around me. Nothing seemed to matter much except the dizziness in my head and the chill ache in my muscles. None of us had eaten anything for over twelve hours. Someone gave us some *lepyoshka*. I tore it into pieces and handed it around. The bread was fresh and delicious, but we had nothing to drink, so it stuck in our throat as we swallowed it down.

A pale desert fox slunk along low in the tumbleweed beside the road. We came around a bend and there was a porcupine frozen in the headlamps. In terror it raised its quills. The driver swung the wheel sharply. He cackled with glee as the tyres squelched over it.

I dozed fitfully, my head beginning to ache. We woke in the middle of the night. Cold stars were strung out for miles above us. We had not seen such stars in Afghanistan where the layers of dust had blurred the night sky.

Hours later the driver stopped. He would go no further. He pulled into a patch of grass next to a *chaikhana* or teahouse. An enormous plane tree stood on the bank of a stream. It must have been hundreds of years old. The water was grey in the canal in front of the *chaikhana*. Beyond it there was a small forest of poplars and I could hear the water rushing through the trees.

It was cold. Someone gave me a thick Russian army jacket with a high woollen collar. He mimed putting it on and pointed at me insistently.

We walked into the *chaikhana*. Someone brought vodka, *lepyoshka*, smoked fish from the canal. I thought I was just hungry and tired, but the drink and the fish with its rubbery bones and dark, oily flesh made me feel even worse.

There was a black and white TV on in the corner. The fuzzy, ghostly images showed Tajik tanks and troops moving towards the border with Afghanistan. The rusting hulk of the nuclear submarine *Kursk* was being raised from the ocean depths. More anthrax had been found in Florida. There were fleeting shots of men in germ warfare suits intercut with lithe young women rollerskating along the beachfront in bikinis. There were B-2 bombers flying in a grey sky, and the *USS Enterprise* rolled along in a blurred sea.

The men around us smoked and drank vodka. They were fascinated by Justin because he could speak Russian. I was beginning to get seriously ill, and it was difficult to follow what was happening around me. There was talk of trouble in the region, of 'Hindustan', meaning India.

Then we were off again, trundling northwards in the night towards Dushanbe. I collapsed in the vehicle. The rest of the journey was a half-conscious blur.

I remembered the yellow curve of a hillside in the moonlight. The red band of a policeman's cap badge as he leaned in the window to look at us and our gear. There was the comforting murmur: '*salaam aleikum*', '*aleikum salaam*'. The officer touched his heart with his hand and waved us on into the darkness.

There were the white walls of a village, and someone gently taking the army coat where it was lying, forgotten, off my lap. There were words floating above my head. I couldn't understand them, but the tone was kind and someone shoved another round, fresh loaf of bread in through the window.

We came to the outskirts of Dushanbe. There were more roadblocks. The police here were hard and unfriendly. The ugly concrete buildings lay bathed in a bluish half-light. Then there was the final, insistent, wave of a flashlight and we were driving down the empty, tree-lined avenues in the first cold, grey light of dawn.

The rest is now history. We never did make it back into Afghanistan. We, like so many other people, were stunned by the rapid collapse of the Taliban. I was already back in London when Mazar-i-Sharif fell. I remember watching in fascination as, one after another, the Taliban lines disintegrated.

Part of me wanted to be there, to see it happening, but another part of me was tired of witnessing war and the suffering it caused. I remembered Lieutenant Frank Ndore and that night long ago on the Uganda/Rwanda border. 'It is impossible to be certain of anything in war,' Lieutenant Frank had said. 'Impossible. The front lines are always shifting.'

I was tired, too, of trying to follow the shifting front lines of war. But I couldn't help watching the images on the TV in my brother's house in London. There were shots of jet fighters high up in the sky, the lines of Northern Alliance soldiers marching in the parched valleys and the occasional snatched shots of American and other special forces. Mostly, though, there was the sound of explosions and the columns of dark smoke rising against the horizon. Even though so much of the war was hidden from us, everything in Afghanistan was changing yet again in a swirl of blood and explosions.

My memories were recent, and vivid. I had been in Afghanistan for only a couple of weeks, but I found myself wondering what was happening to Zamuruddin, to Hakim and to his family trapped under the bombing in Kabul. The winter was coming in fast, and I knew that life would grow even harsher for Latif and Sandek, and their desperately ill grandmother.

I remembered Faizel and his question to us as we stood on the banks of the river Panj at the very edge of Afghanistan. 'What,' he had asked, 'are we going to build out of all this mess?'

I had no answer for him. All any of us could see was the pale dust hanging in the air over the front lines, swirling behind the cold glass curve of the screen. The dust on the horizon was the same pale colour of the dust from the World Trade Center. It made me think of what George Bush had told America, and the world, right in the beginning, only days after the attacks on New York and Washington. We should not expect a single battle, but a long war. One in which there might be some 'dramatic strikes, visible on TV', but it would also include hidden strikes, 'secret even in success'.

I thought, too, of my wife's brother and of all the other people I knew in New York. None of them had been killed on September 11, thank God, but the memory of seeing on television the towers burning, and then falling, still swirled in my mind. The depravity of those secretly planned attacks was likely to influence the rest of my adult life.

There was a terrible irony in this, the first war of the twenty-first century. This was the TV age, but in this war so much would be hidden from our cameras and so from the eyes of the world. Even some successes, we were told, would be secret.

What kind of war would this be where victories might be hidden, but where every loss would be so shockingly, so cruelly visible as the attack on New York had been?

Who would decide when this war was over? What kind of peace would they promise us?

Kuwait. *A long chain of 18-wheeler flatbed trucks carrying tanks and missile launchers moving from the outskirts of Kuwait City towards the Iraqi border – 'It was an awesome sight, seeing that convoy moving through the golden light of late afternoon . . .'*

Tajikistan. *The Haji Yakoub Mosque – the beauty of the tile work and the curves of the archways represented a long-lost heritage.*

Tajikistan. *An ancient caravanserai and the fortress of Hissar with its reconstructed towers. Built in the eighteenth century, the fortress was finally destroyed by the Red Army in 1924.*

Tajikistan. *The bazaar in Dushanbe. I was arrested after taking this picture.*

Afghanistan. *Khuja Bahauddin. The view from my tent of the flat-roofed mud houses breaking the skyline on the ridge.*

Afghanistan. *Northern Alliance fighters watch pictures of themselves being sent around the world by satellite phone.*

Afghanistan. *A truckload of Northern Alliance fighters on the road near Ay Khanoum.*

Afghanistan. *Leaving Afghanistan on the barge across the Panj River – with our twenty-four boxes of equipment and luggage.*

Palestine. *On the Palestinian side of the Erez crossing point into Gaza is a forlorn concrete arch ...*

Palestine. *Gaza: The poverty strikes one immediately. Mostly, people live in drab breeze-block tenements covered in graffiti.*

Palestine. *In the cemetery of the martyrs a freshly dug grave stands empty, waiting for the remains of the next young suicide bomber.*

ISRAEL

THE DIARY OF A CEASEFIRE

Every morning from my hotel window I would watch the helicopter gunships fly over the coast, heading towards Gaza and the West Bank. The Mediterranean sea was a brillant shimmering blue. The Tel Aviv beaches were white and empty, almost deserted in the winter cold, a few footprints of the solitary walkers catching the shadow of the morning light and holding it in their contours.

'Aren't you scared of bombs?' Israelis would ask me.

'No,' I would tell them. I wasn't scared because growing up in the violence that accompanied the end of apartheid I had learned long ago that it didn't pay to think about bombs. One had to be careful, but one had to carry on with life. In my early twenties, in something of a depression over the scourge of apartheid and over the horror of the violence it had spawned, I read Albert Camus' *The Plague*. It had made a great impression on my attitude to life. '*Really it's too damn silly living only in and for the plague. Of course a man should fight for the victims, but if he ceases caring for anything outside that, what's the use of his fighting?*'

It was December 2001, some time since I had last visited the Middle East. The war was still going on in Afghanistan, but the focus of world events had shifted once again back to the continuing war between Israel and the Palestinians. The situation was much worse than it ever had been. The Camp David agreement had come and gone; the Tenet and Mitchell plans and the Oslo peace talks had yielded nothing. Access to the al-Aqsa Mosque and the Dome of the Rock was denied to people who were not Muslims since Ariel Sharon's provocative visit in September 2000.

Israelis, now, were not allowed to visit the Palestinian areas. The government said it was for their own safety. They had a point. In the present climate of mistrust and downright hatred, an Israeli stood a good chance of being torn to pieces by a mob if he or she were caught in the Palestinian areas. I was there in Israel because no Israelis could cross the border into Palestine. Outsiders, though, were safe enough.

This lack of human contact seemed to me to be the greatest tragedy of all. Israelis and Palestinians were drawing farther and farther apart every day. And every day, the television crews were there to report on the dying of the peace process. The images themselves were terrifying. The screams, the shattered glass, the pools of blood on the street. Another Palestinian suicide bomber or attacker had unleashed his cruel brutality on innocent Israeli civilians.

The response was certain, implacable and just as brutal. Tanks rolled into the West Bank and Gaza. They crushed cars and houses alike, reducing whole sections of a town to dust. The F-16s and Apache gunships sent a hail of steel and fire out of the sky, targeting Palestinian Authority buildings, but just as often killing Palestinian civilians.

There are three levels at which this war rages: the fighting on the front lines, the diplomatic wars, and the struggle for supremacy of the images of the conflict.

*

Saturday, 22 December

Yesterday, in response to Yasser Arafat's own call for violence to cease, Hamas ordered an end to suicide bombings and mortar attacks inside the 1967 borders of Israel. Islamic Jihad, though, has not made its position clear. And Hamas has deliberately left the position of Israeli settlements beyond the 1967 border ambiguous. Still, it might be a step towards peace, of a sort.

Earlier I got talking to a man in the lobby of the hotel, an Israeli in his fifties. He was a charming and dignified man who had the confidence of someone who has done well in his life. His parents had fled Poland at the outbreak of World War II. They trekked across the Soviet Union to escape the Holocaust. He was born in a village in Uzbekistan. He smiled. 'My mom always told the story of how I had only two diapers all the way across the continent. She had to wash them every night, even in the winter.'

'Do you like Tel Aviv?' he asked.

'I've only just arrived,' I told him.

He smiled. 'You'll like it, I'm sure of that. There are lots of places to go. You'll see the difference between the buildings built in the socialist times of the '50s and those built later, in the time of capitalism. Tel Aviv now is like Manhattan. In some ways it is like a mini-USA right in the centre of the Middle East.'

But, in truth, he wasn't sure what he really thought of Americans. 'The Americans are too scared. They are too rigid in their thinking. They are an ignorant people. But at least they tell you "no" when they mean "no".'

He wasn't sure what he thought of reporters, either.

'You should know the real story of the situation here. When we took over the West Bank and Gaza in 1968 we gave the Palestinians a better government than they had under those bad leaders. There was no trouble there for ten years or more. They were making money here in Israel. Now the younger generation, they don't remember anything about the bad days when Egypt and Jordan ruled them. They came to Israel and saw what we had here. And they wanted that for themselves. That's when the trouble began. You should remember this, that's all I'm saying.'

By 4:30 pm the light is fading fast. A stunning flamingo pink sunset hangs over a turquoise sea. The air is cool with a sharp nip of winter.

This evening in the lounge of the hotel high up on the eighteenth floor looking out over the lights of Tel Aviv, I meet Nina, John, Dan. All of them, like me, brought in by NBC because outsiders are needed to move freely between Israel and the Palestinian territories. The shadow of war is everywhere tonight. There is the memory of September 11 that still hangs between sentences in people's conversation. The news from outside is filled with the campaign in Afghanistan and threats of war between India and Pakistan. There is the possibility, too, of attacks on Somalia and Iraq. And, of course, there is something of a lull in the fighting here, but everyone knows that the peace, or *relative* peace, is an illusion, because the killing is still going on. Even the little talk of Israeli/Palestinian politics around the table tonight goes around and around and around until it becomes virtually incomprehensible.

John: 'Both sides. They need all this fighting and hate. They need it to be who they are.'

On my last visit here, I found that there was so much more than hate. I found that I liked so many people from both sides. I keep on hoping that this middle ground will prevail here.

Sunday, 23 December

BBC World in the hotel room. There was an attempt to blow up an airliner heading from Paris to the USA. A man was arrested with explosives in his shoes. India and Pakistan have exchanged gunfire on the border.

Relative peace. Seven people were killed yesterday in fighting between Hamas and the Palestinian Authority. Here in Tel Aviv you wouldn't have the slightest idea. Yachts tack far out in a deep blue sea; their sails are white against a sunny blue sky.

The Israeli government of Ariel Sharon has banned Yasser Arafat from going to Christmas ceremonies in Bethlehem. But Arafat has said he intends to go to celebrate Midnight Mass.

I am working with Mohamed Muslemany or 'Muss', a cameraman from Cairo, and Hoda Kotbe, an Egyptian-American. The three of us are to be the crew that travels across the border to work mostly in the Palestinian areas.

This afternoon we met in the office to discuss going to Beit Jala, a town on the outskirts of Bethlehem. It lies on the border between the Palestinian areas and the Jewish settlers. The settlements are just across the valley from the Palestinian town. There is often fighting between the two groups. It is a very tense area. The settlers and the Palestinians trade fire across the valley quite frequently. The settlers call the army and point out where the shooting has come from, and the army bulldozes their house or their field.

'The situation has escalated,' Hoda said, 'because Israel claims that this area is part of the territory agreed on as Israel's after 1967, but there are still a number of Palestinian attacks and Israeli responses. There used to be many tourists, especially over Christmas. But now there are very few, if any.'

In the American Colony Hotel in Jerusalem we meet Aisha, our Palestinian fixer. She is a striking woman with beautiful eyes and dark gleaming hair. She is full of laughter and enthusiasm – a person, clearly, who refuses to live 'only in and for the plague'.

Everyone in the lobby looks up as she strides in. 'I'm sorry I'm late,' she says raising her arms into the air in a gesture of despair. 'But there were three roadblocks on the road here. Can you believe it?'

We drive along the Hebron road to Beit Jala. The sun is beginning to set. It is much colder up here in the hills around Jerusalem than in Tel Aviv. I find myself remembering the olive groves, the rocky hillsides with their white stones catching the last of the day's light.

We come to our first checkpoint. Long lines of cars are waiting to go through. Huge arc lights tower above the Israeli military buildings. There is a watchtower with bullet-proof glass and the Israeli flag rippling in the sunset.

The young soldiers with their M-16s strapped to their chests are patrolling up and down the line of cars.

'They can keep us waiting for hours, these soldiers,' Aisha says. 'If you get impatient it will make it much worse. They really know how to punish people.'

We drive into Beit Jala. The settler village with its high walls is so close, right on the slopes opposite. Some of the buildings in Beit Jala are very beautiful. Crafted from the white stone of the hillsides, their idiosyncratic architecture reflects layers of centuries and of influences – Roman, Turk, Byzantine, and Arab. But many of the buildings here are ruined. Traces of black smoke flares up the stonework of some of the windows, the steel reinforcing twisted and rusting where shells have hit and a fire has blazed. The Paradise Hotel, with its curved stone arches was once a place for tourists who came to Bethlehem. Now all the windows are smashed, the brickwork blackened with the signs of the fire that raged here. 'It was bombed by the Israelis,' Aisha tells us.

We twist and turn through the narrow streets. 'We can't go this way,' Aisha says. 'The Israeli army has taken over a building. It is their headquarters here.' Tomorrow is Christmas Eve, but here on the outskirts of Bethlehem, the birthplace of Christ, the roads are almost completely deserted.

We come to the main town square of Beit Jala. A beautiful white stone church towers over the tiny square. In the centre is a stone carving of St George killing the dragon, the town symbol. A few Christmas lights have been set up on an olive tree, but there is no one around apart from a few taxi drivers.

The cold wind sweeps through the steep streets, the sunset is a gentle pink light behind the steeple of the church. The Palestinian Authority police are patrolling the streets. Some of them are unarmed and wear black uniforms. Others are in camouflage and carry webbing and AK-47s.

Aisha takes us to a Christian school near another ancient stone church further up the hill. A sign outside says it is being restored with help from the Austrian government. We meet Elias, one of the parents of the children at the school.

'We don't have much time for celebration,' Elias says. 'Our minds are filled with trying to survive. We don't have time for anything else. Because we don't know when they are going to come and kill us.'

Aisha has walked a few metres down the road to have a cigarette. 'I wish this Palestinian Authority had never been created,' she says. 'It is worse for us now. The situation is very awful. The Israelis attack us because in their minds the Palestinian Authority with their guns are like soldiers. Before they never used to shoot us like this. But it is a war now.'

It is warm inside the school. The walls are covered with the children's crayon drawings like in any school in the world. Here, though, the drawings are of tanks blowing up buildings, and of helicopters firing orange and purple bullets at the church steeple.

We have asked Elias to organize some Palestinian children to write their wish list for Santa. Or 'Baba Noel', as he is called here.

Some of the kids can write in English. They read their letters out to the camera. *'Pleas Santa come and bring the peas to our country. If you can help us, then doit doit doit.'*

'I am scared from the tenks. My house is full of bullits. I want the peace. I will tell you a secret. I am scared.'

A tiny six-year-old steals the show. *'I want peace and please bring me a Barbie.'*

We drive back in the dark. In a line of shops and houses is a gaping hole of rubble. A tent has been pitched on the rubble. The canvas sides are buffeted by the cold winter wind. A black flag with white Arabic writing flies defiantly from the front tent pole. It is the ancient flag of jihad.

'The Israelis bulldozed her house,' Aisha tells us. 'She had to climb out the back window. She is living in that tent with her four children.'

Further down the street are more smashed windows and piles of crumbled masonry. A patch of land overlooking the valley has been completely flattened by tanks and bulldozers. This whole place is filled with the memory of violence, layer after layer of it.

Monday, 24 December

A stand-off between Arafat and Sharon. The Israeli government say they will lift the ban on Arafat visiting Bethlehem for Midnight Mass if he arrests the militants behind the murder of Rehavam Ze'evi, a right-wing Israeli cabinet minister who was shot dead in Jerusalem's Hyatt Hotel in October.

Muss and I set off for Jerusalem mid-morning. We stop for lunch at an Arab restaurant at the village of Abu Ghosh just off the highway on the outskirts of Jerusalem. Abu Ghosh is the site of the ancient Qiryat Yearim, the place where the Ark rested before it was taken to Jerusalem. It has long been a defensive redoubt. In Roman times the Tenth Legion was based here. The Crusaders rested at Abu Ghosh before attacking Jerusalem in 1099. There was extensive fighting in these valleys on the road between Jerusalem and Tel Aviv in 1948.

Today is peaceful, though. The menu tells us that Moshe Dayan used to come and eat here with his Arab friends. We eat hummus, tahini, tabouleh and falafel under the shade of a mulberry tree. A few chickens are pecking at leftovers of food on the stone veranda outside.

The doorman at the American Colony Hotel is wearing a Santa suit. All the Arab staff call out 'Merry Christmas' as we walk into the lobby. There is something sad and desperate and also courageous about it.

By sundown Arafat has still not been given permission to attend Midnight Mass. He is threatening to walk to Bethlehem. The Israeli army is out in force to prevent him sneaking in. They have set up extra checkpoints all around Bethlehem. In the fading light of day we film the checkpoint at Kalandiya.

Two young Israeli soldiers standing at the checkpoint. One of them is a Russian with close-cropped red hair; the other is an Ethiopian, his hair equally short. There is something fascinating, and moving, to see this gathering of the ancient Jewish tribes, this reforging of a nation after 2 000 years.

Despite the political and diplomatic tension around the question of Yasser Arafat attending Midnight Mass, the atmosphere is relaxed. There is even some joking between the Israeli soldiers and Palestinian people at the checkpoints. It seems very strange to me. Only ten days ago, gunships were flying in the sky above these towns.

'You've got to understand,' Muss says, 'this is the Middle East. It's loose, people's attitudes move up and down. It's flowing. Today I have a gun and I'm a soldier at a checkpoint. Tomorrow maybe we are eating at a table in the same café.'

Like Moshe Dayan and his friends, I think. But what about the day after that?

The checkpoints have slowed the traffic down to a snail's pace. We sit in traffic for nearly two hours. When we finally reach the checkpoint the soldiers joke with us. 'Just wanted to make sure you don't have Arafat in the car with you.'

Finally we make it back to the NBC office in Tel Aviv. The TV screens are filled with the footage of the preparations for Midnight Mass at Manger Square and the Church of the Nativity. Yasser Arafat's trademark red-and-white *keffiyeh* is spread out across an empty chair. It is a potent image that is being beamed to the whole world. Tonight the image of the absence of Yasser Arafat speaks more loudly than the picture of him attending Mass would do. Even the President of Israel, Moshe Katsev, has failed to persuade Ariel Sharon to allow Yasser Arafat to attend Mass. The Israeli Foreign Ministry calls the decision 'stupid'. The Vatican dubs it 'arbitrary'.

One cannot help being affected by the conflict in this country, partly because our mix of world cultures have so many of their roots here. I remember tonight the warm comfort of the Arabs who run the American Colony Hotel. The bright little kids at the school in Beit Jala. But then there is also the joking of the Israeli soldiers, and the friendliness of so many other Israelis at the cafés and bars in Tel Aviv.

I am an outsider here, and when I find myself thinking of the claims of either side my mind swirls with regret, pity and anger that constantly shifts like a seesaw, back and forth.

Tonight the Israelis lost a battle for the image. Yasser Arafat's empty chair at Midnight Mass in Bethlehem will be remembered for a long time to come. Or, at least, until images of the next suicide bombing or Israeli military incursion flood the airwaves.

Muss, in the darkness of the highway back to Jerusalem: 'It all gets too much here sometimes. We in Egypt have understood that neither race can wipe out the other. So Sadat and Begin, both of them old soldiers, understood that they had to bring peace. I was in the '73 war and I saw my friends die, so I know what war is and what a waste of human lives it is.'

25 December. Christmas Day

I wake late this morning to hear two cars with sirens rushing up the street below the hotel. There is the horn of a fire engine in the distance. I wonder what might have happened. Perhaps it is nothing more than an accident, but there is a continual sense of tension here.

Yesterday a Jewish settler was ambushed on the road between Tulkarm and Nablus. It happened late in the afternoon, just about the same time we were being wished 'Merry Christmas' by the staff at the American Colony Hotel. He was seriously wounded, but managed to shoot back at his attackers, killing one of them. I can't help thinking of what Muss said last night and of the parallel fate of human lives.

I look on the map that I picked up in the lobby of the hotel the day I arrived. It is a free map for tourists, given out with the compliments of a jewellery store. It is a surprisingly accurate map and I can see the junction near the village of Ramin where the ambushers waited for the settler. I can see the lines around the two dotted areas of Tulkarm and Nablus. These areas are two islands of Palestinian territory surrounded by Israel.

So many Israelis I meet tell me: 'You can never trust the Arabs.'

'It's not like that,' I protest, thinking of the supreme kindness and hospitality of all the people I met in Beit Jala and other Palestinian areas. And knowing that Israelis can no longer legally go to the Palestinian areas, they cannot truly say that they know Palestinians well.

'It is like that,' the answer comes back. 'You'll see.'

It reminds me of the conversations I used to have with whites in the South Africa of the late 1980s. Very few of them had ever been to a township, but their opinions were implacable, seared into hardness by the separation between peoples, by the regiments of soldiers and by the very walls and fences that had been put in place to protect them.

The imagination collapses into this absence of contact, it is swallowed up by an abyss of fear. Not that both Israelis and Palestinians don't have real fears – the problem is that they can no longer imagine a way out of the situation they find themselves in. And yet, I also know that South Africa was once in the same position. There seemed to be no hope then in those dark years of apartheid, no way to climb out of the abyss . . .

I constantly find myself thinking: 'Yes, it is dangerous, but you've made peace with Egypt and Jordan. Isn't it possible to think that you can make peace with the Palestinians?'

Everything here is about the ownership of land. The land as defined by lines on the map. The first morning I arrived, an Israeli showed me a map of the country. In painstaking detail she showed me how the Green Line ran, separating Israel from Palestine. With her finger she traced the far edge of the West Bank where it comes very close to the sea around Netanya and Hadera.

'This is what we call the narrow waist of Israel. Often visiting politicians are taken up in a helicopter and shown how narrow this point is. They see then how dangerous it would be to give control of it back to the Palestinians.'

I can see the village of Ramin near where the 47-year-old man was attacked. On the map it and the nearby Shavei Shomron settlement that he came from is deep inside the West Bank territory, but it is hardly more than 10 kilometres from the start of that 'narrow waist of Israel'.

At breakfast this morning the conversations about the situation and about Land are still reverberating through my head. I can't help thinking of when we interviewed an Israeli who had come here originally from Canada as a settler. 'We only take the land that is ours. The land that archaeology can prove was lived on by Jews before the diaspora.'

The manager of the hotel lounge is a young Israeli woman in her mid-twenties. She is very friendly, and has that air of competence and confidence of people who mature early in life. She is also a part-time model and was, only recently, a lieutenant in the Israeli army.

'You weren't here last night,' she says brightly.

'No,' I tell here. 'We were in Beit Jala.'

She grimaces and shakes her head. 'I don't like those settlements,' she says.

Immediately I am annoyed. I don't want another lecture on the untrustworthiness of Arabs.

'What don't you like about them?' I ask defensively.

But when she replies, I see that I have misjudged her. She is talking about the Jewish settlement right on the edge of Beit Jala. She is one of the Israelis whose voice has been submerged by the rage of so many of their compatriots. Voices like hers are seldom heard at the moment. In such bloodied times, the horror of the suicide bombings and of the tanks and gunships mean that people like her disappear. The frantic, terrifying whirl of violence, and the necessity of reporting on it, means that they become invisible to the television cameras.

But they are there, all the same, refusing to allow their vision to become swamped by the empty politics of revenge.

'I think,' she says slowly, 'that life is more important than land.'

The ceasefire is beginning to wear very thin. We only hear about it after breakfast, but at dawn this morning an Israeli soldier and four others were wounded when they were ambushed on the Jordanian border. The soldiers fired back and two bodies, presumably those of their attackers, were later found.

All day there are strings of smaller incidents, none of which will make news in the outside world. Palestinians attack an Israeli Defence Force post at Tel Araf near Nablus, and a soldier is slightly wounded by shrapnel. Shots are fired at an IDF vehicle near Zaita, north of Tulkarm. Shots were also fired at an IDF vehicle near Silat a-Daher and at an IDF convoy between Otniel and Adurayim in the southern Hebron hills.

In Gaza, shots were fired at an IDF post near Neveh Dekalim, and grenades thrown at soldiers near Rafah. The papers carry pictures of guns being fired at the Tulkarm funeral of Jamil Abu Atwan who was killed by settler Vitali Binos who returned fire after being ambushed on Monday afternoon. He remains in critical condition in hospital. The IDF captured seven Palestinians from Hamas and Islamic Jihad in a raid on Tamun, north of Nablus.

An extraordinary level of violence permeates the whole society. So much like the old South Africa. On one level it seems to be an invisible war to the strollers and café denizens of Tel Aviv. But that is an illusion. They are all very aware of the dangers around them. They try, like our Palestinian fixer Aisha, living a world away from them in Ramallah, not to submit to the plague. I understand and admire them for it; but the fear, and the anger, permeate the whole consciousness. There is a kind of bleakness that lies under the Mediterranean sunshine, a hollow fear that I remember so well. I felt very depressed walking around the streets yesterday.

My friend Dave, who lives in Israel now, was worried that there was no security guard checking cars as we drove into the basement parking garage of the hotel. 'This is a prime target,' he said. And, of course, it is.

26 December

Today we are going to Gaza. We drive south along the freeway, past the nuclear power facilities, following the heavy electricity pylons. Little patches of beautiful desert landscape survive underneath them. I am struck, as always, by the utilitarian ugliness of our civilization. Nina is looking out the window too. 'We could be driving down the freeway to LA.'

We are going to interview a Palestinian man called Nasser. The group he works with is called 'Pains of Peace'. He meets Israelis who have lost their children. The name of the movement is based on Rabin's statement 'The Pains of Peace are better than the Agonies of War'. We have seen billboards advertising their movement on the highways around Tel Aviv and in Ramallah.

We talk all the time in the car on the way to Gaza about the SITUATION. Nina and Muss make the same point. The Trust has been lost. When Israelis and Palestinians sit together they no longer trust one another. The situation has gone backwards.

'How to regain the trust?' Muss asks.

We arrive at the Erez crossing point. The old simple structure that I went through a few years ago has been superseded by a huge international border post on the Israeli side. It strikes me how permanent this arrangement is. It is a kind of subconscious proof that the radicalism of those on both sides who want to destroy the Other is already meaningless, even while it cruelly takes lives. There will one day be two separate states – no matter how long it takes to get there.

We have to leave our armoured car in the parking lot on the Israeli side. We walk with the gear to passport control. We pass the first group of Israeli soldiers. They are such young kids. One of them has Che Guevara drawn on the back of his bullet-proof vest. Standing alongside him, toting their rifles are two young girls, both of them pretty. One is blonde, the other has her red hair in a fashionable bob. She has a Disney cartoon devil drawn on her bullet-proof vest. She seems to be in charge of the group. She talks on the walkie-talkie and lets us through.

We go through passport control and walk across no-man's-land to where our fixer Wagi is waiting with a yellow minibus. On the Palestinian side of the border is a forlorn concrete arch with the words *Palestinian National Authority. Arrival. WELCOME.*

It is protected by crumbling sand bag barricades. The Palestinian police do a cursory check of our documents and wave us on.

The poverty of this place strikes one immediately. There is rubbish all over the streets and torn plastic bags littering the tiny patches of desert or the few orchards that remain after all the overcrowding. There are some shacks made of wood and plastic sheeting but mostly people live in drab breeze-block tenements covered in graffiti. A man with an AK on his lap sits at the corner of one. One can see the odd man wearing an Arab headdress, but most people are dressed in jeans and sneakers. Donkey carts trundle along the rutted roads.

The Palestinian Authority has checkpoints too. I can't see any real need for them. They certainly would be no use in preventing the Israeli tanks from penetrating the narrow, crowded streets. It is a way of demonstrating power and control to their own people. The Palestinian soldiers are a rather sad-looking, ragtag bunch, it is clear that they are no real match for the Israeli military.

We drive only a short way before we reach Nasser's house. He lost at least one son to Israeli fire. His youngest son was a Palestinian Authority policeman. He was nineteen years old. He was killed trying to restrain radical youths in a Ramallah demonstration, and was shot by Israeli forces.

The crowded living room is hung with pictures of his son in front of the al-Aqsa mosque. It is in fact a studio shot of the young man in his black uniform holding an AK-47. There is one black and white picture of Nasser's son as a baby with his mother. She is dressed in a skirt and tight jacket with her hair done up like Jackie Kennedy.

In the 'Pains of Peace' organization, both sides have lost sons but both sides are trying to find some way to grope towards peace. The Israeli government of Ariel Sharon wouldn't let them go to London recently for a meeting. Or, more accurately, they wouldn't let Nasser and the other

Palestinian members go.

Nasser lives a small flat with his wife and eight other children. Cheap pine furniture and polyester carpets cover the bare concrete floor in the living room. Hanging above the door are two cages of blue and yellow budgies – a splash of colour and song in the drabness of their surroundings.

'I felt bitterness and grief,' Nasser tells us about the death of his son. 'They called me and I also heard the news on the radio. This was on June 5, 2001. Of course the Israelis bear responsibility. What can I say? This is God's will.

'I don't feel that I want revenge. I feel sad that my son was killed. He was a policeman trying to control the situation. He should never have been killed, but I want to find peace.'

After the interview is over, Nasser's ageing father comes into the living room. He is dressed in a black *dishdasha* and wears a *keffiyeh* on his head. He offers us apples and bananas, biscuits and the delicious cardamom-flavoured Arab coffee. He listens to the conversation for a while and when it centres entirely around politics he excuses himself and goes out the room. The women are sitting in another room, but when the old grandfather walks out, Nasser's young daughter comes to join us.

As is often the way, some of the most revealing and touching remarks are made when the camera is switched off.

'I don't agree with Arafat entirely,' Nasser says over coffee. 'But at the moment he is the only one. I don't agree with suicide bombings, but I can understand how they happen. People here have nothing to lose. They are living in terrible conditions. They have lost their land. Everything. I can understand how it happens.'

'I sit with them [the Israelis] because they too have gone through the pain and suffering. They have lost their children and they want to end this situation. I call him the martyr of peace. I hope that he will be the last martyr.'

We leave as it is getting dark. We have to walk back through the checkpoint. The soldier who checks the X-ray machine asks us: 'There are lots of journalists going to Gaza today. Is something happening there?'

'No, not really,' we tell him.

Another soldier, who is also an American citizen, looks at us. 'We can't understand why people want to go there.'

December 29

Today we have come back from spending twenty-four hours in Jenin. The town of Jenin is a tiny enclave of Palestinian territory surrounded by Israel. Since the start of the new *intifada* over eighteen months ago, the town has been virtually sealed off by Israeli tanks and soldiers. As violence has escalated in Israel and the West Bank and Gaza in recent months tensions have spilled over into open conflict. Nearly sixty Palestinians have been killed in fighting with the Israeli military.

Israeli authorities, however, have documented at least twenty-three separate attacks and suicide bombers who they claim have come from the town of Jenin. These attacks have led to well over fifty Israeli deaths. Israeli authorities call Jenin 'a hornet's nest' of terrorist activity.

There are two Israeli checkpoints on the road to Jenin. The first is a simple affair of concrete blocks and a few soldiers next to a jeep. A heavily armoured bulldozer is parked nearby.

The soldiers see our bullet-proof vehicle marked with the letters 'TV'. They wave us through.

We enter the borderland between Israel and the Palestinian Authority areas. Rubbish is strewn all across the rocky ground. A few olive trees, silver-leafed and dark with a hundred seasons of harvests, stand next to the rusting hulks of cars.

The cold winter wind blows across a field of rubble and a row of broken, empty shopfronts. Bleak testimony to the work of the tanks and the bulldozers. No one lives on this land now, neither Jew nor Arab. This borderland is an empty place that lies between people.

A little way down the road, we come to a long line of trucks waiting at the second checkpoint. They are waiting for permission from the Israelis to cross back into the Palestinian areas. 'They can sit for two days or more,' Hassan, a Palestinian colleague, says. 'It depends on the soldiers. They are strangling us with this collective punishment. Sitting there like that for hours with no food, no toilet, it makes you crazy.'

At the second checkpoint an Israeli flag twists against a bright blue sky. Young soldiers, boys and girls in their late teens, stand with their M-16s behind sandbags and barbed wire. The turrets of their emplacement are made of heavy steel and thick bullet-proof glass.

I have crossed hundreds of military checkpoints in my life. I am expecting to be rudely ordered out, and roughly shoved aside as the soldiers search our car. But here the soldiers are polite and professional, even friendly. They ask for our documents. I feel nervous when they ask Hassan, but he is treated with the same courtesy. We are all allowed to pass unmolested. I cannot help thinking how different his fate might be in so many conflict zones where soldiers are little more than bandits.

But inside the town the bomb-shattered ruins of the Palestinian Authority headquarters stand as testimony to the missiles of an F-16 and to the hard, brutal edge of Israeli power. The crushed bodies of cars lie on the kerb beneath the minaret of a mosque. 'The tanks just drive over them,' Hassan says.

The main street is redolent with the smoke of kebab stalls and coffee vendors. The market is filled with the bright colours of fresh fruit and vegetables. There is little outward sign of Islamist extremism. There are fewer women wearing headscarves here than in parts of London.

But the streets are lined with young men who cannot find jobs. On the walls are tattered posters of the others who died as suicide bombers. Their deaths are a ghastly martyrdom to desperation.

In the cemetery of the martyrs a freshly dug grave stands empty, its sandy bottom half-filled with dirty rainwater, waiting for the remains of the next young suicide bomber.

We are still filming as night falls. It is too dangerous to approach the checkpoints after dark. 'The soldiers see only the headlamps and they often shoot,' Hassan says.

We have to spend the night. The call to prayer echoes out in the wintry darkness. A few middle-class men and women in business suits park their cars outside the mosque and go inside to pray.

A full moon rises over the white stones of the old town. A taxi takes us through the narrow alleyways towards a safe house. We stop under the curve of an archway that dates back to the Byzantines. The dark of a cypress tree looms against the stars.

Inside, a young man in black combat gear carrying an M-16 searches our TV equipment. We are shown into a room where a group of leaders from Hamas and Fatah parties are meeting. A pistol lies on the carpet next to a tray of orange slices and glasses of mint tea.

'They are wanted by the Israelis,' Hassan whispers to me. 'But they are safe here. They will never leave Jenin.'

The desperation on the streets is echoed in this small, shadowy room. The outside world they talk of is a confusing mirage of legitimate anger and clichéd slogans. I cannot help thinking that not one of these middle-aged men will ever strap the suicide bombs to his own body. Their leadership could stop the cruel, wasteful deaths of their young men and women.

Just as, I think, with a single order to their troops, the Israelis could stop the terrifying pitilessness of the tanks and the helicopter gunships.

It is freezing cold tonight. Hassan and I are standing on the roof of an apartment building overlooking the town and the land surrounding it.

The pale finger of a mosque stands out against the dark clouds. On the hills beyond Jenin we can see a sprinkling of bright electric lights.

'Those are the Jewish settlements,' Hassan tells me. 'So near to here. Jenin is surrounded.' He points into the shadowy landscape. 'Just after that hill begins Israel.'

Standing there in the dark I think of something I read in an Israeli newspaper a few days before. 'By defining the past, memory creates the present.'

Tonight the past and the present are all around us, almost stifling any hope of a future. I know that Hassan is right. So close, so very close are those Israeli settlements that are a source of implacable rage to the Arabs whose ancestral land has been taken by the Jews.

But I know, too, that the promise of a land of their own has been the unshakeable dream of oppressed Jews for centuries. *Next year in Jerusalem.* For 2 000 years the fragments of hope contained in those words sustained Jews all over the world, even through the worst days of the Holocaust.

Hassan turns to go back inside. He leaves me alone, looking out at these two towns, these two places of light – staring into the cold winter darkness that lies between them.

THE BORDER

It was only weeks ago that I was negotiating the checkpoints in and out of the West Bank. Now I am stuck on one side of yet another border – that between South Africa and Zimbabwe.

The rainy season is drawing to a close in the Limpopo valley. The water in the river is falling as the hard months of the dry season begin. The sky is blue and cloudless. The sun shimmers off the white rocks.

On the South African side of the river runs a long electrified fence. It stretches for hundreds of miles both east and west along the border. It was erected by the apartheid regime, but the ANC government of Thabo Mbeki still maintains this grim frontier. With Zimbabwe's economy in shreds, tens of thousands of refugees are coming south to look for jobs.

On a stretch of the river is a grove of tall, green-barked fever trees. They cast a cool shade over the banks. A concrete weir has been built across the river. It forms a deep pool where the South African farmers draw water for their fields.

There is a gate in the electric fence here. Johannes is the man who maintains the pumps that draw the precious water. He has a key for the gate and lets me in to the pump station.

The concrete weir runs straight across to the Zimbabwean bank. This is one of many invisible breaches in the frontier. I am reminded of Robert Frost:

> Something there is that doesn't love a wall
> No one has seen them made or heard them made
> But at spring mending-time we find them there.

So Frost wrote of the gaps in his stone wall.

Here there is no spring mending-time, only the heat of a late African summer, but people have found the gaps in this electric and razor wire fence.

It would take only a few minutes to walk through the low cascade of water across the border. In the shade of the fever trees Johannes introduces me to his friend Olbert who has crossed over from Zimbabwe.

We squat on our haunches in the clean white sand on the river bank. In the gentle way of Africa, we begin by talking of the rains and of the long drive from Johannesburg.

Johannes is a South African citizen. He is in his mid-forties. He is proud of his job and the money it brings him. He is wearing a clean pressed shirt and a baseball cap. His sandals are new, with car tyre soles. Olbert has walked across the concrete weir from Zimbabwe. He is in his late twenties. A dirty T-shirt and ragged shorts are all he has to wear, while his feet are bare and calloused.

Olbert has no job. Every day he comes down to the river to fish in the deep pool. He smiles broadly as he tells me about the fish. 'They are as fat as this,' he says, pointing to his forearm. 'And their meat is very sweet.'

Johannes has rolled a handmade cigarette. He takes a drag and hands it across. The two men share it between them as we talk.

I suddenly realize that Olbert has no money to buy cigarettes, and that is why Johannes shares his tobacco with him.

The talk of sweet, fat fish is so that Olbert can save face. The truth is that he walks across the border because Johannes is willing, and able, to give him something to eat. It is the oldest custom in Africa – in times of hunger, people must share with others. I have seen it in action amongst the poor all across the continent, from the war zones of Angola to the famine-parched savannas of Sudan.

Soon, the talk turns to politics. Robert Mugabe may have won his election but even here, on the edge of one of the remotest parts of Zimbabwe, his message has failed to convince.

'They chase the whites from the farms,' Olbert says. 'They steal the maize and eat the cattle. Then they kill the kudu and the impala. What will they eat then?'

'People have nothing there,' Johannes says, pointing across the river to Zimbabwe. 'They have no food, no work. That is why they come here.'

Olbert gestures angrily. 'There was a diamond mine there before. The Australians owned it. It is closed now, because of Mugabe. And we have no jobs.

'Our President,' he adds, 'he doesn't want anyone except himself to have anything.'

I know that Robert Mugabe has utterly ignored those of his people like Olbert. They do not matter to him any more. He talks obsessively of how he despises Tony Blair and of how he will never allow Zimbabwe to become a colony of Britain again.

It is the last card left for him to play. Defending the African way of life against the pernicious influence of the West.

But here, on the banks of the Limpopo, it appears to me that Robert Mugabe has fallen into the trap of so many dictators. He has become dangerously isolated from his own people.

In a continent where sharing is the highest virtue, he has placed his own personal power and wealth above the welfare of his people.

Olbert narrows his eyes and shakes his head. 'That Mugabe,' he says softly, echoing an old African saying. 'He eats alone.'

Things change. Old fences come down; new ones go up. In the places I have visited nothing has remained the same. Laurent Kabila is dead, shot by an assassin's bullet. His son Joseph rules the Congo now and, at last, there is some chance of peace.

The civil war continues in Sudan, but there are now some hints that a peace agreement may be reached.

As I write this there is news that twenty-three people have been killed and 120 injured in a suicide bomb attack in Tel Aviv that came after six weeks of relative calm. Soon after, Israeli helicopters fired rockets at a metal-working factory in Gaza city and tanks were moved into Rafah, south of the Gaza strip.

In the Gulf, the signs are that America is moving towards a new invasion of Iraq.

Afghanistan remains dangerously unstable.

Today, the Limpopo is as far as we can go. The others are filming the border fence further along the bank. For a long time I sit with Olbert and Johannes talking of this and that, but listening mostly, trying to gauge the elusive mood of people here about the elections in Zimbabwe. The BBC and other journalists have been banned from working in Zimbabwe. Because of my connections with the BBC, a once familiar place, somewhere I know almost as well as my own home, has become dangerous territory to me. A place I should not go. A country I cannot see for myself, but must witness only through what flickering images I can find on my television screen. The images of someone else's journey.

Olbert points to where the river disappears around a bend. 'There are hippos there, and crocodiles.' This is one of the last rivers in Africa where these animals still live wild. In fact, for those Zimbabweans like himself, driven to head south, crossing the Limpopo is a dangerous passage.

'One day,' I think, 'I will go back, to see for myself.'

But no journey ever takes you exactly where you want to go. I am still searching for the world. I stare across the muddy, swirling waters of the river. That same distance still haunts, and beguiles, my dreams. It is the distance that lies between here and there.

REFERENCES

A New War Across The Border

Farwell, Byron: *Burton – A Biography of Sir Richard Francis Burton*. Penguin, London, 1990
Gourevitch, Philip: *We Wish To Inform You That Tomorrow We Will Be Killed With Our Families*. Macmillan, London 1999
Hemingway, Ernest: *By-Line – Selected Articles and Despatches*. Grafton, London, 1989
Omaar, Rakiya: *Rwanda – Death, Despair and Defiance*. African Rights, London, 1994
Prunier, Gérard: *The Rwanda Crisis – History of a Genocide*. Fountain Publishers, Kampala, 1995
Reader, John: *Africa – A Biography of a Continent*. Penguin, London, 1998
Speke, John Hanning: *Journal of the Discovery of the Source of the Nile*. Everyman's Library, London, 1922

The Last Days of the Leopard King

Alagiah, George: *A Passage to Africa*. Little, Brown, London, 2001
Axelson, Eric: *Congo to Cape*. Harper & Row, New York, 1973
Calder, Ritchie: *Agony of the Congo*. Victor Gollancz, London, 1961
Davidson, Basil: *Africa in History*. Orion Books, London, 1992
Guevara, Ernesto Che: *The African Dream – The Diaries of the Revolutionary War in the Congo*. Harvill, London, 2000
Hoare, Mike: *Congo Mercenary*. Robert Hale, London, 1967
Hochschild, Adam: *King Leopold's Ghost*. Macmillan, London, 2000
Hyland, Paul: *The Black Heart*. Paragon House, New York, 1988
Legum, Colin: *Congo Disaster*. Penguin, London, 1961
Pakenham, Thomas: *The Scramble for Africa*. Jonathan Ball, Johannesburg, 1992
Wrong, Michela: *In the Footsteps of Mr Kurtz*. Fourth Estate, London, 2000

Season of Hunger

Amnesty International: *The Tears of Orphans*. Amnesty International Publications, London, 1995
Buckoke, Andrew: *Fishing in Africa – A Guide to War and Corruption*. Picador, London, 1992
Churchill, Winston: *Frontiers and Wars*. Smithmark, New York, 1995
Evans-Pritchard, E E: *The Nuer*. Clarendon Press, Oxford, 1960
Holt, P M: *A Modern History of the Sudan*. Weidenfeld & Nicolson, London, 1974
Lamb, David: *The Africans*. Vintage Books, New York, 1987
Moorehead, Alan: *The White Nile*. Hamish Hamilton, London 1961

Desert Sunsets, Invisible City, The Diary of a Ceasefire

Bulloch, John & Morris, Harvey: *Saddam's War*. Faber & Faber, London, 1991
Collins, Larry & LaPierre, Dominique: *O Jerusalem*. Steimatzky, Israel, 1993
Friedman, Thomas: *From Beirut to Jerusalem – One Man's Middle Eastern Odyssey*. Harper Collins, London, 1990
Fox, Edward: *Palestine Twilight*. Harper Collins, London, 2001
Gellhorn, Martha: *The Face of War*. Granta Books, London, 1993
Grossman, David: *The Yellow Wind*. Pan Books, London 1989
Lewis, Bernard: *The Middle East*. Phoenix, London, 1996
Murphy-O'Connor, Jerome: *The Holy Land – An Oxford Archaeological Guide from Earliest Times to 1700*. Oxford University Press, Oxford, 1992
Said, Edward: *The End of the Peace Process*. Granta Publications, London, 2002

A Hidden War

Arrian (trans. Aubrey de Sélincourt): *The Campaigns of Alexander*. Penguin, London, 1971
Baxter, Jenny & Downing, Malcolm (eds): *The Day That Shook The World*. BBC Worldwide, London, 2001
Elliot, Jason: *An Unexpected Light – Travels in Afghanistan*. Pan Macmillan, London, 2000
Herodotus (trans. Aubrey de Sélincourt): *The Histories*. Penguin, London, 1965
Hodson, Peregrine: *Under A Sickle Moon*. Penguin, London, 1989
Hopkirk, Kathleen: *Central Asia – A Traveller's Companion*. John Murray,

London, 1993

Hopkirk, Peter: *The Great Game*. Oxford University Press, Oxford, 2001

Levi, Peter: *The Light Garden of the Angel King*. Pallas Athene, London, 2000

Margolis, Eric: *War at the Top of the World*. Routledge, New York, 2001

Polo, Marco (trans. Ronald Latham): *The Travels of Marco Polo*. Penguin, London 1959

Rashid, Ahmed: *Taliban – The Story of the Afghan Warlords*. Pan Macmillan, London, 2001

Thubron, Colin: *The Lost Heart of Asia*. Penguin, London, 1995

Whitlock, Monica: *Beyond the Oxus – the Central Asians*. John Murrary, London, 2002

Wood, Michael: *In the Footsteps of Alexander the Great*. BBC Worldwide, London, 2001

SELECTED INDEX

Abbud, Gen. 135
Abu Ghosh 270
Addis Ababa Agreement 136
'Administrative College' (Zaire) 80
AFDL 43,45,47,50,57,58,62,68,78, 83, 111,119,120,121,123,124
Afghanistan 134,210-262
Ahmed Khan 223
Alagiah, George 60,73,93,96,98,105, 106,109,110,111,112,116,124,144, 145,148,149,150,151,152,169
al-Aqsa Mosque 198,265
Albania 60
Albright, Madeleine 159,177,178
Alexander the Great 185,248,250
Al-Mutla Ridge 191
Amanpour, Christiane 244
American Colony Hotel (Jerusalem) 268,270,271
Amnesty International 137,149,187
Amu Darya (Oxus) River 37,238,248
Angola 7,24,80,84
Annan, Kofi 82,84,167,174,177,178, 184,190,191,192
Antonie, Victor 17
Anya-Nya movement 135
Arafat, Yasser, 266,267,270,271
Asmara 59
Atbara 134
Ay Khanoum 245-250,257
Aziz, Tariq 163,192

Bagaruka, Denis 12-13,15
Bagram 230,243
Bahr-el-Ghazal 134,144

Bakongo empire 64
Baku 219
Balding, Justin 211,216,217,219,220, 229,230,231,232,233,234,235,237, 239,241, 242,245,246, 259,260
Banana 89
Bandundu 68,84
Bangambiki, Emmanuel 26
Bangladesh 130
Banyamulenge 16,24,34,36,37,45,57, 117
Baramoto, Gen. Kpama 91
al-Bashir, Omar 137
Bas-Zaire province 82
BaTwa 19
BBC 14,17,48,53,59,68,169,173,282
Beit Jala 267,268-270,271,272,273
Benn, Tony 163
Berber 134
Berger, Sandy 177,178
Bethlehem 268,270
Bharylai, Gen. 248,249,250
Biafra 130
Biaro camp 83
Blair, Tony 89,163,178,236
Blunt, Byron 73,96,98,100,101,102, 118,120,139,143
Bolongo, Gen. Likulia 62,91,106, 110,112
Bolongo, Gen. Mahele 91,92,109, 110,111,112,113,116,123
Brazzaville 74,77,94,106,113,114
Britain 162,163,235
Brown, Ben 179
Bujumbura 209

Bukango-Lonzo 97
Bukavu 16,17, 22,25,26,28,29,33,34, 35,36,37,40,42,49,68
Bulungu 84
Burns, Nicholas 63
Burr, Richard 212,216,217,218,220, 235,237,240,249
Burundi 39,49,58
Bush, President George 163
Bush, President George W 210,211, 235,240,242,244,261
Byron, Robert 245

Cabinda 89
Camp David agreement 265
Camp Panzi 27,28
Camp Tshatshi 85,96,106,115,118, 119,121-123
Canal Plus 14
Cão, Diogo 64,223
Caspian Sea 219
Caxito (Angola) 81
Central African Republic 58,59
Chad 59
Chatwin, Bruce 245
Chechnya 29
China 163,184
Chirac, Jacques 43
Chrétien, Raymond 45,46
Chu, Jean 240
Churchill, Winston 134,135
CIA 57
Clinton, President Bill 43,163,167, 172,177, 178,191,193
CNN 14,60, 243
Coen, Gad 97,101,102
Cohen, William 177
Congo 7
Congo, People's Republic of 59
Cyangugu 17,22,25,26,28,29,34,36, 41

Dar es Salaam 57
Dawes, Martin 139,141
Dayan, Moshe 270,271
Democratic Republic of Congo 115
Denard, Bob 16

al-Din, Mujir 199
Dinka people (Sudan) 128,134,137, 142,149
Dome of the Rock 198,200,265
Dongola 134
Dowete 82
DSP (Presidential Guard, Zaire) 16, 77,78,86,102,112,116
Dushanbe 211,220-224,229-235,261

Enver Pasha 228
Erez 274
Eritrea 58,59
Ethiopia 58,130,137
European Broadcasting Union 60

Facey, Tim 117
Failaka Island 185
FAR 15,16,58
FAZ 58,83,97,102,108,113,114,120
Firket 134
FNLA 84
Force Publique 79-80
France 58,163

Garang, John 136
Gaza 166,265,266,274-276,277
Gbadolite 44,58,86,91,94,110
Gellhorn, Martha 175-176
Genghis Khan 223
Gisenyi 46,47,50,52,53
Gitarama 18
Golden Horde 223
Goma 16,36,39,44,45,46,47,49,50, 68,117
Gordon, Gen. Charles George 133, 134
Guevara, Che 57
Gulf War 157-159,162,163,166,171, 182,183,184,185,186,191,211
Gulf War Syndrome 168

Habyarimana, Juvenal 20,48,58,110
Hadera 272
Haji Yakoub Mosque 225
Hamas 266,267
Hemingway, Ernest 25-26

Hemingway, Mary 25-26
Henry the Navigator 64
Hissar 222,228
Human Rights Watch 149
Hutu 12,15,19,20,21,36,44,45,49, 50,78,86

Ilebo 82
India 236
Interahamwe 13,15,16,18,22,41,45, 46,47,49,50,58,78,83
Intercontinental Hotel (Kinshasa) 106,114
Iran 134
Iraq 134
Islamabad 242
Israel 195-205,263-279
Ivan the Great 223

Jalalabad 242,251
Japan 163
Jenin 276-279
Jerusalem 1,195-205,268
Johannesburg 57,59
Jonglei Canal 136

Kabila, Joseph 124,282
Kabila, Laurent 37,38,39,40,42,44,46, 47,49,57, 58,59,62,63,66,68,75,78, 83,84, 85,86,87,88,90,91,92,93,94, 98, 99,106,113,115,117,120,124,282
Kabul 230,236,242,243,244,250,251
Kagame, Lt-Col Firman 35
Kagame, Paul 45
Kalandiya 270
Kalemie 57,119
Kalonji, Albert 80
Kamanda, Gerard 115
Kamina army base 59
Kandahar 244,251
Karaha, Bizima 68,97
Karisimbi volcano 51
Kasai province 80
Kasavubu, Joseph 65
Kasese camp 83
Katanga 79-80,82

Katsev, Moshe 271
Kayibanda, Gregoire 48
Kenge 87,89,95,96,97,102,104
Kenya 59
Khalifa, the 134, 135
Khartoum 133,135,137
Khuja Bahauddin 211,229,235,238- 257
Kibumba Camp 45,49
Kigali 13,14,17,18,20,21,26,27,48, 49
Kikwit 84,85,87,97
King Baudouin of Belgium 69
King Leopold of Belgium 64
Kinshasa 16,43,44,46,57,58,59,60— 124,161,168
Kinyarwanda language 19
Kisangani 47,49,58,78,83,84,85,90, 99
Kitchener, Gen. 134,144
Kivu province 16,17,23,57,58
Kokcha River 248,250
Kotbe, Hoda 267,268
Kranz, John 212
Kunduz 230,246,251
Kuwait 155-194
Kuwait City 1,162,164,167,179,184, 185

Lake Kivu 17,22,23,25,26,36,47,52
Lake Tanganyika 22
Lake Victoria 11,26
Levi, Peter 245
Libya 58
Likota, Alain 87-88,89,95,96,99,100, 101,103,104,105,106,112,115,118
Lissala 91
Lissouba, Pascal 59,94
Little, Allan 59,62,68,69,70,96,112, 115,118,119
Lokichokio 127,130,131,132,144, 153
London 8,53,210
Luanda 81,84
Lubumbashi 59,60,62,77,86,115
Lumumba, Juliana 88-89
Lumumba, Patrice 37,57,65,69,80,88

Bukango-Lonzo 97
Bukavu 16,17,22,25,26,28,29,33,34,
    35,36,37,40,42,49,68
Bulungu 84
Burns, Nicholas 63
Burr, Richard 212,216,217,218,220,
    235,237,240,249
Burundi 39,49,58
Bush, President George 163
Bush, President George W 210,211,
    235,240,242,244,261
Byron, Robert 245

Cabinda 89
Camp David agreement 265
Camp Panzi 27,28
Camp Tshatshi 85,96,106,115,118,
    119,121-123
Canal Plus 14
Cão, Diogo 64,223
Caspian Sea 219
Caxito (Angola) 81
Central African Republic 58,59
Chad 59
Chatwin, Bruce 245
Chechnya 29
China 163,184
Chirac, Jacques 43
Chrétien, Raymond 45,46
Chu, Jean 240
Churchill, Winston 134,135
CIA 57
Clinton, President Bill 43,163,167,
    172,177,178,191,193
CNN 14,60,243
Coen, Gad 97,101,102
Cohen, William 177
Congo 7
Congo, People's Republic of 59
Cyangugu 17,22,25,26,28,29,34,36,
    41

Dar es Salaam 57
Dawes, Martin 139,141
Dayan, Moshe 270,271
Democratic Republic of Congo 115
Denard, Bob 16

al-Din, Mujir 199
Dinka people (Sudan) 128,134,137,
    142,149
Dome of the Rock 198,200,265
Dongola 134
Dowete 82
DSP (Presidential Guard, Zaire) 16,
    77,78,86,102,112,116
Dushanbe 211,220-224,229-235,261

Enver Pasha 228
Erez 274
Eritrea 58,59
Ethiopia 58,130,137
European Broadcasting Union 60

Facey, Tim 117
Failaka Island 185
FAR 15,16,58
FAZ 58,83,97,102,108,113,114,120
Firket 134
FNLA 84
Force Publique 79-80
France 58,163

Garang, John 136
Gaza 166,265,266,274-276,277
Gbadolite 44,58,86,91,94,110
Gellhorn, Martha 175-176
Genghis Khan 223
Gisenyi 46,47,50,52,53
Gitarama 18
Golden Horde 223
Goma 16,36,39,44,45,46,47,49,50,
    68,117
Gordon, Gen. Charles George 133,
    134
Guevara, Che 57
Gulf War 157-159,162,163,166,171,
    182,183,184,185,186,191,211
Gulf War Syndrome 168

Habyarimana, Juvenal 20,48,58,110
Hadera 272
Haji Yakoub Mosque 225
Hamas 266,267
Hemingway, Ernest 25-26

Hemingway, Mary 25-26
Henry the Navigator 64
Hissar 222,228
Human Rights Watch 149
Hutu 12,15,19,20,21,36,44,45,49, 50,78,86

Ilebo 82
India 236
Interahamwe 13,15,16,18,22,41,45, 46,47,49,50,58,78,83
Intercontinental Hotel (Kinshasa) 106,114
Iran 134
Iraq 134
Islamabad 242
Israel 195-205,263-279
Ivan the Great 223

Jalalabad 242,251
Japan 163
Jenin 276-279
Jerusalem 1,195-205,268
Johannesburg 57,59
Jonglei Canal 136

Kabila, Joseph 124,282
Kabila, Laurent 37,38,39,40,42,44,46, 47,49,57, 58,59,62,63,66,68,75,78, 83,84, 85,86,87,88,90,91,92,93,94, 98, 99,106,113,115,117,120,124,282
Kabul 230,236,242,243,244,250,251
Kagame, Lt-Col Firman 35
Kagame, Paul 45
Kalandiya 270
Kalemie 57,119
Kalonji, Albert 80
Kamanda, Gerard 115
Kamina army base 59
Kandahar 244,251
Karaha, Bizima 68,97
Karisimbi volcano 51
Kasai province 80
Kasavubu, Joseph 65
Kasese camp 83
Katanga 79-80,82

Katsev, Moshe 271
Kayibanda, Gregoire 48
Kenge 87,89,95,96,97,102,104
Kenya 59
Khalifa, the 134, 135
Khartoum 133,135,137
Khuja Bahauddin 211,229,235,238-257
Kibumba Camp 45,49
Kigali 13,14,17,18,20,21,26,27,48, 49
Kikwit 84,85,87,97
King Baudouin of Belgium 69
King Leopold of Belgium 64
Kinshasa 16,43,44,46,57,58,59,60-124,161,168
Kinyarwanda language 19
Kisangani 47,49,58,78,83,84,85,90, 99
Kitchener, Gen. 134,144
Kivu province 16,17,23,57,58
Kokcha River 248,250
Kotbe, Hoda 267,268
Kranz, John 212
Kunduz 230,246,251
Kuwait 155-194
Kuwait City 1,162,164,167,179,184, 185

Lake Kivu 17,22,23,25,26,36,47,52
Lake Tanganyika 22
Lake Victoria 11,26
Levi, Peter 245
Libya 58
Likota, Alain 87-88,89,95,96,99,100, 101,103,104,105,106,112,115,118
Lissala 91
Lissouba, Pascal 59,94
Little, Allan 59,62,68,69,70,96,112, 115,118,119
Lokichokio 127,130,131,132,144, 153
London 8,53,210
Luanda 81,84
Lubumbashi 59,60,62,77,86,115
Lumumba, Juliana 88-89
Lumumba, Patrice 37,57,65,69,80,88

Lyne, Alistair 24,25,30,144,148,149, 152

Macmillan, Harold 89
Magwenya, Vincent 174
Mahdi, the 133,134,135,143
al-Majid, Ali Hassan 162
Major, John 43
Malualkon 133
Mandela, Nelson 86,89,90,91,92, 103,158
Manhattan 3,5,8,157,210,215
Marais, Fred 89
Massoud, Gen. Ahmad Shah 209,211, 240
Matadi 94,95,99,104,116
Matloff, Judith 115
Matthews, Jimi 60
Mashiyane, Spokes 73
Mazar-i-Sharif 235,243,246,251,261
Mbanza-Congo 111
Mbeki, Thabo 76,280
Mbuji-Mayi 59,124
Memling Hotel (Kinshasa) 60,61,66, 67,109
Middleton, Glenn 62,70,71,90,96, 105,111,114,115,121,122,160,161, 169,170,171,173,174,178,180, 181,182,183,184,187,188,189, 191,193,194
Mobutu, Kongulu 62,71,92,103,109-110,112,113,114
Mobutu, Nzanga 71,92,97,101,102
Mobutu Sese Seko 14,15,16,37,39, 40,42,43,46,47,57,58,59,61,62, 63,65-66,68,69,75-77,79-80,83, 84,85,86,87,88,89,90,91,92,93, 95,97,98,105,106,109,110,111, 112,117
Moi, President 59
Monsengwo, Laurent 97
Mont Ngaliema 119
Morocco 59
Mozambique 7,129,138,140
MPLA 58,81,82,84,95
Mpolo, Maurice 65
MSF 139,141

MSNBC 240,242,243
Mubarak, Hosni 137
Mubarak the Great 185
Mugabe, Robert 281,282
Mugunga Camp 44,45,47,48,49,50
Muiruri, Patrick 17,18,23,24,25,27, 28,29,30,31,32,33,34,37,48
Muluku 102
Mulumba, Kin-Kiey 111,112
Murahaleen, 137,139,146
Murenzi, Gustave 18, 21,23,29,30,33,48,49
Murphy, Dennis 212,216,217,229, 235,237,244,245,246,255,256
Muslemany, Mohamed 267,270,271, 272,274
Mwami, the 20

Nablus 272
Nairobi 144,209
Nanga, Mawapanga Mwana 77
al-Nasser al-Sabah, Saud 174
NBC 211,239
Netanya 272
Newby, Eric 245
New York 8
Ndjili airport (Kinshasa) 61,74,92,98, 104,106
Nile River 128,134,143
el-Nimeiri, Mohammed 136
Nkosi, Milton 60,61,67,96,121,169
Northern Alliance 211,229,230,235, 236,240,241,243,244,248,249, 250,261
'Nouveau Zaire' currency 72-73
Ntaryamira, Cyprien 20
Nuclear Biological Chemical Warfare course 159-162
Nuer people (Sudan) 128,134,137
Nyarubuye 12,150
Nzimbi, Gen. 110

OAU 85
Odessa 216,217
Ogata, Sadako 46
Okito, Joseph 65
Omdurman 134,135

Operation Desert Thunder 172,173
Operation Lifeline Sudan 132
Osama Bin Laden 137,241,244,258
Oslo peace talks 265

Pakistan 211,236
Palestinian Authority 267,269
Palestinians 166,187,190
Panj River 238
Panjshir valley 250
Panthou 129,131.132,133,138-144
Parmehutu 20
People's Revolutionary Party 57
Point-Noire 106
Polo, Marco 245
Pool Malebo 102
Popular Defence Force (Sudan): *see* Murahaleen
Prague 213-214
Prester John 63-64,65

Radio Trottoir 75,118
Rahman, Abdul 170,171,178,179, 180,181,182
Rakhmanov, Imamali 225
Ramallah 202,203,274
Rayson, Chevan 60,73
Reuters 17,48,243
Richardson, Bill 85,86,90
RPF 15,18,20,22,24,29,30,33,47,48, 52
Rumsfeld, Donald 230
Rusizi River 22,23,35,36
Russia 163,184,236
Rusumo (Rwanda) 12
Rwanda 1,9-54,57,58

al-Sabah, Sheik Mubarak 165
Saddam Hussein157,158,159,162, 163,164,171,172,174,177,178,184, 187,189,190,191,192,193,194
Sahel 128,143,145
Salumu, Clyde 62,68,69,70,71,74-75, 83,86,87,89,90,96,98,99,100,101, 102,104,105,112,117,118
Sanders, Kerry 212,213,235
al-Saud, Abdul Aziz 185

Saudi Arabia 164,185
Savimbi, Jonas 209
Seemungal, Martin 144
Shabunda 57
Sharon, Ariel 265,267,270
Shelton, Gen. Henry 167
South Africa 83
Soviet Union 16,224
Speke & Burton 22
SPLA 128,131,136,144,145,151,153
SPLM 132,136
SRRA 132,139,145
SS Outeniqua 85,90,91
Stark, Freya 185
Stimson, Paul 212
Sudan 1,58,125-154
Sudd 136

Tajikistan 211,220-235
Taliban 201,211,230,235,236,241, 242,243,244,246,247,248,249, 250,251,253,256,257,261
Taloqan 230,246,251
Tamerlane 224
Tanzania 58
Tel Aviv 265,266,268
Telecell mobile phone network (Zaire) 71-72
Temple Mount 198,199
Tenet and Mitchell plans 265
Thatcher, Margaret 89
Tokyo 8
Tonj 144-153
Tshikapa 82
Tshisikedi, Etienne 62,63,67,69,70, 88
Tshombe, Moise 80
Tulkarm 272
Turkey 163
Turner, Martin 60,67,96,112,159
Tutsi 12,14,15,16,19,20,21,26,28,36, 41,47,48,78

Uganda 39,58
UN 23,46,50,84,85,127,128,132, 144,149,159,162,184
UNHCR 46,49,83

UNICEF 79,83,85,153
UNITA 58,81,84,95,97,111,209
United States 162,163,235
Uvira 117
Uzbekistan 211

Vaksh River 237
Venter, Sahm 60,61,73

wa Dondo, Kengo 46,62
Walikale 57
Wau 145,146
Wenger, Ian 212,231,235
West Bank 166,265,266,272,273, 277,280
Western Wall tunnels (Jerusalem) 198-200
Williams, Julia 192
Wilson, Ben 67,115,117
World Trade Center 210,261

Zaire 1,14,15,16,22,23,27,36,39,43, 45,55-124
Zaire River 49,61,65,66,90,123
Zambia 58
Ze'evi, Rehavam 270
Zimbabwe 58,59,280,282
Zinni, Anthony 164